CROSSROADS

CREATIVE WRITING EXERCISES IN FOUR GENRES

DIANE THIEL

Taken from:
Crossroads: Creative Writing Exercises in Four Genres
by Diane Thiel

Custom Publishing

New York   Boston   San Francisco
London   Toronto   Sydney   Tokyo   Singapore   Madrid
Mexico City   Munich   Paris   Cape Town   Hong Kong   Montreal

Cover Art: *House, Trees, Land,* by George Herman

Taken from:

Crossroads: Creative Writing Exercises in Four Genres
by Diane Thiel
Copyright © 2005 by Pearson Education, Inc.
Published by Longman
New York, New York 10036

This special edition published in cooperation with Pearson Custom Publishing.

Printed in the United States of America

10 9 8 7 6 5 4 3 2 1

2009420006

DC

Pearson
Custom Publishing
is a division of

www.pearsonhighered.com

ISBN 10: 0-558-13008-9
ISBN 13: 978-0-558-13008-4

For my mother
and the lineage of teachers
who inspired me to write

For writers who teach
For teachers who write

About the Author

Photo by Costa Hadjilambrinos

Diane Thiel is the author of four books of poetry and prose: *Echolocations* (2000), which received the Nicholas Roerich Poetry Prize from Story Line Press; *Writing Your Rhythm: Using Nature, Culture, Form and Myth* (2001); *The White Horse: A Colombian Journey* (2004); and *Resistance Fantasies* (2004). Her work appears in numerous publications, including *Poetry*, *The Hudson Review*, and *Best American Poetry 1999*, and is reprinted in more than twenty major anthologies from Addison Wesley Longman, Bedford, HarperCollins, Beacon, Henry Holt, and McGraw Hill, including *Twentieth-Century American Poetry*. Her work has received numerous awards, including the Robert Frost Award and the Robinson Jeffers Award. Thiel received her BA and MFA from Brown University and has traveled and lived in various countries in Europe and South America. She has been a professor of creative writing for over ten years. Thiel was a Fulbright Scholar for 2001–2002 in Odessa, on the Black Sea, and is on the creative writing faculty at the University of New Mexico.

Contents

PART TWO
Exercises for Exploring Specifics of
Different Genres   85

PART THREE
A Collection of Readings 167

Drama   322

Writers on the Art   386

Preface to the Instructor

As teachers of creative writing, we face a unique challenge. The students in each of our courses have different talents and abilities. We must spark each student's creativity and help him or her develop the skills every competent writer must have. It is often said that creativity cannot be taught. It is my belief, however, that everyone possesses innate creativity, and it is our task, as teachers, to nourish it and give each student the means to express his or her ideas effectively. The teacher of creative writing faces a set of specific challenges and needs a variety of tools in order to meet the needs of his or her students. Over many years of teaching and via discussions with a multitude of other teachers, I arrived at a list of tools most useful to a creative writing classroom, tools featured in this book. The fundamental philosophy that this book embodies is that we learn by example and by practice. As writers, we are also readers, and we learn by emulating those writers who have most inspired us along the way. For this reason, the book includes an extensive selection of readings, and the exercises and discussions are designed to draw from and integrate with these readings.

Features of This Book

- Active lessons, with prompts to have the students writing something nearly every day.

- Exercises to address each element of creative writing separately, while still building toward an understanding of all the elements that go into creating an effective piece of writing.

- Clear, concise discussions of particular techniques of creative writing, followed by practice of these individual techniques.

- Potent, vital examples in an extensive selection of readings that will serve as models to our students.

- An emphasis on the intersections between genres, helping students see what they have in common.

Crossroads: Creative Writing Exercises in Four Genres addresses the varied needs of the creative writing teacher. The purpose of this book is to make the process of creative writing accessible and to help in the development of the necessary tools. The exercises identify and isolate the many elements of creative writing, making them manageable. Thus broken down and explored one at a time, these elements become easier to handle. Some can be extraordinarily useful as steps on the way to longer pieces.

Though the exercises are designed to cover and respond to the fundamentals of writing, they are also motivating and fun. Even as established writers, we set ourselves exercises. We study the techniques of other writers and often model a particular aspect of that writer's work (e.g., how the writer creates the rhythm in a free verse poem; how the point of view shifts so fluidly in a particular scene).

Most of the selections in this book are from contemporary writers, although I do include a few classic pieces, often for the particular needs of an exercise, but also because it is important for students to get a sense of the lineage of writers. When Auden wrote his "Musée des Beaux Arts" in 1940, for example, he was "translating" a sixteenth-century Brueghel painting. Brueghel, in turn, referred quite precisely to the text of the ancient poet Ovid when he chose the figures for his painting. The readings represent writing in a number of different styles, from a number of different cultures and eras.

One important element that sets this book apart from other creative writing textbooks is that the exercises throughout the book emphasize ways in which techniques that are primarily important to one genre can inform and enhance writing in other genres. When teaching creative writing, I often take a passage of prose and examine the different "poetic" techniques that can be found there, such as parallel structures, metaphor, assonance, alliteration, or an underlying iambic or galloping anapestic rhythm. The techniques of writing dialogue, essential in drama, are also quite essential in fiction and in narrative poetry. Creative nonfiction is often made much richer by an attention to the actual dialogue that may have taken place. Emphasis on and examples of these types of connections appear throughout the book.

Organization: Ways to Use This Book

Part One of *Crossroads* emphasizes the connections between genres. You can use these exercises to help students find their individual voices and begin addressing the elements of writing, such as voice, perspective, image, tension, and figurative language. This will give students the sense of the "crossroads" of the writing experience.

The exercises in Part Two delve into specific concerns of nonfiction, fiction, poetry, and drama. The nonfiction section highlights techniques of writing pieces such as memoir or personal opinion. The fiction section addresses elements such as conflict, flashback, and development of character. The poetry section stresses image and metaphor and introduces rhythm, rhyme, and a number of traditional and experimental forms, among other concerns. The drama section addresses issues such as opening scenes, creating dramatic tension, and working with a time line.

Part Three is an anthology of works in the four genres that illustrates various points in the exercises, as well as a short section of writers' comments on the art. Suggestions for reading the pieces included in Part Three accompany many of the exercises in Parts One and Two, often with a cross-genre approach.

You may choose to use the material in this book in the order of its appearance in the table of contents, but the exercises can also be used as the issues arise in workshop. For instance, as discussions arise regarding voice or perspective, you can turn to the exercises that address each particular concern and offer opportunities for practice. Often a work is suggested reading for a variety of different exercises. Revisiting the selections a number of times, to study different aspects of a writer's technique, will give students good examples for emulation and will get them in the habit of "reading as a writer."

Examples of Exercises

As a professor of creative writing for the last twelve years and as an author of books of poetry and prose, I have developed hundreds of exercises that focus on particular elements of creative writing crucial for any poet or prose writer's development. These include exercises addressing such concerns as establishing perspective, creating images and symbols, depicting culture and history, developing a narrative, and attending to form. I approach the essential tools of writing in ways that make each point relevant to the student's own experiences. For instance, in a chapter about perspective, I suggest writing from the perspective of an ancestor, inhabiting a period of history through that voice. In sections that discuss sense of place, I ask students to "revisit" their hometowns and explore the political, geographical, and historical dimensions of the place.

The exercises include opportunities to address specific as well as more expansive elements of writing. Some work well as fifteen-minute free-writing exercises, while others can be used as inspiration for an assignment at home.

The exercises will motivate students and give teachers brief daily lessons for discussion, as well as offer hands-on exercises to follow. Another emphasis of the book is the process of revision. The revision exercises present ways to approach revision, and they include a set of questions that can be used in any workshop of student work.

As mentioned previously, most readings in this book are modern and contemporary, although a few classic readings are chosen particularly because they illustrate effectively certain elements of creative writing and because they give rise to interesting and playful exercises. For instance, the inclusion of Coleridge's "Kubla Kahn" leads to an exercise in which students write a collaborative completion of the poem. The dreamlike, organic nature of Coleridge's "unfinished fragment" allows for a fun exercise in catching the rhythm of a piece, as well as accessing first thoughts.

(For instance, Coleridge's fragment ends in "For he on honeydew hath fed / and drunk the milk of paradise." Students might follow with a line such as "And then he ate a cantaloupe.") I include Poe's "The Tell-Tale Heart" because of an exercise we do with diction: students rewrite the opening paragraph, translating the passage into different dialects (e.g., "Hearken!" might become "Yo!" or "Listen up!").

This book addresses, in creative new ways, aspects of writing that some instructors have found most difficult to teach—poetic meter, for instance. For example, one exercise asks students to emulate an eight-line passage from Shakespeare's *Macbeth*. We study the way the iambic meter of the play shifts to trochaic meter for the casting of the witches' spell and the effect this shift creates. Students then emulate the meter and write spells in trochaic meter, using the witches' spell as a template. This type of exercise (useful in helping the student grasp the concept) is then followed by freer exercises in the particular technique. The book also includes exercises that bring other arts such as music or painting into the conversation in order to better understand the written piece or exercise, while simultaneously emphasizing the connections between different genres, different media, and different eras.

Included in the pages that follow are exercises I have found to be useful in the classroom as well as to my own creative development. As you travel through this book, either in the order of the table of contents or by moving around as the need in workshop arises, I hope you will be inspired to create additional exercises of your own and to find sources of inspiration for your own writing.

Acknowledgments

I would like to thank my thousands of students and many colleagues over the years, as well as the creative writing instructors who reviewed the manuscript in progress: Gail Galloway Adams, West Virginia University; Jennifer Atkinson, George Mason University; Elisabeth Louise Bloomer, Virginia Tech; Brian Kiteley, University of Denver; Jeanne Leiby, University of Central Florida; Thomas C. Marshall, Cabrillo College; John S. Nelson, Dakota State University; Thomas Palakeel, Bradley University; Joy Passanante, University of Idaho; and Jay Rubin, College of Alameda. I am grateful to Joe Terry, Erika Berg, Kristen Mellitt, and Dana Gioia for their assistance at various stages in the process. Thanks to my mother (an inspiring teacher for forty-five years) and all the members of my family. As always, many thanks to my husband, Costa, for his extraordinary assistance at every stage of the writing of this book.

DIANE THIEL

Introduction

If you have opened this book even in curiosity, you have at least wondered about becoming a writer. The idea of writing to be read may be exciting, scary, or both. These feelings are natural, especially if you have not had much experience with it. Whether you have had much practice with writing or little, you should know that you are already a writer. You are a story-teller, even if you don't immediately think of yourself that way. When something exciting happens in your life, what is one of your first impulses? To tell someone else. This is true for every one of us. We tell stories all our lives and use them daily for entertainment, to give advice, to make community.

As a story-teller, you are always looking and listening, consciously or unconsciously, for points of inspiration, and this attention becomes heightened when you start putting your ideas down on the page. It is usually this step, beginning to put your ideas on paper, that seems the most difficult to take. Beginning the process of writing, however, is easier than you may think. The first step is to keep a journal, and, as the first exercise in this book shows, writing in your journal is really no more difficult than observing or imagining a few things that may later become points of departure for a piece.

Although being a writer is as natural as being able to talk, to run, or to throw, being an *effective* writer is no different from being an effective singer or athlete. You must sharpen and improve your natural abilities and reflexes. There is no better way to do this as a writer than by reading widely and trying out the techniques of writers you admire. Renowned twentieth-century author F. Scott Fitzgerald once said, "I want to be able to do anything with words: handle slashing, flaming descriptions like Wells, and use the paradox with the clarity of Samuel Butler, the breadth of Bernard Shaw and the wit of Oscar Wilde. . . . All that is by way of example. As a matter of fact I am a professional literary thief, hot after the best methods of every writer in my generation." Likewise, T. S. Eliot once commented (though he may have stolen it from Ezra Pound), "Good poets borrow. Great poets steal." The real art is in finding the way to emulate something so as to make it your own.

The tradition of writing stretches back to ancient times, and it can be inspiring to recognize ourselves as an extension of that rich and diverse lineage. This book will point out many roads you can take as a writer. It is an exciting process to see your writing as an extension of that ancient path, with a unique landscape of possibilities unfolding before you.

When we write, we tap into a wellspring that is the source of all the arts and that reflects the breadth of our human experience. In this book, we will explore different sources of inspiration, such as music, myth, history, and art, in the process of writing. If we look back in history to the early roots of writing, we can recognize the deep connections between our more recent divisions, such as poetry, drama, story, history, and song. They all stem from the same source and once co-existed in our ancient texts.

As you collect and put on paper ideas for a piece, the question will arise of what form the piece should take. There is a good chance you have begun the process with a notion of the type of writer you would like to be. You may envision yourself as a novelist, poet, short-story writer, a play or screen writer, a journalist or essayist. As you begin to develop your ideas, though, you may find that they push for a piece to take a form you may not have considered.

Sometimes, as you find the need for a different canvas or to explore a different subject matter, another voice begins to emerge. Give yourself permission to explore, to experiment with a variety of forms or genres. Even if all the writing you finally produce belongs to a single genre, your experiments will have been useful, because there are important similarities between the genres, and the specifics of one genre can teach you something about another.

You will find in this book a collection of exercises that address the elements of writing essential to all genres, as well as specific needs of nonfiction, fiction, poetry, and drama. The exercises set simple tasks, the objectives of which are to help you practice your technique. They simultaneously provide inspiration and a delving into particular concerns of creative writing.

This book emphasizes ways in which techniques that are primarily important to one genre can inform and enhance your writing in other forms. If you are interested primarily in poetry, keep in mind that you can learn a great deal from fiction. Plotting dramatic tension, for instance, is one element crucial to good fiction that is extraordinarily useful to poetry as well. Likewise, your fiction can be enhanced by the attention to language and rhythm that poetry provides. If you look closely at a passage of good prose, you can notice the different poetic techniques the author has used, such as parallel structures, metaphor, alliteration, or even an underlying iambic or other notable rhythm (all elements discussed in these pages). The techniques of writing dialogue, essential in drama, are also quite essential in fiction and in narrative poetry. Creative nonfiction can be made much richer by an attention to the actual dialogue that may have taken place.

Each type of writing focuses attention on specific matters that are important to creative writing in general. Even more broadly, there are important connections between all the creative arts that can help you more clearly understand the elements of creative writing. Hemingway commented that he learned about writing through his love of certain composers and their music and learned "as much from painters about how to write as from writers." Discussion of these types of connections is an important element of this book.

Whether you are a beginning or experienced writer, it is important to begin each piece by breaking it down into a number of small explorations.

This process of breaking down, or, alternatively, of beginning with small pieces that you may later synthesize into a larger one, is useful because it makes the task of writing easier to manage and helps you learn by isolating each element of your piece. As you focus your attention on each element, you are better able to determine how you can improve it. One of the greatest questions you will face as a writer is how you are going to *render*, cast or shape, your piece. The idea that sparks a work is important, of course, but, as Robert Frost writes, "how you say a thing" is what ultimately matters in writing.

Often a terrific idea can feel too huge to handle. Many extraordinary ideas remain, unfortunately, at the idea stage. The exercises in this book will help you break down the elements of writing into small ventures that will teach you about the art. All works, no matter how large, are composed in such pieces: a conversation, a scene, an extended metaphor, a line, or a sentence. Poet and prose writer Annie Dillard's crucial question to a young person wanting to become a writer was simply, "Do you like sentences?" Likewise, as the poet and novelist Kate Braverman says, "All good writing is built one good line at a time. You build a novel the same way you do a pyramid. One word, one stone at a time." You always need to address each small component, however expansive the work might become.

The adage about activism applies in writing as well: "Think globally. Act locally." While it is always necessary that you maintain a global vision of the scope and purpose of your piece, this vision can be realized most effectively by paying close local attention to and carefully crafting each word, sentence, and element of the piece.

All writers learn by reading and by setting themselves exercises. This process of sharpening your tools and honing your techniques is necessary in the same way that ongoing training is necessary for an athlete, a musician, a visual artist. I encourage you to return to the exercises and the readings at different stages and to read widely beyond the sample of works included in this book. In fact, what you can learn from the exercises and readings grows and changes as your technique develops.

The art of writing, of course, as any art, is more than just exercise. The poet Rainer Maria Rilke, in his "Letter to a Young Poet," refers to the true source of the art when he says, "I know of no other advice than this: Go within and scale the depths." Although no formulas will assure that you will write a great piece of literature, there are techniques you can develop and practice that will help you truly "scale the depths."

PART ONE

Across the Genres:
Exercises for Developing Craft and Technique

1
Beginning:
Points of Inspiration

Keeping a Journal

Keeping a journal is an indispensable part of being a writer. In a sense, your memory is your journal. The point of both is to record things such as events, thoughts, sensations, and dreams. But as we all know, memory constantly discards details, and that is why it is good practice to keep a written journal. It may even be a good idea to keep more than one. Thoreau, for instance, kept different volumes for his scientific observations and his ideas for literary pieces, but he noted that it became increasingly difficult for him to keep things separate.

Though our technology has developed a multitude of machines to help us write, from recorders to computers to voice recognition systems, there is still no better way for you to begin than writing by hand. You can and should, of course, type things later, as you begin to revise, but it is important that you get started with your pen on paper. The immediate and direct physicality of forming words on the page cannot be substituted because it offers the closest connection between the writing process and its raw material, the word.

The shape and size of your journal are also important. It has to be small enough to carry in your purse or backpack, yet large enough to write in comfortably and fluidly. You should be able to carry it with you conveniently everywhere you go. You might consider your journal as your enhanced memory and write in it everything that can conceivably be of use to you later. Considering that you never know ahead of time what will be useful, the category of things you write in your journal could be very broad: dreams, quotations, overheard bits of dialogue.

Be prepared to "throw away" 95 percent of your writing—or rather, let it go no further than your journal. You will often write ten lines to get a single good one. Think of the journal as a no-pressure situation. There is never a blank page to face, because your hand keeps moving.

Of course, journal entries are far from final pieces. Writers often walk around with an idea for many years—a great idea that hasn't quite found its form, or its connecting force. "Free-writing" (keeping the hand moving, without censoring or revising for the moment) in a journal can help you find these connections, as you record the ebb and flow of your thoughts.

Practically speaking, the journal is a convenient way of keeping thoughts and ideas organized and safe from being lost.

When you are feeling somewhat uninspired, you can turn to the pages in your journal for instantaneous sparks of creativity. You will hardly remember writing some of the things that made it into the pages.

Suggestions for Writing

1. If you don't already have a journal, begin one and record in it such things as:

   Your dream last night

   Quotations from things you are reading

   Overheard snippets of conversation

   Intriguing scientific facts

   An interesting name for a character

   Something unusual you saw on the way home

2. If you have been keeping a journal for a while, revisit some old entries. Open your journal at a random place and read a few pages. Pick a thought, an idea, an image, and explore it from your current perspective. Write a new entry that revisits an old theme.

Personal Stories: History as Your Own Heartbeat

Read/Revisit

Leslie Marmon Silko, "Landscape, History, and the Pueblo Imagination" (see page 192)

Miller Williams, "The Curator" (see page 317)

Researching history can be a way to access the past and connect it to the present and the future. But the research has to mean something. It has to become personal. "History is your own heartbeat," as poet Michael S. Harper says. History, especially your personal history, is a fundamental source and shaper of your ideas. So go ahead and mine it.

Suggestions for Writing

1. Choose an ancestor who has always interested you, and do some research on historical events that took place during his or her life. Do some personal research. Interview your family members about

family history. Record what you hear in your journal. You may find that the story you are seeking has always been at your fingertips.

2. Start by writing about a single incident in your ancestor's life. It might be hard to get started if you think you have to tell a whole life story. So just start with one story: a story the family still tells, one that survived via the oral tradition. This might be a defining moment in the ancestor's life, or a story he or she might tell (or has told) you.

3. Write a three to five page biography of your ancestor. Focus on specific details.

Memory and Imagination

Read/Revisit

James Joyce, from *A Portrait of the Artist as a Young Man* (see page 230)
César Vallejo, "To My Brother Miguel" (see page 315)

Memory is the source of imagination. What we think of, regardless of how imaginative or whimsical, is in one way or another based on what we know. The inventive use of memory is an integral aspect of the creative process. We all remember things differently, so the very act of reconstructing the past is always a creative one. The details we include and the details we exlude help to form our own personal version of events.

Suggestions for Writing

1. Think of your earliest memory. As you write about it, try to inhabit the voice of the child. You might incorporate nonsense words to enhance the effect of the child's particular age, as in the excerpt from Joyce's *Portrait of the Artist*.

2. Write a memory of something you couldn't possibly remember: your grandparents' wedding, your birth, the creation of the earth.

Telling Lies to Tell the Truth

As children, we are all told not to lie, yet, much of our lives, we end up telling lies: tiny, harmless, "white" lies, perhaps, but lies nonetheless. In telling "white" lies, though, we often deny our true selves. Creative writing, on the other hand, is often all about making up stories. It gives us license to tell huge lies. We can invent personas, embody our dreams, tell the tallest of tales. In fact, the taller they are, sometimes the more true they become on the page. We can reveal much of our true selves when we invent personas through which to speak, or create metaphor. It could be said that all figurative language is, in a sense, a lie, because it presents one thing as something else. Yet it so often has the effect of getting closer to the truth. (See the "Figurative Language" chapter for more specifics)

Suggestions for Writing

1. This exercise is a good one to access the true events of your life that are strange enough to sound like lies: Write three short statements or anecdotes about yourself: two lies and one truth, with the same level of believability. In a workshop, it can be fun to read your responses aloud and let others guess which is the truth.

2. Write about fifty words telling an absolute lie that somehow is true to the way you feel.

   For instance, one student wrote about her Spanish teacher vanishing into thin air. Perhaps the student was wishing her away, or perhaps she was turning to magic realism (where reality suddenly becomes fantastic).

2
Voice, Tone, and Style

Finding Your True Subjects

Read/Revisit

> Tim O'Brien, "The Things They Carried" (see page 262)
> Bruce Chatwin, from *In Patagonia* (see page 170)
> Elizabeth Bishop, "One Art" (see page 291)

The term *voice*, when it refers to the writer, is sometimes confused with the term *style*. After all, writers often have both a distinctive voice and style. While *style* refers specifically to a writer's technique, a writer's unique *voice* includes elements of a writer's work that are less tangible than technique. Raymond Carver, in "On Writing," says that voice is "akin to style," but it isn't style alone. "It is the writer's particular and unmistakable signature on everything he writes. It is his world and no other. This is one of the things that distinguishes one writer from another. Not talent. There's plenty of that around. But a writer who has some special way of looking at things and who gives artistic expression to that way of looking: that writer may be around for a time."

What does it mean: to find your voice? What is a writer's voice? While developing your voice includes learning and using effectively elements of style and tone, it also refers to the stories that are your own and the particular insights and worldview that your telling of your stories reveals. So your choice (or discovery) of subjects is one factor that will begin to define your voice. Often, our true subjects may very well be the wounds or difficulties we have undergone. In a way, your subject chooses you. You may not want a certain subject matter, but it is yours anyway, because it is something you may need to work through for a period of time, or even for the rest of your life.

Tim O'Brien's period of service in Vietnam was a catalyst for his finding his subject matter. He returns to this particular setting and the series of external and internal conflicts in many of his works.

One of Bruce Chatwin's recurring concerns is the wandering life. He begins to explore the tendency of humans to be on the road in his first book, *In Patagonia*, and then goes on to refer to this idea in his later books, among them *The Songlines*, which deals with the Australian aboriginal dream tracks on which descendants travel. Chatwin was an incessant traveler, and this is reflected not only in his choice of the travel memoir as a genre but also in his dealing with the idea of *wanderlust,* or a desire to be on the road.

Elizabeth Bishop began dealing with the subject of lost things early in her life. The use of the villanelle form for her poem "One Art" is particularly intriguing, because the form of repetition lends itself well to subject matters that are, in a way, one's obsessions.

Suggestions for Writing

1. Look through your journals. Do any subjects appear again and again? Has someone ever pointed out to you that you talk about the same thing? Often, the word *obsession* has negative connotations, but for writers, obsessions can be the mark of having found a true subject.

2. Keep a dream journal. A true subject might be revealed by the frequency with which you dream about it. Record your dreams for a few weeks. Write down what you remember immediately on waking.

3. Experiment with refrains. See if one of your subject matters would benefit from one of the forms of repetition in poetry. (See the section on "Forms of Repetition" in the "Poetry" chapter in Part Two for more specifics.)

A Question of Style

Read/Revisit

Charlotte Perkins Gilman, "The Yellow Wallpaper" (see page 217)
Alice Munro, "How I Met My Husband" (see page 248)

Style is the way in which a piece of literature is written. As was mentioned before, the term *style* refers to the techniques a writer uses to render a piece. Style reflects the choice of words (diction), sentence structure (syntax), grammatical framework (choice of tense, person, etc.), density (use of figurative or symbolic language), and narrative mode (which includes dialogue, action, inner reflections, and background). Thus, style is the result of the writer's many conscious and unconscious decisions in rendering a piece.

Style is shaped, to a large extent, by the age in which we live—the language of a work written in the nineteenth century will not be the same as the language of a contemporary piece. However, style is also very much a result of the author's choice and inclination. Thus, a writer may develop an individual style that is rather uniform throughout his or her body of work. For example, Ernest Hemingway has an easily identifiable personal style that stamps his writings. On the other hand, a writer may choose to vary his or her style in order to render a piece most effectively.

Suggestions for Writing

Study the styles of Charlotte Perkins Gilman in "The Yellow Wallpaper" and Alice Munro in "How I Met My Husband" (included in Part Three). How does the time period figure into their styles? Gilman's piece is a late-nineteenth-century creation, while Munro's is late twentieth century. Select a paragraph or paragraphs from Charlotte Perkins Gilman and rewrite the sentences, using the much more sparse style of Alice Munro. Now try writing a paragraph from Munro using Gilman's style. Does it work as well, in your opinion?

Conditional Voice

Read/Revisit

> Leslie Marmon Silko, "Landscape, History, and the Pueblo Imagination" (see page 192)

Sometimes voice refers to the grammar of a piece of writing. The conditional voice is a seldom used construction, but some writers have turned it to their advantage. Leslie Marmon Silko, in an essay called "Landscape, History, and the Pueblo Imagination," uses techniques such as the conditional voice to inhabit the world of her ancestors and bring it to life. Study the following paragraph from the essay. Notice the way her recreation of the past is articulated with constructions such as "I imagine," "There might have been," and "the surprise attack would have cancelled."

> I imagine the last afternoon of my distant ancestors as warm and sunny for late September. They might have been traveling slowly, bringing the sheep closer to Laguna in preparation for the approach of colder weather. . . . There might have been comfort in the warmth and the sight of the sheep fattening on good pasture which lulled my ancestors into their fatal inattention. They might have had a rifle, whereas the Apaches had only bows and arrows. But there would have been four or five Apache raiders, and the surprise attack would have cancelled any advantage the rifles gave them.

One of my favorite novels, Marilynne Robinson's *Housekeeping*, frequently returns to the conditional voice to speak about the past. The effect is a dreamlike quality, a drifting between past to present.

> Looking out at the lake one could believe that the Flood had never ended. If one is lost on the water, any hill is Ararat. And below is always the accumulated past, which vanishes but does not vanish, which perishes and remains. If we imagine that Noah's wife when she was old found somewhere a remnant of the Deluge, she might have walked into it till her widow's dress floated above her head and the water loosened her plaited hair. And she would have left it to her sons to tell the tedious tale of generations. She was a nameless woman, and so at home among all those who were never found and never missed, who were uncommemorated, whose deaths were not remarked, nor their begettings.

Suggestions for Writing

1. Using the excerpts from Silko and Robinson as models, try writing about an ancestor or a historical figure using the conditional voice. (Try using constructions like: "My grandmother would have said . . . ," "My great-grandmother would have gone . . . ") See if it helps create the same dreamlike effect.

2. Try reading your favorite piece with grammar-discerning eyes. See how the writer uses, bends, or breaks the rules of grammar for any rhythmic or connotative purposes. Take a paragraph or series of lines and emulate the writer's particular choice of grammar in the passage.

Shifting Tone

Read/Revisit

Wendy Cope, "Lonely Hearts" (see page 295)
Diane Thiel, "*Memento Mori* in Middle School" (see page 313)

Tone in a piece of writing conveys the author's attitude toward the characters of the piece, the subject matter, or the audience. Changes in tone can be used to distinguish between characters or points of view (through, for example, changes in vocabulary, syntax, or linguistic traits such as dialect). Changes in tone can also be used to denote changes in the same character, or changes of attitude toward a character (e.g., a character becoming more anxious in a situation, or a character becoming more sympathetic in the eyes of the author or audience). Tone can be layered (e.g., an overtly light tone can be shaded with the use of images that imply trouble), adding depth and complexity to a piece.

In Wendy Cope's poem, she uses the romance ads as a basis for her form of repetition, the villanelle. Is the tone playful? Do you also feel some degree of longing, or loneliness? Note how a piece might convey two rather different tones at once. While the tone of the ads themselves is light, the fact of romance ads implies the more serious tone of loneliness and longing, thus deepening the meaning of the poem.

The poem "Memento Mori in Middle School" seems to have a playful tongue-in-cheek tone (with the child's interpretation of Dante's Inferno) but, here too, details introduced later in the poem, the "wood of suicides" for instance, convey a much heavier tone.

Suggestions for Writing

Choose a subject for which you could create two different tones. What would the two tones be? What details might you include to establish each particular tone? Write a short free-write using one of the tones. Then try the other.

Breaking the Rules

In *The Writing Life,* Annie Dillard tells a story of a university student who asked her, "Do you think I could be a writer?" Dillard responded by asking, "Do you like sentences?" The student in Dillard's account was surprised and somewhat dismayed by the response. "Sentences? Do I like sentences? I am twenty years old, do I like sentences?"

Dillard's classic story addresses the need to take pleasure in the individual components of the art. Good writing has attention to such elements as rhythm, syntax, diction, smooth or startling arrangements, juxtaposition of images, compression, and development of narrative (all discussed later in this book).

Even grammar can make for exciting revelations. It is important to study the way a writer uses particular techniques of grammar to achieve certain purposes. Tom Wolfe, for instance, in his essay "O Rotten Gotham," breaks many rules of grammar on purpose. He uses a run-on sentence half a page long to convey the feel of the subject he discusses: overcrowding. The sentence itself is overcrowded. He uses the present participle to show the never-ending nature of the congestion:

> In everyday life in New York—just the usual, getting to work, working in massively congested areas like 42nd Street between Fifth Avenue and Lexington, especially now that the Pan-Am Building is set there, working in cubicles such as those in the editorial offices at Time-Life, Inc., which Dr. Hall cites as typical of New York's poor handling of space, working in cubicles with low ceilings and, often, no access to a window, while construction crews all over Manhattan drive everybody up the Masonite wall with air-pressure generators with noises up to the boil-a-brain decibel levels, then rushing to get home, piling into subways and trains, fighting for time and space, the usual day in New York—the whole now-normal thing keeps shooting jolts of adrenaline into the body, breaking down the body's defenses and winding up with the work-a-daddy human animal stroked out at the breakfast table with his head apoplexed like a cauliflower out of his $6.95 semispread Pima-cotton shirt and nosed over into a plate of No-Kloresto egg substitute, signing off with the black thrombosis, cancer, kidney, liver, or stomach failure, and the adrenals ooze to a halt, the size of eggplants in July.

Suggestions for Writing

Using Tom Wolfe's above sentence as a model, write a run-on sentence about the hectic quality of a single day, using the present participle to suggest the ongoing nature of responsibilities.

3
Perspective and Point of View

Perspective

Read/Revisit

Jamaica Kincaid, "Girl" (see page 237)

Some years back, I had the opportunity to take a canoe trip through one of South Florida's cypress forests with some friends, among them a botanist and an ornithologist. To the botanist, the trip was an exciting exploration of the overabundant plant life of the area. Her eye sought the epiphytes growing on the limbs of the tall trees, the vines fighting their way over almost every stump, and the flowers proclaiming the presence of both rare and common species. Not only was she able to identify each plant, but her training allowed her to use clues such as their relative abundance and position to see the state of the ecosystem as we passed through it. To the ornithologist, on the other hand, the forest we were passing through consisted primarily of sounds. Although the birds were mostly hidden in the branches, he was able to identify them through their calls. He could even interpret the calls: mating song, cry of alarm, and so on. Were both to be asked to describe the trip, each would come up with a very different account—each description shaped by the education, experience, and interests of the narrator. The differences in their *perspectives* would give rise to two very different versions.

The perspective from which you choose to tell a story is an essential element of the narrative because it determines what you can reveal about the situation, the characters, and the action, what position you take regarding these things, which details you will focus on and which you will omit, and so on. Perspective is such an integral part of a story that very often it is absolutely clear whose story this is, so there really is no choice to be made about it. Nevertheless, it is always useful to maintain a critical attitude about all elements of the narrative. By challenging even as fundamental an aspect as perspective, by trying out different alternatives, you can be sure that you do not miss an opportunity to strengthen your piece by, for example, choosing a perspective that could offer an unexpected insight.

Choosing a Point of View

The terms *perspective* and *point of view* are often used interchangeably. However, while perspective particularly relates to *whose* eyes we see the story through, point of view generally is understood to also refer to *how* the story is told. Very often, a story gets told from the perspective of one of the characters; however, the story can be narrated using either the *first-person point of view*, where the character narrates the story and refers to himself or herself in the first person (using "I"), or from a third-person point of view, where the narrator is not the character from whose perspective the story unfolds, but, rather, a sort of invisible presence that follows this character and relates to us what the character sees, hears, feels, does, and so on. In the latter case, the character is referred to in the third person (as "he" or "she"), and the particular point of view is called the *third-person limited-objectivity point of view*. The seven possible points of view are described below, with brief discussions of their relative merits.

First Person

Choosing a character within the story as the narrator has the important advantage of immediately engaging the reader. When the narrator is the story's main character, there is a sense of immediacy created. When the narrator is not the main character, use of the first person tends to create an aura of mystery about the main character. Using the first-person point of view makes it difficult to introduce insights into what the characters are thinking—even the narrator, for constructions such as "I thought . . . " tend to become tedious when repeated too often. Drama, which essentially consists of a combination of first-person narratives, is a good example of the possibilities and limitations or challenges inherent in using the first-person point of view.

Second Person

This point of view is not used very commonly in fiction. With it, the narrator invites the reader to pretend that he or she is the narrator. It is not uncommon in nonfiction (particularly the essay) and poetry, probably because the assumption in these genres tends to be that the author is relating personal experiences. Using *you* in either its specific sense (where the writer addresses the audience directly) or its general sense (where *you* is equivalent to *one*) creates a conversational tone and tends to make universal the thoughts and experiences the writer describes.

First-Person Plural

The use and usefulness of this point of view is very similar to that of the second person. The primary objective of the use of the pronoun *we* is to create the impression of a bond between the writer and the reader, and to emphasize the commonality of thought, feeling, and experience.

Third-Person Complete Objectivity

The completely objective point of view places the narrator, and the reader, outside the events described—in the position of simple spectator. The author describes only what can be seen and heard directly, cannot provide any commentary, and is limited in revealing the thoughts and intentions of characters to only what they would speak out loud. Since this point of view is very limiting, it is not used often in fiction. It is more common in nonfiction because of the "documentary" atmosphere it can create. It can be used effectively in fiction and poetry to present characters and events that are extraordinary or difficult to believe. By refusing to comment on what clearly requires a reaction, the author can evoke strong reactions in the reader.

Third-Person Limited Objectivity

Seeing the story through the eyes of one of the characters but placing the narrator just outside this character maintains most of the advantages, and avoids certain of the disadvantages, of the first-person point of view. The immediacy of the story is largely maintained, and the narrator has the advantage of being able to know and reveal everything this character knows and thinks. The advantages of limited objectivity can be extended by shifting perspectives from one character to another. These shifts can be accomplished much more easily in longer pieces, where chapters or other such clear delineations make it easier to signal the reader that the narrative has shifted to the eyes and thoughts of a different character.

Third-Person Limited Omniscience

Choosing a point of view that allows the narrator (who remains detached from all the characters) to reveal what each of the characters knows and thinks increases the possibilities of how the story can be told. Typically, the limitation of the limited omniscience point of view is that nothing can be revealed about the future (nothing that the characters do not yet know, or have not yet thought). The greater freedom this point of view offers, however, carries the danger that the writer will reveal too much about the story, in the process losing all sense of suspense, anticipation, and tension.

Third-Person Complete Omniscience

This point of view gives complete freedom to the writer. The narrator can reveal, at any point in the story, anything that has happened or will happen, and any thoughts and feelings the characters have had or will have.

This degree of freedom creates the ultimate challenge for the writer: how can the interest of the reader be maintained? Complete omniscience is not a natural state—we never really know everything—and having to decide what to reveal and when it should be revealed in the story, when anything can be revealed at any point, is a very difficult task. As a rule of thumb, the complete-omniscience point of view is particularly useful where revelations about the future course of events can actually enhance the tension of the narrative—for example, where the main character is a historical or mythological figure, whose fate is already known, but the point of the story is to reveal something of his or her struggle against the current of events (a common device for both ancient and modern tragedies).

Suggestions for Writing

1. In an earlier exercise, you wrote about your earliest memory. Now take that memory and tell the same story from a variety of different perspectives (e.g., your own, your mother's, your grandfather's). Continue to use first person.

2. You wrote about your earliest memory using first-person point of view. Now write the same memory using third person (refer to yourself as "he" or "she").

3. Imagine a dramatic setting for your character (a battlefield, a courtroom, a family dinner), and write a brief speech for the character in which he or she is trying to convince his or her audience to take some action. Write in first-person plural (using "we").

4. Now try the less common second-person point of view. Kincaid's use of this point of view is effective because the directions, orders, and admonitions the piece is composed of paint a vivid picture of the environment the author grew up in. Think of a point in your life when you had to obey someone or follow that person's instructions and advice for much of your day (as you would in the army, your childhood home, a classroom, a sports team). Describe an incident or a day using only a list of instructions, orders, or admonitions.

5. In his poem, "The Whipping," Robert Hayden shifts from third person ("his") to first person ("my") in the middle of the poem. In the first half of the poem, Hayden, as an outside observer, describes the scene of a boy being beaten by his mother. Then Hayden shifts to the first person and identifies with the boy who is being punished.

   Try a piece that starts out using one point of view and then shifts to a different one for a particular effect.

Embodying a Voice

Read/Revisit

Ursula K. Le Guin, "The Wife's Story" (see page 238)
Miller Williams, "The Curator" (see page 317)

Miller Williams has commented that he wrote "The Curator" after overhearing a Hermitage employee tell the story of what happened at the museum during the siege of Leningrad (now St. Petersburg) in World War II. In the poem, Williams assumes the voice of the curator and tells the story in the first person. In this way, he can relate the experiences, thoughts, and feelings of the curator in an immediate and direct way, giving the story a vibrancy it might not otherwise have.

Suggestions for Writing

1. Think of a story you have overheard someone tell. Or make it a deliberate exercise to listen for pieces of conversation. Record what you overhear someone say.

   Write through that person's perspective. Try to capture the tone and style of the speaker's voice. In "The Curator," for instance, note how the speaker keeps moving deeper and deeper into the point of the story, by such breaks in the text that suggest "here, here is the story I want to tell."

2. Note how the twist of Ursula K. Le Guin's "The Wife's Story" is based on perspective. Think about the reasons Le Guin may have had for concealing the speaker's true identity until the end. What effect does this create for the reader?

   Narrate a story in which the true identity of the narrator is concealed until close to the end of the piece. For instance, you might write a piece in which the narrator appears to be a jealous girlfriend, bothered by a female visitor, but in the end, it becomes clear that the speaker is actually the cat.

Innocent Perspective

Read/Revisit

Craig Raine, "A Martian Sends a Postcard Home" (see page 308)

A newcomer in a society has a unique perspective because of an unfamiliarity with certain linguistic and social conventions. He or she has to deduce meaning from what is observable. There is much we can learn by looking at familiar things with a new perspective. This innocent view has the power to illuminate something obvious but hidden to most observers. Children, for instance, in their naiveté, are often the ones who reveal that the emperor has no clothes.

Writing from a perspective other than one's own can be mind-broadening. It is even more challenging to write about one's own culture through that other perspective. Our daily rituals, as common as they are to us, would seem bizarre to another culture, just as other cultures' rituals often strike us as strange. We have all opened *National Geographic* and been fascinated by the "necks wound round and round with wire," as Elizabeth Bishop says in her poem "In the Waiting Room." But how would our own daily rituals seem to an outsider: acts as common as shaving or applying make-up? What might other cultures think of plastic surgery? It is certainly no less bizarre as a cultural practice than the scarification rituals of certain African tribes, which shock us when we see them depicted in magazines or on television.

We have seen the use of an innocent perspective in mainstream media, in popular TV shows and movies like *Third Rock from the Sun* and *Look Who's Talking*. I have a favorite moment in the movie *Starman*, when the alien has observed and quickly assessed the rules of driving. He says, "I understand. Red means stop. Green means go. Yellow means go very very fast." He misunderstands the rules but reveals a truth we all recognize.

It can be liberating to write from the "limited perspective" of an alien. Craig Raine's poem "A Martian Sends a Postcard Home" is a good example in its depiction of such common items as a clock and a phone. Raine's poem takes on various aspects of contemporary daily life, but it just touches the surface of possibility.

Suggestions for Writing

1. Imitate Raine and explore various aspects of twenty-first-century America through the perspective of an alien. Try writing a poem like Raine's, or you might want to construct a narrative. Or you could write an analytical piece, a report on your findings. Writing from an alien perspective allows satire of many different aspects of human society. You could focus on a bar, a nuclear waste disposal site, a landfill, a school, a jail, a factory, a stripclub, a battlefield. It is a useful way to shake up your own notions about the society in which you live, to look at it with new eyes, the eyes of an outsider who may misunderstand, and, in doing so, reveal a deeper truth.

2. This exercise is a variation of the one above, as it brings up the assumptions archeologists make about past cultures. Imagine yourself arriving on a desolate, uninhabited Earth in some future year. Write through the perspective of an archeologist, digging up the objects of our everyday lives. Focus on the symbolic value of the objects you find. What do they suggest about the culture that lived here? What assumptions can you make about a society that leaves

behind the golden arches of McDonald's and a landfill full of styrofoam? What might a high-heeled shoe, make-up, and a bikini say about the society? Write an assessment of some aspect of twenty-first-century America based on the items that you find. (This exercise works well to fulfill essay assignments, in particular.)

Using Biography

Read/Revisit

Leslie Marmon Silko, "Landscape, History, and the Pueblo Imagination" (see page 192)
Hart Crane, "My Grandmother's Love Letters" (see page 295)
Sor Juana, "She Promises to Hold a Secret in Confidence" (see page 311)

Suggestions for Writing

1. In an earlier exercise, you wrote a biography of a family member or an ancestor. Now narrate a single incident through the voice of the person in the biography. Don't take on too much at once. Choose a dramatic moment of this person's life as a focal point of the narration.

   Sometimes writing with a different voice allows us to explore aspects about ourselves we might not otherwise reveal. And it can allow us to come closer to someone else's experience.

2. Narrate a historical event either from the perspective of a participant or an observer.

3. Write a letter from an ancestor's perspective. Or, if you have any actual old correspondence, use it as a source of inspiration, as in Hart Crane's "My Grandmother's Love Letters":

   > There is even room enough
   > For the letters of my mother's mother,
   > Elizabeth,
   > That have been pressed so long
   > Into a corner of the roof. . . .
   >
   > And I ask myself:
   >
   > "Are your fingers long enough to play
   > Old keys that are but echoes . . . ?"

4
Detail, Image, and Symbol

Detailing a Story

Read/Revisit

    Tim O'Brien, "The Things They Carried" (see page 262)

    As the saying goes, the devil is in the details, and it's true. Think of the world as made up of countless little pieces, the details our senses perceive. There are just too many to include when we describe something in writing. So when we write, we must choose which details are most crucial to the story we are trying to tell or the scene we are trying to depict. We must choose carefully and deliberately because the choice of what we include and what we omit establishes the mood, tone, and direction of our piece.

    Sometimes a work can consist primarily of details. In "The Things They Carried," Tim O'Brien tells the story of each soldier by simply describing what he carries. O'Brien details the soldiers' loads of both physical objects and thoughts and emotions. The apparently casual mixing of these two types of "load" gives each detail a powerful symbolic weight. The story's forward momentum and action spring from the lists of "things they carried"—from the uses and purposes of the physical objects and from the events the objects, thoughts and feelings evoke. The enumeration of details thus carries the narrative, and it is their vivid description and startling juxtaposition that catches and holds the reader's interest throughout.

Suggestions for Writing

    1. Describe a character by the things in that individual's purse, briefcase, desk, office. Let these details reveal something about the character.

    2. Try selecting details that appeal to senses other than vision. What difference is created by the details of the scent of roses as opposed

to a visual description of a rosebush? Describe, for instance, the kitchen of the home you grew up in via the smells you remember.

3. Establish a setting or character. List every detail you can come up with. Now try to select from the list. Which details might have symbolic value and function on more than one level (e.g., a heat wave, which might also imply passion or anger brimming beneath the surface)? Which details help reveal something about the character or setting without stating it directly (e.g., a fur coat and diamonds)?

Turning Abstractions into Images and Action

Read/Revisit

> Anton Chekhov, "Misery" (see page 211)
> Elizabeth Bishop, "One Art" (see page 291)
> April Lindner, "Spice" (see page 304)

One old adage of writing bears repeating: "Show, don't just tell." A little "telling" (or expository discussion about the matter) is sometimes essential, but it shouldn't merely restate or replace the image, and it should be kept in balance with the "showing" (the vivid details). Specificity can actually have a far greater power of universality than vague abstractions. If you write, for instance, about one very specific loss and inhabit the experience with vivid, descriptive language, it will have more far-reaching effects than if you speak about loss in the abstract.

Both Elizabeth Bishop in "One Art" and Anton Chekhov in "Misery" deal with loss. Bishop's poem is about dealing with loss in general, but she makes her point poignant by describing specific losses of increasingly important things. Chekhov also deals with abstract concepts in his story: misery and a society that cares not at all for an individual's pain. His story is effective because he translates these abstract concepts into concrete images and action, such as the snowy weather, the sleigh driver waiting, alone, for a fare, and the uncaring and even abusive clients.

Suggestions for Writing

1. Use an earlier piece of class writing to find examples of abstractions that could be made concrete. Or write down several abstract words, such as several emotions (e.g., anger, happiness, etc.) or any words ending in *ism*. Then use an image or series of images to convey each abstraction. For example: for anger, one might depict a red face or a muscle in the temple twitching. If you are in a workshop, you could scramble and exchange your abstract words with other participants.

2. Note how Bishop depicts loss, ranging from lost door keys to lost continents to a lost love. The poem's list builds in intensity. Write down an abstract idea, such as "loss." Then make a list of specific details that might convey the abstract idea.

3. List a few abstract concepts (e.g., domesticity, longing, love). Now replace each with a common household object, as Lindner does in "Spice." Write a short piece with the common object as its focus. Don't state the abstract concept in your piece.

4. Write a short piece about an emotion, using the emotion as a one-word title. The speaker or main character in your piece feels this emotion but wants to keep it secret. Begin your writing with the following steps:

   a. What kind of weather could reflect or intensify this emotion? List a few images.

   b. What actions by other characters would intensify this emotion? List three or four such actions.

   c. What actions by the main character or speaker would subtly betray this emotion? List three or four.

   d. What images or details about the speaker's or main character's appearance would indicate the emotion? List three or four.

   Next, review your lists to remove any details that would shout the emotion—anything that seems too obvious. Construct your piece using the four sets of remaining images and actions.

Using All of Your Senses

Read/Revisit

William Butler Yeats, "The Lake Isle of Innisfree" (see page 321)
Marianne Moore, "Poetry" (see page 305)
Diane Ackerman, "The Truth about Truffles" (see page 169)

All good creative writing is based on sensory experience. We often think of images as being visual, but they can be auditory, tactile, olfactory, and gustatory as well. Good imagery reveals something with new eyes and ears and hands and turns it around for examination, as in these words from Mariane Moore's "Poetry":

. . . The bat,
holding on upside down or in quest of something to
eat, elephants pushing, a wild horse taking a roll, a tireless wolf under
a tree, the immovable critic twinkling his skin like a horse that
feels a flea . . .

Consider Ezra Pound's poem "In a Station of the Metro":

> The apparition of these faces in the crowd;
> Petals on a wet, black bough.

Ezra Pound (1885–1972)

Although every good writer uses imagery, the above poems are examples of "Imagist" poetry. The Imagists flourished particularly from 1908 to 1917 and included such poets as Wallace Stevens, William Carlos Williams, H. D. (Hilda Doolittle), Carl Sandburg, Ezra Pound, and Marianne Moore. Pound first wrote his famous two-line poem as a thirty-line piece, but he found that the "one-image" poem captured more than a page of words in this case—a single, almost cinematic image (slowed down by the "apparition") that would reverberate afterwards. He thought of the poem as "haiku-like."

Suggestions for Writing

1. Practice the "single image." Write a series of haiku-like poems. Now try incorporating the image in a short paragraph. How does it affect the paragraph to have begun with the heightened image?

2. Try creating imagery using senses other than vision. Let us hear the "lake water lapping" and the "bee-loud glade," as in Yeats's "Lake Isle of Innisfree."

3. The paragraph that opens T. C. Boyle's story "Greasy Lake" is rich in imagery appealing to all of the senses. Read the paragraph below.

   > There was a time when courtesy and winning ways went out of style, when it was good to be bad, when you cultivated decadence like a taste. We were all dangerous characters then. We wore torn-up leather jackets, slouched around with toothpicks in our mouths, sniffed glue and ether and what somebody claimed was cocaine. When we wheeled our parents' whining station wagons out onto the street we left a patch of rubber half a block long. We drank gin and grape juice, Tango, Thunderbird and Bali Hai. We were nineteen. We were bad.

   Make a list of the images in the paragraph and the different senses to which they appeal. Now emulate the paragraph. Write about a place or memory and try incorporating imagery that appeals to all of the senses.

4. Ackerman's piece is creative nonfiction. What elements of poetry and fiction do you notice in her essay? Notice, for instance, the imagined scenario that ends the piece, with the truffle farmer and his sow. Choose a scientific subject, perhaps one from biology (such as the mating rituals of hyenas, for a wild

example). Do some research on the subject. Write a page of research information. Now create an imagined narrative using the research information. Use imagery that appeals to a number of the senses.

Writing from Art

The Fall of Icarus *by Pieter Brueghel the Elder (1520?–1569)*
Source: Scala/Art Resource, NY

Read/Revisit

> W. H. Auden, "Musée des Beaux Arts" (see page 291)
> William Carlos Williams, "The Dance" (see page 319)

Note the way in which Auden's poem "Musée des Beaux Arts" translates Brueghel's painting *The Fall of Icarus*. In the same manner, Brueghel used the text of the first-century Roman poet Ovid when he painted his *Icarus* in the 1500s. References to the ploughman, the fisher, and the shepherd appear in the ancient text. It is also interesting to note that the rhythms of Williams's "The Dance" mimic the rhythms of a dance. (The rhythm in this poem is discussed more extensively in the "Free Verse" and "Rhythm and Refrain" chapters in Part Two.)

All forms of art essentially do the same thing: they explore the nuances of the human experience. It is not surprising, then, that artists working in one form often draw inspiration from works of art in other forms. The connection between literature and painting is particularly strong, perhaps because of the vivid imagery both art forms employ.

Writing from art, known as *ekphrastic* writing, is a great way to hone your sense of the image.

Suggestions for Writing

1. Visit a museum or an art gallery. Or spend some time in a library or bookstore looking through some books with photographs of works of art. Write a response to a work of art that moves you because of its subject or imagery. When you travel and visit museums, carry your journal with you. Wandering through a gallery usually fills you with rich images and inspiration.

2. Give someone a voice: choose someone or something in a painting or sculpture. Write a short piece—a dialogue, an essay, a poem, or a story—from his, her, or its perspective.

3. Riff on a work of art. What does a particular painting make you think about? Where does it send you?

   Write a piece that focuses on a seemingly obscure detail in the piece of art—a cat on the windowsill in the background, for instance.

Symbols, Not Cymbals

Read/Revisit

Richard Wilbur, "The Writer" (see page 316)

Invariably, when we talk about symbols in workshops, someone will ask a question like "Isn't a car ever just a car?" The question recalls Sigmund Freud's famous answer that "sometimes a cigar is just a cigar." Whether something has symbolic value, of course, depends on the context. A car that is used for a getaway, an "accessory" made necessary by the plot, may be just a car, for instance, but your first car usually carries great meaning and symbolism. A symbol asks the reader to ascribe a concept or idea (like freedom) to something tangible (like a car).

Symbols vary from culture to culture, depending on religion, history, landscape, and other elements. However, because they also arise out of our unconscious, there are many similarities between symbols in different cultures. These "universal" symbols or models, such as a flood, a forest, or a fire, are known as archetypes, and they often carry a duality of meaning. A flood is both restorative and destructive, a forest is a place of natural beauty but also danger, and fire gives warmth but has great power to destroy. Symbols often enter one's writing on their own, and only later may the writer realize what has happened on the page. They may carry many layers of meaning.

A piece of writing might be overt about its symbolism, or the symbolism might exist more subtly. An *allegory* is the simplest form of symbolism—a piece in which it is obvious that the elements stand for something. In Nathaniel Hawthorne's well-known story "Young Goodman Brown," for instance, the character named Faith is clearly symbolic. In longer allegorical works such as Dante's *Divine Comedy*, there are often many layers of meaning and interpretation. Because allegory lends itself especially to didactic writing (work that attempts to teach ethical, moral, or religious values), in the wrong hands, it can feel like a sledgehammer to the reader. Overt symbols can easily become loud cymbals if the rest of the music is not kept in balance.

We live in an elaborate symbolic matrix. No one can deny it. We can see the evidence on the average drive to work. Deliberately invented symbols in our society such as words, flags, and road signs are usually referred to by scholars as *signs*. We also have *traditional* or *conventional* symbols, such as flowers or religious icons that have a certain meaning in society and that might appear in a writer's work. Writers might also use *private* or contextual symbols that develop throughout a single piece (such as the whale in *Moby-Dick*) or ones that recur in different works.

Certain people might take on a legendary or symbolic quality in a culture (Attila the Hun, Socrates, Mother Theresa, Elvis, John F. Kennedy). Actions are also sometimes symbolic—in real life and on the page. Actions tell a great deal about a person's character.

Wilbur's "The Writer" uses a starling's struggle to escape from a room as a symbol for the experience of a writer. Although he never explicitly declares the symbolism, the connection is very clear, as the speaker watches the bird, trapped in the room, and connects it to his own and his daughter's experience of being a writer.

Suggestions for Writing

1. As in Wilbur's "The Writer," juxtapose two things: an animal and its actions symbolizing a person and his or her actions.

2. In a workshop, look among your possessions for symbolic items. Take out your wallet or purse, for example. What symbolic items do you have in your possession at the moment? Money is a sign for something, of course, but it also functions on a symbolic level. Pictures? A driver's license? Unmentionables? Do you have a piece of jewelry, clothing, or a tattoo that is symbolic? Write a short piece that makes the symbolism of the item clear, but subtle. (You might also use symbolic items in your vicinity—a tree, a blackboard, a painting.)

5
Figurative Language

What you say is important, of course, but *how* you say it often makes the difference. As Robert Frost says, "All the fun's in how you say a thing."

The "how" is made up of a great variety of elements operating simultaneously, some of which have been discussed in other chapters: diction (word choice), syntax (the arrangement of words), figurative language, form. Each of these elements contributes to the *tone* (the stance or attitude) of the piece. Titles might be used to set up the tone from the beginning.

The following is a brief review of types of figurative language, with examples of poetry and prose. Most of the terms derive from the Greek (which gives them their unwieldy quality in English). The techniques, not the terms themselves, are the essential element, although you will probably also learn the terms as you try your hand at them:

apostrophe: addressing something not usually spoken to: an historical figure, a poem, an object, an idea, something in nature.

O wind, rend open the heat

H. D. (1886–1961)

Milton! Thou shouldst be living at this hour.

WILLIAM WORDSWORTH (1770–1850)

personification: giving human characteristics to something nonhuman (an animal, inanimate object, abstract idea, etc.).

A tattered coat upon a stick, unless
Soul clap its hands and sing, and louder sing
For every tatter in its mortal dress

WILLIAM BUTLER YEATS (1865–1939)

The great crane still swung its black arm from Oxford Street to above their heads.

DORIS LESSING (B. 1919)

30

synesthesia: (from Greek, meaning "blended feeling") the association of an image perceived by one of the senses with one perceived by another.

And taste the music of that vision pale

JOHN KEATS (1795–1821)

Perfumes there are as sweet as the oboe's sound
Green as prairies, fresh as a child's caress

CHARLES BAUDELAIRE (1826–1867)

hyperbole: (from the Greek, "throwing beyond") exaggeration.

I lost two cities, lovely ones. And vaster,
some realms I owned, two rivers, a continent.

ELIZABETH BISHOP (1911–1979)

And from far up, ringing from peak to peak of the summits over us, came a cry of such unutterable and ecstatic joy that it sounds down across the years and tingles among the cups of my quiet breakfast table.

LOREN EISELEY (1907–1977)

understatement: something phrased in a restrained way.

. . . for destruction ice
Is also great
and would suffice.

ROBERT FROST (1874–1963)

litotes: (from the Greek, "plain or meager") a type of understatement that makes a point by denying the opposite, such as "He's no angel."

metonymy: referring to something by using the name of something associated with it (e.g., the Church, the Crown, the White House, the silver screen). There are many categories of metonymy, such as using the name of the place for the institution ("Wall Street is jittery") or the object for the user ("The factories are on strike"). Note how scepter, crown, scythe, and spade represent social classes in the following passage:

Scepter and crown must tumble down
And in the dust be equal made
With the poor crooked scythe and spade.

JAMES SHIRLEY (1596–1666)

synecdoche: (from the Greek, "taking whole") a type of metonymy in which a part refers to the whole.

proud (orgulloso) of his daughter's pen

RHINA P. ESPAILLAT (B. 1932)

Every day brings a ship,
Every ship brings a word;
Well for those who have no fear,
Looking seaward well assured
That the word the vessel brings
Is the word they wish to hear.

RALPH WALDO EMERSON (1803–1882)

paradox: (from the Greek meaning, "contrary to expectation") a statement that seems like a contradiction but which reveals another layer of truth. Shakespeare's poetry is filled with paradox.

When most I wink, then do mine eyes best see. . . .
All days are nights to see till I see thee.

When my love swears she is made of truth
I do believe her, though I know she lies.

WILLIAM SHAKESPEARE (1564–1616)

Sylvie did not want to lose me. She did not want me to grow gigantic and multiple, so that I seemed to fill the whole house.

And below is always the accumulated past, which vanishes but does not vanish, which perishes and remains.

MARILYNNE ROBINSON (B. 1944)

oxymoron: compressed paradox, like "jumbo shrimp," or "sweet sorrow."

Parting is such sweet sorrow.

WILLIAM SHAKESPEARE (1564–1616)

allusion: reference to another literary work, history, art, event, etc. An allusion might be direct or subtle. Sometimes a work declares an influence directly, such as the quotation from Dante that opens T. S. Eliot's "Love Song of J. Alfred Prufrock." Names are another method of creating allusion, such as Melville's choice of the biblical tyrant Ahab for the captain's name in *Moby-Dick*.

An allusion might also be more subtle, such as the use of a quotation or paraphrase from another author within the piece. Sometimes the allusion has an archetypal quality about it, recalling an age-old story, such as the reference to the Flood in Alice Munro's short story "The Found Boat":

At the end of Bell Street, McKay Street, Mayo Street, there was the Flood. It was the Wawanash River, which every spring overflowed its banks. . . . Light reflected off the water made everything bright and cold, as it is in a lakeside town, and woke or revived in people certain vague hopes of disaster. . . . There were always things floating around in the Flood— branches, fence-rails, logs, road signs, old lumber; sometimes boilers, washtubs, pots and pans, or even a car seat or stuffed chair, as if somewhere the Flood had got into a dump.

ALICE MUNRO (B. 1931)

metaphor: a comparison in which something is directly described as being something else.

Young as she is, the stuff
Of her life is great cargo

RICHARD WILBUR (B. 1921)

She had horses were bodies of sand.
She had horses who were maps drawn of blood.
She had horses who wore skins of ocean water.

JOY HARJO (B. 1951)

1. **extended metaphor**: a metaphor that expands on an original comparison. Many poems operate on this principle, as do many prose passages, sometimes extensive works.

In her room at the prow of the house
Where light breaks, and the windows are tossed with linden,
My daughter is writing a story.

I pause in the stairwell, hearing
From her shut door a commotion of typewriter-keys
Like a chain hauled over a gunwhale.

Young as she is, the stuff
Of her life is great cargo, and some of it heavy:
I wish her a lucky passage.

RICHARD WILBUR (B. 1921)

2. **simile**: a type of metaphor using such words as *like, as, seems, appears.*

And like a thunderbolt he falls.

ALFRED LORD TENNYSON (1809-1892)

For the letters of my mother's mother
. . . are brown and soft,
And liable to melt as snow.

HART CRANE (1899-1932)

   3. **implied metaphor**: a metaphor that uses neither a connective such as *like* nor a form of the verb *to be*.

In her room at the prow of the house

RICHARD WILBUR (B.1921)

There are no stars tonight
But those of memory.

HART CRANE (1899-1932)

In Mississippi I wandered among some of the ghosts and bones, and it is my great lesson to have learned to stop trying to evade and forget what I have seen and heard and understood and now must know, but rather to embrace the ghosts and cradle the bones and call them my own.

ANTHONY WALTON (B. 1960)

analogy: a kind of reasoning (used in the sciences, math, history, and other disciplines) that is based on metaphor and crucial to our process of thinking and making connections. Terry Tempest Williams uses analogy and extended metaphor, as well as other figurative language, in "Peregrine Falcon":

Our urban wastelands are becoming wildlife's last stand. The great frontier. We've moved them out of town like all other low-income tenants. . . . I like to sit on the piles of unbroken Hefties, black bubbles of sanitation. . . . The starlings gorge themselves, bumping into each other like drunks. They are not discretionary. They'll eat anything, just like us. . . . Perhaps we project on to starlings that which we deplore in ourselves: our numbers, our aggression, our greed, and our cruelty. Like starlings, we are taking over the world.

TERRY TEMPEST WILLIAMS (B. 1955)

Writers often use many figures of speech within a single passage, as in the following familiar soliloquy from Shakespeare's *Macbeth* (Act V, Scene 5), which uses nearly all of them.

Tomorrow, and tomorrow, and tomorrow
Creeps in this petty pace from day to day
To the last syllable of recorded time;
And all our yesterdays have lighted fools
The way to dusty death. Out, out, brief candle!
Life 's but a walking shadow, a poor player,
That struts and frets his hour upon the stage,
And then is heard no more. It is a tale
Told by an idiot, full of sound and fury,
Signifying nothing.

Suggestions for Writing

1. Look at the passage above from *Macbeth*. How many figures of speech can you identify?

2. A fun way to practice the techniques of figurative language (and simultaneously generate ideas) is to write the terms defined and discussed above on scraps of paper. Now pick three out of a hat. Write a short piece containing all three elements.

3. For a fun but rather challenging exercise, write down several (or all) of the above types of figurative language on scraps of paper. Then write a poem, selecting a different technique at random for each line. "Following orders" in this fashion can help you grasp a particular figure of speech, but the random sequence will also provide you with some unique variations that might not have otherwise arisen—lines or thoughts to use later. In some rare instances, the initial results might actually produce a lasting poem. This exercise often yields rather surreal connections.

   For instance, use the following devices in the order they are introduced:

   line:

one (apostrophe):	Address something nonhuman
two (personification):	Personify something
three (synesthesia):	Use an image mixing sensory perception
four (hyperbole):	Exaggerate
five (understatement/litotes):	Use understatement/Deny the opposite
six (metonymy/synecdoche):	Refer to something by using something related/Use a part for a whole
seven (paradox/oxymoron):	Write a compressed contradiction
eight (allusion):	Allude to something
nine (metaphor):	Use a metaphor
ten (simile):	Extend the metaphor, using simile
eleven (implied meta-phor/analogy):	Extend the metaphor further, using implied metaphor or analogy

4. For a later, much greater challenge using the preceding exercise, you might also incorporate rhyme and meter (see the sections on rhyme and meter in Part Two). The following student response uses nearly all of the above devices in the following order: apostrophe, personification, hyperbole, paradox, synecdoche, allusion, simile, metaphor, extended metaphor.

Valentine

O, my blood, you are so red and busy,
You must get frustrated and want a drink.
So I will fix you hundreds of them, for
Alcohol poisoning might make you think.
Vintage bottles burst forth tiny red cells,
Gentle white ones with the power to kill.
Then, a funeral in my platelets,
Empty as E. Dickinson's windowsill.
You, like the silent chair in which she sat.
I more mischievous, a Cheshire cat,
Her cold fingers stroke my mane . . . life's chess game.

JENNIFER PEARSON, STUDENT

5. In a workshop, the above "following orders" exercise might be done as a collaborative poem with a random quality (the results will likely be even more surreal than the previous exercises). Each person writes the first line, then passes the paper to the right. Then each person writes the second line and passes the paper, and so on.

Using too much figurative language in a piece of writing, of course, might weigh it down or cause confusion. Some combinations of metaphor might be useful to create a surreal effect, but be wary of creating unintentional *mixed* or *warring* metaphors such as "Language is the river that opens doors" or "The curves on the road unfolded."

6
Diction

Origins of Words

Word choice in English can be particularly daunting, probably because English derives from so many languages. Following is a list of words that derive from Germanic/Anglo-Saxon roots and corresponding words from Greco-Latin roots. Words of Anglo-Saxon origin are often monosyllabic, which makes them particularly useful when writing metrical verse or for achieving the effect of a sparse style.

Germanic/Anglo-Saxon	*Greco-Latin*
house	domicile
woods	forest
dark	obscure
mad	insane
eat	consume
speak	discourse
sorrow	anguish

Suggestions for Writing

1. Write a short piece incorporating only words from the first column. Then rewrite the piece incorporating only words from the second column. Do you notice any difference in the tone?
2. Rewrite the piece in the preceding exercise using words from both columns.

Parts of Speech

Read/Revisit

Tim O'Brien, "The Things They Carried" (see page 262)
Jamaica Kincaid, "Girl" (see page 237)

Suggestions for Writing

1. Notice how Tim O'Brien's "The Things They Carried" is driven, in particular, by nouns. Write a short piece that lists a series of nouns (a noun is a person, place, or thing) that have symbolic weight. O'Brien organizes according to the *things* the soldiers carried.

2. Verbs are the strongest part of speech, and using active verbs is one of the best ways to energize your writing. Notice how Jamaica Kincaid's "Girl" is organized according to the verbs and the use of the imperative. Imitate this piece, using a series of verbs that explore your own particular environment and upbringing.

3. Take other parts of speech, such as adjectives, and try creating new verbs with them (e.g., the river blued).

4. Adjectives and adverbs are often excessive and can weaken a piece of writing. Write a few brief sentences with adverbs, such as the following:

She sank lazily into the chair.

He angrily disagreed.

Now rewrite each construction without the adverb. Perhaps choose an image that will depict the adverb.

Foreign Flavor

Read/Revisit

Rhina P. Espaillat, "Bilingual/Bilingüe" (poem and essay) (see pages 297 and 391)
Milcha Sanchez-Scott, *The Cuban Swimmer* (see page 372)

Sometimes the use of a word or words in another language seems essential to conveying aspects of a particular setting. If you grew up with a second language, you may have memories of events that took place in another language. Or you might be writing about a travel experience that would benefit from the occasional foreign word. The challenge is to let the words add flavor to the rendering in English without overburdening the piece.

Notice how Rhina Espaillat uses the register of two languages to write about the conflict of generations. Consider the effect of the parentheses and the reason for the lack of them in the final stanza. Milcha Sanchez-Scott relies heavily on Spanish in her play. However, this reliance does not make it difficult for a non-Spanish speaker to follow the dialogue in the play. The context of the situation and the actions of the characters make the meaning of the Spanish words clear to everyone.

Suggestions for Writing

1. Write a piece in which you substitute certain words with their equivalent in another language. This probably works best if you are bilingual, but if you are not, you might think of the words you do know in another language. Why do you remember them? Is there a story behind the words or phrases—how they planted themselves in your brain? Use one of these words or phrases as the impetus for a piece. Some words struck me as extraordinarily memorable the first time I heard them, because of their musicality, their root, or their meaning. The Spanish *sueño* feels dreamlike to me. I've always liked the French *plume* because of the feather and pen connection. *Besuchen*, German for visit, contains the word *suchen*, to seek.

2. Study Milcha Sanchez-Scott's use of foreign words in her play. Write a bit of dialogue between two characters, one of whom speaks only in English but the other mixes a word or phrase from another language with English. Write the dialogue so the context of the situation and the action of the speakers make it clear what the non-English words mean.

Surrealist Game

Read/Revisit

Lewis Carroll, "Jabberwocky" (see page 294)

Suggestions for Writing

The following exercise derives from a favorite practice of the surrealists, who enjoyed such collaborative, random exercises to produce writing. It was named *Cadavre Exquis* (Exquisite Corpse) allegedly because of a famous line that resulted from it: "The Exquisite Corpse Drinks New Wine." Random though it appears, the exercise is based in the logic of syntax, and it will produce some coherency amidst the random connections.

To do this exercise on your own, you could fill in the blanks as quickly as possible, without giving clear coherency from line to line, and see what results. In a workshop, everyone should begin by filling in the blanks of the first line, (try to make the individual line make sense), then pass it to the right. Each person then should write the second line and pass it to the right, and so on. When all the lines are completed, read the results aloud. (For even more surreal results, you could fold the paper to hide each completed line before you pass it.)

> At dawn, the <u>sound adjective, noun type of machine</u>
> began to <u>verb adverb</u>
> next to the <u>color adjective, noun place</u>.
> The <u>smell adjective noun, animal</u>
> <u>verb (past tense) adverb</u>
> on the <u>texture adjective, noun piece of furniture</u>.
> Later that morning, the <u>emotional adjective, noun musical instrument</u>
> <u>verb(past tense) adverb</u>
> through the <u>taste adjective, noun element of landscape</u>.
> This caused the _____.

Example:

> At dawn, the noisy dishwasher
> began to chuckle hysterically
> next to the blue house.
> The rancid cat
> complained loudly
> on the soft couch.
> Later that morning, the sad piano
> howled ferociously
> through the bitter mountains.
> This caused the windows to break.

Simplify

Although some exercises in this chapter suggest ways to use words in fresh, innovative, sometimes surreal arrangements, diction certainly need not be difficult or bizarre to have a powerful effect.

Read/Revisit

> Robert Frost, "The Road Not Taken" (see page 297)
> William Stafford, "Traveling through the Dark" (see page 312)

In Paule Marshall's essay "Poets in the Kitchen," she speaks about the major influences on her writing life as having been her relatives talking around the kitchen table. She speaks about the value of "common speech and the plain workaday words" that are the "stock in trade of some of the best fiction writers." The richness of her family's idiomatic expressions from Barbados found their way into her work. She learned more from them than from the established writers she could name as influences.

Robert Frost was known for the simple, yet evocative choice of language in his work. Consider Frost's well-known poem "The Road Not Taken" with new eyes and ears. Read it aloud to appreciate its full impact. The choice of simple, but precise words in the poem, such as *diverged, undergrowth, traveler*, and *way*, build the poem's intensity. Frost's poem also builds on a single image. It extends one central metaphor. One of the most evocative lines in the poem is "Yet knowing how way leads on to way"—an inventive syntax that repeats the most simple of words: *way*. Notice, also, how Frost keeps the rhyme fresh by using different parts of speech (noun, adjective, verb, noun adverb, pronoun, preposition) at the end of each line.

Suggestions for Writing

1. Think of your own history, your earliest memories of language, your introduction to your own identity. What "poets" do you recall (of the kitchen, poolhall, corner of fifth and Main, etc.)? Focus on one person or one group that was somehow crucial to your language, your views, your voice.

2. Try emulating Frost's simplicity. Take some cryptic lines from your journal and think about what stories they are concealing. Have the courage to just "tell it straight," as Frost often does.

    Or, write a response to Frost's poem in particular, a conversation with the idea of two roads that forked in your own life.

3. William Stafford's "Traveling through the Dark" uses simple diction and a straightforward manner of narration. Consider the effect of Stafford's choices. Try emulating his style.

Tell-Tale Dialect

Read/Revisit

Edgar Allan Poe, "The Tell-Tale Heart" (see page 275)

Dialect is a difficult element to master in writing, particularly if you are using a dialect with which you are not completely comfortable. Sometimes writers work with linguists or natives of a region to make sure that their characters' speech sounds authentic. The exercise below will get you thinking about the way using a different dialect can entirely change a piece of writing.

Suggestions for Writing

"Translate" a famous passage into a different form of English. For instance, use the opening paragraph of Edgar Allan Poe's "The Tell-Tale Heart," and have the murderer use a different dialect (e.g., from the deep South, a Brooklyn youth, Spanglish, etc.).

> True!—nervous—very, very dreadfully nervous I had been and am; but why *will* you say that I am mad? The disease had sharpened my senses— not destroyed—not dulled them. Above all was the sense of hearing acute. I heard all things in the heaven and in the earth. I heard many things in hell. How, then, am I mad? Hearken! and observe how healthily—how calmly I can tell you the whole story.

It is impossible to say how first the idea entered my brain; but, once conceived, it haunted me day and night. Object there was none. Passion there was none. I loved the old man. He had never wronged me. He had never given me insult. For his gold I had no desire. I think it was his eye!— yes, it was this! He had the eye of a vulture—a pale blue eye, with a film over it. Whenever it fell upon me, my blood ran cold; and so, by degrees— very gradually—I made up my mind to take the life of the old man, and thus rid myself of the eye forever.

Example:

Word!—nervous—I was mad scared, yo! But why you got to be say I'm trippin', you know? The disease woke me up—I ain't sleepin'. My ears was on fire with knowledge! I heard things in da' heaven above and da' earth, and all the way down to Hell. How am I nuts? Peep this! 'Cuz I got a story to tell.

I don't know how it got in my head, yo, but once it was there, yo boom—it haunted me day and night. There was no beef, no hype, 'cuz I had mad love for the old geezer! I ain't got no reason, ain't got no rhyme. He never dissed me. I wasn't trying to take his paper. But he had this nasty ol' lookin' eye. He had eyes like a vulture, blue, all glazed and all! Whenever he peeped me, my blood ran cold, and so over time, I decided to cap him before he got me.

STUDENTS: MICHELLE BYNUM, JEREMY GOLDSMITH,
JENNIFER PEARSON

You could, of course, use any of many well-known works for this exercise. The passage is a good, albeit eerie choice, because of the urgent voice: the madman who tries to convince us of his sanity. It also contains several archaic words such as *hearken*, which offer opportunity for humorous translations.

7

Setting

Setting with Personality

Read/Revisit

> Doris Lessing, "A Woman on a Roof" (see page 241)
> Charlotte Perkins Gilman, "The Yellow Wallpaper" (see page 217) and
>   "Why I Wrote the Yellow Wallpaper" (see page 394)

An important question for the writer to answer early on is "Where are we, and when?" Readers and (in the case of drama) viewers generally need the details of a concrete setting in order to enter the story and imagine themselves in it. Sometimes, particularly in shorter pieces, and especially in poetry, the title helps to place the narrative in space and time. Maxine Kumin says that titles are "geography, chronology, or furniture."

Charlotte Perkins Gilman's "The Yellow Wallpaper" has an intriguing focus on the setting. The tiny room, with its maddening wallpaper, is a crucial element of the story because it reflects the protagonist's deteriorating mental state: as the character descends into mental illness, the setting shifts from concrete external reality to essentially a landscape of the mind.

Though in most creative writing the setting is concrete (i.e., represents a specific time and place), in some cases, especially in poetry, the setting might describe purely a state of mind—thoughts or emotions. Other times, the setting may be a dream world, as in Coleridge's well-known poem "Kubla Khan." In all these cases, however, the setting is both specific and an essential element of the narrative.

The importance of the setting depends, of course, on context. Notice how crucial the setting is in Doris Lessing's "A Woman on a Roof." The heat wave in "A Woman on a Roof" might have been merely an opportunity to get a tan, but for the men working in the heat, it becomes an anger-inducing element.

Suggestions for Writing

1. Choose a limited setting and write a paragraph using that setting. Try to select an area or a place that might have symbolic resonance

on a number of levels (a church, your grandmother's attic, a cabin in the woods).

In a workshop, you might all come up with ideas for evocative settings and then decide on a single one. Each person should then write an opening paragraph using the same setting. It would be interesting to read these aloud and hear how much they differ in tone, or perhaps don't, depending on the setting selected and the different contexts.

2. Write a poem or a story that takes place in a dream, or an essay about a dream you hope could become real. Describe how the world would be if your dream were realized.

3. Sometimes the setting can be so significant it almost becomes a character in the story. The movie *The Money Pit*, for example, is about everything that can go wrong in restoring an old house. In this case, the old house is a character in the story. In "A Woman on a Roof," the oppressive heat takes on a life of its own. And in "The Yellow Wallpaper," the wallpaper begins to drive the main character mad, as she observes: "The front pattern does move— and no wonder! The woman behind shakes it! Sometimes I think there are a great many women behind, and sometimes only one, and she crawls around fast, and her crawling shakes it all over."

Create a scenario and describe the aspects of your setting in terms of a character. Try not to use a cliché like "the angry sea," although you may certainly describe the ways in which the sea is angry.

Setting from Family History

Read/Revisit

Fred D'Aguiar, "A Son in Shadow" (see page 172)
Bruce Chatwin, from *In Patagonia* (see page 170)

Bruce Chatwin's travel narrative, *In Patagonia*, opens with the memory of a piece of brontosaurus skin in his grandmother's dining room cabinet. This memory from childhood sparked an interest in Patagonia, which was where this particular brontosaurus had supposedly lived. Chatwin uses this image to establish a personal link to the region of Patagonia, as he begins to introduce the setting of the narrative.

A travel narrative is, by its very nature, largely concerned with setting and sense of place. Chatwin's personal connection with Patagonia through family history and the recounting of his early memories of the piece of brontosaurus skin creates a charge which has the effect of drawing the reader into the narrative.

In Fred D' Aguiar's "A Son in Shadow," D' Aguiar's imagines his father and mother meeting in mid-Fifties Guyana. His reconstruction of their courtship is assisted by his keen sense of the location and time in which the event took place:

> Georgetown's two-lane streets with trenches on either side mean a mostly single-file walk, she in front probably looking over her shoulder when he says something worthy of a glance, or a cut-eye look if his suggestions about her body or what he will do with it if given half a chance exceed the decorum of the day—which is what, in mid-Fifties Guyana? From my grandmother it's "Don't talk to a man unless you think you're a big woman. Man will bring you trouble. Man want just one thing from you. Don't listen to he. Don't get ruined for he. A young lady must cork her ears and keep her eye straight in front of she when these men start to flock around. . . .

Suggestions for Writing

1. Re-imagine a family story using details of place to help re-create the past, as in D'Aguiar's use of Georgetown's two-lane streets.

2. Write about a place where you have traveled or would like to travel. Try Chatwin's approach of linking the place to a family story or personal memory which will entice the reader to join you on the adventure.

3. Choose a natural setting from your family history, and use it to make a comment about a personal or societal issue. For instance, is there a part of your town that you think has been ruined? How does it connect with your own personal history? The history of the country?

4. Choose a place or a building that has evocative memories for you. Let your piece stay focused on the place as a "container" for memories.

Setting Your Hometown

How much do you really know about your hometown? What questions might you want to ask about it? When was it founded and by whom? Are there any political incidents which you think define it? How are they connected with the geography, the climate? Approaching your hometown from these different angles will let you see it both as a specific entity and a place that represents the connections and tensions between nature and culture.

Your memories and questions are likely to lead you toward further research, into archives. Start with what you do know about your hometown. You will be surprised how many of your preconceptions get shaken up. Look for original sources. It can be very exciting to hold first editions and letters in your hand. There is an immediacy about a letter that can be very inspiring. Consider Ernest Hemingway's account of the 1935 hurricane in Key West, which took so many lives. He wrote it first as a letter and then as an article, revealing the combination of failures in particular, that led to the death of a large number of WWI veterans—the failure of the Weather Bureau to issue a proper warning, and of the people in charge of the veterans who failed to take the precaution of sending a train early enough to move them out of the area:

> We were the first in to Camp Five of the veterans who were working on the highway construction. Out of 187 only 8 survived. . . .
>
> The veterans in those camps were practically murdered. . . .
>
> What I know and can swear to is this; that while the storm was at its height on Matecumbe and most of the people already dead the Miami bureau sent a warning of winds of gale strength on the keys from Key Largo to Key West and of hurricane intensity in the Florida straights [straits] below Key West. They lost the storm completely.

Hemingway's eyewitness testimony has a distinctive energy of its own.

Suggestions for Writing

1. Return to your hometown, even if you have never left. Try to see it as you have never seen it before. Visit the natural regions of your hometown. Describe what you see. Look up the geological, natural, and human history. Focus on the names of places. Research their origin. Do you find any ironies in them? Have any natural phenomena defined the place: floods, hurricanes, droughts? Have you experienced them? What images do you remember?

2. Think about how landscape helps to shape identity. Do you consider more than one place your home? Write about how the places you have lived in have influenced who you are. Focus on elements such as climate, culture, history, etc.

8
Plot and Tension

Foundations of Plot

Read/Revisit

> Charlotte Perkins Gilman, "The Yellow Wallpaper" (see page 217)
>   and "Why I Wrote the Yellow Wallpaper" (see page 394)
> Jacquelyn Reingold, *Creative Development* (see page 365)
> Sharon Oard Warner, "A Simple Matter of Hunger" (see page 279)

The term *plot* is often used interchangeably with the terms *story* and *action*. In the language of creative writing, however, the three terms are not equivalent, and a great deal can be learned by understanding the distinction between them.

Story usually refers to the whole piece, whether it be a poem, short story, or book of nonfiction. Thus the term has a broad meaning that encompasses more than what happens. It also includes the *point of view*, the *setting*, the *characters*—in short it refers to all the elements of a work of creative writing. A term that can be used interchangeably with *story* is *narrative*.

Action refers to everything that happens in a story. This includes everything that happens in the characters' minds (*internal action*), as well as everything that is done by or to the characters (*external action*).

In Gilman's story "The Yellow Wallpaper," most of the action essential to the story is internal. The story's objective is to show the process of a person's plunge into insanity. In contrast, the action in Reingold's play *Creative Development* is exclusively external. This should not be surprising, because a character's thoughts are particularly difficult to show in drama. Drama often contains a great deal of external action, some of which will reveal the character's internal conflict.

The action can be categorized in terms of its importance to the development of the story. *Significant action* is essential to the story's development. *Incidental* or *peripheral action* is not essential to the story's development but is useful because it can enhance the realistic feel of the story: for example, characters must be shown to perform at least some routine functions, such as sleeping or eating; background action can provide context for the significant action; events happening to characters totally unrelated to the main characters or to the significant action can be used to illustrate the broader effects of the significant action.

Plot refers to the arrangement of the significant action in a story. One can think of plot as the skeleton of the story—the layout of each significant action in sequence. For example, the plot of Reingold's play can be outlined as follows: woman playwright comes to a meeting with a studio's creative director in order to pitch her play for a movie script. The creative director shoots down her proposal even though he has not seen the play. When the playwright questions him, the creative director reveals he has no respect for the theater. The playwright reveals herself as a Muse and brings in her sister muses to pass judgment on the creative director. Pleading for his life, the director promises to change his ways and respect true creativity. The Muse proposes to him a script that is a combination of various blockbuster hit movies. When the director accepts it, it is the last straw, and his fate is sealed.

Each sequence of significant action in a story reveals information that is important for the development of the story. When outlining a plot, the writer must decide when it is most effective to reveal certain information. Withholding information from the reader or viewer until just the right moment increases the tension in the plot and makes the story more effective. In "A Simple Matter of Hunger," for instance, Sharon Oard Warner does not reveal the fact that the baby has AIDS until several pages into the piece. This creates a sense of suspense that increases the reader's interest and involvement in the story.

It is important to remember, however, that the plot of a story or play is only the skeleton and has to be fleshed out into the complete story by adding the other basic elements, such as setting, definition of characters, dialogue, and peripheral action.

Suggestions for Writing

1. A fundamental plot underlying many pieces of literature is that of a hero setting out on a journey to obtain something of vital importance, and then meeting and overcoming obstacles on the way. Write an outline, following this simple, but effective model. For your hero, choose an ordinary person. Choose an objective that can only be attained by traveling somewhere. Place three obstacles on the character's path: another character, a natural obstacle (e.g., weather, a natural disaster, a mountain), and a situation (e.g., airline strike, car crash, family demands). After you have sketched out an outline, write a short story about how your hero overcomes these obstacles.

2. Write a short scene or one-act play entitled "Boy (or Girl) Lost in the City." Begin by laying out the plot, then add peripheral action, and finally write the dialogue. Then write a short story with the same title. In what ways can the plot of the short story be different from

that of the play? (For example, the action in the story can easily move from one physical locale to another, whereas the action in the play is essentially restricted to one locale by the limitations of staging.) How can the peripheral action be different? (For example, in the short story, peripheral action has to be sequential and it does not need to depict typical activity of a city street in any detail. In a play, peripheral action, which must include typical street activity, can be simultaneous with the significant action.)

3. Consider, in Sharon Oard Warner's evocative story "A Simple Matter of Hunger," the way the baby's illness is not named for the first few pages. The reader wonders what is wrong with the baby. How does this approach affect the tension in the piece? Warner has commented that some readers suggested to her that she should have given the baby a different illness. But in what ways might this radically change the story? Do you think it crucial to her story that the baby has AIDS? Emulate Warner's approach to enhancing the tension in her story and write a short narrative in which an important detail is concealed until the story is well underway.

Reversing the Plot

Our universe is expanding, with the galaxies speeding away from each other. One of the fundamental questions of cosmology is what the universe's ultimate fate will be. Several theories have been proposed. One of these asserts that the expansion will eventually stop, and the universe will begin to collapse. The physicist Stephen Hawking has suggested that if this theory is correct, the arrows of time will not point in the same direction for the whole history of the cosmos. At the point the universe begins to contract, time as we know it will move backwards.

Martin Amis's book *Time's Arrow* uses Hawking's idea to explore questions of time. He narrates a life story backwards, with a soul trying to make sense of a backwards world. In doing so, he comments satirically about society—from the weighty and grave to the comic and irreverent. The following passage from the novel describes rain, lightning, and earthquakes from a backwards perspective:

> I know I live on a fierce and magical planet, which sheds or surrenders rain or even flings it off in whipstroke after whipstroke, which fires out bolts of electric gold into the firmament at 186,000 miles per second, which with a single shrug of its tectonic plates can erect a city in half an hour. Creation . . . is easy, is quick.

The conversations in the book, too, are backwards:

> "Don't go—please."
> "Goodbye, Tod."
> "Don't go."

"It's no good."

"Please."

"There's no future for us."

Which I greet, I confess, with a silent "Yeah, yeah." Tod resumes:

"Elsa," he says, or Rosemary or Juanita or Betty-Jean. "You're very special to me."

"Like hell."

"But I love you."

"I can't look you in the eye."

I have noticed in the past, of course that most conversations would make much better sense if you ran them backward. But with this man-woman stuff, you could run them any way you liked—and still get no further forward.

While recent discoveries provide support for the competing theory that the universe will continue to expand forever, reversing the flow of time in the plot remains a useful literary device. One task for which it is particularly useful is uncovering the true magnitude of events or actions.

W. S. Merwin's "Unchopping a Tree" uses the reversal of time to achieve this effect. In the description of the mammals, the nests, the insects that would have to be returned, the splintered trunk reconnected, one senses the enormity of the destruction in the felling of a single tree. In describing the process backwards, he makes a comment about the intricate balance of nature that, once destroyed, is impossible to restore:

> With spiders' webs you must simply do the best you can. We do not have the spider's weaving equipment, nor any substitute for the leaf's living bond with its point of attachment and nourishment.

Suggestions for Writing

Describe something backwards. Create your reverse-time version in order to make a comment about something that has been done that might be better undone (e.g., undevelop a new development, unpollute a river, etc.).

Trading Characters, Settings, and Conflicts

The mind searches for ways to make sense of disparate elements, to make narrative. Although the following exercise might not always yield the best story, it is a good challenge, and the mere combinations alone often make for good humor: (e.g., Napoleon, in class, stage fright; Madonna, Buckingham Palace, UFO sighting).

The combinations that arise can be kernels of later, more substantial pieces.

Suggestions for Writing

1. Have each person write down a character, a place, and an event on three separate scraps of paper. Collect them in piles. Then each participant will select one from each pile. Construct a short narrative using the three elements you have chosen. Try to use each of the elements in an equally significant way. Note the following student example:

> (a student, a ramshackle cabin, world domination)
> The school had called a snow day, and Tom had been hunting all day down in the state forest. When he came back to the house, he had no idea where Billy was or what he was up to. He saw the diffuse glow of a single hanging lightbulb coming from the guest cabin located in the far end of the field behind their house. As he brushed through the overgrown reeds in his rubber boots, he saw tiny fireworks bursting sporadically in one of the broken out windows. Billy was doing something with the scraps from the rusted out brick wagon. Tom crept closer. Little glints of light flew, and as Tom felt along the splintery wood walls, it became obvious to him what his brother was doing. The mildewed map of the world was dangling on the wall. The little flags were posted precariously. Billy was at it again.
>
> EMILY BUSCH, STUDENT

2. Assign each other titles, based perhaps on heritage and inclinations. The titles might send you where you otherwise would not have gone. Or try a different approach and use titles randomly. In a workshop, come up with titles and then scramble them. Write a piece with the title you receive.

Reverberating Closure

Read/Revisit

Evan Connell, from *Mrs. Bridge* (see page 215)
Alice Walker, "Am I Blue" (see page 207)
Alice Munro, "How I Met My Husband" (see page 248)
Elizabeth Bishop, "One Art" (see page 291)
Diane Thiel, *Memento Mori* in Middle School" (see page 313)
Nikos Kavadias, "A Knife" (see page 302)
Edwin Arlington Robinson, "Richard Cory" (see page 310)

Robert Frost says, "Anyone can get into a poem. It takes a poet to get out of one. William Butler Yeats believed good closure occurred when a poem would "come shut with a click, like a closing box." What gives a piece of writing that click? It is hard to identify, but we know it when we see or hear it. Evan Connell's vignettes in his novel *Mrs. Bridge* shut like a door at the end, yet also echo into the next chapter. Perhaps that is the quality closure should have—it should reverberate.

A poignant or startling event, scene, image, or moment can make for good closure, in drama, prose, or poetry. Alice Walker's example in her narrative essay "Am I Blue," for instance, ends with the speaker spitting out "misery." Likewise, the poem "*Memento Mori* in Middle School" closes with the image of children yelling after school, showing off "their darkened red and purple tongues."

Closure is sometimes influenced by form. Sonnets, for instance, traditionally closed with a philosophical commentary. And several poetic forms, such as the villanelle, have refrains that often carry a slightly different meaning in the end (see Elizabeth Bishop's "One Art"). A piece might also be left mysterious.

Some writers favor the ironic ending, which usually has to be set up from the beginning. The irony of Ursula K. Le Guin's vignette, "The Wife's Story," for instance, becomes clear close to the end of the story, as it becomes apparent that the speaker is a wolf. In Alice Munro's "How I Met My Husband," the title and first 12 pages prepare you for one kind of story, as they describe how the speaker met and fell in love with a dashing air-show pilot. However, a radical shift occurs in the last two paragraphs. Edie, the main character, has been waiting for a promised letter from her first love, going down daily to meet the mail:

> Till it came to me one day there were women doing this with their lives, all over. There were women just waiting and waiting by mailboxes for one letter or another. I imagined me making this journey day after day and year after year, and my hair starting to get gray. . . . So I stopped meeting the mail. . . .
>
> I was surprised when the mailman phoned the Peebles' place in the evening and asked for me. He said he missed me. He asked if I would like to go to Goderich, where some well-known movie was on, I forget now what. So I said yes, and I went out with him for two years and he asked me to marry him, and we were engaged a year more while I got my things together, and then we did marry. He always tells the children the story of how I went after him by sitting by the mailbox every day, and naturally I laugh and let him, because I like for people to think what pleases them and makes them happy.

Poems often carry an element of surprise at the end. Dorothy Parker's poems, for instance, are known for their ironic twists, such as one of my favorites, "One Perfect Rose," which is set up as a love poem, with a refrain of "one perfect rose" that the speaker's love always brings. The twist comes in the last stanza, when the speaker wonders why her love has never sent her "one perfect limousine, do you suppose?"

Consider the effect of the closure in Edwin Arlington Robinson's "Richard Cory." The end of the poem "makes" the poem, because it is unexpected. The ending works not just because of the element of surprise, but because it reflects accurately the way such events feel when they occur.

Nikos Kavadias's ballad "A Knife" carries a similar element of surprise at the end. We are drawn into the story being narrated by the old dealer, and though filled with the intensity of the violence surrounding the history of the knife, we are still somewhat unprepared for the final line, which continues reverberating after the poem is finished.

There is an old German proverb regarding closure: "Beginning and end shake hands with each other." Sometimes, when we are writing, we know we have reached the end, and it happens naturally, perhaps with an organic, circular structure that contains elements of the opening. Other times we have an idea, but it takes a while to find the right words. And sometimes a piece does not seem to find an end. Try not to force it. It might be telling you to continue down that road.

Suggestions for Writing

1. Try writing a piece with an ironic closure, one that surprises the reader because the opposite of what is expected takes place. Play the trickster. Some real-life stories have a natural irony when they occur, with a clear closure, a line of dialogue, perhaps.

2. Look with new eyes at the closure of a piece you have written. Are there any other ways your piece could end? Write an alternative closure and compare the two. Discussions about closure should be an important aspect of a workshop. Often, as writers, we don't know when to stop; a natural closure might already exist in the piece. Other sets of eyes can help identify what is missing or what can be cut.

9
Rhythm

Finding Your Rhythm:
Poetry in Prose

Rhythm is an organic part of our everyday lives—in the tides, crickets in the night, our heartbeats. What makes rhythm in a piece of writing? Rhythm is defined as a systematic variation in the flow of sound. In poetry, rhythm might be regular, via the use of meter. Or it might be based on the unit of breath. The repetition of key words and phrases is a technique of free verse and the prose poem. (Rhythm in poetry is discussed extensively in "Rhythm and Refrain" and "Hearing the Beat: Using Meter" in Part Two.) But there is much that good prose can learn from poetic technique as well.

Consider the following passage from Marilynne Robinson's novel *Housekeeping*:

> Looking out at the lake one could believe that the Flood had never ended. If one is lost on the water, any hill is Ararat. And below is always the accumulated past, which vanishes but does not vanish, which perishes and remains. If we imagine that Noah's wife when she was old found somewhere a remnant of the Deluge, she might have walked into it till her widow's dress floated above her head and the water loosened her plaited hair. And she would have left it to her sons to tell the tedious tale of generations. She was a nameless woman, and so at home among all those who were never found and never missed, who were uncommemorated, whose deaths were not remarked, nor their begettings.

Robinson's choice of language is a beautiful example of poetry within prose. If you read the above passage aloud, you will notice the rhythm of the sentences, the near iambic lines such as "If one is lost on the water, any hill is Ararat," "If we imagine that Noah's wife when she was old," or "whose deaths were not remarked nor their begettings." She even uses internal assonance (such as *past* and *vanish*, or *tale* and *hair*) and alliteration (such as *tedious tale*). There are parallel structures such as "which vanishes but does not vanish, which perishes and remains" and "who were never found and never missed, who were uncommemorated, whose deaths were not remarked." Notice also the variation of sentence length and structure. Much of the music of this type of passage is best heard, however, when read aloud.

President Lincoln, in his Gettysburg Address, employed poetic techniques so effectively that the speech has been often called a poem, and it is one of the very few speeches (and perhaps the only presidential address) to be considered a piece of literature. Phrases such as "we cannot dedicate—we cannot consecrate—we cannot hallow this ground" employ repetition and variation to full rhythmical effect. Certain portions of the speech even employ meter: "The world will little note nor long remember what we say" is in perfect iambs.

> Four score and seven years ago our fathers brought forth upon this continent a new nation conceived in Liberty, and dedicated to the proposition that all men are created equal.
>
> Now we are engaged in a great civil war, testing whether that nation or any nation so conceived and so dedicated can long endure. We are met on a great battlefield of that war. We are met to dedicate a portion of it as the final resting place of those who here gave their lives that that nation might live. It is altogether fitting and proper that we should do this.
>
> But in a larger sense we cannot dedicate—we cannot consecrate—we cannot hallow this ground. The brave men living and dead who struggled here have consecrated it far above our poor power to add or detract. The world will little note nor long remember what we say here, but it can never forget what they did here. It is for us, the living, rather to be dedicated here to the unfinished work that they have thus far so nobly carried on. It is rather for us to be here dedicated to the great task remaining before us—that from these honored dead we take increased devotion to that cause for which they here gave the last full measure of devotion—that we here highly resolve that the dead shall not have died in vain—that the nation shall, under God, have a new birth of freedom—and that governments of the people, by the people, and for the people, shall not perish from the earth.

Suggestions for Writing

1. Try to discover what your natural rhythm might be. Take a passage of your writing and study various elements. For instance, what is the ratio of short to long sentences? What repetition of sentence structure do you see? Do you notice repetitions of words?

2. Take a favorite passage of prose that has an evocative rhythm. Look at it closely and examine what elements contribute to that rhythm. What poetic techniques can you identify in the passage?

Parallel Structures

Read/Revisit

Sherman Alexie, "Indian Education" (see page 290)
Sherman Alexie and Diane Thiel, "A Conversation with Sherman Alexie" (see page 386)
Joy Harjo, "She Had Some Horses" (see page 300)

Parallel structures are another type of rhythmical tool in prose or poetry. The repetitions are often used to reinforce a statement and effect a certain rhythm. Great orators were known for employing this structure, as Martin Luther King Jr. does in works such as the famous "I Have a Dream" speech and "Letter from Birmingham Jail." One well-known example of parallelism is the following verse:

> For want of a nail, the shoe was lost,
> For want of a shoe, the horse was lost,
> For want of a horse, the rider was lost,
> For want of a rider, the battle was lost,
> For want of a battle, the kingdom was lost,
> And all for the want of a horseshoe nail.

BENJAMIN FRANKLIN (1706–1790)

Walt Whitman often uses a parallel structure to create rhythm in his free verse. The following is an excerpt from "When Lilacs Last in the Dooryard Bloom'd," Whitman's famous elegy mourning the death of Abraham Lincoln. The repetition of the first word of a line as the first word in succeeding lines is known as *anaphora*. Notice the way the parallel structure builds the rhythm and contributes to the intensity of the traveling coffin:

> Coffin that passes through lanes and streets,
> Through day and night with the great cloud darkening the land,
> With the pomp of the inloop'd flags with the cities draped in black,
> With the show of the States themselves as of crape-veil'd women standing,
> With processions long and winding and the flambeaus of the night,
> With the countless torches lit, with the silent sea of faces and the unbared heads,
> With the waiting depot, the arriving coffin, and the sombre faces,
> With dirges through the night, with the thousand voices rising strong and solemn,
> With all the mournful voices of the dirges pour'd around the coffin,
> The dim-lit churches and the shuddering organs—where amid these you journey,
> With the tolling bells' perpetual clang,
> Here, coffin that slowly passes,
> I give you my sprig of lilac.

WALT WHITMAN (1819–1892)

Parallel structures exist in Native American traditions as well. Joy Harjo often uses such repetition, as in "She Had Some Horses," a poem filled with contradictions:

> She had horses who called themselves "horse."
> She had horses who called themselves "spirit," and kept
> their voices secret and to themselves. . . .
> She had horses who whispered in the dark, who were afraid to speak.
> She had horses who screamed out of fear of the silence, who
> carried knives to protect themselves from ghosts.
> She had horses who waited for destruction.
> She had horses who waited for resurrection.

JOY HARJO (B. 1951)

Sherman Alexie uses similar parallel structures in many of his poems, as in "Indian Education," where the repetition of "Crazy Horse" creates an element of rhythm in the poem. In the interview included in Part Three of this book, Alexie speaks about his artistic and cultural reasons for using parallel structure and repetition.

Many writers also use a parallel structure called *chiasmus* (crossing), in which the word order of one phrase is inverted in the next, as in the lines that open Christian Wiman's long narrative poem in blank verse, "The Long Home." The effect is one of elegance within simple language:

> We drove all day on roads without a speck
> Of paving, not knowing but knowing not
> to ask when we would stop or where.
>
> CHRISTIAN WIMAN (B. 1966)

A good example of chiasmus in prose is the following sentence from Marilynne Robinson's *Housekeeping*: "Every sorrow suggests a thousand songs, and every song recalls a thousand sorrows."

Suggestions for Writing

1. Write a short prose piece using a parallel structure to emphasize your point and give the passage a certain rhythm.

2. To practice chiasmus, list several pairs of words that create an interesting meaning or rhythm. The word "not" works well with many different verbs, but also try to think of some other pairings. Now incorporate each set into a sentence. A caution: chiasmus can add spice to writing, but just a pinch is often enough.

3. When describing something, the natural tendency is to list its characteristics. But it can be powerful to list what it is not, instead. Describe something by stating what it is not. Create a parallel structure of negative statements.

Listening to Nature

Read/Revisit

William Butler Yeats, "The Lake Isle of Innisfree" (see page 321)

The natural world is filled with songs. We can learn a great deal about the rhythms of nature by just listening. Go to the ocean, a waterfall, a river near your home. Listen for a while. Then try writing as you listen. How does it affect your rhythm?

Go into the woods and listen to the trees. Listen to the wind in the trees. Stay very still and listen to bird calls for a while. Then write. What might they be saying? Can you tell the tone of their songs? Do you hear the scolding shriek of a bluejay, the wild laugh of a loon, or the lyrical song of a warbler? Do they sound like anything you know?

You might also be able to discern certain rhythms with your eyes. A good example is a lizard's dewlap. I have sat mesmerized by the hypnotic beat of the dewlap concealed in the throat, revealing itself again and again.

Think about your own voice. What physical realities make the sounds and words emerge? Why do people from different regions have different accents? Do we train our mouths to move in a certain way? In a favorite novel of mine, David Malouf's *An Imaginary Life*, there is a passage where the Roman poet Ovid is teaching a wild boy to speak. The boy can imitate all the birds and animals of the woods, but rather than merely mimicking, he seems to become the creature:

> His whole face is contorted differently as he assumes each creature's voice. If he were to speak always as frog or hawk or wolf, the muscles of his throat and jaw might grow to fit the sound, so intimately are the creatures and the sounds they make connected, so deeply are they one. . . . I have begun to understand him. In imitating the birds, he is not, like our mimics, copying something that is outside him and revealing the accuracy of his ear or the virtuosity of his speech organs. He is being the bird. He is allowing it to speak out of him.

Try making the sounds you hear. What new muscles do you use? One interesting and easy exercise to do in the wild will attract many birds to you. Conceal yourself well and make repeated *psh psh psh* sounds. The sounds imitate the scolding calls of many birds. It can also be a meditative experience to remain still and call like that. Listen to the responses you get. Are there rhythms, repetitions? Imagine yourself as an arriving bird. What are you hearing? What are you thinking as you respond?

In Malouf's book, as Ovid learns more about the wild boy, he realizes how deeply the boy is connected to the universe. If he is to understand the child, he needs to "think as he must: I am raining. I am thundering."

Suggestions for Writing

1. Imitate the rhythm of a sound you hear—a bird call, the ocean. Let your form reflect something in the natural world. Robinson Jeffers's long lines, for instance, reflect the rhythm of the dramatic Pacific tides.

2. You might also listen for the rhythms of something other than the natural world. Let the rhythms of everyday speech find their way into your writing. (See the "Dialogue" chapter.) You might also try to capture the pace of a city—the positives or the negatives. (See Tom Wolfe's use of the chaotic run-on sentence in the section on "Breaking the Rules.")

3. In "Ode to a Nightingale," John Keats reflects on the unchanging music of the nightingale throughout history:

> Perhaps the selfsame song that found a path
> Through the sad heart of Ruth, when sick for home,
> She stood in tears amid the alien corn
> The same that oft-times hath
> Charmed magic casements, opening on the foam
> Of perilous seas, in faery lands forlorn.
>
> JOHN KEATS (1795–1821)

Let the music in nature take you to another realm. Write about another era in which this song was heard.

4. Some words seem to have sounds as their origin—crunch, growl, splash, hum—an effect known as *onomatopoeia*, from the Greek, meaning "name-making." A sophisticated use of onomatopoeia can be heard in the following well-known lines by Alfred Lord Tennyson:

> The moan of doves in immemorial elms,
> And murmuring of innumerable bees.
>
> ALFRED, LORD TENNYSON (1809–1892)

As you listen to sounds around you, repeat the sounds, listening to your own voice for the words they bring to mind. Keep a list of such words. Incorporate them in a piece of writing.

10
Character and Speaker

Populating a Piece

Read/Revisit

> Nikos Kavadias, "A Knife" (see page 302)
> Alice Walker, "Am I Blue" (see page 207)

Just as the real world is populated by living things, literature is populated by characters. The term "living things" is used here deliberately, to emphasize that nonhuman characters figure prominently in many important pieces of literature—especially certain forms such as children's literature, fairy tales, myths, science fiction, and nature writing.

Characters in literature can be described via a number of literary devices. While some of these devices may be specific to a genre, there are three that are common to all four genres: description, dialogue (direct or indirect), and thoughts. The process of presenting a character is called *characterization*.

Characters can be presented in varying detail or *depth*. When little detail is provided, the character is superficial or two-dimensional—*flat*. When the characterization provides more details, the character is more realistic or three-dimensional. Typically, it is the secondary characters in a piece that are flat, but there are important exceptions. The lack of depth in characterization tends to produce characters that are stereotypes, such as the tall, dark, handsome lover or the ugly, crude villain. Consequently, flat characterization of main characters is particularly appropriate for parody, allegory, or a lighter piece that is intended purely to amuse.

Suggestions for Writing

> 1. Describe an interesting stranger you came across in the street (or the park, airport, etc.). Focus your description exclusively on appearance and what it conveys about the character.

2. Create a nonhuman character and a human character and write a story or a poem about a special relationship that develops between them, as Alice Walker does in "Am I Blue." Endow the nonhuman character with human characteristics. You might also take the relationship further than Walker does and imagine a fantastic relationship, one that can never happen in reality.

Assuming a Voice

Read/Revisit

Robert Browning, "My Last Duchess" (see page 292)

Robert Frost once wrote, "When I say me in a poem, it's someone else. / When I say somebody else, it might be me." Sometimes writing with a different voice allows us to explore aspects about ourselves we might not otherwise reveal. Sometimes it allows us to come closer to someone else's experience. Try inhabiting one of the characters in a story (with whom you identify perhaps) and write from the *persona* you create. You could give someone a voice who previously had none. You might, for instance, inhabit an animal from a myth or fairy tale.

Victorian poet Robert Browning developed the form of the *dramatic monologue* (a speech that creates a dramatic scene) in a poem. He often used the form to explore the psyches of weak, troubled, or crazy characters. His "My Last Duchess," likely the most famous dramatic monologue ever written, takes on the voice of an Italian Renaissance duke:

> She thanked men,—good! but thanked
> Somehow—I know not how—as if she ranked
> My gift of a nine-hundred-years-old name
> With anybody's gift.
>
> ROBERT BROWNING (1812–1889)

The narrator of David Malouf's novel *An Imaginary Life* assumes the voice of the Roman poet Ovid, who is exiled to a region where no one can speak his language. It is this element of the story that Malouf enters most fully:

> I have come to a decision. The language I shall teach the Child is the language of these people I have come among, and not after all my own. And in making that decision I know I have made another. I shall never go back to Rome. . . . More and more in these last weeks I have come to realize that this place is the true destination I have been seeking.

Suggestions for Writing

1. Make a list of historical or mythological figures you would like to "inhabit." Consider the particular aspect of their lives that intrigues you. You might need to do some research in order to have your facts straight. Try a dramatic monologue from one of your chosen perspectives, focusing on a particular "story" of the figure's life. You may be surprised how the voice comes when you call it, as in the following student example:

> (Inhabitation of Federico Garcia Lorca)
> People think that being a poet means that every minute there's a poem in your head, that every time of silence, there are little mechanisms in your creative fiber that produce stanzas and lines of love and pain, the only two emotions that are valuable. But it's not that simple. It's not like jumping into a pool and coming out with all sorts of ideas and dreams and stories. Sometimes a poem is written in blood—it comes to you in pain and agony. Sometimes it is like sweet nectar so soothing to the palate. . . . Poetry is fire and ice, my friend.
>
> JORGE FERNANDEZ, STUDENT

2. Inhabit an animal, or an inanimate object, or a natural phenomenon, like a hurricane.

3. Repeat the preceding exercise as a group project, one that will emphasize the web of connections. Each person might choose to be a different voice of a certain ecosystem. I have done this exercise with groups of college students as well as young kids. A group of middle school students made a skit out of the voices, called "The Everglades Council," with the council being made up of various members of the ecosystem. I was pleased to see that students chose to be the tiny things as well as the large: the apple snail and the snail kite, as well as the alligator. Some students chose to be the voice of the sun, the water, the wind. One chose to be the human.

4. In another variation of the preceding exercises, write through the voice, but make it a riddle of sorts, never directly stating what you are. This is a useful exercise to see if your description is effective.

Inside a Character's Mind

Dialogue or a character's response to a setting or situation can tell a great deal more about her or his personality than straight physical description or abstract words (see, for instance, the excerpt from Evan Connell's *Mrs. Bridge*).

Another way of revealing character is via the workings of that character's mind. Although early novels often contained an omniscient or all-knowing narrator, many modern novels have no narrator at all. Rather, novelists such as James Joyce and Virginia Woolf bring us into the twists and turns of a character's mind, via a *stream-of-consciousness* approach. The following passage of Virginia Woolf's *The Waves*, for instance, shows the character Bernard in turmoil about writing a letter to the girl he loves. The layers of character development are numerous here, as Bernard admits to creating another persona for the letter:

> Yes, all is propitious. I am now in the mood. I can write the letter straight off which I have begun ever so many times. I have just come in; I have flung down my hat and my stick; I am writing the first thing that comes into my head without troubling to put the paper straight. It is going to be a brilliant sketch which, she must think, was written without a pause, without an erasure. Look how unformed the letters are—there is a careless blot. All must be sacrificed to speed and carelessness. I will write a quick, running small hand, exaggerating the down stroke of the 'y' and crossing the 't' thus—with a dash. The date shall be only Tuesday, the 17th, and then a question mark. But also I must give her the impression that though he—for this is not myself—is writing in such an offhand, such a slapdash way, there is some subtle suggestion of intimacy and respect. I must allude to talks we have had together—bring back some remembered scene. But I must seem to her (this is very important) to be passing from thing to thing with the greatest ease in the world. . . . I want her to say as she brushes her hair or puts out the candle, "Where did I read that? Oh, in Bernard's letter." It is the speed, the hot, molten effect, the lava flow of sentence into sentence that I need. Who am I thinking of? Byron, of course. I am, in some ways, like Byron. Perhaps a sip of Byron will help to put me in the vein. Let me read a page. No; this is dull; this is scrappy. This is rather too formal. Now I am getting the hang of it. Now I am getting his beat into my brain (the rhythm is the main thing in writing). Now, without pausing I will begin, on the very lilt of the stroke—
>
> Yet it falls flat. It peters out. I cannot get up steam enough to carry me over the transition. My true self breaks off from my assumed. And if I begin to rewrite it, she will feel, "Bernard is posing as a literary man; Bernard is thinking of his biographer" (which is true). No, I will write the letter tomorrow directly after breakfast.

Suggestions for Writing

1. Free-writing, in effect, reveals our own stream of consciousness. Try getting in character, and free-writing as that character, in order to create the mental wanderings of the character's mind. (One caution: go deeply into your character, but leave more than a trail of bread crumbs to find your way back.)

2. Use dialogue or a sequence of actions to reveal a character's personality.

3. Write a description of a character's physical qualities, using details such as bumping one's head on the doorway or wearing shoe-lifts, or causing a stir when he or she walks into the room.

11
Dialogue

Dialogue Makes Character

Read/Revisit

Jamaica Kincaid, "Girl" (see page 237)
James Joyce, from *A Portrait of the Artist as a Young Man* (see page 230)

Much of a character's nature can be revealed by what he or she says and does. A piece like Jamaica Kincaid's "Girl," for instance, is built entirely on the mother's voice as a series of instructions for her daughter; this unique piece becomes a mother's monologue, actually, although the daughter's voice is heard twice in the piece. We can gather a great deal about the mother/daughter relationship from the barrage of words we hear the former speak, as well as the very few words we hear from the latter.

In James Joyce's *A Portrait of the Artist as a Young Man*, we gain a sense of Stephen Dedalus's character through the stream-of-consciousness technique that shows the inner workings of his mind as well as the dialogue with other characters. In the excerpt from the novel included in Part Three, we can tell a great deal about Stephen Dedalus through the dialogue with his classmates. Consider the following interaction:

Nasty Roche had big hands. He called the Friday pudding dog-in-the-blanket. And one day he had asked:
—What is your name?
Stephen had answered: Stephen Dedalus.
Then Nasty Roche had said:
—What kind of a name is that?
And when Stephen had not been able to answer Nasty Roche had asked:
—What is your father?
Stephen had answered:
—A gentleman.
Then Nasty Roche had asked:
—Is he a magistrate?

The simple dialogue speaks volumes about the interaction between Stephen Dedalus and Nasty Roche and begins to prepare us for the violence Stephen experiences from the other boys.

Suggestions for Writing

1. Write a short dialogue in which you reveal a character through dialogue with another character.

2. Tape one of your own conversations at a café or a bar and then transcribe it. Then select the most distinctive portions that would work well in a story. How much of the actual conversation can be discarded? What elements might be kept to convey a certain rhythm of the conversation, even if they aren't information rich?

The Unsaid

Read/Revisit

Evan Connell, from *Mrs. Bridge* (see page 215)

Dialogue can often be most revealing by what is not said. In Evan Connell's novel *Mrs. Bridge*, we get a strong sense of Mrs. Bridge's character by the way she skirts issues and chooses her words so decidedly. Often, while it appears she is trying to be polite, she actually becomes quite offensive. When her daughter Carolyn wants to go to her black friend Alice's party, the precise details and what remains unsaid in the dialogue carry great weight:

"Where does Alice live?"
"Thirteenth and Prospect."
Mrs. Bridge took up a little silver knife and began to cut a slice of peach which was rather too large to be eaten in one bite. She knew where Thirteenth and Prospect was, although she had never stopped there. It was a mixed neighborhood.
"Can I go?"
Mrs. Bridge smiled affectionately at Carolyn. "I wouldn't if I were you."

Suggestions for Writing

Create a character who has something to conceal. Place him or her in a controversial conversation. Now emulate Connell's Mrs. Bridge, in the way the character says a great deal with what she chooses not to say.

Dropping from the Eaves

We all have a natural curiosity about other people's lives. If we didn't, story-telling would have no place in our world. Tuning in to other people's lives, particularly in places where we are anonymous, can offer inspiration. Of course, many people today eavesdrop in chatrooms on the Internet, which can be an interesting experience in itself. But people don't tend to tell elaborate stories on the Internet, and there is something about the *overheard* story that can give a richness and reality to your listening, and later to your writing.

Eavesdropping—the word itself is like a poem, like the words dropping magically from the eaves into your own writing.

Suggestions for Writing

1. Here is your license to eavesdrop. Go to a public space: a café, the beach, a bus, a train, any place where you might mingle with people from many walks of life. Give yourself different "listening" exercises. Try to catch some dialogue, intonation. Transcribe the actual words people say. (But be as discreet as possible. People tend to sense an ear bending toward them to hear better.)

   Hallelujahs mask oh-no-she-didn'ts. . . .
   She didn't invite who to the wedding?
   Guess who's not invited to the mother's banquet.
   Deacon Wiley's sleeping with who?
   No wonder she hasn't been to choir practice. . . .
   Sister Jones is testifying once again
   Going on about how the Lord brought her a Lexus.

   MICHELLE BYNUM, STUDENT

2. Use the eavesdropping to create a *dramatic monologue*. Let the character's speech create a dramatic scene.

12
Conversations between Texts

Making the Old Story New

Read/Revisit

> Ursula K. Le Guin, "The Wife's Story" (see page 238)
> R. S. Gwynn, "Shakespearean Sonnet" (see page 300)
> W. H. Auden, "Musée des Beaux Arts" (see page 291)
> Diane Thiel, "*Memento Mori* in Middle School" (see page 313)

Our stories never change. They simply take on different forms. Once we learn to recognize archetypes (patterns or models present in the unconscious as well as in our heritage of art), we can often see them at work in sources as varied as fairy tales, nursery rhymes, ancient myths, contemporary stories, and in our own writing.

There are countless sources available today that show how archetypes can be used to understand various aspects of our lives—from psychology, to relationships, to job-related issues. The works of psychologist Carl Jung and mythologist Northrop Frye are classic sources. A rather accessible source as an introduction to archetype is Joseph Campbell. His *Hero with a Thousand Faces* draws on the idea of the same stories existing in different cultures, with the heroes and dragons wearing different faces but undergoing similar journeys, trials, and revelations. ("The Hero's Adventure," in particular, in a series of videotaped interviews with Campbell called *The Power of Myth* provides an excellent introduction.)

Of course, there can be a danger in being too aware of archetypes as we recreate them. And one can say this about any kind of art—that, on some level, it is good not to be too aware. Sometimes, the first conscious efforts at using myth or archetype can yield rather clunky results. Nonetheless, it is good practice to let the mind connect story to story, to become familiar with recurring themes, symbols, and sequences of action: the battle, the cycle of life, the forest, the flood, the fountain, the journey. Then they will begin to wander your writing with more fluidity.

All works of art can be explored for archetypal ideas. Certain works have become patterns after which so many other pieces are modeled. Some works declare the influence of such a text in the very title: James Joyce's *Ulysses* or Derek Walcott's *The Odyssey* or *Homeros*, for example, establish the connection with Homer's *Odyssey* and the archetype of the journey.

Many writers use other works of literature, from ancient texts to fairy tales, as explicit points of departure. They might use means such as exploring a particular character or sequence of action, or add an ironic twist or ending. American humorist James Thurber retells the story of "Little Red Riding Hood," a classic example of the archetypal encounter in the dark forest. Thurber's version, however, ends with the girl pulling a revolver out of her basket and shooting the wolf dead. The moral that ends the parody is: "Little girls aren't as foolish as they used to be."

Sometimes a writer will choose to write from the point of view of a character who doesn't have much of a voice in the original work. John Gardner's novel *Grendel*, for instance, tells the story of Beowulf from the perspective of the monster, Grendel. Likewise, Jean Rhys's novel *Wide Sargasso Sea* tells the story of Rochester's insane first wife, who has no voice in Charlotte Bronte's *Jane Eyre*.

R. S. Gwynn's "Shakespearean Sonnet" uses the form of a Shakespearean sonnet to reflect on 14 Shakespeare plays in 14 lines. Gwynn received the inspiration for the poem from a blurb in an issue of *TV Guide* that reduced *Hamlet* to the unintentionally iambic line, "A man is haunted by his father's ghost." The compression of each of the plays supplies much of the humor in the poem.

The poem "*Memento Mori* in Middle School" recounts a childhood project about Dante's *Inferno*. The poem uses a middle school setting to explore a journey on many levels. Dante himself, in his epic, used the classic archetype of the journey and descent into the dark. The poem offers an interesting example of subject finding form—a loosely rhymed terza rima in homage to Dante. Note the variation of different types of rhyme: exact, slant, assonantal. (See "Committing a Rhyme" in Part Two.)

Suggestions for Writing

1. Choose a myth, fairy tale, or other well-known story, and use the general motif or plot to reflect on something or narrate a story (perhaps make it contemporary). You might also change the tale somewhat for comic purposes, as in James Thurber's version of Little Red Riding Hood, mentioned above. There are numerous models to follow, several of which are included in this book. A few suggestions: Yeats's poem "Leda and the Swan," Auden's poem "Musée des Beaux Arts," Anne Sexton's poems in her collection *Transformations*, Ursula K. Le Guin's story "The Wife's Story." If

you like, the symbols or patterns of action in the fairy tale or myth might provide more subtle undercurrents for your piece, rather than a retelling (Alice Munro's story "The Found Boat" and Joyce Carol Oates's story "Where Are You Going, Where Have You Been?" are a few examples you might use as inspiration).

2. Find folk tales or myths from different cultures: Native American, African, Chinese, for example. Note any connections to stories with which you are familiar. Write a piece that explores an archetypal theme or symbol in the stories: creation, a flood, transformation, etc. Perhaps use a line from the tale as an epigraph. (Your response might have a contemporary slant. For instance, write about a flood in your hometown.)

3. Respond to a well-known work of literature, perhaps by taking on a character's voice (perhaps one who doesn't have much of a voice in the original)

4. Respond to a work of art, emulating the shape and progression of the piece, as in "*Memento Mori* in Middle School," which, in a tongue-in-cheek manner, uses the archetype of the journey (moving, instead of through the circles of Hell, from red posterboard to red posterboard in a middle school project) and unites the trials of the *Inferno* with a trial-filled middle school experience.

5. Use a form for a distinct purpose of responding to a text. R. S. Gwynn writes his one-line compressions of Shakespeare's plays as a Shakespearean sonnet. "*Memento Mori* in Middle School" responds to Dante by using a variation of Dante's terza rima. Respond to a well-known piece, using the form of the piece to do so.

6. The most well-known poems can be excellent choices for *parody* (an imitation of a work, or a writer's style, often mocking, for humorous purposes). For instance, try writing a parody of Frost's "The Road Not Taken." Maybe use two roads that diverge in your hometown (e.g., one goes to school, the other to the bar).

Song and Story

Read/Revisit

William Butler Yeats, "The Stolen Child" (see page 320)
Edwin Arlington Robinson, "Richard Cory" (see page 310)

Music, of course, is a great source of inspiration and has been closely linked to literature throughout ages and cultures, as in the traditional ballads of Ireland or the operas and ballets that have set many great works of literature to music. In the oral tradition of ancient Greece, poetry was often set to music. The choruses of tragedies and comedies were sung, with or without instrumental music. This tradition in Greece continues to this day. A great many contemporary Greek musicians set famous ancient and modern poems to music. Many composers elsewhere do the same, though not to the same degree, perhaps.

We can explore different angles on works of literature via contemporary versions, such as Greg Brown's rendition of Blake's *Songs of Innocence and Experience* or Loreena McKennitt's renditions of folk songs and poems such as Yeats's "The Stolen Child."

Many contemporary musicians allude to works of literature. Dire Straits has an interesting "Romeo and Juliet," which gives the old story contemporary language such as "juliet the dice were loaded from the start."

Paul Simon adopts Edwin Arlington Robinson's poem "Richard Cory" for his 1960s song of the same title. Simon chooses a different form for his song, a ballad. He also makes a number of changes in diction and pronouns, using the first person instead of the third.

Many twentieth-century songs use traditional forms, such as the ballads of Woody Guthrie and Bob Dylan. Dylan's "Boots of Spanish Leather" is particularly powerful because of its poignant closure and its intriguing dialogue. The song tells the story of someone going off to sea. It is sung in two voices, and in Dylan's original, it appears that the man is being left behind and the woman is going off to sea. But in numerous renditions by other artists, the woman is left behind, and the man is heading off to sea. This possibility of performing the lyric either way makes it particularly intriguing. The leaver asks several times what gift might be desired, but repeatedly, the one being left behind just asks for the leaver to come back "unspoiled."

When the one at home gets a letter from the one at sea, which states the uncertainty of return, "depending on how I'm feeling," the one left behind knows the score and in graceful, but practical resignation, finally agrees to accept a gift and asks for boots of Spanish leather.

Song, story, and poetry are linked in the form of the ballad, which offers a good sense of the lineage in music. Tracing the influences on contemporary music can be an enlightening process: rock and roll emerged, for instance, out of rhythm and blues. (See "Blues Poetry" in Part Two.)

Songs may be where people go to find their poetry, perhaps because of the artificial distinctions between poetry and song in our culture. In truth, the two are more linked than it would sometimes appear.

Suggestions for Writing

1. Listen to poems you know that have been set to music. See what emerges beneath your pen during or after. Do you feel differently about the poem after you hear it sung?

2. Listen to your favorite songs (rock, rap, country, hip-hop, etc.) with the intention of free-writing afterwards. Use the song as a leaping-off point. Perhaps use a line as an epigraph.

3. Imitate the rhythm of different kinds of music with your lines or sentences. Let the rhythm of your lines or sentences reflect the influence of the beat.

4. Listen to songs in a language you don't know. Can you tell the tone of the song—longing, joy, reverence? "Translate" the song via the tone.

5. Listen to classical music. Try writing as you listen. Try Beethoven's Sixth Symphony, particularly the "Storm Passage" created by violins and cellos. (If you introduce it to others who do not know the piece, you might withhold the name at first, to see what kind of "stormy" feelings get evoked and appear beneath the pen.)

6. Loreena McKennitt may have chosen to set "The Stolen Child" to music because of the refrain, which made it a natural candidate. Try writing a poem with a refrain.

7. Choose a poem from a different era, and write a new version of it, as Paul Simon did in "Richard Cory."

"Kubla Khan" Continued

"Kubla Khan" is Samuel Taylor Coleridge's famous 54-line fragment. In a prefatory note to the poem, Coleridge explains that an entire poem (200–300 lines) appeared to him in a dream. In ill health, he had fallen asleep after taking a painkiller (probably laudanum). He was reading *Purchas His Pilgrimage*, most likely the following sentences: "Here the Kubla Khan commanded a palace to be built, and a stately garden thereunto. And thus ten miles of fertile ground were inclosed with a wall." Coleridge believed he composed the entire poem in his sleep but adds: "if that indeed can be called composition in which all the images rose up before him as *things*, with a parallel production of the correspondent expressions, without any sensation or consciousness of effort." On waking, he began to write down what he remembered. He was interrupted, however, by a person on business who took him away from the poem for more than an hour. When he returned to his room, Coleridge found that the rest of the poem had escaped his memory. This account, however, has often been considered a fictitious story that Coleridge created about the poem.

Like other Romantics, Coleridge believed writing to be an "organic" rather than a mechanical act. He rejected the notion of a work of art as being "mechanically" contrived to please a certain audience, for instance. He spoke of art as a living entity, growing and developing as one. This philosophy may have had something to do with his refusal to finish the fragment, which he felt had come to an unfortunate, untimely end. Or the fragment may, indeed, have been a fiction, meant to represent the subconscious and the organic nature of art. Because conflicting accounts from Coleridge himself exist, the circumstances surrounding the poem remain somewhat mysterious.

One can certainly relate to the notion of the interrupted process or idea, though our accounts may not be as dramatic as Coleridge's loss of 200 composed lines. Many poets have since attempted to complete the famous fragment, reproduced below. (The Khan is a reference to the first khan, or ruler of the Mongol dynasty in thirteenth-century China. The named places are fictitious, as is the topography.)

Kubla Khan

Or a Vision in a Dream. A Fragment

In Xanadu did Kubla Khan
A stately pleasure dome decree:
Where Alph, the sacred river, ran
Through caverns measureless to man
    Down to a sunless sea.
So twice five miles of fertile ground
With walls and towers were girdled round:
And there were gardens bright with sinuous rills,
Where blossomed many an incense-bearing tree;
And here were forests ancient as the hills,
Enfolding sunny spots of greenery.

But oh! that deep romantic chasm which slanted
Down the green hill athwart a cedarn cover!
A savage place! as holy and enchanted
As e'er beneath a waning moon was haunted
By woman wailing for her demon lover!
And from this chasm, with ceaseless turmoil seething,
As if this earth in fast thick pants were breathing,
A mighty fountain momently was forced:
Amid whose swift half-intermitted burst
Huge fragments vaulted like rebounding hail,
Or chaffy grain beneath the thresher's flail:
And 'mid these dancing rocks at once and ever
It flung up momently the sacred river.
Five miles meandering with a mazy motion
Through wood and dale the sacred river ran,
Then reached the caverns measureless to man,
And sank in tumult to a lifeless ocean:
And 'mid this tumult Kubla heard from far
Ancestral voices prophesying war!

    The shadow of the dome of pleasure
    Floated midway on the waves;
    Where was heard the mingled measure
    From the fountains and the caves.
It was a miracle of rare device,
A sunny pleasure dome with caves of ice!

    A damsel with a dulcimer
    In a vision once I saw:

It was an Abyssinian maid,
And on her dulcimer she played,
Singing of Mount Abora.
Could I revive within me
Her symphony and song,
To such a deep delight 'twould win me
That with music loud and long
I would build that dome in air,
That sunny dome! those caves of ice!
And all who heard should see them there,
And all should cry Beware! Beware!
His flashing eyes, his floating hair!
Weave a circle round him thrice,
And close your eyes with holy dread,
For he on honey-dew hath fed,
And drunk the milk of Paradise.

SAMUEL TAYLOR COLERIDGE (1772–1834)

Suggestions for Writing

Though you might endeavor to complete the poem on your own, you could also try writing a collaborative closure.

In a group, read the poem aloud. Notice how Coleridge uses rhyme, though not in a recurring pattern. The poem also has a generally iambic beat. Sometimes the line has five beats, sometimes four. (See Part Two, "Hearing the Beat: Using Meter.")

After noting such elements, read the poem aloud again, to get back into the rhythm. Each person should then write the next line of the poem, keeping in mind the general iambic beat and changing rhyme scheme. Don't give the meaning of the line too much thought, but allow the unconscious to take over somewhat. Try to catch the rhythm. Take only a minute or two per line. Then pass the papers to the right.

Feel free to go with your first thoughts, however odd. For instance, one participant, after Coleridge's lines "For he on honey-dew hath fed, / And drunk the milk of paradise," began with the line "And then, he ate a cantaloupe."

Each person then writes a second line and passes the paper. This continues until the papers have traveled around the room, and you have the one with which you began. Complete the poem with your own final line. Read a few of the completing lines aloud.

13
Revision

Rereading, Reimagining, Reshaping

So, you have finished the first draft of your piece. Reward yourself with something, and get ready for the next stage of writing: revising.

Begin by rereading your piece. Be critical. Evaluate the parts as well as the whole. Try asking yourself why anyone would want to read this piece—what is its meaning and purpose. A writer rarely begins a piece knowing what its meaning will be; even when he or she does, the intended meaning will change in the process of writing. In creative writing, meaning and purpose emerge organically, as the piece is shaped. As Joan Didion said, "I write to find out what I'm thinking." Meaning and purpose become clearer as the piece is finished. Identifying and articulating them can be an iterative process that helps you reimagine, reorganize, and reshape your piece until it is finished.

Suggestions for Rewriting

1. Read your piece carefully, slowly. Then write down what is at stake in it, what its meaning and purpose are. The longer your answer, the more likely the stakes are not well defined and not high enough. Pare down your answer to one or two sentences. Make sure that what is at stake is compelling enough. If the meaning and purpose of your piece are not very compelling, restate them so they are.

2. Reimagine your piece. What do you need to change in it—what scenes, images, statements do you need to delete, insert, or revise— to achieve the revised meaning and purpose?

3. Repeat the process described above until you can describe the central idea of your piece in a single short, concise sentence. Now reduce the meaning of this sentence to a short list of words (as few as one and no more than five). Express each word in your list in an image, a statement, or a short dialogue. Insert these in your piece and read it again. Does the added material strengthen your piece? Does it clarify the piece's meaning and purpose?

What's in a Name:
Finding a Title

Read/Revisit

> Alice Munro, "How I Met My Husband" (see page 248)
> Craig Raine, "A Martian Sends a Postcard Home" (see page 308)
> William Stafford, "Traveling through the Dark" (see page 312)

An important aspect of revision can be finding a title for your work. Maxine Kumin says that titles are "geography, chronology, or furniture." By furniture, she means some element present in the poem that becomes the title. In a poem like Craig Raine's "A Martian Sends a Postcard Home," the title tells us precisely where we are, and the poem itself can become the postcard home. William Stafford's title "Traveling through the Dark" has resonance on more than one level. It tells us where we are and what we are doing, but it has evocative, symbolic interpretations as well.

Alice Munro's short story "How I Met My Husband" adds another dimension to the possibilities of a title. The title of this story lures the reader into believing that the romance being described throughout the story will lead to the marriage, when, in actuality, only the final paragraph of the story introduces the main character's prospective husband. The title serves the purpose of misleading the reader so we are further drawn into the twists and turns of the main character's experiences.

A title can also serve subtle, but symbolic purposes. Evan Connell selected *Mrs. Bridge* as both the name of his main character and the name of his book because of the bridge-playing, country club society he was exposing. He was also implying the social reality that one could ignore "less pleasant" aspects of society by simply crossing over them on a bridge.

Sometimes a title arrives early in the process. But more often the selection of titles can make for a good story in itself. The title of James M. Cain's famous novel *The Postman Always Rings Twice* (adapted into two movies, a play, and an opera) has an intriguing story. Cain gave two different accounts of the origin of the title. He said that while he was working on the novel, the postman would ring twice if the mail carried bills and once if a personal letter. The arrival of bills every day drove the writer into a state of frustration as he worked on his novel. But in Cain's other account of the title's genesis, he says that the postman would ring twice if he carried rejection letters, and once if an acceptance letter. When Cain's novel was accepted, and the doorbell rang once, he celebrated by giving the novel its name.

Suggestions for Writing

1. Take a piece of your writing that has, in your opinion or others', a mediocre working title. Apply Kumin's concept of "geography, chronology, or furniture." Give the piece a title that places us somewhere. Now find the "furniture"; look for an extraordinary line or image already present in the writing that might work as the title. If you do use it as the title, you might consider removing it from the text.

2. Try a symbolic title. Can you identify a particular element in the piece that has resonance on both a literal level as well as a symbolic one?

Finding the Form:
A Revision Narrative

Read/Revisit

Diane Thiel, "*Memento Mori* in Middle School" (See page 313)

For years, I had the idea to write about a memory of an odd middle school project I did on Dante's *Inferno*. The narrative itself existed (in my mind and my memory), but the piece hadn't yet quite found its form. Would it be cast as an essay, a story, a poem? Choosing poetry to tell the story of first encountering Dante's epic seemed most appropriate, but the choice of terza rima for the poem occurred later in the process. An early draft of the poem is reproduced on the pages following. It is not the first draft (I write everything initially by hand) but the first typed draft.

In the early stages of writing a poem, I often find myself putting "Notes for a Poem" at the top of the page because I hardly think of the draft as a poem, but more as a free-write. As I looked through the twenty-some drafts of this poem, I chose this one to illustrate the revision process because it is the point at which a crucial realization about the form of the poem took place. What could I do with this story? How should I render it? And then it came to me—terza rima—of course! The form Dante invented for *The Divine Comedy* suddenly seemed the only choice! The form is particularly suited to narratives, because its interlocking rhyme scheme provides a natural forward motion. I knew it should work well for my telling this story.

In the first typed lines of this draft, as well as in my handwritten reworking in the lower right-hand corner, you can see the new incarnation of the poem beginning to take shape. The first lines are rewritten with a tentative terza rima, testing out the new idea. Subsequent drafts show my reworking of various parts of the poem to arrive, finally, at a version of terza rima. I say "version" because although the lines in the finished poem are metrical and rhymed, the rhymes are often somewhat muted. You can see, even in this early reworking of the opening, that I chose to soften the rhymes into *chimes*, perhaps, by using assonance and off-rhyme. The exact rhymes then attain a more emphatic quality when they are heard.

Most of the narrative details are already present in this early draft. In the case of this particular poem, the introduction (or deletion of events and ideas) was not a crucial part of the revision. Creating the poem had to do, mostly, with finding the right lyrical path. The heightening and clarification of certain details, however, became an important aspect of revision. In the second line of the poem, for instance, adding the small detail about "gifted class" gives the narrative more credibility. An average class of twelve-year-olds would not be reading the *Inferno*. The detail also begins establishing the tongue-in-cheek tone. How odd those gifted-class projects (and students) were! The union of the *Inferno* with that trial-filled middle school age became a reflection of threshold crossings that burn themselves into our memories.

One important point that had to be expanded in later drafts was the introduction of Fred, whom the children thought of at the wood of suicides. In the early draft, the narrative moves quickly past what may have happened to him, but this detail becomes the dark heart, the *memento mori* (recognition of our mortality), perhaps even the motivation for the poem. The mention of Fred needed a longer moment to reverberate.

The change in title from "Presenting the Divine Comedy" to "*Memento Mori* in Middle School" reflects the importance of this point in the narrative and sets up both the dark and the light in the poem. You can see the new title making its first appearance at the top of the second page of the draft, close to the point where Fred is introduced. The lighter aspects of the poem, with all the details about a child's interpretation of Dante's poem, might make a reader laugh aloud, but the suggestion of Fred's likely suicide gives the poem important contrasting darker shades.

Suggestions for Writing

1. Take a piece of your writing and try recasting it. If it is a short story, try boiling it down to its essence and see how it works as a narrative poem. If it is a poem, try prose or a dramatic scene, or possibly an entirely different form for the poem.

2. Look at a short piece of your writing (from your journal or perhaps a more developed piece). What details are most crucial to creating the tone or tones of the piece? Do any important details need further elaboration?

3. An important aspect of revision is knowing when to stop, an issue that often troubles both beginning and established writers. Save drafts of each poem and number them. You may find yourself returning to earlier drafts, or at least sections of earlier drafts. It is useful to put poems aside for a while before revising. Take a particular poem that has several drafts, and write a short piece of prose describing what your revision process has been with the poem. You might begin to notice your own patterns of revision.

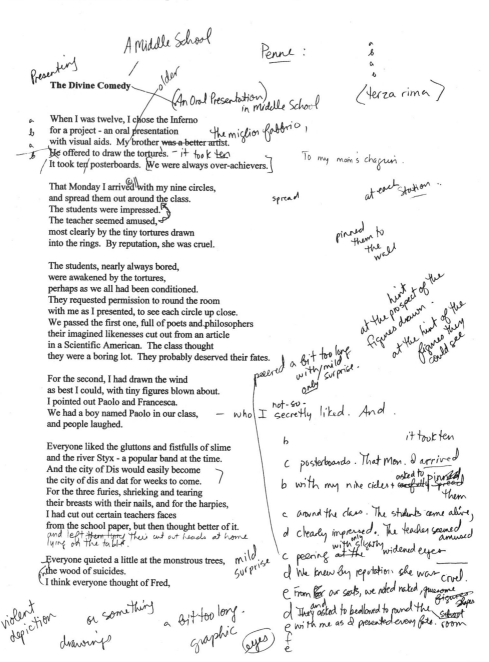

Presenting

A Middle School
/ older

The Divine Comedy

(*An Oral Presentation*)
in middle school

Penne :

(*terza rima*)

When I was twelve, I chose the Inferno
for a project - an oral presentation
with visual aids. My brother was a better artist.
He offered to draw the tortures. - it took ten
It took ten posterboards. We were always over-achievers.

the miglion fabbrio,

To my mom's chagrin.

That Monday I arrived with my nine circles,
and spread them out around the class.
The students were impressed.
The teacher seemed amused,
most clearly by the tiny tortures drawn
into the rings. By reputation, she was cruel.

spread   at each station ..

pinned to
them the
wall

The students, nearly always bored,
were awakened by the tortures,
perhaps as we all had been conditioned.
They requested permission to round the room
with me as I presented, to see each circle up close.
We passed the first one, full of poets and philosophers
their imagined likenesses cut out from an article
in a Scientific American. The class thought
they were a boring lot. They probably deserved their fates.

hint of the
at the prospect of the
figures drawn .
at the hint of the
figures they
could see

peered a bit too long
with mild
only surprise.

For the second, I had drawn the wind
as best I could, with tiny figures blown about.
I pointed out Paolo and Francesca.
We had a boy named Paolo in our class,
and people laughed.

— who I not-so-
secretly liked. And .

Everyone liked the gluttons and fistfulls of slime
and the river Styx - a popular band at the time.
And the city of Dis would easily become
the city of dis and dat for weeks to come.
For the three furies, shrieking and tearing
their breasts with their nails, and for the harpies,
I had cut out certain teachers faces
from the school paper, but then thought better of it.
and left them lying their cut out heads at home
lying on the table.

it took ten

b

c posterboards. That Mon. I arrived
        asked to pinned
b with my nine circles + carefully spread
                                              them
c around the class. The students came alive,
d clearly impressed. The teacher seemed
                with slightly   amused
c peering at the   only widened eyes
d We knew by reputation she was cruel.
e From for our seats, we noted naked, gruesome
d They asked to be allowed to round the school room
        and   figures shapes
e with me as I presented every foto. room
f
e

Everyone quieted a little at the monstrous trees,
in the wood of suicides.
I think everyone thought of Fred,

mild
surprise

violent
depiction
                or something
        drawings

a bit too long.
        graphic (eyes)

First Typed Draft of Diane Thiel's "Memento Mori in Middle School"

Memento Mori

though no one said a word.

People moved on quickly to Geryon
and rode the flying monster down.
The wicked counselors we knew by name.
They occupied the office right below us.
But again, I had resisted pasting in their faces.
A last minute decision. Their little cut-out heads
remained on the table at home.

For the ice in the last circle, where my brother
had expertly drawn the traitors with unfeeling hearts,
my mother had insisted I take with me
a freezer full of popsicles —— to end on a lighter note,
she said. After all, it is a comedy isn't it?
Always a bit disturbed by my projects, she hadn't seen
the end result. But she thought, by the end,
everyone would need it.

Encouraged by the treat, the class moved quickly
to the last circle, and chose their colors.
The teacher, mildly confused, but knowing
they would melt, reluctantly allowed them.
And when the bell announced the change of class,
we left her room with red and purple mouths.

*always wanted to know
what ~~about~~ happened to
those sweet
poems I used to write.*

— I wanted to be liked.

became kids again.

nearly forgotten

*the concerns
amidst the
nearly forgotten by everyone.
I carried the posters back
home.*

we all had secrets by then.

*Bird
Imagery
(Penne :
wings) . . .
Francesca.*

Present some philosophy   —

A + E — fortunate fall

We understood descent.

*and still have them
somewhere in the house
that.*

Workshop: Thirteen Ways
of Looking for Revision

Writers often have a hard time evaluating their own pieces for the purpose of revising—especially pieces they have recently been working on. Workshopping offers the opportunity to get another perspective on your work, to get feedback from your potential audience. If you do not have the opportunity to participate in a formal workshop, you could ask a peer to read your piece critically. The following questions can be used by the reader of your piece to obtain insights into how the piece might be revised so it can become more effective. You may use these questions yourself, but it is often useful to attain some "distance" from your piece, perhaps by putting it aside for a period of time, before you review it.

Questions for Revising

1. What effect does the title have on the piece? Does it add anything? Could you think of something else that would serve a functional or symbolic purpose?

2. Is the opening effective? Is there another scene or image in the piece that might serve as a stronger way to begin?

3. Does the piece work best in its current form? Can you imagine another possibility for rendering it?

4. Does the chosen perspective present the piece most effectively? How would the piece work told from someone else's perspective?

5. How does the setting work for this piece? How soon, as readers, do we know where (and when) we are? How does the writer give us this information? Could it be more subtle? Direct? If the setting is generic on purpose, does this work?

6. Does the piece hold your interest throughout? What creates the dramatic tension in the piece and is there enough of it? Does the tension drop at any points? What might be done to maintain the intensity?

7. Is the language general or specific? Is it abstract or concrete? Note any abstract words that could be replaced with fresh images. Can you suggest any images?

8. Is the voice or dialogue of the speakers or characters believable? Is there consistency? What creates inconsistencies? How might this be refined? If there is meant to be intentional inconsistency, is that working?

9. Read a passage aloud. Does the language of the piece have rhythm? How might the piece be made more rhythmical?

10. How is the piece structured? Does the series of scenes or images work effectively? Can you think of another arrangement that might work better?

11. Does every word, sentence, scene have a purpose? What can be cut?

12. Is there anything that may confuse the reader unnecessarily? How might the confusing passage be clarified?

13. Does the closure reverberate? Does it effectively give an ending without restating too much? Does it leave the reader thinking? Is this piece really finished, or could you envision a different, more effective ending? Does the piece go on beyond what might be a more effective closure?

PART TWO

Exercises for Exploring Specifics of Different Genres

14
Nonfiction

From Memory to Memoir

Read/Revisit

Naomi Shihab Nye, "Three Pokes of a Thistle" (see page 183)

In a sense, all creative writing springs from personal experience. However, when the focus of a piece is on relating personal experiences as truthfully and accurately as possible, then the piece is a *memoir* or *autobiography*. Usually an autobiography is a book-length piece that describes the events of the author's life in their entirety (or at least over a long period) up to the point that the piece is written. A memoir, on the other hand, tends to focus more on a specific event or events that took place at a specific location. Of course, the boundaries between autobiography and memoir are not very precise, and neither are those between memoir and other types of nonfiction such as the travel narrative and the historical account.

This is where your memory (the word *memoir*, after all, springs from the same root) and your journal, which is an extension of your memory, are of crucial importance. You will need to mine them for topics. What you write about need not be earthshaking or exotic. It does need to capture the interest of your readers, but often the experiences we have in common are what we find compelling. One thing you must keep in mind, however, when you are relating personal experiences is that you must be honest about your feelings. Insincerity is very difficult to hide, and there is nothing like it for turning off a reader.

Suggestions for Writing

1. Think of a special occasion you were a part of (Christmas, wedding, Thanksgiving dinner, graduation, etc.) when not everything went as planned—when something unexpected, either good or bad, happened. Why is the occasion one you still remember? Write a short piece describing what happened, what you felt, and what you think other participants felt about the situation.

2. Make a list of memorable moments in your life: when you were the happiest, saddest, angriest, most afraid. Pick one and write a short piece describing the events that led up to the moment. Discuss how these events affected you. How did you resolve your feelings? Did the situation change you in some way?

3. Personal experience and growth are almost synonymous. The experiences that help you mature are, therefore, natural topics for personal narratives. Recount an important experience that led to significant personal growth. Was a relationship with another person instrumental in this situation? How did your experience affect relationships with parents, siblings, friends?

4. Emulate Naomi Shihab Nye's style in "Three Pokes of a Thistle," and write a short piece about a very specific memory. Perhaps focus on a specific object as symbolic of something, like the first bra in "Bra Strap." Is there a related piece that might work as another "poke of the thistle"?

Researching a Life:
Biographical Sketch

Read/Revisit

Fred D'Aguiar, "A Son in Shadow" (see page 172)

Some of the most popular and powerful works of creative nonfiction are biographies. Works such as Walter Isaacson's biography of Benjamin Franklin and David McCullough's biography of John Adams are best-sellers. Some, like Sylvia Nasar's biography of mathematician John Nash, *A Beautiful Mind*, have become successful major motion pictures. But just as you don't need to be famous to produce an interesting memoir or autobiography, you don't need a famous subject to produce a compelling biography. In fact, if you don't have much experience in biographical writing, it is best that you begin with the people and subjects that are most familiar to you: your family, immediate or extended. And since who your family is has much to do with who you are, a biographical sketch may well be an interesting and important component of a more personal piece such as a memoir.

Biographical writing, like much of creative nonfiction, requires a research effort. Characterization is crucial in writing an effective biography or even a biographical sketch. You have to bring your subject to life, and make him or her compelling to the reader, just as in a good piece of fiction—only in this case, the details about the character have to be true. Think of your subject as a puzzle whose pieces you must find before you can put them together.

Judith Ortiz Cofer, in her memoir, *Silent Dancing*, recreates her family's past via a home movie of a party. She returns several times to this movie, which becomes a leaping-off point for her imagination about the relatives and family friends involved:

> The movie opens with a sweep of the living room. It is "typical" immigrant Puerto Rican decor for the time: the sofa and chairs are square and hard-looking, upholstered in bright colors (blue and yellow in this instance, and covered in the transparent plastic) that furniture salesmen then were adept at making women buy. The linoleum on the floor is light blue, and if it was subjected to the spike heels as it was in most places, there were dime-sized indentations all over it that cannot be seen in this movie. The room is full of people dressed in mainly two colors: dark suits for the men, red dresses for the women. I have asked my mother why most of the women are in red that night, and she shrugs, "I don't remember. Just a coincidence." She doesn't have my obsession for assigning symbolism to everything.

Sometimes one only has the tiny fragments of a biography and must reimagine the rest. Fred D'Aguiar's "A Son in Shadow" (discussed more fully in the "Finding the Emotional Truth" section later in this chapter) works with the idea of what the writer knows about his father, as well as what he doesn't.

Suggestions for Writing

1. Interview a member of your family. Grandparents and great aunts and uncles would be good choices because they are more likely to surprise you with information you did not know. They also might be more likely to open up to you than your parents or siblings would be. Record the interview or keep extensive notes. Choose five events or thoughts you find particularly compelling, and develop a biographical sketch around them.

2. Try Judith Ortiz Cofer's approach of creating a "home movie" about your family home. Describe a few scenes the movie would capture. Now go back in time, and perhaps place (another city or country, perhaps). What scenes would the movie capture before you were "in the picture"?

3. Choose a historical figure you admire. Research your subject's life. Get a volume of his or her correspondence and read it. Write a short piece about the relationship between your subject and one or more of the correspondents. How did the relationship influence your subject's life?

Taking a Stand: Personal Opinion

Read/Revisit

Jonathan Swift, "A Modest Proposal" (see page 201)
Alice Walker, "Am I Blue" (see page 207)

The most familiar form of personal opinion piece is the newspaper editorial. However, this type of writing is often not considered *creative* writing because, unlike an essay, it usually does not pay the close attention to language that is the mark of a literary work. Because the distinguishing characteristic of the literary essay is the *style* of the writing, the best way to understand this form is to read and compare essays written by several different authors.

Conventional and literary opinion essays share a common goal: in both types of piece, the author argues a particular position on a specific issue. The value of the literary opinion piece is that the argument is structured in terms of concrete images rather than abstract concepts. This distinctly creative approach has the potential to make a powerful argument because it addresses the reader on both the intellectual and emotional levels. Swift in "A Modest Proposal," for example, never states explicitly what his point is. Instead, he makes a forceful point about the need for a civilized society to care for its less fortunate members by constructing an absurd argument in which he proposes the opposite.

Everything you write is, ultimately, shaped by your feelings, opinions, and beliefs about the world. Consequently, every piece of writing is a "personal opinion" piece in some respect. The personal opinion essay can be distinguished by the fact that the author makes it clear that the piece's intent is to argue an opinion (even when the opinion itself is not stated directly). You can always identify the author's central position by summarizing the theme of the essay in a single sentence that begins with: "The author believes (or thinks) that . . . " When you write essays of your own, such words will likely be edited out as your piece develops, but it is always a good idea to write down your thesis before you begin working on your essay.

One of the powers of a good story is its ability to strengthen an argument. A narrative can be one of the best ways to convince a reader. In essays, in particular, the modes of discourse often get divided—expository, narrative, descriptive writing. But try bringing these elements closer together.

Alice Walker's "Am I Blue" is a good example of a narrative used to express Walker's opinion about an issue. She tells a story of her experience with a horse, Blue, and how his grief over his mate being removed makes her think about slavery. She looks at the penned horse through the window and likens his life to the experience of her ancestors. Blue is crazed at the loss of his mate and looks human in Walker's eyes. His grief makes her move through history, through beliefs people have held at different times. The essay courses through history to arrive at a statement about choices of what we will tolerate, what we will support with our actions. Walker reads the message clearly reflected in Blue's eyes: "Everything you do to us will happen to you; we are your teachers, as you are ours. We are one lesson."

Suggestions for Writing

1. Begin by writing down a thesis. Outline your essay by selecting details that will support your thesis: personal experiences, what you like and dislike, what your interest and emotional investment in the world is.

2. Write out the theme for a personal opinion essay. Choose something you are passionate about. Now emulate Swift and structure an argument (a "modest proposal") for an opposite position that is so extreme and unacceptable that it implicitly supports your thesis.

3. As Walker does, think of a story from your life that you might use to create a convincing argument. Try writing the piece as an argumentative essay. Then write your personal story. Which one makes the more compelling argument? You might find that the two join together at some natural point. Perhaps the argument will begin to reveal itself as an extension of the story.

Living Sources: Gathering and Using Information

Read/Revisit

Diane Ackerman, "The Truth About Truffles" (see page 169)
Mimi Schwartz, "Memoir? Fiction? Where's the Line?" (see page 187)

Research is not something you do only for a class project. You collect and analyze information every moment you are awake (and, some claim, even while you sleep): everything you see, hear, smell, taste, or touch gives you information about your surroundings. You may not think of this process as "research" because the collection and analysis of the information are mostly not conscious, but there are still many occasions in your everyday life where the process is conscious (for example, each time you make a conscious decision).

Becoming aware of all the information you collect every moment of your life, and of the ways you use it, can give you important insights about what research really means. Research is a natural process. You do research when you collect and use information. The collection of information is not necessarily a "formal" process—information is not found only in the library or online. What you see, feel, and think is also information, and this type of information is especially important in creative writing. Think of your poetry and fiction—of the way in which you communicate your feelings, perceptions, and ideas about the world.

This type of communication is also very important in creative nonfiction, in pieces such as Ackerman's "The Truth About Truffles," and Schwartz's "Memoir? Fiction? Where's the Line?" These rather different pieces are designed to present information about and discuss specific topics and, therefore, offer some "hard" data (information from authoritative sources). Ackerman's piece uses primarily scientific information, but presents it in a poetic and humorous way, having the reader enter the piece by imagining the feelings of the sow searching for truffles. Mimi Schwartz uses direct observation of students as well as personal insights to discuss the blurring of the line between memoir and fiction. The use of both "hard" data and creative techniques in each of these pieces makes them particularly effective.

Suggestions for Writing

1. Think of the decisions you've had to make recently: buying a car or a stereo, choosing a college or a major, getting a job, moving. Pick one decision that entailed a major commitment from you. How did you make your decision? You can detail your decision-making process by making two lists. Title the first list "Personal Experience" and in it include things you did or thought about that led you to your decision. For example, if the decision you are analyzing is your choice of the college you currently attend, include in this list things such as a visit to this and other colleges; your thoughts about location, cost, and other factors; and whether you've always wanted to go to this school. Title the second list "Outside Sources" and in it include information you obtained from sources other than your own personal experience. Here you would include things such as college rankings, student/faculty ratio, job placement of graduates, and other information that you got from catalogues, your high school counselor, magazines, and other sources. Note that some of the information may be hard to categorize. Should you list your talking about the school with someone who is enrolled in it or graduated from it under "Personal Experience" or under "Outside Sources"? If what you got from your discussions was only a sense of what you might like, list this under "Personal Experience." If, on the other hand, you got concrete information or advice, list this under "Outside Sources." If you got both, list the information in both categories.

   When you are done with your lists (be exhaustive), go over them and decide whether you relied mostly on personal experience or outside sources in making your decision. In a few sentences, explain why you chose as you did (relying on one type of information more than the other). Now look only at the list of outside sources. Did you trust some sources more than others? Write a few sentences explaining why. Finally, write a few sentences about what additional information (of both types) you would have liked to have in making your decision, and discuss why that information would have been useful to you.

2. Think of a topic you are interested in and write it down as a title. Do a ten-minute free-write, putting on paper anything that comes to mind about this topic: facts, questions, beliefs, and so on. Read what you wrote and begin to organize it. Group together those things that seem to be connected. Write one sentence for each group, stating an idea that the group seems to represent. Are some of these ideas connected? If yes, join those that are. Which of the ideas do you think it would be practical to research? Choose one and phrase it as a question. Break this main question into as many smaller questions as you can (when you answer all of these subquestions, you will have answered the main question). Use each of these subquestions as a heading, and under it list all of the information you will need to have in order to answer it. Also list where you believe you will be able to find this information.

Reflecting on the World

Read/Revisit

Diane Ackerman, "The Truth about Truffles" (see page 169)

The basic difference between a reflective piece and an essay is style. Reflective pieces tend to convey the tone of introspective monologue, weaving and turning, usually moving from image to image. Annie Dillard's "Seeing," for instance, in the spirit of the classical essay, meanders through personal story, collected narratives, and factual information to make her point about perception—how we all have different perceptual filters through which we view the world.

"The lover can see, and the knowledgeable," Dillard points out, calling nature a "now-you-see-it, now-you-don't affair":

> It's all a matter of keeping my eyes open. Nature is like one of those line drawings of a tree that are puzzles for children: Can you find hidden in the leaves a duck, a house, a boy, a bucket, a zebra, and a boot? Specialists can find the most incredibly well-hidden things. A book I read when I was young recommended an easy way to find caterpillars to rear: you simply find some fresh caterpillar droppings, look up, and there's your caterpillar.

In "The Truth about Truffles," from *A Natural History of the Senses*, Diane Ackerman, in writing about the "world's homeliest vegetable," uses biology, chemistry, history, and poetic narrative to reflect on her subject. Consider her final paragraph and the bizarre narrative she creates for the truffle farmer and his sow, who (confused by the similarity of truffle smell to male pig) digs furiously in the earth, trying to reach the "sexiest boar she's ever encountered in her life, only for some reason he appears to be underground."

While the tone of the reflective piece is introspective, it generally conveys more than the personal thoughts of the author—it is more than a piece from the author's personal journal. It presents information, often from solid scholarly research. But, unlike a research report, it integrates that information with the author's personal experience. This method has the effect of bringing the information down to earth, presenting it through the lens of personal understanding, and ultimately making it more accessible to the reader.

Suggestions for Writing

1. Choose a topic you are interested in but that you know relatively little about. Research the topic. Make note of interesting images that illustrate important aspects of your topic. Write a reflection piece in which you present your topic primarily by listing these images.

2. Dillard's "Seeing" discusses more than the sense of vision—it addresses some of the fundamental ways in which people relate to the world around them. Write a reflective piece about one of the senses other than vision (i.e., hearing, touch, smell, and taste) and the ways in which it helps us relate to the world. Use an equal measure of research data and personal experiences to make your argument.

Writing about Place

Read/Revisit

Bruce Chatwin, from *In Patagonia* (see page 170)
Leslie Marmon Silko, "Landscape, History, and the Pueblo Imagination" (see page 192)

From the ancient Greek writer Pausanias, to the articles in the "Travel" sections of every modern major newspaper, travel narrative has a particularly long and continuous history and popularity. This should not be surprising in light of the fact that "the journey" is one of the fundamental, archetypal motifs of literature. By definition, the travel narrative takes the reader along for the ride. What distinguishes the *literary* narrative from its cousins that every week grace the pages of countless newspapers is that the literary travel narrative also guides the reader through an internal journey of the author—one of mental, spiritual, or emotional change.

Bruce Chatwin's travel narrative, *In Patagonia*, is an intriguing blend of memoir, history, and natural history. The book is composed of a series of short vignettes which present different aspects of Patagonia and effectively allow us to experience the place. Sometimes the place is depicted through encounters with particular people Chatwin meets on his journey:

> The poet lived along a lonely stretch of river, in overgrown orchards of apricots, alone in a two-roomed hut. He had been a teacher of literature in Buenos Aires. He came down to Patagonia forty years back and stayed.
>
> I knocked on the door and he woke. It was drizzling and while he dressed I sheltered under the porch and watched his colony of pet toads.
>
> His fingers gripped my arm. He fixed me with an intense and luminous stare.
>
> 'Patagonia!' he cried. 'She is a hard mistress. She casts her spell. An enchantress! She folds you in her arms and never lets go.'

The travel narrative, however, is only one category of writing about place (which, in turn, is one category of the personal narrative). Another important aspect of this type of writing is the piece that relates the special significance a particular place has for the writer. Silko's "Landscape, History, and the Pueblo Imagination" relates the significance of place not only for the author but for her ancestral Laguna Pueblo culture as well.

Suggestions for Writing

1. Write a short piece about a place you have traveled to. Begin by making a long list of details about the place. Pay attention to all of your senses—write not only about the sights but also about the smells, the sounds, and other sensory impressions. Make another list of events that happened as you traveled there and back, and during your stay. Make a third list about the feelings the place or the events surrounding it evoked. Be sure to include negative and mixed as well as positive feelings. Look through your lists to identify unique or particularly interesting aspects of the place and your experiences. Structure your piece around these elements.

2. Write a piece in which you describe your connection with the land. What particular landscape do you find compelling? This could be an urban landscape, but if this is the case, also discuss your feelings about the nature the urban landscape is located within. Describe your connection at the physical, emotional, and spiritual levels.

A Piece of History

History is a great source for both fiction and nonfiction writing. The historical novel is a well-established and popular form, one that sits at the end of the spectrum opposite from the "academic" history. Historical creative (or literary) nonfiction sits between them. While the historical novel introduces fictional characters in a real, well-researched historical setting, the creative nonfiction piece sticks to real people. And while the nonliterary history is primarily concerned with completeness, accuracy, and documentation, the literary piece is primarily concerned with bringing a historical period or event to life, and therefore pays close attention to the use of language and style.

Of course, the lines dividing these categories are not always very clear. The farther back the historical period, and the more obscure the event, the less is likely to be known about it, and the more the writer will have to fill in with guess, supposition, or imagination. Also, the better the writer of the "academic" history, the more likely she or he is to write vividly and bring the period to life. The earliest histories we have, written by Herodotus, Thucidides, and other ancient Greek and Roman writers, are to a large part accounts of events that were directly witnessed by the authors, or that happened during their lifetimes. Thus, they take the form of personal accounts, and because the authors were also talented writers, these histories are regarded as classic works of literature.

The one thing that all forms of historical writing share is the need for attention to detail and aptitude for research on the part of the author. This is so even if the piece is an account of the writer's personal experiences within a historical event or setting, such as O'Brien's *If I Die in a Combat Zone, Box Me Up and Ship Me Home*. Details in this book remain as essential as in O'Brien's fiction piece, "The Things They Carried," and the author's story is enriched with information he learned only after he was shipped to Vietnam—information that was given to him by his comrades:

> During the first month, I learned that FNG meant "fuckin' new guy, "and that I would be one until the Combat Center's next shipment arrived. I learned that GI's in the field can be as lazy and careless and stupid as GI's anywhere. They don't wear helmets and armored vests unless an officer insists; they fall asleep on guard, and for the most part, no one really cares; they throw away or bury ammunition if it gets heavy and hot. I learned that REMF means "rear echelon motherfucker"; that a man is getting "Short" after his third or fourth month; that a hand grenade is really a "frag"; that one bullet is all it takes and that "you never hear the shot that gets you"; that no one in Alpha Company knows or cares about the cause or purpose of their war: it is about "dinks and slopes," and the idea is simply to kill them or avoid them. Except that in Alpha you don't kill a man, you "waste" him. You don't get mangled by a mine, you get fucked up. You don't call a man by his first name—he's the Kid or the Water Buffalo, Buddy Wolf or

Buddy Barker or Buddy Barney, or if the fellow is bland or disliked, he's just Smith or Jones or Rodríguez. . . . You can go through a year in Vietnam and live with a platoon of sixty or seventy people, some going and some coming, and you can leave without knowing more than a dozen complete names, not that it matters.

While O'Brien's piece overlaps the categories of memoir and opinion essay, it is primarily a historical account because the author's objective is to bring the reader into a particular historical period. *If I Die in a Combat Zone, Box Me Up and Ship Me Home* represents the *personal* approach to historical narrative, as contrasted to the *objective* approach, which considers the general history of a period or event, rather than the author's personal involvement with it.

Suggestions for Writing

1. Choose a historical person and an important or interesting event that this figure participated in. Research both the person and the event. Write a story about the role of the person in the event.

2. Make a list of current or recent events about which your family, friends, schoolmates, teachers, or community have different opinions. Choose the event that seems to you to incite the widest and strongest conflicting opinions. Interview at least six people, three on one side of the opinion divide and three on the other. Write a story about the event and about the reactions it elicited in people.

Finding the Emotional Truth

Read/Revisit

Fred D'Aguiar, "A Son in Shadow" (see page 172)
Mimi Schwartz, "Memoir? Fiction? Where's the Line?" (see page 187)

Writers of memoir are presented with a unique challenge. On the one hand, a writer of memoir is writing nonfiction and thus wants to stay as close as possible to the truth. On the other hand, the "truth" must always be an individual affair. We all have varying accounts of the same reality. Have you ever found yourself recounting a family story only to have a sibling insist that it didn't happen that way? You each had stored your own "truth."

Interesting arguments arise among memoir writers about what constitutes "fictionalizing" a piece. Most memoir writers use techniques of fiction in the way they construct the intensity of the narrative and in their selection of details. Some critics argue that too much fictionalizing goes on in memoir.

As a memoir writer myself, I recognize that in the process of writing a nonfiction narrative, the most essential thing is to find the "emotional truth," a phrase now commonly associated with memoir. Perhaps a detail is slightly changed for the purpose of the story, but the feeling of the experience (the emotional truth) remains. As writers, we are always creating our own versions of the truth—by the details we decide to include, the details we leave out, and the way we shape the narrative.

Mimi Schwartz, in her essay "Memoir? Fiction? Where's the Line?" addresses these essential questions that writers of memoir must ask themselves. She uses detailed examples of working with students to discover the scope of this process. She recounts several stories of trying to find the line between fiction and memoir. In Tim O'Brien's short story "How to Tell a True War Story" (included in the fiction section of this book), the author makes the point that one cannot tell a true war story because, in the fog of war, perceptions are altered, and much of the account is based on the perceptions of the people involved. However, one could argue that the "emotional" truth is still being realized in such "stories."

Fred D'Aguiar, in his piece about his father's meeting his mother, "A Son in Shadow," acknowledges from the first sentence what he doesn't know: "I know nothing about how they meet." As he invites the reader to join him on the process of discovery, he reimagines aspects of their lives together, but he often returns to the refrain of what he doesn't know: "Most of the puzzle is missing." And later: "I try to fill the gaps, piece together the father I never knew. I imagine everything where there is little or nothing to go on."

The result is a vital, intriguing piece that uses techniques of nonfiction, fiction, and metawriting (writing about the process of his own invention). It is the missing fragments that intrigue us most as readers, perhaps because we all have family stories like this, particularly from our childhood, stories in which we can only reimagine the "truth."

Suggestions for Writing

Imagine a significant moment in your parents' lives that occurred before you were born or before you were old enough to remember. Sketch out the details you have heard them recount. What details do you need to invent?

Now try D'Aguiar's method of acknowledging what he does not know about the past. Make this awareness of invention part of your process as you write the piece about your parents.

Revision: Beyond the Frame

Sometimes what is necessary in the process of revision is to reimagine various aspects of the piece. In nonfiction in particular, the selection of details is crucial to the telling of the story. It is important to recognize that the choice of details creates a certain kind of "truth" in the account, as does the absence of details.

Think of the natural story-tellers you know. The way they select details has a great deal to do with why people ask them to recount stories, saying that they "tell it better." Some writers include far too many details to get to the point, boring the reader (or listener) with twice as many details as necessary. Others tell too little, leaving out the background information or atmosphere that might make the piece more poignant.

Looking at a piece of writing with fresh eyes and a willingness to move far outside the frame of the original shape can be an essential part of the revision process. Writers need to be willing to expand from the outside as well as internally.

Suggestions for Rewriting

1. Choose a nonfiction piece that you have written, and write one or more scenes that describe events that happened before the beginning of the story. Do any of these add something important to the narrative? Do the same with the end of the story. Do scenes describing events that happened after the end of the narrative add something important?

2. Adding elements of the narrative might make your piece longer than you first intended. Look at your piece of writing and underline all the specific details. Is there any non-essential information that might be cut? Can any points be shortened if you move beyond the original frame? Perhaps these could be replaced with a subtle flashback or flashforward in time.

3. In an expository piece, examine the details both within and outside the frame of the discussion. Sketch out the main points you want to get across. Add the sequence of information, thoughts, and arguments you use to make each point. Are any superfluous? Are you missing something? Is the sequence logical? Can some of the main points be combined into one? Are they what you intended to argue when you began the piece?

15
Fiction

Populating a Plot

Read/Revisit

Ursula LeGuin, "The Wife's Story" (see page 238)
Evan Connell, from *Mrs. Bridge* (see page 215)

A rather common misconception about writing fiction is that an interesting plot is the most important element of an effective story—a plot that offers action and surprises. The truth is, however, that no matter how dramatic, action-packed, or clever the plot is, the story will be only as effective as the characters are interesting. This basic truth becomes evident if you look at any presentation of real-life situations that are naturally imbued in drama: sports, criminal investigations, war reporting. In every case, the stories are much more powerful when they are told in a way that brings the main characters to life (broadcasting of the Olympics is filled with the life stories of the athletes).

Given this truth, it is most useful to understand plot as more than the pattern of events that make up a story. Rather, you should think of plot as the ways in which the characters in a story perceive and deal with the circumstances of the situations they are placed in by you, the author. To write an effective story, you must first bring to life a compelling character (or characters), and then place your characters in an interesting situation, one that allows for surprising reactions.

Suggestions for Writing

1. List ten favorite stories or novels. Make a list of five characters, picking a main character from each of five of the stories. In listing the characters, describe only their primary attribute (e.g., in *Mrs. Bridge*, the description for Mrs. Bridge would be "upper middle class housewife"). Now from the five remaining stories, make a list of the main premise or situation in each story (e.g., in "The Wife's Story" the situation would be "one spouse suspects there is something strange going on with the other spouse"). Pair a character from the first list with a situation from the second and write a short scene.

2. In a workshop, each participant describes one character in terms of a main attribute, such as occupation, and one situation, writing each description on a separate piece of paper. Then each participant passes the character description to the person on the right and the situation description to the person on the left. Each person then writes a short scene using the paired descriptions.

A Spell of Trouble: Conflict and Tension

Read/Revisit

Doris Lessing, "A Woman on a Roof" (see page 241)
Sharon Oard Warner, "A Simple Matter of Hunger" (see page 279)

Trouble makes an interesting story. While a perfect day at the beach with the sun shining, the water calm and just the right temperature, and a nice tan with no sunburn as the outcome is very pleasant and desirable, in real life, such a day is uneventful and, thus, does not make an interesting story to tell others. Consequently, most effective stories follow pretty much the same fundamental path of development—the *narrative arc* of *conflict* (and its complications), *crisis*, and *resolution*; often, the crisis is followed by *falling action* before the resolution is achieved.

Conflict is the beating heart of a narrative. It provides the dramatic tension that keeps the story alive. So a crucial task of every author is to weave conflict into the story in a way that is natural and appropriate. To do this, it is important to note that the source of all conflict is the *desires* of the characters that populate the story. Conflict results from obstacles the characters encounter in the pursuit of fulfilling their desires. Such obstacles can only come from a limited set of sources: other characters, society at large, nature, and from within each character. Even though this means that there are only four basic types of conflict—with individual people, with society, with nature, and internal conflict—the possibilities within each category are virtually unlimited.

Note, for example, that a complex set of conflicts drives the story in "A Woman on a Roof." There are overt conflicts: between the three men working on the roof and the woman, between the three men, and between the men and the weather. There are also more subtle conflicts: the internal conflict Tom has about the woman, and the social conflict that is highlighted by the very different effect the weather has on the workers and the woman on the roof.

Categorizing types of conflict is useful in analyzing plot structure, but it also holds the danger of making it appear as if the conflict should be simple and direct—between hero and villain, or hero and society, for example.

The concept of "hero" tends to tempt writers, especially beginning writers, to see characters as isolated entities, struggling alone to overcome the obstacles in their path. In fact, stories that explore relationships between characters are richer and more interesting. This is true even when there is an overarching conflict between a protagonist and some force placing obstacles in his or her path. It is therefore important to understand that relationships entail conflict between characters, and the narrative arc can be conceived as a set of conflicts leading to a variety of crises. For example, Sharon Oard Warner's "A Simple Matter of Hunger" is driven by the social conflict caused by the stigmatization of AIDS. Note, however, how this overarching conflict is given immediacy and depth by being expressed as a series of personal conflicts: between Eleanor and her husband, between her and the doctor's staff, and between her and Jancey's grandmother.

It is also important to note that for each conflict to be able to provide enough tension in the story to hold the reader's attention, the two sides of the conflict must be closely balanced so that the outcome of the conflict is in question.

Suggestions for Writing

1. Describe a character, a desire he or she has, and an obstacle to this desire that is imposed by society. Repeat this with an obstacle imposed by nature, then an obstacle imposed by the character.

2. Begin with one character and his or her desire to have the perfect wedding. Make a list of twenty possible obstacles. Be sure to include at least two obstacles from each category: obstacles presented by people, society, nature, and within the character. Each of these obstacles is the foundation of a conflict. Now examine each of these conflicts and determine how evenly matched the two sides are. How likely is the character to overcome each obstacle and prevail in the conflict? Order the list so that the conflicts whose outcomes are most in doubt are at the top. Write an outline for a story that utilizes the top five conflicts on this list.

Writing between the Lines: Subtext

Read/Revisit

Jamaica Kincaid, "Girl" (see page 237)
Evan Connell, from *Mrs. Bridge* (see page 215)

Do you always say everything that comes to your mind? It is not very likely that you do—none of us really do, because if we always said exactly what we thought, we would likely have no friends. Communication, however, takes place at levels other than the verbal. Gestures, body position, and facial expressions make up what is often referred to as "body language." Body language and other nonverbal cues, such as tone of voice, heart rate (and its consequences such as flushing), and eye movement, are not as easy to control as our words. When we try to hide something, often we are betrayed by our body language.

This subtle level of communication (the nonverbal) is not as easy to present in writing, but it is well worth the trouble because it enlivens our stories—it increases the subtlety and richness of our writing. The easiest way to reveal that a character's words do not express true feelings is by revealing his or her thoughts. However, this can become cumbersome if used too much and it lacks subtlety. When it comes to describing the thoughts of characters, a good rule of thumb is to reveal the absolute minimum amount necessary.

A good story means more than it says; therefore, it has both *text* (what is stated in a situation) and *subtext* (what remains unsaid but is implied or otherwise communicated). The subtext operates at a deeper level than the action and dialogue of our story. Jamaica Kincaid's "Girl" is a prime example of the importance of subtext. Almost all that is interesting about the story is left unsaid: what it was like to be a girl in the Antigua of Kincaid's childhood; what the status of women was and how it was maintained.

Suggestions for Writing

1. Describe an event from the perspective of two characters. Focus your description on actions rather than thoughts. The two characters are related in some way (e.g., parent and child, or husband and wife). Each character remembers the event differently (one may hardly remember it at all). Let the differences reveal something important about the relationship. See the "Preliminary Training" excerpt from Evan Connell's *Mrs. Bridge* for an example.

2. Write a short scene involving two characters. One or both characters are not able to reveal everything they feel. Reveal one character's feelings through his or her thoughts and the other character's through the description of nonverbal cues.

How You See It; How You Don't: Points of View

Read/Revisit

Edgar Allan Poe, "The Tell-Tale Heart" (see page 275)
Tim O'Brien, "The Things They Carried" (see page 262)

As discussed in the "Perspective and Point of View" chapter in Part One, most fiction is written in either the first or third person. Which point of view you choose depends on how much distance you want to place between the reader and your characters. For example, the power and effectiveness of Edgar Allan Poe's story "The Tell-Tale Heart" come from the immediacy that is achieved by using the first-person point of view. The crucial element of the story is that the murderer is haunted by the sound of a heartbeat that no one else hears. This element is made most effective by the particular choice of point of view.

Generally, once you choose a point of view, you must keep it fixed—point of view implies a particular distance, and any change in it can be jarring. This does not mean, however, that *perspective* must also remain fixed. If you choose a point of view that relates events from the perspective of a character in the story (such as the first-person or the third-person limited objectivity point of view) rather than from the perspective of a totally external narrator, you may choose to weave a narrative of the perspectives of more than one character. In "The Things They Carried," for example, Tim O'Brien has a unique approach to introducing each character's perspective: describing things that each person carried and the significance of the items. The technique allows the reader to engage with each of the characters as a distinct individual, with a unique perspective and experience in the situation.

The device of changing perspective is particularly useful when each character has information or insights that are unique. Such information could be conveyed by an omniscient narrator, but the choice of either the limited or complete omniscience point of view means that a greater distance between the reader and the characters is created.

While transitions in perspective need not be jarring, they still need to be executed with finesse. These transitions are easier in longer works such as novels, because they can be facilitated by such handy devices as chapter breaks—they may even be indicated by putting the name of the character whose perspective we shift to in the chapter title. Transitions in perspective are more difficult to execute smoothly in shorter pieces, and especially when the first-person point of view is chosen.

In another story, "How to Tell a True War Story," Tim O'Brien weaves the perspectives of several characters together in a piece that is narrated from the first-person point of view. The changes in perspective are integral to the story: the author's point is that there is no such thing as a "true" war story because of the subjective nature of each experience. O'Brien comments in the piece that "a true war story is never moral. It does not instruct, nor encourage virtue, nor suggest models of proper human behavior, nor restrain men from doing the things men have always done." In his story, O'Brien accomplishes transitions smoothly by having a character tell a story to the narrator:

In other cases you can't even tell a true war story. Sometimes it's just beyond telling.

I heard this one, for example, from Mitchell Sanders. . . . The occasion was right for a good story.

"God's truth," Mitchell Sanders said. "A six-man patrol goes up into the mountains on a basic listening-post operation. . . .

Suggestions for Writing

1. Write a scene with three characters, each of whom has a different perspective on what he or she is doing. Use the third-person, limited objectivity point of view. Do not use the character's name in the first sentence written from his or her perspective; try other ways to indicate the shift in perspective.

2. Choose a natural disaster (an earthquake, a tornado, a flood) and write a short piece describing the event through the experiences of three characters. Let each character have a very different perspective from any of the others (e.g., a police officer, a traveler who happens to be driving through town, a local resident at home).

Setting the Story

Read/Revisit

Anton Chekhov, "Misery" (see page 211)
Doris Lessing, "A Woman on a Roof" (see page 241)

Often, setting is thought of as background, providing a necessary backdrop for the story to unfold; it is there to orient the reader in space and time, to provide an answer to the inevitable question "Where am I?" But setting can serve many important functions in a piece of fiction. It can create an atmosphere that sets the mood of a piece. It can have symbolic value, emphasizing the point the story is trying to get across. The setting can act as a motivating force for the characters, and it can sometimes take on the attributes of a character—for example, when a conflict exists between the setting and one or more of the characters.

In both Chekhov's "Misery" and Lessing's "A Woman on a Roof," the setting serves most, if not all, of these functions. It is interesting to note that in both pieces, the details about what is typically thought of as "setting"—those details that describe where and when the story takes place—are rather sparse. In Chekhov's piece, were it not for the names of the characters, and had "Petersburg" not been mentioned in the dialogue, the story could easily be taking place in any city of the far northern regions of our planet, any winter up to the first decade of the twentieth century. Lessing's piece is equally vague on the details of place and time. The story could take place at any relatively modern city in the summer. It is the weather that sets the mood and plays a symbolic role in both pieces. In "Misery" the cold intensifies the atmosphere of misery and is emblematic of the cold indifference the main character has to contend with. In "A Woman on a Roof," the progressively intensifying heat not only creates the atmosphere and is symbolic of the rising anger and desire of the three workmen, but it is also the motivating force of the story: were it not for the heatwave, the story could not be taking place.

Suggestions for Writing

1. Write a scene in which extreme weather plays one of the following roles:

   One or more characters struggle against it.

   It motivates conflict between two characters.

   It intensifies and is symbolic of the conflict between two characters.

2. Write a scene in which a character is uncomfortable in a setting. Reveal the nature of the character's discomfort (is he or she feeling afraid, lost, threatened, inadequate) by describing his or her reactions to the setting. What specific elements of the setting evoke reactions by the character? The feeling of discomfort implies a conflict between the character and the setting, so be sure to intensify the conflict as much as possible and to reveal the character's motivations.

3. Write a scene in which two characters are engaged in a conflict over the setting (e.g., one wants to change something about the setting and the other does not, or one wants to leave while the other wants to stay). Again, be sure to intensify the conflict. Choose an interesting setting: because the setting is a motivating force for the conflict (though not necessarily the only motivating force), the more interesting the setting, the more interesting the conflict.

The Passage of Time

Read/Revisit

Alice Munro, "How I Met My Husband" (see page 248)

The passage of time is the most fundamental underpinning of the telling of a story. Every piece of fiction, from beginning to end, moves through time—almost always forward. The *way* in which it moves through time is the most basic element of the structure of the plot.

Because a story is an abstraction of reality, it must discard those elements of reality (objects, people, events, etc., that would have been part of the situation had the story been actually happening in the real world) that are not essential to the story. Consequently, a story almost never moves through time at an even and steady pace. In "How I Write Short Stories," Alice Munro comments about her nonlinear process of writing:

> I don't take up a story and follow it as if it were a road, taking me some-where, with views and neat diversions along the way. I go into it, and move back and forth and settle here and there, stay in it for a while. It's more like a house. Everybody knows what a house does, how it encloses space and makes connections between one enclosed space and another and presents what is outside in a new way.

A story consists of episodes. Each episode consists of a set of events that take place sequentially and move rather evenly and steadily through time. Episodes are separated by a jump in time, a change in setting, or the appearance or departure of an important character, or a combination of these discontinuities. In fiction, these episodes are called *scenes*, and their arrangement is what we call *plot*.

Alice Munro's "How I Met My Husband" is structured in a number of scenes that are spaced fairly close in time (about a day or so between each). The story progresses slowly, until just before the end. The last scene leaps forward in time, first weeks, then months, and finally years into the future.

Even though plot almost always moves forward in time (in other words, the end of a story is at a point in time later than the beginning), it rarely does so continuously. Very often several scenes happen at the same time (they show events that happen in different places and involve different characters). These are *parallel* scenes, and they are a very useful way for the writer to describe the experiences of different characters either as a consequence of or in preparation for a significant event.

Another device that is used very frequently is the *flashback*—a scene that takes place at an earlier time than the main flow of the plot (the *base time* of the story). Flashbacks show the reader significant past events that help explain current actions and events—they help layer the motivation of characters.

Moving forward in time in a *flashforward* is a much less frequently used technique. It invariably has the effect of distancing the reader from the characters and is therefore useful when the writer wants to inject objectivity and decrease the impact on the reader of situations that affect the characters strongly.

Suggestions for Writing

1. Write a short piece based on the following premise. Two characters who used to be friends have a chance meeting. One begins to apologize to the other for the action or actions that caused the demise of their friendship. Use flashbacks to reveal the event that caused the end of the friendship and to layer the motivation of each of the characters for the events taking place in the present. For example, why has one decided to apologize? Will the other accept the apology or not? Why?

2. Write a short piece about two characters who are involved in a romantic relationship. They are having a fight. They either break up or make up. Open the piece with a flashforward that shows what happens to each of the characters and their relationship some years later.

Compelling Characters

Read/Revisit

James Joyce, from *A Portrait of the Artist as a Young Man* (see page 230)
Ursula K. LeGuin, "The Wife's Story" (see page 238)

As pointed out in the section on "Populating a Plot," populating your piece with compelling characters is of primary importance. Unless you are writing a piece such as satire, where there is a good reason for presenting *flat* characters, you must bring your characters to life and make the reader care about what happens to them.

Effective *characterization* (i.e., presenting a character) is very similar to getting to know someone in real life. We first perceive people through our senses: we see them and hear them and, to a lesser extent, smell them, feel them, and even taste them. It is therefore important to give some physical details about our characters. But be careful not to overburden the reader—be judicious in selecting those details that are relevant to the story. Do let the reader feel (or feel along with) the character through some of the less frequently used senses if possible—such details give unexpected, subtle brushes to the character's portrait. Note how the stream of consciousness approach that James Joyce uses in *A Portrait of the Artist as a Young Man* gives the reader a sense of intimacy with the main character, Stephen Dedalus, and makes it easier to reveal his distinctive voice.

As we get to know someone better, we begin to be able to predict how he or she would react in a situation. Similarly, we get to know what our character would say in a given siutation, and how he or she would say it, both verbally and nonverbally. We get to know what our character would do and how he or she would do it. Think of your character as a dynamic being—

someone who reacts in specific ways to given situations and who changes as a result of his or her experiences. Give your character a distinctive voice. In "The Wife's Story," Ursula K. Le Guin slowly builds her main character by letting the character narrate the story, giving the reader progressively deeper insights into who and what she is. "The Wife's Story" is particularly effective because by the time the main character's identity becomes apparent, the reader has come to identify with her—and is now placed in the position of having to look at the human species with the eyes of a wolf.

As we become intimate with others, we begin to understand why they act in particular ways. To build a fully rounded character, you must help the reader understand what the character thinks and wants in any given situation. You can give this information to the reader directly, by using a narrator who can reveal such intimate details, or you can use dialogue, nonverbal cues, and action to let the reader uncover your character's motivation. While the former approach gives you more latitude, the latter may be more effective in bringing the reader closer to the character.

Suggestions for Writing

1. Build a character by describing one attribute from each of the four categories below:
   a. Physical appearance (e.g., height, weight, hair color, age).
   b. Voice (e.g., sound, tone, accent).
   c. Smell, feel, taste.
   d. Accessories (e.g., clothes, jewelry, objects carried).

2. Write a scene with two characters. One character speaks while the other responds nonverbally. Do not reveal directly the thoughts of either character. Extend the scene past the point where the two characters part. How do they part? What does each character do after they part?

Vignettes

Read/Revisit

Evan Connell, from *Mrs. Bridge* (see page 215)

We all tell anecdotes of our lives, and jokes. The vignette is this type of form—short prose, complete on its own, but often woven with other vignettes into a larger piece. Although a vignette is short, it may actually be difficult to write because of this very compression.

Evan Connell's novel *Mrs. Bridge*, for instance, is arranged as a series of vignettes, each of which seems to stand on its own as a moment captured in a life. Note the way the final sentence of each vignette also provides a fine example of the distance a single sentence can travel, through layers of meaning.

Eduardo Galeano, in his three-volume *Memory of Fire*, tells the history of the Americas in a series of short, poignant depictions, which reverberate because of their compression:

1908, San Andrés de Sotavento

The Government Decides That Indians Don't Exist

The governor, General Miguel Marino Torralvo, issues the order for the oil companies operating on the Colombia coast. The Indians do not exist, the governor certifies before a notary and witnesses. Three years ago, Law No. 1905/55, approved in Bogotá by the National Congress, established that Indians did not exist in San Andrés de Sotavento and other Indian communities where oil had suddenly spurted from the ground.

Suggestions for Writing

1. Write about an event in history. Imitate Galeano's compression of events.

2. Write a vignette about family life. Start, perhaps, with your favorite anecdote, one that you have only shared aloud. Choose one that has a clear opening and closure. Let it find its way to paper. As you write others, you may find that, together, they build a continuous story: of a family, a job, a love.

Writing inside the Story: Metafiction

Read/Revisit

Fred D'Aguiar, "A Son in Shadow" (see page 172)

Your journal holds many ideas for stories you did not develop because they seemed to go nowhere. Perhaps you had a good beginning, but nothing seemed to work in trying to develop a story from it. Perhaps a story seems flat; it may have an interesting premise, but you haven't been able to render it in an interesting way. Is there anything you can do, you wonder, with these ideas and fragments?

It is possible that the process of rendering a piece could make for a more interesting story than the piece itself. Perhaps the different beginnings you tried tell an interesting story when put together. Perhaps you had an interesting conversation with a friend or relative when talking about a story you've been working on. This type of writing—called *metafiction*—can open up interesting possibilities for the story. Writing about the process of writing, of course, injects a direct and clear element of reality into the piece, blurring to some degree the genre distinction between fiction and nonfiction. In his "A Son in Shadow," D'Aguiar straddles genre boundaries. On the one hand, his story is about real people in real situations, but on the other, the author has to imagine events that he doesn't know much about, and he lets us know he is doing so.

Suggestions for Writing

1. From your journal, pick an idea for a beginning of a story you have not been able to develop successfully. Write the beginning to the story. Emulate D'Aguiar and write several different versions of this beginning (sketch five to ten). For each version, change a few details of the scene but keep the physical setting the same. For some of the versions, try extending the story slightly beyond the original scene. What could happen right before? Right after? Write each version on a separate piece of paper (or two). When you are done, try different arrangements. How do the versions work when put together as a single story?

2. Write a short story about the workshop experience. Be sure to keep the story purely fictional. Center the story around a single very short piece of fiction written by the central character. Include in your story two versions of the piece: the first draft presented to the workshop, and a second draft that incorporates some of the critiques offered in the workshop. What were the responses of the workshop participants to the first draft? What were their responses to the revised piece? What do these comments reveal about the workshop participants? What are the central character's thoughts about the process? What do these reveal about him or her? How much did the piece benefit from the workshop?

Revision: Reimagining Character and Conflict

As was already discussed, a fundamental element of effective characterization is character motivation: what do your characters want? In evaluating your story, you need to review what your characters are willing to risk in order to get what they want. If your characters do not care enough to risk something important, neither will the reader. The stakes must be high enough to keep the reader engaged. On the other hand, if the stakes are too high, the story and the characters may not be believable.

Sometimes the resolution of the conflict might seem too obvious. We have all been frustrated by films and novels that spell out their resolutions long before we reach them. One solution might be to reimagine different possibilities for resolving the central conflict of the story. Could you imagine a variety of ways the action and intensity might reach their peak?

Suggestions for Rewriting

1. Take your piece apart. Are there places where the story is thin? Are some characters too flat? Are there places where the action lags? Does the sequence of scenes or chapters work? Do you get the feeling something might be missing? Does the story feel unfinished? Make notes of your criticisms in the margins or in a notebook.

2. Have one of your main characters write a letter, either to another character in the story or to someone outside the story (which works better?), describing what has been happening in the story. What possibilities does this open up for the piece?

3. Revise a scene in which a conflict is resolved. Pick a scene you think is problematic. Rewrite it reversing the outcome of the conflict. How does that affect the scene? What possibilities does it open up for the piece?

16
Poetry

Sound, Sense, and Nonsense

Read/Revisit

Lewis Carroll, "Jabberwocky" (see page 294)
James Joyce, from *A Portrait of the Artist as a Young Man* (see page 230)

A 12-year-old girl gave me the idea for the following exercise. She had written about the hoppergrass, the name she had given the grasshopper. That day, we flipped words around. We made a list of some of the words, which we read together as a single poem:

Hoppergrass
lifewild
flybutter
grownover
fedunder
lesschild
lesscare
grass-saw
dozerbull
centershopping
stormthunder
fallrain
flyfire
lightmoon
lifewild
gladesever

Turning each word around gave it a new kind of resonance. e. e. cummings loved wordplay and the sounds of words. "anyone lived in a pretty how town" is one of my favorites. It is a nature poem, a love poem, a poem about the existential experience, a poem carried by sound. It is a poem that opens up further by discussion. When I first came across the lines "he sang his didn't he danced his did," somehow, I knew instinctively this was a philosophy of life I wanted to follow.

It can be useful to try opening the language in poetry like e. e. cummings's, or in prose like James Joyce's. At this point, though, you might not want to sustain it for as long as, say, Joyce's 628 pages of *Finnegan's Wake*, which begins:

riverrun, past Eve and Adam's, from swerve of shore to bend of bay, brings us by a commodius vicus of recirculation back to Howth Castle and Environs.

Sir Tristram, violer d'amores, fr'over the short sea, had passencore rearrived from North Armorica on this side the scraggy isthmus of Europe Minor to wielderfight his penisolate war: nor had topsawyer's rocks by the stream Oconee exaggerated themselse to Laurens County's gorgios while they went doublin their mumper all the time: nor avoice from afire bellowed mishe mishe to tauftauf thuartpeatrick: not yet, though venissoon after, had a kidscad buttended a bland old isaac: not yet, though all's fair in vanessy, were sosie sesthers wroth with twone nathandjoe. Rot a peck of pa's malt had Jhem or Shen brewed by arclight and rory end to the regginbrow was to be seen ringsome on the aquaface.

The fall (bababadalgharaghtakamminarronnkonnbronntonnerronnt uonnthunntrovarrhounawnskawntoohoohoordenenthurnuk!) of a once wallstraight oldparr is retaled early in bed and later on life down through all christian minstrelsy.

Joyce began using invented words in his early work. In the first pages of *A Portrait of the Artist as a Young Man* (included in the fiction section of Part Three), he uses babytalk to capture the age and the inner thoughts of the main character, Stephen Dedalus.

After Joyce's *A Portrait of the Artist* and *Finnegan's Wake* in particular, Lewis Carroll's "Jabberwocky" seems like plain English. Despite its many made-up words, the events of the story are clear, possibly because of the archetypal pattern of the slaying of a dragon, the conflict of David and Goliath.

Suggestions for Writing

1. Make a list of compound words that could be grouped under one subject. Flip the words, as in "Hoppergrass." Make a list poem.

2. Choose one of the words you created in the preceding exercise and use it as a point from which to leap. Call your piece "Gladesever," for instance.

3. Mix up the parts of speech. Let verbs become nouns and nouns become adjectives. Let yourself be carried by the language. You can worry later about what it means.

4. Imitate "Jabberwocky." Give it a contemporary flair. Write about an encounter with a physical or metaphysical "jabberwocky" of your own. Notice the meter and rhyme scheme that give the poem its shape and sound. Try to imitate this aspect as well: iambic tetrameter, with iambic trimeter in the last line of each stanza, and a rhyme scheme of abab (see "Hearing the Beat: Using Meter").

5. I read *Finnegan's Wake* in a reading group with many Joyce scholars and the help of a published skeleton key. But a first

approach to Joyce's style might be to see how much sense can be gleaned from the sound. Read each sentence in the above passage aloud, and then paraphrase it without too much thought. In a workshop, it is fun to see the many different interpretations that result.

Random Connections

Elizabeth Bishop got her inspiration for the poem "The Man-Moth" from a misprint for "mammoth" in a newspaper. Typographical, grammatical, or foreign-language translation errors can be a great source of inspiration. I have saved them for years, from various sources:

- A sign in a Paris hotel elevator: *Please leave your values at the front desk.*

- A wrong answer on a high school science test: *H_2O is hot water. CO_2 is cold water.*

A student in one of my classes repeated the phrase "as I lied in bed last night" several times in a writing assignment. I couldn't resist asking her in the margin whom she was lying to.

Use these mishaps as leaping off points. In *Leaping Poetry*, Robert Bly refers to the "long floating leap . . . from the conscious to the unconscious." Writing is very much about the accidental connection, and about allowing these connections to occur. I am reminded of Lawrence Ferlinghetti's poem about Chagall, the painter known for his startling juxtaposed images such as horses eating violins. Ferlinghetti plays with the command in the title, "Don't Let that Horse Eat that Violin," imagining it as a directive from Chagall's mother. Ferlinghetti suggests that poets must allow such bizarre connections, must let the horses eat the violins, at least some of the time.

An important element in all good writing is fresh, innovative *diction* (word choice) and *syntax* (arrangement of words). The source of the right word is sometimes one of those mysterious, elusive elements of writing. Sometimes the right word arrives as a gift. Found poems and other serendipitous exercises help charge the imagination with new combinations.

Suggestions for Writing

1. "Found poems" are poems that are literally found (whole or almost in their entirety) in unexpected places. Try finding a poem in your belongings: the ingredients on a candy bar, the fine print on an I.D., a page of your chemistry book, a funny or disturbing memo you received at work, an overheard conversation. First, stick as close

to the original as you can. You might find that you have an entire poem, or it might become the kernel of something more elaborate, perhaps an element of a story.

2. "Random connections" is a fun exercise and a good game. Participants should break into sets of two. Without consulting each other, one person should come up with a "Why?" The other should come up with a "Because." Some of the links work beautifully. Others are bizarre, but they might work even more beautifully. You could try this exercise with other links: if, then; I used to, but now. The following are several examples from students:

Why do I see the things I see in your eyes?
Because the T.V. is on.

Why do we wear clothes?
Because we feel like dancing.

Why do I have to grow up?
Because you broke it.

If frogs ruled the world,
then birds would swim.

I used to be afraid of the dark,
But now I can't see a thing.

I used to fall in love at the drop of a pin,
But now I sleep with my eyes open.

I used to think my teachers weren't human,
But now I can drive.

3. Refrigerator magnet words can be useful for sparking ideas (and you can use them while making dinner). Even self-proclaimed nonwriters have found them inspiring. In a workshop, you could also use word lists or cards. Make lists or piles of nouns, verbs, adjectives, etc., and then pick from the piles to see what constructions result. You could select consciously, or you might close your eyes and pick randomly. It is rare, of course, that a whole poem or story will emerge from such serendipitous exercises, but perhaps a new image or idea will appear. I confess that occasionally a line from my refrigerator finds its way into a piece of writing.

Making Metaphor: Image, Symbol, Metaphor Revisited

Read/Revisit

Richard Wilbur, "The Writer" (see page 316)
Robert Frost, "Poetic Metaphor" from "Education by Poetry" (see page 394)

As discussed in Part One, in the sections on "Figurative Language" and "Detail, Image, and Symbol," the various kinds of figurative language refer to all the genres. They are, perhaps, most heightened in poetry.

The word *metaphor* comes from the Greek, meaning "to carry over." In Greece, I noticed that moving trucks bear the word *Metafores* on the side. The mind organizes material by trying to link something new to what it already knows. It wants to make metaphor. Essentially, when using metaphor, we speak about one thing in terms of something else. We use metaphor many times a day, without even realizing it.

Sometimes, as I begin to talk about the term in a class and ask the class to give me a metaphor, students sit searching their minds until someone finally comes up with a meager one. Yet they have all probably used several rich ones in their last conversation. Metaphor fills our language, from our daily accounts to our insults to our terms of endearment.

Robert Frost, in his essay "Education by Poetry," suggests that poetry plays an important role in the development of thinking. He discusses the importance of analogy in reasoning and emphasizes the practical nature of using metaphor, how we learn to link one thing to another. This kind of association challenges our minds and builds associative muscles. Aristotle (384–322 BCE) believed that metaphor (the word is sometimes used to mean all figurative language) was the most important skill of an educated person. He wrote:

> By far the greatest thing is to be a master of metaphor. It is the one thing that cannot be learned from others. It is a sign of genius, for a good metaphor implies an intuitive perception of similarity among dissimilars.

Although Aristotle may have been right in suggesting that mastery of metaphor cannot be learned from others, we all use metaphor in our daily language. Practicing the different means of making figurative language is a way to understand its use, bring it into our own writing and speech, and exercise our ability to draw connections in the world. By consciously practicing, we can improve our use of figurative language and become masters of metaphor.

Suggestions for Writing

1. Write about an animal you resemble. I have often thought that people resemble certain animals, either by sheer physical appearance or by their actions. We all have our bearlike friends, our nervous, hopping sparrows, our darting lizards, languid cats.

2. Compare humans in general to some other animal or plant, in order to make a statement. One student's rather insightful response compared humans to the maleluca, a water-sucking exotic plant originally introduced to help dry up the Everglades but now threatening the entire ecosystem as it spreads swiftly through the region and wipes away native plants. The comparison led into a good discussion about the dangers of introducing exotics into an ecosystem and helped others see the effect humans are having on the world.

3. As in Wilbur's "The Writer," compare the act of writing to something in nature, using an extended metaphor. This kind of exercise also helps us realize how techniques of poetry can be used for more expository purposes.

Free Verse: Origins and Seasons

Read/Revisit

W. H. Auden, "Musée des Beaux Arts" (see page 291)
Walt Whitman, "When I Heard the Learn'd Astronomer" (see page 316)

Free verse is the translation of *vers libre*, which arose in France in the late nineteenth century, partially in response to strict structural rules for poetry regarding such things as precise placement of caesura (or pause) in the line, and counting of syllables. Vers libre began as a relaxation of these rules. The early twentieth century in America brought free verse to the forefront, and the new philosophy about poetry was encapsulated in Ezra Pound's famous statement that one should "compose in the sequence of the musical phrase, not the metronome."

The name *free verse*, however, has often been debated and called inaccurate and misleading because it implies that there are no limitations or guiding principles. Other terms are sometimes preferred—*open form poetry*, for instance.

Ironically, memorable poetry in open form can be very difficult to write because of the discipline that such freedom demands. The unit of free verse is often described as being a breath. The form requires an attention to the cadences of language. Each phrase should be weighed carefully, as should the length of a line. Rhythm is a vital aspect of open form. One of the dangers of free verse is that it sometimes implies to beginners that "anything goes." Much poetry being written today exists on the page, but not in the ear. Arbitrary line breaks and a lack of rhythm can be the unfortunate result.

As any teacher knows, students sometimes want to declare "open season" on all rules (grammatical, formal, etc.). However, certain "seasons" in one's writing can be useful (as many exercises in this book suggest). It is important to remember (though I don't love extending the hunting metaphor) that open season does not mean obliterating all of the animals in the forest.

When discussing the origins of free verse, it is vital to remember that the poets who introduced it into their contemporary society had been trained in traditional forms. Poets such as Whitman, Pound, Eliot, and Stevens have undercurrents of form in their free verse. But even earlier "formal" poets such as John Milton, William Blake, and Matthew Arnold used radical departures from meter or rhyme schemes before such action had name and popularity.

There are different conjectures as to the reasons for the development of free verse in America. American writers may have been endeavoring to cast off English forms. Walt Whitman is often named as our most familiar American writer of free verse. The great musicality and rhythm in his lines are often said to reflect the landscapes of his American heritage. His lines often have a rising quality or a falling quality, based on the rhythm. One often hears pairs of lines with the same meter. Whitman often creates rhythms using parallel structures. In "When I Heard the Learned Astronomer," for instance, notice the way the rhythm builds with the increasing number of beats in the first few lines.

Whitman also employs other techniques of repetition to make rhythm, such as the grammatical use of the present participle to achieve a "continual" effect, as in the following lines from "Song of Myself":

Many sweating, ploughing, thrashing, and then the chaff for payment receiving.
A few idly owning, and they the wheat continually claiming.

WALT WHITMAN (1819–1892)

Poems in open form sometimes follow a basic metrical pattern and might occasionally be characterized in metrical terms. A poem might be said to have a loose *dactylic* rhythm, for instance (see "Hearing the Beat: Using Meter").

Poetry often has an attention to the shape on the page, which translates to the ear. *Visual* or *concrete* poetry is the term for the particular kind of poetry in which the words form actual shapes: a bird, wings, a flower, etc. But any open form poetry can take on interesting shapes based on subject, and all should have good reason for their line breaks. May Swenson's "The Shape of Death" is an example of a poem whose form on the page was altered to create a distinct rhythm and meaning. Swenson wrote the poem ten years after the bombing of Hiroshima and Nagasaki. Originally, the poem was structured:

there is a clap of sound, a white blossom
belches from the jaw of fright,
a pillared cloud churns from white to gray
like a monstrous brain that bursts and burns,
then turns sickly black, spilling away,
filling the whole sky with ashes of dread

In a later version, Swenson rearranged the lines of her poem, "remembering" them by dismembering them, creating the effect of what is blown apart:

There is a
clap of sound. A white   blossom belches from the
jaw of fright. A   monstrous brain that bursts
and burns—then turns   sickly black, spilling
away, filling the whole   sky with ashes of dread.

MAY SWENSON (1919–1982)

Good open form poetry has rhythm, whether it be a fluidity or an intentionally jarring pattern of sound to create a certain effect. One element is essential in all writing: poets need to train and use their ears.

Suggestions for Writing

1. Read aloud some free verse poems whose lines have remained with you. Identify any metrical patterns within (see "Hearing the Beat: Using Meter"). What kind of patterns exist? Can you identify a reason for each line break?

2. Experiment with line breaks. Consider Swenson's deliberate jarring effect in the above excerpt. Choose a subject that would benefit from such a chaotic structure and rhythm and use the line breaks to create meaning.

3. In all writing (but in free verse, in particular) the rhythm often relies on word choice or particular combinations of sound, such as internal rhyme or alliteration (see "Committing a Rhyme"). Combinations of words can create a fluid pace or a harsh breaking rhythm. Sometimes such rhythms appear beneath your pen. Harvest your free-writing to find some of these combinations. Build on the structures you find.

4. Notice how Auden's "Musée des Beaux Arts," though decidedly free verse, has interesting rhyme schemes throughout the poem. Notice the structure of long and short lines as well. Try Auden's use of alternating long and short lines.

Making and Breaking the Line

Read/Revisit

Sherman Alexie, "Indian Education" (see page 290)
William Carlos Williams, "The Dance" (see page 319)

In the previous section, "Free Verse: Origins and Seasons," different possibilities for creating the rhythm and lyricism of a free verse poem are discussed. Attention to "the line" as poetry's main unit is of major importance to both formal and free verse poems. In much formal poetry, the line is determined by an established length and a particular rhythm that forms the foundation of its lyricism.

With free verse, attention to the line is particularly vital because much of the music is determined by the poet's choices regarding the line. When writing poetry, essentially, we "teach" the reader how to read the poem by where we break the line, often using an unexpected pause to achieve a certain effect.

In Sherman Alexie's "Indian Education," for instance, note how the pause created by the line break allows for a moment of expectation to build from the first line of the poem:

Crazy Horse came back to life
in a storage room of the Smithsonian

The poem also closes with particularly evocative line breaks:

although Crazy Horse measured himself
against the fact of a mirror, traded faces
with a taxi driver and memorized the city,
folding, unfolding, his mapped heart.

The line breaks allow each idea of how the speaker "measured himself" and then "traded faces" to reverberate for a moment before the poem moves on to the mirror and the taxi driver, respectively. The measured pauses allow the final stanza to build toward the striking closing image of "his mapped heart."

In "A Supermarket in California," Allen Ginsberg, in writing about Walt Whitman, emulates Whitman's long lines, lists, and parallel structures. Ginsberg's choice of line length has the effect of establishing an affinity with Whitman on a level deeper than the imagined appearance of Whitman in the supermarket.

William Carlos Williams's poem "The Dance" (discussed also in "Rhythm and Refrain") has intriguing line breaks that suit its subject matter. Note how lines two and three seem to break in odd places:

In Brueghel's great picture, The Kermess,
the dancers go round, they go round and
around, the squeal and the blare and the
tweedle of bagpipes

What could be the reason for these odd line breaks? What might they have to do with the subject matter of the poem?

Suggestions for Writing

1. Study the Williams poem mentioned above. Now write a few lines that depict a particular movement (e.g., a dance, running long distance, climbing a ladder). Play with the line breaks to depict the movement that is the subject of the poem.

2. Look at each of the poems noted above. Do you see other particular reasons the poet breaks the line where he or she does? Take a poem you have written and experiment with breaking the lines differently. Have someone else read it aloud in its original form and with its different line breaks. How does it change the reading of the poem?

Stanzas

Many poems (open form poems as well as those with more traditional forms) are organized in stanzas, or groups of lines. *Stanza* comes from the Italian, meaning "room, or stopping place." The following is a very brief overview of stanza forms with a few examples, as well as a few suggestions of other poems to seek out on your own. The overview is intended to give you a sense of the way you might break your own poems into traditional stanza forms, or use such structures as points of departure. Poems broken into stanzas need not necessarily rhyme, of course, but the following examples offer both classical and contemporary examples of rhyme.

Some poems are arranged in couplets (units of two lines), from the heroic verse of Dryden and Pope to such familiar poems as Blake's "The Tyger." Often couplets are distinguished only by the rhyme scheme (aab-bcc, etc.) rather than visual space. Some couplets are arranged in a structure of two-line stanzas, as in Rhina P. Espaillat's "Bilingual/Bilingüe,"

My father liked them separate, one there
one here (allá y aquí), as if aware

that words might cut in two his daughter's heart
(el corazón) and lock the alien part

RHINA P. ESPAILLAT (B. 1932)

Three-line stanzas, or *tercets*, might carry different rhyme schemes, or all three lines of the tercet might also rhyme:

The Angel that presided o'er my birth
Said little creature formed of joy and mirth
Go love without the help of anything on earth.

WILLIAM BLAKE (1757–1827)

The following example breaks the rhythm and alters the rhyme for the purpose of slowing the poem down at its closure:

Stillness after motion,
the creaky music cranking, cranking down,
the carnival preparing to leave town.

RACHEL HADAS (B. 1948)

Another common rhyme scheme for a three-line stanza is terza rima (triple rhyme) such as Dante used. The rhyme scheme is aba, bcb, cdc, etc., and the middle rhyme of each tercet becomes the first and third rhyme of the next stanza. The interlocking form weaves the stanzas together and gives the poem movement, propelling it forward.

Marilyn Nelson's "Chosen" uses tercets with a varying rhyme scheme to form part of a sonnet. For a variation on terza rima, see my poem, "*Memento Mori* in Middle School." (Both are included in Part Three.)

The *quatrain*, or four-line stanza, is the most common in European literature. A common quatrain is the ballad stanza, with four beats in the first and third lines, three or four in the second and fourth lines. Note the structure and rhythm of the following stanzas from Nikos Kavadias's "A Knife."

I remember, as if it were now, the old dealer
who looked like a Goya oil painting,
standing next to long swords and torn
uniforms—in a hoarse voice, saying,

"This knife, here, which you want to buy—
legend surrounds it. Everyone knows
that those who have owned it, one after another
have all, at some time, killed someone close.

NIKOS KAVADIAS (1913–1975)
TRANSLATED BY DIANE THIEL

The five-line stanza allows for many combinations of rhymes and line lengths. Edgar Allan Poe uses the familiar quatrain and adds an additional rhyming line:

To Helen

Helen, thy beauty is to me
    Like those Nicéan barks of yore,
That gently, o'er a perfumed sea,
    The weary, way-worn wanderer bore
    To his own native shore.

On desperate seas long wont to roam,
    Thy hyacinth hair, thy classic face,
Thy Naiad airs have brought me home
    To the glory that was Greece,
And the grandeur that was Rome.

Lo! in yon brilliant window-niche
    How statue-like I see thee stand,
    The agate lamp within thy hand!
Ah, Psyche, from the regions which
    Are Holy-Land!

EDGAR ALLAN POE (1809–1849)

For another example of the five-line stanza, see Robert Frost's "The Road Not Taken" (included in Part Three).

The six-line stanza might contain one of many different patterns of rhyme and meter. The "Venus and Adonis stanza", named for Shakespeare's poem, is a quatrain with a couplet: ababcc. The "Burns stanza" or "Scottish stanza" follows a pattern of aaabab—the a lines are tetrameter (four feet), the b lines are dimeter (two feet). R. S. Gwynn's "The Classroom at the Mall" uses a rhyme scheme of abccab:

Our Dean of Something thought it would be good
For Learning (even better for P.R.)
To make the school "accessible to all"
And leased the bankrupt bookstore at the Mall
A few steps from Poquito's Mexican Food
And Chocolate Chips Aweigh. So here we are—

R. S. GWYNN (B. 1948)

The *sestina* is a type of poem that uses six-line stanzas in which end words repeat in a precise pattern. There is a section on the sestina in the "Forms from Various Cultures and Traditions" section.

The seven-line stanza also offers many possibilities. *Rime royal* (so named because it was used by British King James I) is the most common. It contains iambic pentameter, rhyming ababbcc. But many contemporary poets have created their own seven-line structures:

My frowning students carve
    Me monsters out of prose:
This one—a gargoyle—thumbs its contemptuous nose
At how, in English, subject must agree
With verb—for any such agreement shows
    Too great a willingness to serve,
        A docility

CHARLES MARTIN (B. 1942)

Ottava rima is the most widely known eight-line stanza: iambic pentameter, abababcc—familiar to many through Yeats's "Among School Children" and Byron's witty *Don Juan*:

His classic studies made a little puzzle,
    Because of filthy loves of gods and goddesses,
Who in the earlier ages raised a bustle,
    But never put on pantaloons or bodices;
His reverend tutors had at times a tussle,
    And for their Aeneiads, Iliads and Odysseys,
Were forced to make an odd sort of apology,
    For Donna Inez dreaded the Mythology.

        GEORGE GORDON, LORD BYRON (1788–1824)

Fred D'Aguiar's *Bloodlines* is a contemporary narrative in ottava rima:

And now I have to make a confession.
I said way back that I can't die, sure,
but the real truth is I won't die, not as long
as slavery harnesses history, driving her
over the edge, into the ground, to exhaustion.
I refuse to lie in ground whose pressure,
shaped like my body, is not six feet of soil,
but slavery; not history on me, but forced toil.

        FRED D'AGUIAR (B. 1960)

Timothy Steele's "The Library" is a good contemporary example of a nine-line stanza:

I could construct a weighty paradigm,
The Library as Mind. It's somehow truer
To recollect details of closing time.
Someone, at slotted folders on a viewer,
Tucks microfiche squares in their resting places;
Felt cloth's drawn over the exhibit cases;
The jumbled New Book Shelves are set in shape;
The days' last check-outs are thumped quickly through a
Device that neutralizes tattle-tape.

        TIMOTHY STEELE (B. 1948)

The Spenserian stanza (used in Edmund Spenser's *The Faerie Queen*) is a special nine-line form. The first eight lines are iambic pentameter and the ninth is an alexandrine (with twelve syllables). The rhyme scheme is ababbcbcc. Byron, Shelley, and other Romantics enjoyed the elaborate musical quality of the interlacing form. The following is the first stanza of Shelley's famous *elegy* for John Keats, "Adonais":

I weep for Adonais—he is dead!
Oh, weep for Adonais! though our tears
Thaw not the frost which binds so dear a head!
And thou sad Hour, selected from all years
To mourn our loss, rouse thy obscure compeers,
And teach them thine own sorrow, say: with me
Died Adonais; till the Future dares
Forget the Past, his fate and fame shall be
An echo and a light unto eternity!

        PERCY BYSSHE SHELLEY (1792–1822)

Some forms of poetry have no fixed stanzas; they continue until they end. *Blank verse* (unrhymed iambic pentameter) is the best known pattern for poems in English. Most parts of Shakespeare's plays are in blank verse, as is Milton's *Paradise Lost.* Many twentieth-century writers such as Robert Frost and Elizabeth Bishop found blank verse an ideal form for conveying the natural rhythms of language. (See, for instance, Frost's "Out Out—," included in Part Three. Frost found the subject for this chilling poem in a newspaper article and rendered the subject matter in blank verse.)

Numerous contemporary writers, such as Mark Jarman, Emily Grosholz, Dave Mason, Mary Jo Salter, and Christian Wiman (to name just a few), continue in this tradition, often using the blank verse form to sustain longer narrative poems, sometimes book-length works.

Suggestions for Writing

Try your hand at the different stanza forms. Pay attention to certain shapes and structures that may emerge in your journal. Notice, for instance, if a poem seems to be developing in couplets. Model your favorite poets. You will probably find that certain divisions suit your particular voice or certain subjects better than others.

Rhythm and Refrain

Read/Revisit

Alfonsina Storni, "Ancestral Burden" (see page 312)
William Carlos Williams, "The Dance" (see page 319)
Naomi Shihab Nye, "Famous" (see page 307)

As discussed briefly in sections on "Free Verse: Origins and Seasons," "Making and Breaking the Line," and "Parallel Structures" in particular, there are a variety of inventive ways to create rhythm in a free verse poem. Yusef Komunyakaa, in "Rhythm Method," speaks of the organic nature of rhythm, how we feel it in every aspect of our lives, even in the worms easing through the earth "beneath each footstep." Naomi Shihab Nye's repetition of "famous" in her poem, "Famous," creates a poignant and rhythmical effect:

The river is famous to the fish.

The loud voice is famous to the silence,
which knew it would inherit the earth
before anybody said so.

The cat sleeping on the fence is famous to the birds
watching him from the birdhouse.

The tear is famous, briefly, to the cheek.

Sometimes the rhythm of a free verse poem has an undercurrent of a formal element, such as the undercurrent of the triple rhythms in William Carlos Williams's "The Dance." In Alfonsina Storni's "Ancestral Burden," note how both the repetition in the first few lines, as well as the structure of the sapphic-like stanza (after Sappho, with three longer lines and then a short one), creates a unique rhythmical effect in the poem:

> You told me my father never cried
> You told me my grandfather never cried
> The men of my lineage never cried
> They were steel inside.

A number of writers have "found their rhythm" in various poems via inspiration from sources such as jazz refrains. Michael S. Harper's "Dear John, Dear Coltrane" names its influence quite directly in the title. Consider how the poem itself feels like a jazz tune. Note the repetitions throughout the poem. When Harper reads this poem, he performs it, singing the refrain: "a love supreme."

Suggestions for Writing

1. Listen to jazz for inspiration. Try to emulate some of the rhythms you hear as you free-write in your journal. Follow a pattern and then break off in an unexpected direction.
2. Naomi Shihab Nye's repetition of "famous" creates a poignant and rhythmical effect in "Famous." Try emulating her use of repetition in the poem.
3. In Williams's "The Dance," consider the undercurrent of rhythm throughout the poem. How do the triple rhythms affect the subject matter: a dance? Write some lines of free verse in which the rhythm carries an emphatic meaning.

Hearing the Beat:
Using Meter

Rhythmical patterns of poetry are referred to as *meter* (from the Greek meaning "measure"). Hearing or reciting a poem with meter gives us a physical as well as an intellectual or emotional pleasure. Theorists have different conjectures about this physical reaction. Some suggest that it has to do with meter's hypnotic power. Others suggest that because the accents in much metered verse are faster than our heartbeats, they excite and speed up our hearts.

Frederick Turner, in his essay "The Neural Lyre," speaks about the effect of metered verse on the brain—that it encourages the left brain to communicate with the right brain. He suggests that our left-brain activity of understanding language becomes infused with our more hard-wired, right-brain pattern-recognition abilities, that meter, essentially, tunes up the brain, combining a rhythmic organization with a variety of syntactical possibilities. He speaks of the brain as a "*Penelope*, whose right hand weaves the shroud of meaning and whose left hand disentangles the thread or clue of understanding."

Turner traces how societies have evolved using meter, a cultural universal, perhaps because of its hypnotic power to cast a spell in the mind—a rhythmic reality rooted in science. Dana Gioia, in *Can Poetry Matter*, draws on this recognition of meter as an ancient technique used when there was very "little, if any distinction among poetry, religion, history, music, and magic." All were performed using an incantatory meter.

Poetry written with meter is sometimes called *verse*, from the Latin *versus*, meaning "turned around or back." The structural unit of the line in most poetry (metered or unmetered) has this element of the "turn." The word *line* derives from the Latin *linea*, associated with linen, or thread. One might think of poetry as lines spun together on a loom. The rhythms of language have meaning and are a powerful element of the weave.

It is a good idea to become familiar with the various meters (both the patterns of regularity as well as different methods of variation) and to try your hand at them. It will help you recognize why certain lines have always remained with you, and it will give you additional tools for writing. You may even begin to notice meter in prose passages or in everyday speech. Many lines of everyday speech in English, for instance, tend to be iambic, a pattern of alternating unstressed and stressed syllables.

The Basic Patterns

The unit whose repetition creates the rhythm in a line is called a *foot*. Following are examples of iambic, trochaic, anapestic, and dactylic feet. Boldface type in the examples indicates a stressed syllable, and words have been broken up to show the individual syllables in some of the lines.

Iambic lines consist primarily of *iambs*. An iamb is an unstressed syllable followed by a stressed syllable.

I **all** / a **lone** / be **weep** / my **out** / cast **state**

WILLIAM SHAKESPEARE (1564–1616)

Woke **up** / this **mor** / nin', **blues** / all **round** / my **bed**

TRADITIONAL BLUES LYRIC

Trochaic lines consist mainly of *trochees*. A trochee is a stressed syllable followed by an unstressed syllable. Trochaic meter is often used to convey a kind of mystical quality, as in the following:

Once up / **on** a / **mid** night / **drear** y, / **while** I / **pon** dered, / **weak** and / **wear** y,

Over many a quaint and curious volume of forgotten lore—
While I nodded, nearly napping, suddenly there came a tapping,
As of someone gently rapping, rapping at my chamber door.
"Tis some visitor," I muttered, "tapping at my chamber door—
Only this and nothing more."

EDGAR ALLAN POE (1809–1849)

Anapestic lines consist mainly of *anapests*. An anapest is two unstressed syllables followed by a stressed syllable. Note the galloping pace of these lines from Robert Browning's "How We Brought the Good News from Ghent to Aix," created by the use of the anapest:

And his **low** / head and **crest**, / just one **sharp** / ear bent **back**
For my voice, and the other pricked out on his track;
And one eye's black intelligence,—ever that glance
O'er its white edge at me, his own master, askance!

ROBERT BROWNING (1812–1889)

In "Confederacy," by contemporary poet Elise Paschen, the anapests feel like a dance, like Paschen's "two-stepping" subject:

Wear the **heart** / like a **home**
as in Patsy Kline's song,
what we're two-stepping to

ELISE PASCHEN (B. 1959)

Dactylic lines consist mainly of *dactyls*. A dactyl is one stressed syllable followed by two unstressed syllables.

This is the / **for** est pri / **me** val. The / **mur** mur ing / **pines** and the / **hem** lock
HENRY WADSWORTH LONGFELLOW (1807–1882)

June Jordan chose to use dactyls in her poem for Phyllis Wheatley—the poet slave who, in the eighteenth century, was the first woman, as well as the first African American, to publish a book in North America. Jordan's choice of form for this poem echoes Wheatley's poetry:

Viewed like a / **spe** cies of / **flaw** in the / **live** stock
JUNE JORDAN (B. 1936)

Variations in Meter

Variations in regularity—or metrical substitutions—are a vital aspect of meter. There are many ways one can create variation. In iambic meter, for instance, trochaic feet often appear at the beginning of lines for emphasis. In "Bilingual/Bilingüe," the trochaic feet, "English" and "Spanish" further emphasize the imperative in the father's words:

> to what he was—his memory, his name
> (su nombre)—with a key he could not claim.
>
> **Eng**lish / out**side** / this **door**, / **Spa**nish / in**side**,"

RHINA P. ESPAILLAT (B. 1932)

The *pyrrhic* unit is another common substitution, consisting of two unstressed syllables, as in "dom for" below":

> A **horse**! / A **horse**! / My **king** / dom for / a **horse**!

WILLIAM SHAKESPEARE (1564–1616)

The *spondee* contains two stressed syllables, as in "full kiss" below:

> Yet **once** / more **ere** / thou **hate** / me, **one** / **full kiss**.

ALGERNON CHARLES SWINBURNE (1837–1909)

In "Single Sonnet," Bogan struggles with what she calls the "heroic mould" of the sonnet, which "proves" its strength and returns to iambic in her final line:

> **Staunch me** ter, **great song**, it is **yours**, at **length**,
> To **prove** how **strong** er **you** are **than** my **strength**.

LOUISE BOGAN (1897–1970)

Two other ways to add variety to a line are use of the *caesura*, or pause, usually indicated by punctuation, and use of *enjambment*, or running on to the next line without a pause (as opposed to using an *end-stopped* line). The following two lines illustrate both devices:

> Lose something every day. Accept the fluster
> of lost door keys, the hour badly spent.

ELIZABETH BISHOP (1911–1979)

Samuel Taylor Coleridge wrote the following lines to help memorize the different feet. Each line depicts the type of foot it describes:

> Trochee trips from long to short;
> From long to long in solemn sort
> Slow Spondee stalks, strong foot, yet ill able
> Ever to come up with Dactyl trisyllable.
> Iambics march from short to long;
> With a leap and a bound the swift Anapests throng.

SAMUEL TAYLOR COLERIDGE (1772–1834)

Iambic and anapestic feet are called *rising* feet, as they move from unstressed to stressed syllables. Trochaic and dactylic feet are called *falling*. Timothy Steele comments that he sees the meter of lines as landscape, with hills and valleys of different size or levels of stress. The feet create the basic pattern, which then allows certain variations to have more impact. The amount of variation in a poem can range from very little to extensive changes, often depending on the subject.

The Basic Metrical Lines

The length of a line is essential to the rhythm of metered poetry as well as open form. (In open form, in particular, a line might break at a certain, perhaps unexpected point for the purpose of creating a particular rhythm or meaning—see the "Free Verse: Origins and Seasons" section.) Pentameter, the most common meter, contains five feet. Monometer, dimeter, trimeter, tetrameter, hexameter, heptameter, and octameter contain one, two, three, four, six, seven, and eight beats, respectively.

Monometer (one beat), a rare line length, is used in the following epigram:

Adam
Had 'em.

ANONYMOUS

For more about epigrams, see the section, "Forms from Various Cultures and Traditions."

Dimeter (two beats) is used in the following lines from Tennyson's "The Charge of the Light Brigade." Note that the basic pattern is dactylic.

Cannon to right of them,
Cannon to left of them,
Cannon in front of them
Volleyed and thundered;

ALFRED, LORD TENNYSON (1809–1892)

Trimeter (three beats) is used in the following lines. Read the lines aloud and note where the stresses fall, as in the words "Up," "bronze," and "saw" in the first line.

Up from the bronze, I saw
Water without a flaw

LOUISE BOGAN (1897–1970)

Tetrameter (four beats) is used in the following lines. Each line has four feet and an iambic pattern that creates four stresses in the line.

Whose woods these are, I think I know.
His house is in the village, though;
He will not see me stopping here
To watch his woods fill up with snow.

ROBERT FROST (1874–1963)

Pentameter (five beats) is the most common line in English. This brief example is from Milton's *Paradise Lost* (Book IX, lines 115–123). Notice, however, that the fourth and ninth lines of the excerpt break the meter and have six beats. (The list of "rocks, dens, and caves" recalls an earlier description in Book II of the epic: "Rocks, caves, lakes, fens, bogs, dens, and shades of death"—see octameter, below.)

If I could joy in aught; sweet interchange
Of hill and valley, rivers, woods, and plains,
Now land, now sea, and shores with forest crowned,
Rocks, dens, and caves! But I in none of these
Find place or refuge; and, the more I see
Pleasures about me, so much more I feel
Torment within me, as from the hateful siege
Of contraries; all good to me becomes
Bane, and in Heaven much worse would be my state.

JOHN MILTON (1608–1674)

Hexameter (six beats), sometimes called an *alexandrine*, is used in the following stanza from "The Lake Isle of Innisfree":

I will arise and go now, and go to Innisfree,
And a small cabin build there, of clay and wattles made.
Nine bean-rows will I have there, a hive for the honey-bee,
And live alone in the bee-loud glade.

WILLIAM BUTLER YEATS (1865–1939)

Heptameter (seven beats) lines, often called *fourteeners*, were common in the Renaissance but are rather uncommon now. "Casey at the Bat" is a famous American poem in heptameter:

The outlook wasn't brilliant for the Mudville nine that day;
The score stood four to two with but one inning more to play.

ERNEST LAWRENCE THAYER (1863–1940)

Some metrists suggest that ballad meter is a derivation of heptameter, with its pattern of four stresses, then three, as in the following excerpt from "The Rime of the Ancient Mariner":

Since then, at an uncertain hour,
That agony returns:
And till my ghastly tale is told,
This heart within me burns.

SAMUEL TAYLOR COLERIDGE (1772–1834)

Octameter (eight beats) is a very uncommon line in English. Swinburne's "March" is one example. Some octameter lines exist as a dramatic variation from the basic pattern of a poem, such as this line from Book II of *Paradise Lost*, which varies from the poem's basic meter (see pentameter, above):

> Rocks, caves, lakes, fens, bogs, dens, and shades of death.
>
> JOHN MILTON (1608–1674)

Lines longer than eight beats exist, but they are quite rare, probably because of the limitations imposed by the natural rhythm of breathing.

Other Metrical Lines

Some poets, such as W. H. Auden, Marianne Moore, and Dylan Thomas, have enjoyed working in **syllabic verse**, arranging lines by the number of syllables but without attention to meter. A well-known syllabic poem is Dylan Thomas's "Fern Hill." Note in these first two lines how each contains 14 syllables.

> Now as I was young and easy under the apple boughs
> About the lilting house and happy as the grass was green
>
> DYLAN THOMAS (1914–1953)

Syllabic verse is sometimes confused with accentual verse. **Accentual verse** refers to the amount and pattern of stresses, not merely the number of syllables. Ballad meter, for instance, contains a wide variety of syllable counts per line, but there is a precise pattern of stresses or accents. (See the "Ballad and Ballade" section in "Forms from Various Cultures and Traditions.") Richard Wilbur's "Junk" is a good example of a contemporary use of accentual meter, with four beats in each line.

> An **axe angles**
>   from my **neighbor's ash**can
>
> RICHARD WILBUR (B. 1921)

Accentual iambic meter is sometimes called *loose iambics*. **Accentual syllabic verse** is the term for meter that keeps a precise pattern of syllables and accents, with variation occurring in the accents. Accentual syllabic meter is the basis for standard English meters such as iambic pentameter. **Quantitative meter,** common among the classical forms of the ancient Greeks and Romans, is based on the principle of vowel length (the time it takes to say a syllable).

Sapphic verse (named for the Greek poet Sappho, but also used by Catullus and Horace) are four-line stanzas in the meter of the example below. The term *sapphics* is also used to refer to the meter of the first three lines. The English Sapphic stanza consists of three 11-syllable lines—

hendecasyllables—followed by a five-syllable line, with the stresses noted in contemporary poet Annie Finch's "Sapphics for Patience":

> **Look** there—**some** thing **rests** on your **hand** and **even**
> **lingers, though** the **wind** all a**round** is **ask**ing
> **it** to **leave** you. **Pass**ing the **open passage**,
> **you** have been **cho**sen.
>
> Seed. Like dust or thistle it sits so lightly
> that your hand while holding the trust of silk gets
> gentle. Seed like hope has come, making stillness.
> Wish in the quiet.
>
> If I stood there—stopped by an open passage—
> staring at my hand—which is always open—
> hopeful, maybe, not to compel you, I'd wish
> only for patience.

ANNIE FINCH (B. 1956)

A difficulty of the Sapphic stanza may be its inflexible meter (due to an attempt to imitate classical syllable quantities), which may not allow for shifts in rhythm to create meaning. Some poets have used the basic structure of the Sapphic stanza with small metrical variations, or with a looser pattern of five beats per line, for instance.

For a far more extensive discussion of the many intricacies of meter, a comprehensive source is Timothy Steele's book on meter, *All the Fun's in How You Say a Thing*.

Practicing Meter

When using meter, our minds and bodies respond to both the regularity and the change. As Robert Bridges said, the rhythm beneath allows the poem to lift off. Practicing different meters is also likely to give your free verse and your prose a more lyrical quality, as you train your ear.

Suggestions for Writing

1. Try writing lines with the different basic meters (iambic, trochaic, etc.). You might listen to everyday speech and write down lines that have a particular rhythm. One small caution (from experience): you need not mention your identification of meter to your sources. Not everyone appreciates such a discerning ear. And there's bound to be trouble if you respond to a statement like "Let's go! We're going to be late again" with "Hey, that line is iambic pentameter!"

2. Find a passage of prose in which a few sentences follow basic metrical patterns. Break them into lines and then *feet* (the metrical subdivisions of a line) and note their *scansion* (their patterns of stress).

3. Note how such elements as caesura and enjambment affect rhythm. Try writing lines with these elements (also see the "Making Rhyme Fresh" section).

4. Write a poem in iambic pentameter. Find one or more places in the poem where a break in the meter might be used to create a particular meaning (as in the examples of variation noted). Practice techniques of variation (e.g., using trochaic, pyrrhic, or spondaic feet to vary the iambic pattern).

5. Practice writing lines that have *accentual* rhythm. Create a pattern of a certain number of beats per line (e.g., tetrameter, pentameter, etc.).

6. Read your own writing aloud (poetry and prose). It will help you hear the undercurrents of your own rhythm or identify where it needs work.

Trochaic Meter and Spells

When we think of the incantation that accompanies a spell, we think of a hypnotic arrangement, containing rhyme and meter. Scan the following lines from Poe's "The Raven." Read them aloud to hear the rhythm.

> Once upon a midnight dreary, while I pondered, weak and weary,
> Over many a quaint and curious volume of forgotten lore
>
> EDGAR ALLAN POE (1809–1849)

In Shakespeare's *Macbeth*, when the witches cast their well-known spell, the blank verse of the play changes to a trochaic meter (a pattern of alternating stressed and unstressed syllables) with rhyme and a repetition of sounds to heighten the effect of the magic. The word *trochee* derives from the Greek *trochos*, meaning "wheel." Trochees have a forward-skipping rhythm that is particularly suitable for creating a hypnotic effect.

> Eye of newt, and toe of frog,
> Wool of bat, and tongue of dog,
> Adder's fork, and blindworm's sting,
> Lizard's leg, and howlet's wing—
> For a charm of pow'rful trouble.
> Like a hell-broth boil and bubble.
> Double, double, toil and trouble,
> Fire burn and cauldron bubble.

Suggestions for Writing

Using a basic trochaic meter, write an emulation of the above spell. In the first four lines of your spell, list the necessary ingredients. Try using ingredients of this day and age. The choice of ingredients can be a good way to talk about symbol. The items used in the spell could be chosen for their symbolic purpose: a love letter, a test, a dress, eye of newt? (Hopefully not!) List the elements and procedures for the spell as a kind of recipe. Laura Esquivel's novel *Like Water for Chocolate* has this "magically real" element of symbolic food bringing about certain events.

In the second half of your spell, include an incantation (with words such as "double, double, toil and trouble") and the intent of the spell.

When I use this exercise in classes, I like to suggest that students frame their wishes in the positive (for obvious reasons). For instance, if you want to get someone out of your life, try a spell for something positive that will take the person far far away from you.

Committing a Rhyme

Early on in workshops, my students often ask me if they are "allowed to rhyme" in a poem. Much of the modern work they come across has no meter or rhyme, which may seem like out-dated concepts. Earlier in this century, I imagine students asked for permission *not* to rhyme. Most of the models of rhyme that an average anthology contains are poems from other centuries, so when students try to use certain patterns of sound, they often write using archaic language and syntax. Many people have not come in contact with good contemporary models of poems using rhyme (other than songs, which are often considered another category). We learn by example, and it is important to learn from the great poets of our history, but also to have contemporary models.

In Bruce Meyer's interview with British poet James Fenton in the late 1980s, Fenton suggests that there are many poets writing today who are terrified of "committing a rhyme." He states that one must defy the unspoken and spoken rules of the critics and the fads:

> Absolutely defy it. If you don't defy it, you're going to be a prisoner of your time. . . . When I was teaching in Minnesota, I learned a lot about how people can be cowed into submission by critical opinion. The terror with which they treated the question of form, as if there is a question of form. There isn't a question of form. There is poetry. There is this terrific art which has been handed down from generation to generation to read with immense pleasure. But there are some people who are sitting there terrified of committing a rhyme.

Rhyme requires practice and a good ear, or it can fail miserably. A bad poem in rhyme is more loud (cacophonous, perhaps) and noticeable than a bad free verse poem, which might just quietly die on the page. English is a difficult language in which to use rhyme, for it contains far fewer rhyming words when compared with Spanish or Italian, for instance. Variations broaden the musical possibilities in English and often allow for lines that sound more natural to the ear. There are many ways to create variation, either by using the following different types of rhyme, or by alternating the parts of speech at the end of lines, or by such techniques as *enjambment* (discussed in the exercises following). Writers often use these techniques without realizing what has created the music. After a while, these methods become second nature.

Rhyme and its variations must have meaning, just as rhythm does. A deliberate off-rhyme (defined below) among exact rhymes, for instance, might create the effect of disorder or letdown.

The following are patterns of sound and types of rhyme (defined as the repetition of the identical or similar stressed sound).

exact rhyme: differing consonant sounds followed by identical stressed vowel sounds, as in "state, gate" and "lies, surprise."

slant-rhyme: also called off-rhyme, half-rhyme, near rhyme, approximate rhyme, oblique rhyme. The sounds are similar, but not exactly alike. In the most common type of slant rhyme, the final consonant sounds are identical, but the stressed vowel sounds differ. This effect might exist at the end or in the middle of a line and is referred to as **consonance**, as in "good, food" and "soot, flute" (see Shirley Geok-Lin Lim's "Pantoum for Chinese Women" in Part Three).

assonance: the repetition, in proximity, of identical vowel sounds, preceded and followed by differing consonant sounds, as in "ten, them" and "time, mine" (see my poem "*Memento Mori* in Middle School" in Part Three).

alliteration: the repetition of initial consonant sounds, as in "baby boy," or sometimes the prominent repetition of the first consonant, as in "*after life's final*."

masculine rhyme: also known as single rhyme. The final syllables are stressed and, after their initial consonant sounds, are identical in sound, as in "spent, meant, intent" (see Elizabeth Bishop's "One Art", among many examples).

feminine rhyme: also known as double rhyme. Stressed rhymed syllables are followed by identical unstressed syllables, as in "master, disaster, fluster" (see "One Art"), "despising, arising" (see Shakespeare's "When in Disgrace with Fortune and Men's Eyes" in Part Three).

triple rhyme: a form of feminine rhyme in which identical stressed vowel sounds are followed by two identical unstressed syllables, as in "goddesses, bodices, Odysseys" and "apology, mythology." This type of rhyme works well occasionally, but it has the greatest likelihood of slipping into light verse. It might be best employed in deliberately humorous verse (see the excerpt from Byron's *Don Juan* in the "Stanzas" section).

eye-rhyme: the sounds do not rhyme, but the words look as if they would rhyme, as in "rough, bough."

end rhyme: also known as terminal rhyme, the rhymes that appear at the end of lines.

internal rhyme: rhyme that appears within the line.

Two important cautions, to avoid the most common failures of rhyme in contemporary verse: First, don't go for the easiest rhyme. Rhyme should surprise. Second, don't use awkward syntax just to squeeze in a rhyme. Trying to force something to fit didn't work for Cinderella's stepsisters. Or, to reference another tale, if you force a rhyme, it will beat like a tell-tale heart in the center of your poem.

Suggestions for Writing

1. Write lines practicing each of the above elements of rhyme (exact rhyme, slant rhyme, etc.).

2. Running one line into the next, or *enjambment* (also discussed in "Hearing the Beat: Using Meter"), rather than using end-stopped lines, can enhance the flow and keep rhymes from sounding too lockstep. Notice the enjambment in Rhina P. Espaillat's "Bilingual/Bilingüe" below. Practice using enjambment to soften the sound of exact rhymes.

3. Another way to keep rhyme fresh and interesting (exact rhyme, in particular), is to vary your choice of parts of speech for the rhyming word. Write some lines that vary the parts of speech. End your lines with a verb, then a noun, then an adjective, etc., as in the example below, by Rhina P. Espaillat. (Also see Espaillat's essay "Bilingual/Bilingüe" in Part Three.)

Bilingual/Bilingüe

My father liked them separate, one there,	*(adverb)*
one here (allá y aquí), as if aware	*(adjective)*
that words might cut in two his daughter's heart	*(noun)*
(el corazón) and lock the alien part	*(noun)*
to what he was—his memory, his name	*(noun)*
(su nombre)—with a key he could not claim.	*(verb)*
"English outside this door, Spanish inside,"	*(preposition)*
he said, "y basta." But who can divide	*(verb)*
the world, the word (mundo y palabra) from	*(preposition)*
any child? I knew how to be dumb	*(adjective)*
and stubborn (testaruda); late, in bed,	*(noun)*
I hoarded secret syllables I read	*(verb)*
Until my tongue (mi lengua) learned to run	*(verb)*
where his stumbled. And still the heart was one.	*(noun)*
I like to think he knew that, even when,	*(conjunction)*
proud (orgulloso) of his daughter's pen,	*(noun)*
he stood outside mis versos, half in fear	*(noun)*
of words he loved but wanted not to hear.	*(verb)*

Forms from Various Cultures and Traditions

The following pages present examples of several specific *fixed*, or closed, poetic forms:

Sonnet
Forms of repetition: sestina, villanelle, rondeau, triolet, pantoum
Short forms: epigrams, haiku, tanka, renga
Ballad
Acrostic
Blues poetry

Practicing each form is an exercise in itself, because of the framework the rules for the form provide. You will find that following these rules can actually be quite liberating—it can often bring you to a place in your stream of consciousness that you might not otherwise have found. Structure, in a way, can enable freedom, just as grammar allows us to communicate. Attempting these exercises will also shed light on great poems of history written in these forms. And being familiar with them gives you additional tools for your own writing. Writing a villanelle or triolet, for instance, can hone the skill of using a repeated line or refrain. Once you have a good grasp of the form, you can use its influence to your best advantage—either by using the form itself or using it as inspiration for your own variations. When you find a form that particularly suits or intrigues you, search out its more elaborate history and the many examples in literature.

Working in form can help to train your ear and can have the effect of making your free verse and prose more lyrical and rhythmical. It is also vital to note, however, that a competent exercise in a particular form is not necessarily a great poem. As I have mentioned several times in the book, we must keep in mind that the source of true art remains on many levels an enigma.

Remember, also, that it may take a while for a subject to discover its true shape. Form should have meaning and purpose in a particular piece and find its subject organically. Writers spend decades, sometimes, working on a single short poem. It is a good idea to think of much of your writing as "exercise." It takes the pressure off, opens up the field to many possibilities, and keeps you going.

Sonnet

Read/Revisit

Marilyn Nelson, "Chosen" (see page 307)
William Shakespeare, "When in Disgrace with Fortune and Men's Eyes" (see page 311)
R. S. Gwynn, "Shakespearean Sonnet" (see page 300)

The sonnet is a 14-line poem and one of the most well-known verse forms. The word *sonnet* comes from the Italian *sonetto*, meaning "a little song or sound," which previously came from the Latin *sonus*, meaning "sound." The sonnet form is thought to have been invented by Giacomo de Lentino around the year 1200.

Many traditional sonnets were written in iambic pentameter: five feet or ten syllables to every line, with every other syllable stressed. There are different traditional rhyme schemes for the sonnet, the best known being the following:

Shakespeare: abab cdcd efef gg
Spenser: ababbcbccdcdee
Petrarch: abba abba with the sestet rhyming cdcdcd, cdecde, cdccdc, or some other variation that doesn't end in a couplet.
Wordsworth: abbaacca dedeff

The first eight lines or *octave* of the Petrarchan sonnet presents the theme and develops it. In the following *sestet*, the first three lines reflect upon the theme and the final three lines bring it to a close. The Shakespearean sonnet allows a break between octave and sestet, but is generally composed of three quatrains, each with different pairs of rhymes, and a final couplet with its own rhyme. An important feature of the Shakespearean sonnet is this last couplet, which closes the poem with a climax, or a philosophical reflection on what has been presented. Spenser's form has an octave followed by a sestet that includes a final couplet. Many other poets, such as Milton and Wordsworth, have developed other variations of the sonnet.

Sonnets are sometimes written in a *sequence* or cycle. Some of these cycles (such as a crown or garland of sonnets) have a particular number and elaborate structure. The *garland* of sonnets used by several Russian poets, for instance, consists of 15 poems. They are arranged so that the final sonnet contains only lines repeated from the preceding poems.

Considering the many sonnets written by such poets as Yeats, Frost, Millay, Nelson, and Gwynn, to name just a few, one can see that the form has thrived into modern and contemporary work. Many contemporary sonnets are written with nontraditional meters and rhyme schemes, or without rhyme, and contain a variety of subjects.

Marilyn Nelson's "Chosen," uses both exact and slant rhyme and shapes the sonnet into tercets and a concluding couplet. She uses the form's compression to articulate a terrible incident that has a historical weight. Consider how Nelson's "Chosen" and Gwynn's "Shakespearean Sonnet" both use tradition and bend it, in both the form and choice of subjects.

Suggestions for Writing

1. Try the sonnet. You could select a rhyme scheme. Or, as you write the first few lines, a rhyme scheme may begin to emerge. To better understand the form, I encourage you to use iambic pentameter (with minimal variations) at first (see "Hearing the Beat: Using Meter"). Later, you can experiment with more variations. Though the subject of love often conjures up a sonnet, don't feel limited

to this. Consider the startling subjects of Gwynn's and Nelson's contemporary sonnets. Perhaps use the compression of a sonnet to depict a traumatic event, as Marilyn Nelson does. Note, also, Nelson's use of paradox (or contradiction) to deal with the terror.

2. "Translate" Shakespeare's sonnet into a love poem in contemporary English or, perhaps, a different character's voice.

Forms of Repetition: Sestina, Villanelle, Rondeau, Triolet, Pantoum

Sestina

Read/Revisit

Dana Gioia, "My Confessional Sestina" (see page 299)

The word *sestina* comes from the Italian *sesto*, meaning "sixth" (from the Latin root *sextus*). This form is based on sixes and is an ideal exercise for the mathematical mind. The elaborate repetitions are reminiscent of the patterns we see in the natural world. The form is thought to have been invented in Provence in the thirteenth century by the troubadour poet Arnaut Daniel. Dante admired Daniel's poetry and popularized the form by writing sestinas in Italian.

The sestina has six unrhymed stanzas of six lines each, with the end words repeating in a precise pattern throughout the poem. The repeated words create a rhyme-like effect that occurs at seemingly unpredictable intervals as the pattern changes from stanza to stanza. The poem then ends with a three-line stanza, each line containing two of the words. The pattern would be as follows, with the capital letters representing end words:

ABCDEF / FAEBDC / CFDABE / ECBFAD / DEACFB / BDFECA / AB,CD,EF

The final poem therefore contains 39 lines made up of 6 + 6 + 6 +6 + 6 + 6 + 3.

When used to the poem's advantage, the repetitions create a forward movement, and the words serve different functions in the progression of the poem. They might also create a cyclical effect.

Many poets have enjoyed working in the sestina form, including Algernon Charles Swinburne, Rudyard Kipling, Ezra Pound, Elizabeth Bishop, W. H. Auden, Donald Justice, and Mona Van Duyn. Dana Gioia's "My Confessional Sestina" uses the form to make a satirical comment about workshop poems, as well as confessional poetry.

Suggestions for Writing

1. In a workshop (ignoring Gioia's wry comment on the workshop sestina for the moment), to make sense of the form, you might work with a group to write a collective sestina. Choose six words and write them on the board. Set up a grid for the poem. Have participants call out lines that end with the appropriate words. Don't expect an exquisite poem to emerge, but it is a fun way to make sense of the form, and some interesting lines will likely appear.

2. Though it may be easy to follow the rules and "fill in the blanks" to create a passable sestina, writing a good one is not an easy task. It is definitely not the form for all subjects. Sestinas tend to lag midway, and a good one needs a serious charge or turn of events, perhaps a narrative twist. Try to choose a subject that will have some shift at its center. Another hint is to change the grammar of the chosen words, as in Gioia's use of "taste."

3. Adopt (and adapt) six words from a writer who has influenced you. Give credit to your source. Use them to write an "homage," perhaps. Donald Justice did this in his "Sestina on Six Words by Weldon Kees."

4. Since so many sestinas seem to lag, the form might provide a good opportunity to invent a new form. Use the concept and pattern of repetition, but try a half sestina, a *sestria*, perhaps.

5. As Gioia does, make a comment about a particular form while using the form. Many writers have done this. Louise Bogan, for instance, in "Single Sonnet," chooses the form of a sonnet to address the "heroic mould" of the sonnet.

Villanelle

Read/Revisit

Elizabeth Bishop, "One Art" (see page 291)
Wendy Cope, "Lonely Hearts" (see page 295)

The word villanelle comes from *villanella*—a type of old Italian folk song. The villanelle contains six stanzas: five stanzas of three lines and one stanza of four lines. The first and last lines of the first stanza are repeated throughout the poem in the intricate pattern of A^1bA^2 / abA^1 / abA^2 / abA^1 / abA^2 / abA^1A^2. (The capitals refer to *repeated* lines and the lower case letters to *rhymes* with the repeated lines. The numbers 1 and 2 refer to the two lines that repeat precisely.) The poem has a rhyme scheme of aba throughout, with a variation in the last stanza.

The pattern of repetition in the villanelle can create a cyclical, hypnotic effect, like a tide coming back in. The form also reinforces the ideas expressed in the poem.

Elizabeth Bishop's "One Art," is a powerful example of the possibilities of the villanelle. In this poem, she is talking about loss, and the poem moves through the different kinds of loss one might experience. The subject is a good one for this form, in which the repetition has a deliberate function. Notice that she does not repeat the A^2 line exactly, but she repeats its meaning. She also alters the A^1 line in the last stanza. The variation is enchanting.

The villanelle can also be an appropriate form to convey an element of humor or irony. Wendy Cope's "Lonely Hearts" uses the villanelle to explore the personal ads, which seem more and more a reality of modern life. The form in this poem enhances the subject. The repetition has a distinct purpose here, as does the rhyme. Otherwise, the poem might read as a mere series of ads.

The villanelle form is a good one as an exercise because it helps to hone the skill of using a repeated line, like the refrain of a song. In a case such as "One Art," it might allow one to explore the many layers that surround a single subject, such as loss. In "Lonely Hearts," the repetition achieves the "listing" effect of newspaper ads, and provides a humorous commentary on how similar all the ads tend to sound.

Other contemporary poets have found the villanelle useful for conveying various subjects. Carolyn Beard Whitlow, for instance, has used the villanelle as a blues poem, another form with a structure of repetition. (See the "Blues Poetry" section, later in Part Two.)

Suggestions for Writing

Try writing a villanelle. You might choose a subject that has many angles to explore, so the repetition has a purpose and does not become tedious. Allow the form to work for you. Try to create movement within the poem by exploring different layers of meaning in the repeated line or by creating a narrative within.

Rondeau and Triolet

Read/Revisit

Gerry Cambridge, "Goldfinch in Spring" (see page 293)
Paul Laurence Dunbar, "We Wear the Mask" (see page 296)
Frederick Morgan, "1904" (see page 306)

The word *rondeau* comes from the French *rond*, meaning "round," as each line comes round, or is repeated. The rondeau consists of 13 lines divided into three stanzas. The first and last stanzas contain five lines, and the second stanza contains three lines (not including the refrains). There are two rhymes in the poem. The opening words of the first line (or sometimes the whole first line) form unrhymed refrains in the second and third stanzas, often puns. The pattern is: aabba, aabR, aabbaR. (The R signifies the refrain):

The *triolet*, essentially a shorter version of the rondeau, was popular among French medieval poets such as Eustace Deschamps. It was revived by Jean de la Fontaine in the seventeenth century and remained popular into the nineteenth century.

The triolet is another form particularly useful for subjects that contain several angles or layers, or a cyclical quality. Frederick Morgan's "1904" is a good variation on the form, where the single repetition enhances the idea of a secret kept for years.

Suggestions for Writing

Try a triolet or rondeau. Choose a subject that might benefit from the reinforcement of a line, like the cycles felt (or heard) in contemporary Scottish poet Gerry Cambridge's "Goldfinch in Spring" or the passage of time in Frederick Morgan's "1904." In Cambridge's poem, note also the effect of the varying grammar of each line.

Get a handle on each form by trying to adhere to it at first. Later, you can experiment with variations, and use the repetition to its greatest advantage in your particular poem.

Pantoum

Read/Revisit

Shirley Geok-Lin Lim, "Pantoum for Chinese Women" (see page 303)

The *pantoum*, of Malaysian origin, is another form using repetition. Victor Hugo first described the pantoum in the West. It became a popular form (with some variations) among French poets such as Louisa Siefert and Charles Baudelaire. It became prevalent in England in the late nineteenth century, but was not used much in America until the last half of the twentieth century.

The poem is made up of four-line stanzas: lines two and four of one stanza are repeated as lines one and three of the next. The poem can have any length. Sometimes the final stanza uses the first and third lines of the first stanza as its second and fourth lines. This creates the effect of completion, giving the poem a feeling of having come full circle.

Shirley Geok-Lin Lim's "Pantoum for Chinese Women" (included in Part Three) takes on the heavy subject of Chinese female infanticide as a result of the one-child law. The "soot" in the poem refers to a common method of smothering girl children. Of her choice of form for this poem, Lim has stated that she believes poetry must give pleasure and that use of meter and rhyme are ways to enhance the musicality. She believes that sometimes the most terrible subjects might best be cast in language that gives the most pleasure, as if to somehow rise beyond the horror.

Suggestions for Writing

As a pantoum can be of any length, start with a few stanzas. Be willing to change your initial lines if you find yourself heading in a different direction—which often happens with such a form.

Short Forms: Epigram, Haiku, Tanka Renga

Epigram

The epigram is a short, often witty poem, meant to be remembered. The word *epigram* derives from the Greek word meaning "write on," as on a gravestone or a wall, for instance. Such writing tended to be brief, given the limited space, not to mention the labor of carving each letter in stone. Epigrams have survived from antiquity in many languages (probably because they were carved in stone) and convey such subjects as history, irony, and love. The following is a translation of an early Persian poet:

> I'll hide within my poems as I write them
> Hoping to kiss your lips as you recite them.

> AMAREH (11TH CENTURY);
> TRANSLATED BY DICK DAVIS

An epigram need not rhyme or follow a particular meter, although very many do, given the nature of the form as one to be remembered. Rhyme certainly enhances that intention.

> Sir, I admit your general rule,
> That every poet is a fool:
> But you yourself may serve to show it,
> That every fool is not a poet.

> ALEXANDER POPE (1688–1744)

> John, while swimming in the ocean,
> rubbed sharks' backs with suntan lotion.
> Now the sharks have skin of bronze
> in their bellies, namely John's.

> X. J. KENNEDY (B. 1929)

> Adam
> Had 'em

> ANONYMOUS

Haiku, Tanka, Renga

Japanese forms have also found their way into English poetry. For over a thousand years, tanka have been written: five-line poems with 31 syllables, following the pattern 5, 7, 5, 7, 7. The popular haiku (which means "beginning verse" in Japanese) derives from the first lines of tanka. The haiku (or hokku), a poem of 17 syllables (5, 7, 5), often depicts something in nature, but it carries in its compressed style a mystical suggestion of other interpretations. It is important to note, however, that the Japanese syllable is quite a different entity than the English syllable. Therefore, an English haiku need not necessarily have 17 syllables, but rather three short lines. The poem might have one of many tones, from somber to humorous. The most important thing is the leap contained in the poem's compression. The poem should reverberate.

> Under cherry trees 5
> Soup, the salad, fish, and all . . . 7
> Seasoned with petals. 5
>
> MATSUO BASHO (1644–1694)

> Cricket, watch
> out! I'm rolling
> over!
>
> KOBAYASHI ISSA (1763–1827)

Haiku were also used as the first three lines for a series of tanka called *renga*. Renga were often collaborative poems, and many Japanese poets wrote books of rules for the form. Each stanza would connect to the previous one (through an image, perhaps, or a play on words), but not to the stanza before. The rules would also describe the pacing from beginning to end. The first six or eight stanzas would set up the poem. The middle stanzas would become quite elaborate, include humor, and move through a great range of subjects and emotions. The final six or eight stanzas would move quickly, with rapid, closely related images like simple farewells at the end of a gathering. Often the final stanza would contain an image of spring, indicating hope and rejuvenation. Traditionally, Japanese renga might involve over two hundred poets writing a single poem.

Matsuo Basho, considered one of the great writers of haiku, preferred renga of 36 stanzas. He spoke of the linking technique as having the essential quality of *hibiki*, or echo. He believed that the second stanza should echo the first, via a thread of connection, as in the following (the poem need not rhyme, of course, although the following translation does):

> From this day on,
> I will be known as a wanderer
> leaving in morning showers.

You will sleep your nights
Nestled among *sasanqua* flowers.

MATSUO BASHO (1644–1694);
TRANSLATED BY DIANE THIEL

Basho is known also for his travelogues—which were written as a mosaic of prose and poetry, and which often contained linked poems, the parts often identified as "written by host" or "written by guest," a kind of call and response.

Japanese forms have been much revived in contemporary verse, and have often been used in innovative ways. W. H. Auden's "Elegy for JFK," for instance, is formally intriguing in its use of a series of haiku. And many poets, such as Mexican poet Octavio Paz, have revived the tradition of collaborative renga, with one poet producing the first three lines and another poet the following two.

Suggestions for Writing

1. Try writing an epigram. Choose a subject that would benefit from getting right to the point. Make a statement about love. Give advice. Use irony. One common type of epigram presents the poet pretending to be something inanimate, and is often a riddle.

2. Try writing haiku and tanka. In a group setting, you might revive the ancient tradition of renga and attempt poems in collaboration. The first person would write the first stanza of three lines, the second person would write the next stanza of two lines, the third person would write the following stanza, again of three lines, as discussed above.

3. Just for fun, you might try the types of links discussed in the exercises in "Random Connections," in Part One, to see what kind of "accidental" connections arise. Write your tanka (or haiku) individually, but read them as if they were a renga written in collaboration. See what mysterious echoes appear.

Ballad

Read/Revisit

Nikos Kavadias, "A Knife" (see page 302)
Dudley Randall, "Ballad of Birmingham" (see page 309)

The ballad has been traditionally used for the purpose of story-telling and expresses the tradition of the link between poetry, story, and song. Any narrative song might be called a ballad. Traditionally, ballads would shift and change as they traveled from place to place. Sir Walter Scott, a renowned collector of Scottish folk ballads, angered a few of his sources by the act. One woman said to him, "They were made for singing and no' for reading, but ye ha'e broken the charm now and they'll never be sung mair." Perhaps something of the oral tradition does get lost in the act of transcribing a ballad—it freezes it in time. On the other hand, the transcribers of ballads and other forms of folklore certainly preserved much of our culture that would have otherwise been lost.

Ballad meter varies, but the traditional ballad stanza is four lines rhymed abcb or abab, with alternating beats of 4, 3, 4, 3. If the feet are iambic, the quatrain is said to have *common measure*, as in eighteenth-century English hymnist John Newton's "Amazing Grace":

> Amazing grace! how sweet the sound
> > That saved a wretch like me!
> I once was lost, but now am found,
> > Was blind, but now I see.

The ballad has often been used as a form to convey historical events, and it has been adopted by contemporary writers for this purpose. Consider Dudley Randall's "Ballad of Birmingham," for instance (the poem is included in Part Three). The subject matter of ballads ranges from the comic and irreverent to very serious and poignant depictions of events, as in Kavadias's and Randall's poems.

Suggestions for Writing

1. Ballad scholar Albert B. Friedman has said that the events of ballads are frequently "the stuff of tabloid journalism—sensational tales of lust, revenge and domestic crime." Use a tabloid newspaper to select subjects for your ballads. (In all honesty, you could probably use any newspaper, considering the nature of much of today's sensationalism in the everyday news.)

2. Note how both Randall's ballad and Kavadias's ballad have more than one voice. Try writing a narrative poem for more than one voice.

Acrostic

Read/Revisit

David Mason, "Acrostic from Aegina" (see page 305)

The *acrostic* originated in ancient times. Some of the Hebrew psalms of the Bible are acrostics. The word derives from the Greek *acros* (outermost) and *stichos* (line of poetry). In an acrostic, the letters of the lines spell a vertical word, or group of words. A double acrostic has two vertical arrangements in the middle or at the end of the line. And a (rare) triple acrostic has three vertical arrangements.

The acrostic has been enjoyed over time as a game—from the Greeks to Boccaccio to Chaucer to Edgar Allan Poe. In its design, the acrostic often contains a secret or riddle. It might carry the name of a beloved, as in David Mason's "Acrostic from Aegina."

With its hidden word or message, the acrostic can have a subversive quality. Mason names his poem as an acrostic, but sometimes the acrostic is concealed. *The New Yorker*, for instance, once unknowingly published an acrostic that named and insulted a prominent anthologist. (There is, in fact, a tradition of the insult poem, which makes use of humor and exaggeration and often contains an element of "call and response," as one might imagine—a trading of insults. The epigram has also been a popular form for insult poems.)

Suggestions for Writing

1. Write an acrostic that spells the name of your beloved, honors or dishonors a person in history, contains a riddle, or is an insult poem. Choose a subject that would truly benefit from the "secret message" nature of the poem.

2. Try an *abecedarian*, a variant of an acrostic. In this form, each line begins with a letter of the alphabet, in order.

Blues Poetry

Read/Revisit

Carolyn Beard Whitlow, "Rockin' a Man Stone Blind" (see page 315)

Blues poetry has its roots in music and in the experience of African Americans. The earliest form was the work song: the call and response from one person to another working in the field. These work songs are often referred to as "field hollers." The songs were sometimes secret messages passed back and forth. Slaves were often silenced for fear of the subversive nature of their songs.

Blues poetry emerged from blues music, via such poets as Langston Hughes and Sterling Brown. Although "the blues" is traditionally associated with painful experience, it also has as its center the idea of the triumph of the human spirit.

Some blues poetry adheres to no particular form but is considered blues because of its content. Some has both the content and structure of repetition that old blues songs contain. The traditional blues stanza had three lines, with the first line repeated (with variations) in the second line, and then a third rhyming line. Some blues songs have a structure of four lines.

> In the evenin', in the evenin', momma, when the sun go down,
> In the evenin', darlin' I declare, when the sun go down,
> Yes it's so lonesome, so lonesome, when the one you love is not around.
>
> TRADITIONAL

> I woke up this mornin' feelin' round for my shoes
> Know about that, I got these old walkin' blues
> I woke up this mornin' feelin' round for my shoes
> I know about that, I got them old walkin' blues
>
> ROBERT JOHNSON (1911–1938)

Some contemporary poets have used the blues tradition in innovative ways. Carolyn B. Whitlow, for instance, writes her poem "Rockin' a Man Stone Blind" in the form of a villanelle (see "Villanelle").

Many of us, when we compare our lives to conditions in other eras or geographic locations, might feel that we can't possibly be true to the blues, which emerged out of such tremendous human suffering. This kind of poem might provoke some unmasking, or some serious thought about the conditions of our lives (and possibly about our apathy). But we all have cultural and historical memory we can access.

The persistent problems of human society—war, oppression, cruelty to human beings as well as animals—can be subjects one might draw upon as inspiration for the blues. Poems about such universal conditions might have the power to open up our minds to the enduring questions about human existence.

Be true to your sorrow, or the sorrows you feel around you in the world. Singing them out can be one way of addressing them.

Suggestions for Writing

1. Write a blues poem. Try listening to blues music before you write. You might try Robert Johnson, Blind Lemon Jefferson, or Lightnin' Hopkins, to name a few. This exercise in workshops might produce some serious blues poems, or it might be a forum for participants to find out their concerns.

2. What is your deepest sorrow? There is a repeated motif in the blues tradition, of meeting the devil at the crossroads. You might write about your own such encounter, a crossroads of your own life. Try the structure of repetition.

3. Try writing a blues poem from someone else's perspective. Think of someone who has undergone something very difficult, and write from that perspective.

Performing the Poem: Reading, Slam, Performance

Read/Revisit

Dudley Randall, "Ballad of Birmingham" (see page 309)
Nikos Kavadias, "A Knife" (see page 302)

Poetry is a genre particularly conducive to performance. In their earliest incarnations, poems were intended to be performed. The stories and history of cultures were passed down in poetry via meter and rhyme, useful as tools to enhance our memory. When we speak of the oral tradition, we often think of times as distant as ancient Greece, of Homeric songs carried from one place to another by memory. Modern Greece, however, is a good example of a place where the oral tradition has survived—perhaps because for many centuries Greece was under foreign rule. Writing could be censored, but no one could suppress or confiscate songs.

Learning poems by heart is another way to honor our oral traditions. As a child, did you learn any poems by heart? Think of what the words suggest: "by heart." We enter a poem more fully when we make it part of our memory. We claim it as our own.

Suggestions for Performance

1. In a workshop, have everyone in your group share a favorite poem. In your recitations, try to inhabit the poem as fully as possible with your voice. Later, share a poem you have written yourself and have committed to memory.

2. Choose a poem that has more than one voice, such as Nikos Kavadias's "A Knife" or Dudley Randall's "Ballad of Birmingham." Choose a partner and practice a performance of the poem. Commit your lines to memory. In a group, you might also have two sets of people perform the same poem, in order to see how different interpretations of the poem might change the presentation.

3. Select a poem in translation and perform the poem with a partner, having one person recite the English version and the other person recite the poem in the original language.

4. Select a poem that does not necessarily have more than one voice. With a partner, figure out an inventive way to share the lines. Then perform the poem.

5. Be creative and figure out an inventive way to dramatize a poem, either by yourself or with a partner. You could use props, music, dramatic gestures, etc.

6. Have a class "slam." Choose three judges. Each of the remaining students will perform a poem. Or, if a poem lends itself to more than one voice, you may break up in groups of two or three and perform one together.

Revision: Drafts and Discovery

Read/Revisit

Elizabeth Bishop, "One Art" (see page 291)
Wendy Cope, "Lonely Hearts" (see page 295)

Elizabeth Bishop provides a wonderful example of the importance of revision in writing a poem. It is extraordinarily useful to examine a writer's drafts of a particular piece, both to understand his or her progress and to help develop your own. Bishop left quite a paper trail and is known for spending decades to complete some of her poems. Her famous "The Moose," for instance, took about twenty years to complete. Her villanelle "One Art," Bishop has declared, was surprisingly easy, "like writing a letter." Yet 17 drafts exist of the poem. For Bishop, 17 drafts was an *easy* process.

"One Art" is a great example of what can happen in the process of revision and the discoveries that can be made in the process of developing an idea. Brett C. Millier writes:

> Elizabeth Bishop left seventeen drafts of her poem "One Art" among her papers. In the first draft, she lists all the things she's lost in her life—keys, pens, glasses, cities—and then she writes "one might think this would have prepared me / for losing one average-sized not exceptionally / beautiful or dazzlingly intelligent person . . . / But it doesn't seem to have at all . . ." By the seventeenth draft, nearly every word has been transformed, but most importantly, Bishop discovered along the way that there might be a way to master this loss.

Following is the first draft of Bishop's poem. Compare this free verse version to her final, intricately crafted "One Art." Notice the compression that took place, as well as the change in thought process from the first to the final version.

HOW TO LOSE THINGS /? / THE GIFT OF LOSING THINGS?

lost   *cont*

[Draft 1]

One might begin by losing one's reading glasses
oh 2 or 3 times a day - or one's favorite pen.

THE ART OF LOSING THINGS

The thing to do is to begin by "mislaying".

Mostly, one begins by "mislaying":
keys, reading-glasses, fountain pens
- these are almost too easy to be mentioned,
and "mislaying" means that they usually turn up
in the most obvious place, although when one
is making progress, the places grow more unlikely
- This is by way of introduction. I really
want to introduce myself - I am such a
fantastic lly good at losing things
I think everyone shd. profit from my experiences.

loss

easily

thrill

instinct
          26/ed

          my

You may find it hard to believe, but I have actually lost
I mean lost, and forever two whole houses,
one a very big one.   A third house, also big, is
at present, I think, "mislaid" - but
maybe it's lost, too. I won't know for sure for some time.
I have lost one/long peninsula and one island.
I have lost - it can never be has never been found
a small-sized town on that same island.
I've lost smaller bits of geography, like   and many smaller bits of geography or scenery
a splendid beach , and a good-sized bay.
Two whole cities, two of the
world's biggest cities (two of the most beautiful
although that's beside the point)
A piece of one continent -
and one entire continent.   All gone, gone forever and over.

One might think this would have prepared me
for losing one average-sized not especially------- exceptionally
beautiful or dazzlingly intelligent person
(except for blue eyes)   (only the eyes were exceptionally beautiful and
But it doesn't seem to have, at all...   the hands looked intelligent)
                              the fine hands

a good piece of one continent
and another continent - the whole damned thing!
He who loseth his life, etc. - but he who
loses his love - neever, no never never never again -

A
  ×
B

First Draft of Elizabeth Bishop's "One Art"

Suggestions for Writing

1. Notice how Bishop's "One Art" and Cope's "Lonely Hearts" (both villanelles) are developed via a "listing" effect. Make a list (of at least twenty lines) in your journal. For instance, you might try a topic such as "things I should have said to him," or "bits of gossip." As you work with the list, see if a refrain begins to naturally emerge. As you discard or add, see how the drafts begin to change. What discoveries did you make in the process of reworking?

2. Choose one of your own poems for which the process of revision has been giving you difficulty. It may not have found its best form or incarnation. Put the poem aside and begin again. Perhaps write the poem from a different viewpoint (e.g., use the grandmother's voice instead of the father's) or make it more of a narrative instead of focusing on a lyrical moment.

17
Drama

Drama in Action

Read/Revisit

David Ives, *Time Flies* (see page 350)
Susan Glaspell, *Trifles* (see page 339) and "Creating Trifles" (see page 395)

While fiction, creative nonfiction, and poetry are all forms of story *telling*, drama is essentially story *acting*. This implies a number of fundamental differences between drama and the other three genres:

- Drama is primarily a *visual* art form. Because it is meant to be seen by the audience, the author must pay close attention to visual details. In fact, because the story has to be told directly by the actors and the setting, the visual elements (such as the appearance and dress of the actors, and the physical objects that make up the setting) tend to be perceived immediately by the audience as cues that help them place the story in time and space.

- Drama is also an *aural* art form. With the exception of stage directions, which are not meant to be read by the audience, every word in a script is dialogue that is meant to be heard by the audience. Consequently, the author must pay close attention to how the words he or she has written actually sound. Sherman Alexie says "screenplays are more like poetry than like fiction." He is correct, in that poetry, and particularly formal poetry, is meant to be read aloud and must, therefore, pay much closer attention to the sound of words than fiction.

- Drama has to be physically produced—enacted. This implies that, whether the work is meant for the stage (theater) or for film or television, the author must keep in mind the physical limitations of each medium and the cost of production of the work.

- Drama is essentially a continuous art. The performed work must be able to capture and hold the interest of the audience for the duration of the performance. The opening must immediately grab the audience's attention and build a momentum that the performance must increase and sustain. In addition, because the audience does not have the capability to return to earlier points in the action to review things they may have missed, it is imperative for the author to spell out characters and events boldly, and to use devices such as repetition to make sure that nothing important *is* missed in the first place. This makes form an important aspect of drama, again making it more similar to poetry than fiction.

These unique characteristics of drama shape the form in interesting ways. Because of the physical and continuous nature of the dramatic form, almost all plays and most movies cover directly a limited period of time. Covering too long a span would require characters to age, and although aging is relatively easy to handle in fiction, it is much more difficult in drama. Make-up and the use of younger actors are possibilities, but they are costly (which is the reason you really only see them used in movies). The physical nature of drama also means that there are real limits to the length of the piece: neither plays nor movies generally last more than two hours. Speaking words takes much longer than reading them (try timing yourself reading a piece both silently and aloud), so this doesn't leave room for a lot of dialogue or action. These particular constraints mean that, in drama, the action typically begins in the middle (actually, almost always close to the end) of the story.

Consider Glaspell's *Trifles* and Ives's *Time Flies*. Glaspell's play could be relatively easily converted into a short story. Its setting could be easily described in prose, and its definite story line, balance of action, and dialogue facilitate the play's conversion into fiction. Ives's play, on the other hand, has an abstract setting and includes very little action. The play relies very heavily on dialogue and does not really present a story. For these reasons it would be quite a challenge to render it as a prose fiction piece.

Suggestions for Writing

1. Look at the ideas for stories you have recorded in your journal. If you don't have any in your journal, do a 15-minute free-write to come up with as many story ideas as you can. Which of these ideas could be developed effectively into play? Evaluate each idea using the following criteria:

   - How well can the story be told using only dialogue?
   - How many characters are necessary for the story to unfold? (More than six or seven would make for an unwieldy play.)
   - How expansive is the setting necessary for the story? (If the story takes place in more than three different settings, it would be difficult to render in even a long play.)
   - How long is the story's timeline?

Choose the idea you think would work best as a play. Write a list of characters. Decide how many acts (based on major changes of setting) your play will have. Write a description of the setting for each act.

2. Consider turning either Sharon Oard Warner's story "A Simple Matter of Hunger" or Doris Lessing's "A Woman on a Roof" into a play. How much of the story will you be able to show directly? How many acts will the play need? Where would your play begin? Write setting descriptions for each act. Write the opening scene of the play.

Opening Scenes

Read/Revisit

Susan Glaspell, *Trifles* (see page 339) and "Creating Trifles" (see page 395)

David J. LeMaster, *The Assassination and Persecution of Abraham Lincoln* (see page 360)

The beginning of the story that we see enacted on stage or on screen is called the *exposition*. The exposition gives the audience necessary background information about the setting and the characters so they can make sense of what is going on. This information is given through visual cues such as the appearance and dress of the actors and the appearance of the set, and through dialogue.

The *inciting incident* is one or more events that happened before the exposition—events that create the situation in which the characters find themselves at the beginning of the action. In *The Assassination and Persecution of Abraham Lincoln*, David J. LeMaster presents the inciting incident to the audience through the voice of a radio announcer. Glaspell uses a very similar method in *Trifles*, having the character Hale relate at the opening of the play the details of how he found John Wright murdered.

As was discussed already, drama must immediately capture and then hold the attention of the audience. Both Shakespeare and Glaspell accomplish this by posing the *dramatic question* right at the outset. In *The Assassination and Persecution of Abraham Lincoln*, the dramatic question is posed by the surreal situation the audience is presented with at the opening of the play. The audience is set wondering "What is this about?" In *Trifles*, the dramatic question is much more direct and clear: whether or not Mrs. Wright murdered her husband. Again, the question is posed at the opening of the play, with the revelation of the inciting event and by the dialogue immediately following.

Suggestions for Writing

1. Make a list of five dramatic questions that you think have potential. Write each one as a complete sentence. Pick one and write an opening scene of three to five pages.

2. Write a one-act play in which all of the characters are college students. Limit the cast to no more than five characters. Before you begin writing the play write the following items:

   ▪ A list with the name of each character and one or two sentences about each one.

   ▪ The dramatic question in a single complete sentence.

   ▪ The inciting incident, if any.

   ▪ A short paragraph describing in detail the place where the action will happen.

Writing on the Edge: Desire and Dramatic Tension

Read/Revisit

David LeMaster, *The Assassination and Persecution of Abraham Lincoln* (see page 360)

Dramatic tension in drama has to be set in clear, bold terms. The tension is always the result of some *conflict*, and because every human being is motivated by *desire*, the conflict is the outcome of the characters' attempts to satisfy their desires. For the story to be interesting, for there to be dramatic tension, there must be obstacles to the characters' satisfying their desires. The characters' attempts to overcome the obstacles are what create conflict and tension. The conflict is between the character and the obstacle, and the tension results from the audience's curiosity about the outcome of the conflict.

There are a limited number of obstacles that come between us and our desires: other people, nature, circumstances (fate, our social position, our wealth, etc.), ourselves (internal conflict). This short list, however, opens up virtually unlimited possibilities, especially if you consider that several obstacles can be combined to create a complex conflict.

Dramatic tension is created through posing a series of dramatic questions that are subsidiary to the main dramatic question. In *The Assassination and Persecution of Abraham Lincoln*, the primary dramatic question is "What is happening?"—a situation that is common in nonrealistic or absurdist drama. This central question is never resolved explicitly by the play. The audience has to answer it by themselves. However, a number of secondary dramatic questions—"Why did Lincoln stage his fake assassination?" "Will

he get away with the help of Booth?" "Why does Booth think Lincoln's acting was only 'alright'?"—sustain tension and keep the play interesting.

Suggestions for Writing

1. Write a short one-act play with two characters. The fundamental
   conflict is between the characters, who are in a romantic
   relationship—the relationship is in trouble. Choose a secondary
   conflict from one of the four types of obstacles: other people,
   nature, circumstances, ourselves. Have the resolution of the
   secondary conflict facilitate a resolution of the primary conflict.

2. Take as the basic premise two characters dividing a number of objects
   between them. Make a list of the possible motivations (desires) for
   each character. Make a list of the possible conflicts. Determine which
   conflict or set of conflicts has the greatest potential to sustain dramatic
   tension for an extended scene (10–12 minutes). Write the scene.

Writing along the Timeline

Read/Revisit

Sherman Alexie, from *Smoke Signals* (see page 322)
Sherman Alexie and Diane Thiel, "A Conversation with Sherman
   Alexie" (see page 386)

Movement in time is much more constrained in drama than in the other
literary forms. (See "The Passage of Time" section in the "Fiction" chapter.) This is especially true for a stage play, where flashback, flashforward,
and parallel scenes are extremely difficult if not impossible to execute.
The scenes of a play are sequential, moving in one direction in time (almost
always forward). Large elapsed intervals between scenes and acts are also
difficult to execute and are, therefore, generally avoided. Information about
the past (and sometimes the future) is conveyed through dialogue—often
through one character telling a story to another.

The timeline in a screenplay is more flexible, because the camera medi-
ates between the audience and the action. Time can be announced directly
by printing it on the screen (a printed message like this is called a *title card*,
and it can also be used to convey information such as place), by zooming
in on a clock, or by fading out from a character and fading in to a scene
with a dreamlike quality that communicates "flashback." Even so, large jumps
in the timeline are usually avoided in screenplays as well as plays, because
they tend to disrupt the action.

In Sherman Alexie's screenplay *Smoke Signals*, the inciting action is put
on the screen in the opening scene. The time is established by audio cues: disco

music, and the voice of a disc jockey who announces that it is "2:45 a.m. on a hot Bicentennial Fourth of July in 1976." After the opening sequence of a house fire, there is a significant time jump to 1988. These scenes are separated from the main action of the screenplay by the opening credits. After that, however, the action progresses sequentially, with minimal time jumps between scenes. Close to the end of the screenplay (not included in the excerpt in Part Three), there is one flashback to the scene of the house fire. The flashback is signaled by the same disco music heard in the opening scene, and it is facilitated by the fact that it presents an already familiar scene.

Suggestions for Writing

1. Write the opening stage directions for a play to convey the following times and places:

   Townhouse, Chicago, December 7, 1941.
   Oval office, Washington, D.C., April 4, 1968.
   Suburban house, U.S.A., the present.

2. Note how Alexie jumps considerable distances in place and time in the opening scenes of *Smoke Signals*. Convert this piece for a stage performance. Write detailed stage directions to describe the setting for each scene. Remember that lighting can be used to change the focal action on the stage. If you choose to leave a scene out because it would complicate the setting too much, you must reveal the information contained in the deleted scene in the dialogue. Remember that you don't have the luxury of using onscreen titles to show the audience how much time has elapsed, so you must convey the information in some other way.

3. Write three short, consecutive scenes for a stage play, each of which moves forward several days. Write stage directions that do not require any change in the stage setting between the scenes.

4. Write a scene in which a past event is revealed through dialogue.

Dramatic Twist: From the Real to the Fantastic

Read/Revisit

Jaqueline Reingold, *Creative Development* (see page 365)
Milcha Sanchez-Scott, *The Cuban Swimmer* (see page 372)

Modern drama often departs from the traditional concepts of characterization, setting, plot, and timeline and introduces nonrealistic elements. Sometimes the characters may be nonrealistic but placed in a realistic setting—for example, a historical figure from long ago might be placed in a modern setting. Sometimes the setting may be nonrealistic, or it might be abstract or represent no specific place. Some plays might use a realistic setting, such as a forest, but place nonrealistic elements in it, such as living-room furniture. The plot may develop in an illogical sequence of events, or time may be ignored or distorted.

The degree of nonrealism and abstraction can vary, from minimal to total, but the greater the departure from reality, the more difficult the play will be to carry through without losing the interest of the audience. The nonreal elements should have meaning and should make a point in an interesting way. But you should be aware that you will need to maintain a delicate balance if you choose to render a piece as nonrealistic drama. On the one hand, you must avoid confusing the audience, and on the other, you must avoid making the point so directly that the audience feels that the play is lecturing or preaching.

One way to maintain the necessary balance is to maintain a general sense of reality throughout the action, but use a specific departure from reality in order to surprise, but not necessarily shock, the audience into some new insight. In *Creative Development*, Jaqueline Reingold injects a surprising, unreal element halfway through the play. In a dramatic, humorous twist, the character Diane reveals she is a Muse, and from that point on, the action evolves in an alternate reality (one in which Muses with supernatural powers exist). Reingold does give some hints of what is coming, via the unusual things Diane pulls from her purse, but by the time the objects start becoming totally unrealistic, the twist is not far away.

In contrast, in *The Cuban Swimmer*, Milcha Sanchez-Scott maintains realism up until the last scene of the play. The surprising, magically real ending extends the meaning of her play, making it more than a drama about family, as it highlights the religious symbolism of the play, half-hidden until now. Note the final lines of the play: "This is indeed a miracle! It's a resurrection! Margarita Suárez, with a flotilla of boats to meet her, is now walking on the waters, through the breakers . . . onto the beach, with crowds of people cheering her on. What a jubilation! This is a miracle!"

Suggestions for Writing

1. Pick one aspect of modern culture to expose, and emulate Reingold's approach in *Creative Development*. Write an outline for a one-act play in which the action begins as totally realistic, but a dramatic twist into the unreal takes place at some point in the middle of the play. Can you make the twist humorous as well as symbolic? Think of three subtle hints you can give in the action before the twist (like Reingold's use of the items in the purse) that suggest everything is not what it seems. Make these clues improbable, but not impossible; do not yet cross the line into the unreal. Where in the action do you place each clue? Can you make them funny? Do they create a sense of suspense?

2. Look through the ideas for possible plays you have written in your journal. Do you have ending scenes for all of them? How would a scene that departs from reality work as an ending? Pick one for which you think such a scene might work, and write an outline of the play.

3. Begin at the end. Write an unreal scene that could conclude a play you haven't even thought of yet. Revise the scene until it works well as a stand-alone piece. Now write some ideas about what action (which stays in the confines of the real) would work well with the scene. Develop one or more of these ideas into an outline.

Making Dialogue Dramatic

Dialogue is the primary vehicle for conveying information in drama, especially stage drama. Film may draw on other techniques, using more visual and nondialogue audio cues, but these are more limited in stage drama. Dialogue must reveal who the characters are, what they know and think, what they feel, and often where they are in space and time, as well as what has happened in the past. Dramatic dialogue is necessarily more packed with information than dialogue in real life, yet it must appear to be natural.

If you do not have much experience in writing drama, you will be tempted to begin by writing dialogue and let that carry the action. However, because you must pack so much information in the dialogue, writing it should be the last step in the process. Think of your stage or screen play as a sequence of scenes. First map out this sequence, and then map in detail what will happen in each individual scene. Typically each scene will begin with the entrance or exit of a character. List, in detail, each progression of action: who enters (or exits) and how, where does this character go, what do other characters in the scene do. Each sequential bit of action constitutes a *beat*. If two or more characters are doing different things in the same instant, their actions are part of the same beat. Only after you know what you want to happen in each beat—which particular bit of information you want to reveal—should you write the dialogue and stage directions for the beat, constructing the scene from the ground up.

Suggestions for Writing

1. Write the dialogue and stage directions for two characters who are discussing a third character. Let the scene reveal several important characteristics of the third character. For example, what is the character's occupation? Age? What does the character want? Is the character trustworthy? Map out the scene first, before you write the dialogue and directions.

2. Map a short scene (one to two pages) between two characters who are related (husband and wife, parent and child, siblings, etc.). Write the dialogue and stage directions to reveal important information for each of the characters (e.g., are they happy? is one trying to hide something from the other? what does each want? how does each feel about the other? etc.).

3. Map a short scene (two to three pages) for three characters. Two of the characters know something that the third does not. They want to reveal this information to the third character but may not tell him or her directly. Write out the scene.

Look Who's Talking:
Unique Characters

Read/Revisit

David Ives, *Time Flies* (see page 350)

Characterization in drama presents some unique challenges but also offers some unique opportunities. The most obvious limitation is that revealing the characters' thoughts is not as easy as in fiction or poetry. Usually there is no narrator in drama; thoughts are related to the audience through dialogue or action. There is a bit more flexibility in screen drama, where voice-over can be used to reveal characters' thoughts, but this is a technique that should be used carefully and sparingly, as it tends to interrupt the action.

In addition, because drama has rather strict limitations in terms of length, and because there are even more severe limitations on the amount of information that can be conveyed in the available amount of time (as has already been discussed, it takes longer to speak a certain amount of text than to read it), characters must be developed very quickly. Consequently characters in drama are often more exaggerated and more intense than in the other genres and in real life.

Every writer of drama faces the question: "How do I create memorable characters quickly and effectively?" One answer is to create characters that are unique. From Oedipus to Forrest Gump, drama is filled with characters whose unique characteristics or situations make them memorable. Surprising characters, such as the mayflies in David Ives's *Time Flies*, are also unique, and therefore memorable. Ives's characters are particularly effective because who they are (mayflies, which only live about a day) makes the play's point about the value of time particularly poignant.

Suggestions for Writing

1. Emulating David Ives's poignant choice of mayflies as characters, write a scene or very short play in which two nonhuman characters discuss one of the following issues.

   Overpopulation

   Pollution

   Travel

2. Write a scene in which two people who become romantically interested in each other meet for the first time. Give one characteristic to one character that makes him or her immediately memorable. It might be a physical characteristic such as weight, or an attribute such as wealth or total lack thereof. Or the character might be a famous historical figure, or named after someone famous.

Setting the Stage

Read/Revisit

Milcha Sanchez-Scott, *The Cuban Swimmer* (see page 372)

Writing a stage play presents unique limitations on the possible settings. Unlike fiction, poetry, and even screenplays, where the action can range over a large number of physical settings, stage plays must set action to take place within a very few different physical settings—typically no more than three. The theatrical stage can only be set during a break in the action such as an intermission between acts, and each different setting must be designed so it can be easily assembled and disassembled, or moved into and out of place. Creative lighting can alleviate some of these difficulties: more than one setting can be onstage at once, and if you light only one, the audience can be convinced to ignore the presence of the others.

Stage directions are as much a part of a play as the dialogue. They can be very elaborate or very skeletal and short. Since the size, structure, and capabilities of the stages of today's theaters vary tremendously, most modern plays call for rather simple staging. To allow for greatest flexibility in the ways their plays can be staged, most playwrights today do not include elaborate staging directions.

As a writer of plays, you should always be conscious of the staging possibilities as you are developing your pieces. Even if you do not write detailed staging directions, you should be able to visualize how your play can be staged. The best way to develop a sensitivity about what is possible, what is difficult, and what is impossible in terms of staging is to watch plays. The more plays you see, staged in a variety of theaters, the better you will hone your staging instincts. While you should be mindful of possible difficulties and do what you can to avoid them, you also should not compromise an interesting story line because of what you perceive as staging difficulties.

For example, though Sanchez-Scott provides few staging directions for *The Cuban Swimmer*, and though the work is a one-act play, requiring only one set, the staging of the play presents a serious challenge: how to depict a swimmer, in the ocean, next to a boat in which most of the action takes place, and also allow for a helicopter hovering above, and a distant beach the swimmer will reach at the end.

Suggestions for Writing

1. Stage directions are an important part of a play, and it is important for you, as a writer, to be able to visualize how a play may be staged. Take on the challenge of staging *The Cuban Swimmer*. Write a detailed description about how you would stage the play.

2. Choose a challenging setting (such as open country in the Wild West). Write a scene, including the stage directions, to depict action that takes place in this setting.

Revision: Heightening Conflict

The arrangement of scenes can have a great deal to do with the heightening of tension in a play. Sometimes a new juxtaposition can create a certain charge. A mystery, for instance, could be established by gradually imparting information in scene after scene. Our tendency might be to write a play with a chronological timeline. However, reenvisioning the sequence of action might be a clue to raising the level of intensity.

In drama in particular, so much of the intensity must be imparted through the characters' speech and actions. Are your characters engaged in enough action as they speak? What creates the tension in their interaction with others? Sometimes as writers, we need to go past the point of reality. We can always rein the level of drama back in, but pushing it beyond the edge can let us see how much is too much, as well as pointing out how little is too little.

Suggestions for Rewriting

1. Write an outline containing every scene of your play. Are the scenes in the best possible order? Is each scene necessary—what would happen if you removed it? Is there an important scene missing? This might work best if you took scissors to the outline and cut it up, with each scene on a separate strip of paper. Shuffle the strips and rearrange them in a random order. Move them around so that the

sequence starts making sense. Remove some that might be superfluous. See if you are able to combine some sets of scenes into one. Add a strip with a new scene if one comes to you. How is what you end up with different from the original outline? Use the new outline as a map for your revisions.

2. In your outline, identify each scene in which there is a conflict. Reread the corresponding sections of your manuscript. Rewrite each section, intensifying the conflict. Focus on the characters' lines and corresponding actions. Suspend your good sense and be extreme: exaggerate the conflict between characters, as well as each character's internal conflict, to the point you have a caricature. How does the story read now? Revisit the same passages and scale back the intensity a bit if necessary.

PART THREE

A Collection of
Readings

Nonfiction

Diane Ackerman (B. 1948)

The Truth about Truffles

"The world's homeliest vegetable," it's been called, but also "divinely sensual" and possessing "the most decadent flavor in the world." As expensive as caviar, truffles sell for over $500 a pound in Manhattan these days, which makes it the most expensive vegetable on earth. Or, rather, under earth. Truffle barons must depend on luck and insight. A truffle may be either black (*melanosporum*) or white (*magnata*), and can be cooked whole, though people usually shave raw slivers of it over pasta, eggs, or other culinary canvases. For 2,000 years it's been offered as an aphrodisiac, prized by Balzac, Huysmans, Colette, and other voluptuous literary sorts for its presumed ability to make one's loins smolder like those of randy lions. When Brillat-Savarin describes the dining habits of the duke of Orleans, he gets so excited about the truffles that he uses three exclamation points:

> Truffled turkeys!!! Their reputation mounts almost as fast as their cost! They are lucky stars, whose very appearance makes gourmands of every category twinkle, gleam, and caper with pleasure.

One writer describes the smell of truffles as "the muskiness of a rumpled bed after an afternoon of love in the tropics." The Greeks believed truffles were the outcome of thunder, reversed somehow and turned to root in the ground. Périgord, in southwest France, produces black truffles that ooze a luscious perfume and are prized as the ne plus ultra of truffles, essential black sequins in the famous Périgord goose-liver pâté. The best white truffles come from the Piedmont region, near Alba in Italy. Napoleon is supposed to have conceived "his only legitimate son after devouring a truffled turkey," and women throughout history have fed their male companions truffles to rouse their desire. Some truffle dealers use trained dogs to locate the truffles, which tend to grow close to the roots of some lindens, scrub oaks, and hazelnut trees; but sows are still the preferred truffle hunters, as they have been for centuries. Turn a sow loose in a field where there are truffles, and she'll sniff like a bloodhound and then dig with manic passion. What is the sow's obsession with truffles? German researchers at the Technical University of Munich and the Lübeck School of Medicine have discovered that truffles contain twice as much androstenol, a male pig hormone, as would normally appear in a male pig. And boar pheromone is chemically very close to the human male hormone, which may be why we find truffles arousing, too. Experiments have shown that if a little bit of androstenol is sprayed into a room where women are looking at pictures of men, they'll report that the men are more attractive.

For the truffle farmer and his sow, walking above a subterranean orchard of truffles, it must be hysterically funny and sad. Here this beautiful, healthy sow smells the sexiest boar she's ever encountered in her life, only for some reason he seems to be underground. This drives her wild and she digs frantically, only to turn up a strange, lumpy, splotched mushroom. Then she smells another supermacho boar only a few feet away—also buried underground—and dives in, trying desperately to dig up that one. It must make her berserk with desire and frustration. Finally, the truffle farmer gathers the mushrooms, puts them in his sack, and drags his sow back home, though behind her the whole orchard vibrates with the rich aromatic lust of handsome boars, every one of them panting for her, but invisible!

1990

Bruce Chatwin (1942–1989)

From *In Patagonia*

In my grandmother's dining-room there was a glass-fronted cabinet and in the cabinet a piece of skin. It was a small piece only, but thick and leathery, with strands of coarse, reddish hair. It was stuck to a card with a rusty pin. On the card was some writing in faded black ink, but I was too young then to read.

"What's that?"

"A piece of brontosaurus."

My mother knew the names of two prehistoric animals, the brontosaurus and the mammoth. She knew it was not a mammoth. Mammoths came from Siberia.

The brontosaurus, I learned, was an animal that had drowned in the Flood, being too big for Noah to ship aboard the Ark. I pictured a shaggy lumbering creature with claws and fangs and a malicious green light in its eyes. Sometimes the brontosaurus would crash through the bedroom wall and wake me from my sleep.

This particular brontosaurus had lived in Patagonia, a country in South America, at the far end of the world. Thousands of years before, it had fallen into a glacier, travelled down a mountain in a prison of blue ice, and arrived in perfect condition at the bottom. Here my grandmother's cousin, Charley Milward the Sailor, found it.

Charley Milward was captain of a merchant ship that sank at the entrance to the Strait of Magellan. He survived the wreck and settled nearby, at Punta Arenas, where he ran a ship-repairing yard. The Charley Milward of my imagination was a god among men—tall, silent and strong, with black mutton-chop whiskers and fierce blue eyes. He wore his sailor's cap at an angle and the tops of his sea-boots turned down.

Directly he saw the brontosaurus poking out of the ice, he knew what to do. He had it jointed, salted, packed in barrels, and shipped to the Natural History Museum in South Kensington. I pictured blood and ice, flesh and salt, gangs of Indian workmen and lines of barrels along a shore—a work of giants and all to no purpose; the brontosaurus went rotten on its voyage through the tropics and arrived in London a putrefied mess; which was why you saw brontosaurus bones in the museum, but no skin.

Fortunately cousin Charley had posted a scrap to my grandmother.

My grandmother lived in a red-brick house set behind a screen of yellow-spattered laurels. It had tall chimneys, pointed gables and a garden of blood-coloured roses. Inside it smelled of church.

I do not remember much about my grandmother except her size. I would clamber over her wide bosom or watch, slyly, to see if she'd be able to rise from her chair. Above her hung paintings of Dutch burghers, their fat buttery faces nesting in white ruffs. On the mantelpiece were two Japanese homunculi with red and white ivory eyes that popped out on stalks. I would play with these, or with a German articulated monkey, but always I pestered her: "Please can I have the piece of brontosaurus."

Never in my life have I wanted anything as I wanted that piece of skin. My grandmother said I should have it one day, perhaps. And when she died I said: "Now I *can* have the piece of brontosaurus," but my mother said: "Oh, that thing! I'm afraid we threw it away."

At school they laughed at the story of the brontosaurus. The science master said I'd mixed it up with the Siberian mammoth. He told the class how Russian scientists had dined off deep-frozen mammoth and told me not to tell lies. Besides, he said, brontosauruses were reptiles. They had no hair, but scaly armoured hide. And he showed us an artist's impression of the beast—so different from that of my imagination—grey-green, with a tiny head and gigantic switchback of vertebrae, placidly eating weed in a lake. I was ashamed of my hairy brontosaurus, but I knew it was not a mammoth.

It took some years to sort the story out. Charley Milward's animal was not a brontosaurus, but the mylodon or Giant Sloth. He never found a whole specimen, or even a whole skeleton, but some skin and bones, preserved by the cold, dryness and salt, in a cave on Last Hope Sound in Chilean Patagonia. He sent the collection to England and sold it to the British Museum. This version was less romantic but had the merit of being true.

My interest in Patagonia survived the loss of the skin; for the Cold War woke in me a passion for geography. In the late 1940s the Cannibal of the Kremlin shadowed our lives; you could mistake his moustaches for teeth. We listened to lectures about the war he was planning. We watched the civil defence lecturer ring the cities of Europe to show the zones of total and partial destruction. We saw the zones bump one against the other leaving no space in between. The instructor wore khaki shorts. His knees were white and knobbly, and we saw it was hopeless. The war was coming and there was nothing we could do.

Next, we read about the cobalt bomb, which was worse than the hydrogen bomb and could smother the planet in an endless chain reaction.

I knew the colour cobalt from my great-aunt's paintbox. She had lived on Capri at the time of Maxim Gorky and painted Capriot boys naked. Later her art became almost entirely religious. She did lots of St Sebastians, always against a cobalt-blue background, always the same beautiful young man, stuck through and through with arrows and still on his feet.

So I pictured the cobalt bomb as a dense blue cloudbank, spitting tongues of flame at the edges. And I saw myself, out alone on a green headland, scanning the horizon for the advance of the cloud.

And yet we hoped to survive the blast. We started an Emigration Committee and made plans to settle in some far corner of the earth. We pored over atlases. We learned the direction of prevailing winds and the likely patterns of fall-out. The war would come in the Northern Hemisphere, so we looked to the Southern. We ruled out Pacific Islands for islands are traps. We ruled out Australia and New Zealand, and we fixed on Patagonia as the safest place on earth.

I pictured a low timber house with a shingled roof, caulked against storms, with blazing log fires inside and the walls lined with the best books, somewhere to live when the rest of the world blew up.

Then Stalin died and we sang hymns of praise in chapel, but I continued to hold Patagonia in reserve.

1977

Fred D'Aguiar (B. 1960)

A Son in Shadow

I know nothing about how they meet. She is a schoolgirl. He is at work, probably a government clerk in a building near her school. At the hour when school and office are out for lunch their lives intersect at sandwich counters, soft-drink stands, traffic lights, market squares. Their eyes meet or their bodies collide at one of these food queues. He says something suggestive, complimentary. She suppresses a smile or traps one beneath her hands. He takes this as encouragement (as if any reaction of hers would have been read as anything else) and keeps on talking and following her and probably misses lunch that day. All the while she walks and eats and drinks and soaks up his praise, his sweet body-talk, his erotic chatter and sexy pitter-patter, his idle boasts and ample toasts to his life, his dreams about their future, the world their oyster together.

Am I going too fast on my father's behalf? Should there have been an immediate and cutting rebuttal from her and several days before another meeting? Does he leave work early to catch her at the end of the school day and follow her home just to see where she lives and to extend the boundaries of their courtship? Throwing it from day to night, from school to home, from childhood play to serious adult intent? Georgetown's two-lane streets with trenches on either side mean a mostly single-file walk, she in front probably looking over her shoulder when he says something worthy of a glance, or a cut-eye look if his suggestions about her body or what he will do with it if given half a chance exceed the decorum of the day—which is what, in mid-Fifties Guyana? From my grandmother it's, "Don't talk to a man unless you think you're a big woman. Man will bring you trouble. Man want just one thing from you. Don't listen to he. Don't get ruined for he. A young lady must cork her ears and keep her eye straight in front of she when these men start to flock around. The gentleman among them will find his way to her front door. The gentleman will make contact with the parents first. Woo them first before muttering one thing to the young lady. Man who go directly to young ladies only want to ruin them. Don't want to make them into respectable young women—just whores. Mark my words." My grandfather simply thinks that his little girl is not ready for the attentions of any man, that none of them is good enough for his little girl, and so the man who comes to his front door had better have a good pretext for disturbing his reverie. He had better know something about merchant seamen and the character of the sea, and about silence—how to keep it so that it signifies authority and dignity, so when you speak you are heard and your words, every one of them, are rivets. That man would have to be a genius to get past my grandfather, a genius or a gentleman. And since my father is neither, it's out of the question that he'll even use the front door of worship. His route will have to be the yard and the street of ruination.

So he stands in full view of her house at dusk. It takes a few nights before her parents realize he is there for their daughter. Then one day her father comes out and tells him to take his dog behavior to someone else's front door, and the young man quickly turns on his heel and walks away. Another time her mother opens the upstairs window and curses him, and he laughs and saunters off as if her words were a broom gently ushering him out of her yard. But he returns the next night and the next, and the daughter can't believe his determination. She is embarrassed that her body has been a magnet for trouble, that she is the cause of the uproar, then angry with him for his keen regard of her at the expense of her dignity, not to mention his. Neighbors tease her about him. They take pity on the boy, offer him drinks, some ice-cold mauby, a bite to eat, a dhalpouri, all of which he declines at first, then dutifully accepts. One neighbor even offers him a chair, and on one night of pestilential showers an umbrella, since he does not budge from his spot while all around him people dash for shelter, abandoning a night of liming (loitering) and gaffing (talking) to the persistence and chatter of the rain. Not my father. He stands his ground with only the back of his right hand up to his brow to shelter his eyes zeroed in on her house. She steals a glance at him after days of seeming to ignore the idea of him, though his presence burns brightly inside her heart. She can't believe his vigilance is for her. She stops to stare in the mirror and for the first time sees her full lips, long straight nose, shoulder-length brunette hair, and dark green eyes with their slight oval shape. Her high cheekbones. Her ears close to her skull. She runs her fingers lightly over these places as if to touch is to believe. Her lips tingle. Her hair shines. Her eyes smile. And she knows from this young man's perseverance that she is beautiful, desirable. She abandons herself to chores, and suppresses a smile and a song. She walks past windows as much as possible to feed the young man's hungry eyes with a morsel of that which he has venerated to the point of indignity. She rewards his eyes by doing unnecessary half-turns at the upstairs window. A flash of clavicle, a hand slowly putting her hair off her face and setting it down behind her ears, and then a smile, a demure glance, her head inclined a little, her eyes raised, her eyelids batted a few times—she performs for him though she feels silly and self-conscious. What else is there for a girl to do? Things befitting a lady that she picked up from the cinema. Not the sauciness of a tramp.

Her mother pulls her by one of those beautiful close-skulled ears from the window and curses her as if she were a ten-cent whore, then throws open the window and hurtles a long list of insults at this tall, silent, rude, good-for-nothing streak of impertinence darkening her street. The father folds his paper and gets up, but by the time he gets to the window the young man is gone.

My mother cries into the basin of dishes. She rubs a saucer so hard that it comes apart in her hands. She is lucky not to cut herself. She will have to answer to her mother for that breakage. In the past it meant at least a few slaps and many minutes of curses for bringing only trouble into her mother's house. Tonight her mother is even angrier. Her father has turned his fury against her for rearing a daughter who is a fool for men. Her mother finds her in the kitchen holding the two pieces of the saucer together and then apart—as if her dread and sheer desire for reparation would magically weld them whole. Her tears fall like drops of solder on that divided saucer. Her mother grabs her hands and strikes her and curses her into her face so that my mother may as well have been standing over a steaming, spluttering pot on the stove. She drops the two pieces of saucer and they become six pieces. Her mother looks down and strides over the mess with threats about what will happen if her feet find a splinter. She cries but finds every piece, and to be sure to get the splinters too she runs her palms along the floor, this way and that, and with her nails she prizes out whatever her hand picks up. She cries herself to sleep.

The next night he is back at his station, and her mother and father, their voices, their words, their blows sound a little farther off, fall a little lighter. His presence, the bare-faced courage of it, becomes a suit of armor for her to don against her mother's and father's attacks. She flies through her chores. She manages under her mother's watchful eye to show both sides of her clavicle, even a little of the definition down the middle of her chest— that small trench her inflated chest digs, which catches the light and takes the breath away, that line drawn from the throat to the upper-most rib exuding warmth and tension, drawing the eyes twenty-five yards away with its radiance in the half-light of dusk, promising more than it can possibly contain, than the eye can hold, and triggering a normal heart into palpitations, a normal breath into shallowness and rapidity.

"Miss Isiah, howdy! How come you house so clean on the west side and not so clean on the east? It lopsided! Dirt have a preference in your house? Or is that saga boy hanging around the west side of your house a dirt repellent?" The gossip must have been rampant in the surrounding yards, yards seemingly designed deliberately so people could see into one another's homes and catch anything spilling out of them—quarrels, courtships, cooking pots, music—and sometimes a clash of houses, a reaction against the claustrophobia of the yard, but not enough yards, not enough room to procure a necessary privacy in order to maintain a badly sought-after dignity—clean, well dressed, head high in the air on Sundays—impossible if the night before there is a fight and everyone hears you beg not to be hit anymore, or else such a stream of obscenities gushes from your mouth that the sealed red lips of Sunday morning just don't cut it.

My father maintains his vigil. Granny threatens to save the contents of her chamber pot from the night before and empty it on his head. Could she have thrown it from her living room window to his shaded spot by the street? Luckily she never tries. She may well be telling him that he doesn't deserve even that amount of attention. If there is any creature lower than a gutter rat—one too low to merit even her worst display of disdain—then he is it. How does my father take that? As a qualification he can do without? How much of that kind of water is he able to let run off his back? Poor man. He has to be in love. He has to be wearing his own suit of armor. Lashed to his mast like Odysseus, he hears the most taunting, terrible things, but what saves him, what restores him, are the ropes, the armor of his love for my mother. Others without this charm would have withered away, but my father smiles and shrugs at the barrage of looks, insults, gestures, silence, loneliness.

Watch his body there under that breadfruit or sapodilla tree; the shine of his status as sentry and his conviction are twin headlights that blind her parents. They redouble their efforts to get rid of his particular glare, then are divided by the sense of his inevitability in their daughter's life. My grandmother stops shouting at him while my grandfather still raises his cane and causes the young man to walk away briskly. My grandmother then opens the windows on the west side, ostensibly to let in the sea breeze but really to exhibit in all those window frames a new and friendly demeanor. My grandfather shouts at her that he can smell the rank intent of that black boy, rotten as a fish market, blowing into his living room and spoiling his thoughts.

But the windows stay open. And my mother at them. With the love Morse of her clavicles and her cleavage as she grows bolder. Smiling, then waving. And no hand in sight to box her or grip her by the ear and draw her away from there. Until one night she boldly leaves the house and goes to him and they talk for five minutes rapidly as if words are about to run out in the Southern Hemisphere.

My father's parents wonder what has become of their Gordon.

"The boy only intend to visit town."

"Town swallow him up."

"No, one woman turn he head, stick it in a butter churn and swill it."

"He lost to us now."

"True."

They say this to each other but hardly speak to him except to make pronouncements on the size of foreign lands.

"Guyana small?"

"What's the boy talking about?"

"Why, England and Scotland combined are the size of Guyana."

"How much room does a man need?"

"That woman take he common sense in a mortar and pound it with a pestle."

The two voices are one voice.

Opportunity is here now. The English are letting go of the reins, a whole new land is about to be fashioned. And he is planning to leave! What kind of woman has done this to our boy? The boy is lost. Talking to him is like harnessing a stubborn donkey. This isn't love but voodoo, obeah, juju, some concoction in a drink, some spell thrown in his locus. A little salt over the shoulder, an iodine shower, a rabbit foot on a string, a duck's bill or snake head dried and deposited into the left trouser pocket, a precious stone, lapis lazuli, amethyst, or anything on the middle finger, a good old reliable crucifix around the neck, made of silver, not gold, and at least one ounce in weight and two inches in diameter. A psalm in papyrus folded in a shirt pocket next to the heart. A blessing from a priest, a breathing of nothing but incense with a towel over the head. A bout of fasting, one night without sleep, a dreamless night, and a dreamless, sleepless, youngest son restored to them. He wants to stay around the house, he shows them why he loves his mummy and poppy and the bounteous land. There is no plan to flee. There is no city woman with his heart in her hand. And his brain is not ablaze in his pants. His head is not an empty, airless room.

They have one cardboard suitcase each, apart from her purse and his envelope tied with a string that contains their passports and tickets, birth certificates, and, for him, a document that he is indeed a clerk with X amount of experience at such-and-such a government office, signed "supervisor"—a worthless piece of shit, of course, in the eyes of any British employer. But for the time being, these little things are emblematic of the towering, staggering optimism that propels them out of Georgetown, Guyana, over the sea to London, England.

So what do they do? My mother is a shy woman. My father, in the two photos I've seen of him, is equally reserved. Not liable to experimentation. The big risk has been taken—that of leaving everything they know for all that is alien to them. My mother knows next to nothing about sex, except perhaps a bit about kissing. My father may have experimented a little, as boys tend to do, but he, too, when faced with the female body, confronts unfamiliar territory. Each burns for the other, enough to pull up roots and take off into the unknown. Yet I want to believe that they improvise around the idea of her purity and respect it until their marriage night. That they keep intact some of the moral system they come from even as they dismantle and ignore every other stricture placed on them by Guyanese society: honor your father and mother; fear a just and loving God; pledge allegiance to the flag; lust is the devil's oxygen. All that circles in their veins.

Over the twelve days at sea they examine what they have left and what they are heading toward. At sea they are in between lives: one life is over but the other has not yet begun. The talking they do on that ship without any duties to perform at all! My mother tells how her father, despite his routine as a merchant seaman, finds time to memorize whole poems by the Victorians: Tennyson, Longfellow, Browning, Jean Ingelow, Arnold, and Hopkins. The sea is his workplace, yet he makes time to do this marvelous thing. She tells how when he comes back to land he gathers them all in the living room and performs "The Charge of the Light Brigade" or "Maud" or "My Last Duchess" or "Fra Lippo Lippi" or "The High Tide on the Coast of Lincolnshire" or "Dover Beach" or "The Kingfisher" or "The Wreck of the Deutschland." He recites these poems to his creole-thinking children, who sit there and marvel at the English they are hearing, not that of the policeman or the teacher or the priest, but even more difficult to decipher, full of twists and impossible turns that throw you off the bicycle of your creole reasoning into the sand. If any of them interrupts my grandfather he stops in midflow, tells them off in creole, and resumes his poem where he left off. When particularly miffed by the disturbance he starts the poem from the beginning again. Does my grandfather recite these verses before or after he gets drunk, swears at the top of his voice, and chases my grandmother around the house with his broad leather belt?

But when my parents are out at sea, they have only the King James Bible in their possession. What they plan and rehearse is every aspect of their new life.

"Children. I want children."

"Me too. Plenty of them."

"I can work between births."

"Yes, both of us. Until we have enough money for a house. Then you can stay home with the kids."

"A nanny. Someone to watch the kids while we work. What kind of house?"

"Three bedrooms. A garden at the front, small, and back, large. A car—a Morris Minor. With all that room in the back for the children and real indicators and a wood finish." Neither has a notebook or dreamed of keeping one. They do not write their thoughts, they utter them. If something is committed to memory, there has to be a quotidian reason for it, apart from bits of the Bible and a few calypsos. My grandfather's labor of love, his settling down with a copy of Palgrave's *Golden Treasury* and memorizing lines that bear no practical relationship to his life, must seem bizarre to his children. Yet by doing so he demonstrates his love of words, their music, the sense of their sound, their approximation to the heartbeat and breath, their holding out of an alternative world to the one surrounding him, their confirmation of a past and another's life and thoughts, their luxury of composition, deliberation, their balancing and rebalancing of a skewered life. I imagine my mother benefits from this exposure in some oblique way—that the Victorians stick to her mental makeup whether she cares for them or not, that a little of them comes off on me in the wash of my gestation in her.

There is an old black-and-white photo (isn't there always?) and fragments of stories about his comings and goings, his carryings-on, as the West Indian speak goes, his mischief. "Look pan that smooth face, them two big, dark eye them, don't they win trust quick-time? Is hard to tie the man with them eye in him head to any woman and she pickney them. He face clean-shaven like he never shave. He curly black hair, dougla-look, but trim neat-neat. The man got topside." His hair, thick and wavy because of the "dougla" mix of East Indian and black, exaggerates an already high forehead. Automatically we credit such an appearance, in the Caribbean and elsewhere, with intelligence—"topside." And a European nose, not broad, with a high bridge (good breeding, though the nostrils flare a bit—sign of a quick temper!). And lips that invite kisses. "They full-full and pout like a kiss with the sound of a kiss way behind, long after that kiss come and gone." He is six feet tall and thin but not skinny, that brand of thin that women refer to as elegant, since the result is long fingers and economic gestures. Notice I say economic and not cheap. A man of few words. A watcher. "But when he relax in company he know and trust, then he the center of wit and idle philosophizing. He shoot back a few rums, neat no chaser, with anyone, and hold his own with men more inclined to gin and tonic. He know when to mind he Ps and Qs and when to gaff in the most lewd Georgetown, rumshop talk with the boys. What chance a sixteen-year-old closeted lady got against such a man, I ask you?"

But most of the puzzle is missing. So I start to draw links from one fragment to the next. He begins to belong—fleetingly, at first—in my life. As a man in poor light seen crossing a road mercifully free of traffic, its tar-macadam steamy with a recent downpour. As a tall, lank body glimpsed ducking under the awning of a shop front and disappearing inside and never emerging no matter how long I wait across the street, watching the door with its reflecting plate glass and listening for the little jingle of the bell that announces the arrival and departure of customers.

Or I cross Blackheath Hill entranced by the urgent belief that my father is in one of the cars speeding up and down it. Blackheath Hill curves a little with a steep gradient—less than one in six in places. It's more of a ski slope than a hill. Cars and trucks, motorbikes and cyclists all come down the road as if in a race for a finish line. Going up it is no different. Vehicles race to the top as if with the fear that their engines might cut off and they will slide back down. I want to be seen by my father. I have to be close to his car so that he does not miss me. I measure the traffic and watch myself get halfway, then, after a pause to allow a couple of cars to pass on their way up, a brisk walk, if I time it right, to allow the rest of the traffic to catch up with me, to see the kid who seems to be in no particular hurry to get out of their way looking at them. I step onto the sidewalk and cherish the breeze of the nearest vehicle at my back—Father, this is your son you have just missed. Isn't he big? Pull over and call his name. Take him in your arms. Admonish him. Remind him that cars can kill and his little body would not survive a hit at these high speeds. Tell him to look for his father under less dangerous circumstances.

I am searching the only way I know how, by rumination, contemplation, conjecture, supposition. I try to fill the gaps, try to piece together the father I never knew. I imagine everything where there is little or nothing to go on. And yet, in going back, in raking up bits and pieces of a shattered and erased existence, I know that I am courting rejection from a source hitherto silent and beyond me. I am conjuring up a father safely out of reach and taking the risk that the lips I help to move, the lungs I force to breathe, will simply say "No." No to everything I ask of them, even the merest crumb of recognition.

"Father." The noun rings hollowly when I say it, my head is empty of any meaning the word might have. I shout it in a dark cave but none of the expected bats come flapping out. Just weaker and weaker divisions of my call. "Father." It is my incantation to bring him back from the grave to the responsibility of his name. But how, when I only know his wife, my mother, and her sudden, moody silence whenever he crops up in conversation?

You ever have anyone sweet-talk you? Fill your ears with their kind of wax, rub that wax with their tongue all over your body with more promises than the promised land itself contains, fill your head with their sweet drone, their buzz that shuts out your parents, friends, your own mind from its own house? That's your father, the bumblebee, paying attention to me.

My sixteenth birthday was a month behind. He was nearly twenty. A big man in my eyes. What did he want with me? A smooth tongue in my ears. Mostly, though, he watched me, my house, my backside when he followed me home from school. His eyes gleamed in the early evening, the whites of his eyes. He stood so still by the side of the road outside my house that he might have been a lamppost, planted there, shining just for me.

My father cursed him, my mother joined in, my sisters laughed at his silence, his stillness. They all said he had to be the most stupid man in Georgetown, a dunce, a bat in need of a perch, out in the sun too long, sun fry his brain, cat take his tongue, his head empty like a calabash, his tongue cut out, he look like a beggar. They felt sorry for him standing there like a paling, his face a yard long, his tongue a slab of useless plywood in his mouth. "Look what Ingrid gone and bring to the house, shame, dumbness, blackness follow she here to we house to paint shame all over it and us. Go away, black boy, take your dumb misery somewhere else, crawl back to your pen in the country, leave we sister alone, she got more beauty than sense to listen to a fool like you, to let you follow her, to encourage you by not cursing the day you was born and the two people who got together to born you and your people and the whole sorry village you crawl out of to come and plant yourself here in front of we house on William Street, a decent street, in Kitty, in we capital."

I should have thanked my sisters; instead I begged them to leave him alone. Ignore him and he'll go away. My father left the house to get hold of the boy by the scruff of his neck and boot his backside out of Kitty, but he ran off when my father appeared in the door frame. With the light of the house behind him and casting a long, dark shadow, he must have looked twice his size and in no mood to bargain. Your father sprinted away, melting into the darkness. I watched for his return by checking that the windows I'd bolted earlier really were bolted, convincing myself that I had overlooked one of them, using my hands to feel the latch as I searched the street for him. But he was gone for the night. My knight. Shining eyes for armor.

My mother cursed him from the living room window, flung it open and pointed at him and with her tongue reduced him to a pile of rubble and scattered that rubble over a wide area then picked her way through the strewn wreckage to make sure her destruction was complete: "Country boy, what you want with my daughter? What make you think you man enough for her? What you got between your legs that give you the right to plant yourself in front of my house? What kind of blight you is? You fungus!"

As she cursed him and he retreated from the house sheepishly, she watched her husband for approval. These were mild curses for her, dutiful curses, a warm-up. When she really got going her face reddened and her left arm carved up the air in front of her as if it were the meat of her opponent being dissected into bite-size bits. That's how I knew she was searching for a way to help me but hadn't yet found it. Not as long as my father was at home. Soon he would be at sea, away for weeks, and things would be different.

That is, if my onlooker, my remote watcher, my far-off admirer wasn't scared off forever. And what if he was? Then he didn't deserve me in the first place. If he couldn't take a few curses he wasn't good for anything. If I wasn't worth taking a few curses for . . . well, I didn't want a man who didn't think

I was worth taking a few curses for! I loved him for coming back night after night when all he got from me was a glance at the window. Sometimes less than a glance. Just me passing across the window frame as I dashed from chore to chore under four baleful eyes.

It seemed like he was saving all his breath and words for when he could be alone with me. Then he turned on the bumblebee of himself and I was the hapless flower of his attentions. He told me about my skin that it was silk, that all the colors of the rainbow put together still didn't come close to my beautiful skin. That my face, my eyes, my mouth, my nose, the tip of my nose, my ears, my fingertips, each was a precious jewel, precious stone. He likened the rest of me to things I had read about but had never seen, had dreamed about but had never dreamed I would see: dandelions, apples, snow, spring in England's shires, the white cliffs of Dover. In his eyes my body, me, was everything I dreamed of becoming.

That was your father before any of you were a twinkle in his eye. More accurately, that was my lover and then my husband. Your father was a different man altogether. Suddenly a stranger occupied my bed. His tongue now turned to wood. All the laughter of my sisters, the half-hearted curses of my mother, my father's promise of blue misery, all came true in this strange man, this father, this latter-day husband and lover.

I saw the change in him. My hands were full with you children. He went out of reach. He cradled you as if he didn't know which side was up, which down. He held you at arm's length to avoid the tar and feathers of you babies. Soon I earned the same treatment, but if you children were tar and feathers I was refuse. His face creased when he came near me. What had become of my silk skin? My precious features disappeared into my face, earning neither praise nor blame—just his silence, his wooden tongue, and that bad-smell look of his. I kept quiet for as long as I could. I watched him retreat from all of us, hoping he'd reel himself back in since the line between us was strong and I thought unbreakable; but no. I had to shout to get him to hear me. I shouted like my mother standing at the upstairs window to some rude stranger in the street twenty-five yards away. I sounded like my father filling the door frame. My jeering sisters insinuated their way into my voice. And your father simply kept walking away.

Believe me, I pulled my hair and beat the ground with my hands and feet to get at him in my head and in the ground he walked on that I worshiped. Hadn't he delivered England to me and all the seasons of England, all England's shires and the fog he'd left out of his serenades, no doubt just to keep some surprise in store for me? The first morning I opened the door that autumn and shouted, "Fire!" when I saw all that smoke, thinking the whole street on fire, all the streets, London burning, and slammed the door and ran into his arms and his laughter, and he took me out into it in my nightdress, he in his pajamas, and all the time I followed him, not ashamed to be seen outside in my thin, flimsy nylon (if anyone could see through that blanket) because he was in his pajamas, the blue, striped ones, and his voice, his sweet drone, told me it was fine, this smoke without fire was fine, "This is fog."

He walked away and everything started to be erased by that fog. That smoke without fire crossed the ocean into my past and obliterated Kitty, Georgetown, the house on William Street, everything he had touched, every place I had known him in. I swallowed that fog. It poured into my ears, nose, eyes, mouth. He was gone. I got a chest pain and breathlessness that made me panic. There wasn't just me. There were you children. I had to breathe for you children. The pain in my chest that was your father had to be plucked out, otherwise I too would be lost to you all, and to myself.

The first time I see him is the last time I see him. I can't wait to get to the front of the queue to have him all to myself. When I get there my eyes travel up and down his body. From those few gray hairs that decorate his temples and his forehead and his nose to the cuffs at his ankles and sparkling black shoes. He wears a black suit, a double-breasted number with three brass buttons on the cuff of each sleeve. He lies on his back with his hands clasped over his flat stomach. There is too much powder on his face. Let's get out of this mournful place, Dad. We have a lot of catching up to do. He has the rare look—of holding his breath, of not breathing, in between inhaling and exhaling—that exquisitely beautiful corpses capture. For a moment after I invite him to leave with me, I expect his chest to inflate, his lids to open, and those clasped hands to unfold and pull him upright into a sitting position as if he really were just napping because he has dressed way too early for the ball.

There are myths about this sort of thing. Father enslaves son. Son hates father, bides his time, waits for the strong father to weaken. Son pounces one day, pounces hard and definite, and the father is overwhelmed, broken, destroyed with hardly any resistance, except that of surprise and then resignation. Son washes his hands but finds he is washing hands that are not bloodstained, not marked or blemished in any way. He is simply scrubbing hands that no longer belong to him—they are his father's hands, attached to his arms, his shoulders, his body. He has removed a shadow all the more to see unencumbered the father in himself. There is the widow he has made of his mother. He cannot love her as his father might. While his father lived he thought he could. The moment his father expired he knew his mother would remain unloved.

I alight too soon from a number 53 bus on Blackheath Hill, disembark while the bus is moving, and stumble, trip from two legs onto all fours, hands like feet, transforming, sprouting more limbs, becoming a spider and breaking my fall. That same fall is now a tumble, a dozen somersaults that end with me standing upright and quite still on two legs with the other limbs dangling. Onlookers, who fully expected disaster, applaud. I walk back up the hill to the block of council flats as a man might, upright, on two legs. My other limbs dangle, swing as if they are two hands. Some days I will be out of breath, I will gasp and exhale, and the cloud before me will not be my winter's breath but the silken strands of a web, or worse, fire. Other days I might look at a bed of geraniums planted on the council estate and turn all their numberless petals into stone. A diamond held between my thumb and index finger crumbles in this mood, in this light, like the powdery wings of a butterfly.

I stare out of an apartment on the twenty-fourth floor of a tower block overlooking the nut-brown Thames. That wasp on the windowpane nibbling up and down the glass for a pore to exit through, back into the air and heat, tries to sting what it can feel but cannot see. My father is the window. I am the wasp. Sometimes a helping hand comes along and lifts the window, and the wasp slides out. Other times a shadow descends, there is a displacement of air, and it is the last thing the wasp knows. Which of those times is this? I want to know. I don't want to know. I am not nibbling nor trying to sting. I am kissing, repeatedly, rapidly, the featureless face of my father. It feels like summer light. It reflects a garden. Whose is that interfering hand? Why that interrupting shadow? My child's hand. My child's shadow. My son or my father? My son and my father. Two sons, two fathers. Yet three people. We walk behind a father's name, shoulder a father's memory. Wear another's walk, another's gait. Wait for what has happened to their bodies, the same scars, maladies, aches, to surface in ours.

I want to shed my skin. Walk away from my shadow. Leave my name in a place I cannot return to. To be nameless, bodiless. To swim to Wallace Stevens's Key West, which is shoreless, horizonless. Blackheath Hill becomes Auden's Bristol Street, an occasion for wonder and lament. Blackheath at 5:45 a.m. on a foggy winter morning becomes Peckham Rye. There are no trees on Blackheath, but angels hang in the air if only Blake were there to see them. On the twenty-fourth floor towering above the Thames, water, not land, surrounds me. Everything seems to rise out of that water. Look up at ambling clouds and the tower betrays its drift out to sea.

1999

Naomi Shihab Nye (B. 1952)

Three Pokes of a Thistle

Hiding inside the Good Girl

"She has the devil inside her," said my first report card from first grade. I walked home slowly, holding it out from my body, a thistle, a thorn, to my mother, who read the inside, then the note on the back. She cried mightily, heaves of underground rivers, we stood looking deep into the earth as water rushed by.

I didn't know who he was.

One day I'd smashed John's nose on the pencil sharpener and broken it. Stood in the cloakroom smelling the rust of coats. I said No. No thank you. I already read that and it's not a very good story. Jane doesn't do much. I want the spider who talks. The family of little women and their thousand days. No. What I had for breakfast is a secret. I didn't want to tell them I ate dried apricots. I listened to their lineage of eggs. I listened to the bacon crackle in everyone else's pail. Thank you.

What shall we do, what shall we do? Please, I beg you. Our pajamas were flying from the line, waists pinned, their legs fat with fabulous air. My mother peeled beets, her fingers stained deep red. She was bleeding dinner for us. She was getting up and lying down.

Once I came home from school in the middle of the day in a taxi. School gave me a stomachache. I rode in the front passenger seat. It would be expensive. My mother stood at the screen door peering out, my baby brother perched on her hip. She wore an apron. The taxi pulled up in front of the blue mailbox I viewed as an animal across from our house—his opening mouth. Right before I climbed out, another car hit the taxi hard from behind so my mother saw me fly from the front seat to the back. Her mouth wide open, the baby dangling from her like fringe. She came toward us running. I climbed up onto the ledge inside the back window to examine the wreckage. The taxi driver's visored cap had blown out the window. He was shaking his head side to side as if he had water in his ears.

You, you, look what a stomachache gets you. Whiplash.

The doctor felt my neck.

Later I sat on the front steps staring at the spot where it had happened. What about that other driver? He cried when the policeman arrived. He was an old man coming to mail a letter. I was incidental to the scene, but it couldn't have happened without me. *If you had just stayed where you belonged. . . .* My classmates sealed into their desks laboring over pages of subtraction, while out in the world, cars were banging together. Yellow roses opened slowly on a bush beside my step. I was thinking how everything looked from far away.

Then I was old. A hundred years before I found it, Mark Twain inscribed the front of his first-edition leatherbound book, "be good—and you will be lonesome." In black ink, with a flourish. He signed his name. My friend had the book in a box in her attic and did not know. It was from her mother's collection. I carried it down the stairs, trembling. My friend said, "Do you think it is valuable?"

Language Barrier

Basically our father spoke English perfectly, though he still got his *bs* and *ps* mixed up. He had a gentle, deliberate way of choosing words. I could feel him reaching up into the air to find them. At night, he told us whimsical, curling "Joha" stories which hypnotized us to sleep. I especially liked the big cooking pan that gave birth to the little pan. My friend Marcia's

father who grew up in the United States hardly talked. He built airplanes.
I didn't think I would want to fly in anything he made. When Marcia asked
him a question, he grunted a kind of pig sound. He sank his face into the
paper. My father spilled out musical lines, a horizon of graceful buildings
standing beside one another in a distant city. You could imagine people
living inside one of my father's words.

He said a few things to us in Arabic—fragrant syllables after we ate, bless-
ings when he hugged us. He hugged us all the time. He said, "I love you" all
the time. But I didn't learn how to say "Thank you" in Arabic till I was fourteen, which struck me, even then, as a preposterous omission.

Marcia's father seemed tired. He had seven children because he was
a Catholic, Marcia said. I didn't get it. Marcia's mother threw away the left-
overs from their table after dinner. My mother carefully wrapped the last
little mound of mashed potato inside waxed paper. We'd eat it later.

I felt comfortable in the world of so many different people. Their voices
floated around the neighborhood like pollen. On the next block, French-
Canadians made blueberry pie. I wanted a slice. It is true that a girl knocked
on our door one day and asked to "see the Arab," but I was not insulted.
I was mystified. Who?

Sometimes Marcia and I slept together on our screened-in back porch,
or in a big green tent in her yard. She was easy to scare. I said the giant harvest moon was coming to eat her and she hid under her pillow. She told
me spider stories. We had fun trading little terrors.

When I was almost ready to move away, Marcia and I stood in Dade
Park together one last time. I said good-bye to the swings and benches
and wooden seesaws with chipped red paint. Two bigger boys rode up on
bicycles and circled us. We'd never seen them before. One of them asked
if we knew how to do the F-word. I had no idea what they were talking
about. Marcia said she knew, but wouldn't tell me. The boys circled the basketball courts, eyeing us strangely. Walking home with Marcia, I felt almost
glad to be moving away from her. She stuck her chest out. She said, "Did
you ever wish someone would touch you in a private place?"

I looked in the big dictionary at home. Hundreds of F-words I didn't
know reached their hands out so it took a long time. And I asked my
mother, whose face was so smooth and beautiful and filled with sadness
because nothing was quite as good as it could be.

She didn't know either.

Bra Strap

It felt like a taunt, the elastic strap of Karen's bra visible beneath her
white blouse in front of me in fifth grade. I saw it even before Douglas
snapped it. Who did she think she was, growing older without me?

I spent the night with her one Saturday. In the bathtub together, we
splashed and soaped, jingling our talk of teachers, boys, and holidays. But
my eyes were on her chest, the great pale fruits growing there. Already
they mounded toward stems.

She caught me looking and said, "So?" Sighing, as if she were already tired. Said, "In my family they grow early." Downstairs her bosomy mother stacked cups in a high old cabinet that smelled of grandmother's hair. I could hear her clinking. In my family they barely grew at all. I had been proud of my mother's boyishness, her lithe trunk and straight legs.

Now I couldn't stop thinking about it: what was there, what wasn't there. The mounds on the fronts of certain dolls with candy-coated names. One by one, watching the backs of my friends' blouses, I saw them all fall under the spell. I begged my mother, who said, "For what? Just to be like everybody else?"

Pausing near the underwear displays at Famous and Barr, I asked to be measured, sizing up boxes. "Training Bra"—what were we in training for?

When Louise fell off her front porch and a stake went all the way through her, I heard teachers whispering, "Hope this doesn't ruin her for the future." We discussed the word "impaled." What future? The mysteries of ovaries had not yet been explained. Little factories for eggs. Little secret nests. On the day we saw the film, I didn't like it. If that was what the future meant, I didn't want it anymore. As I was staring out the window afterwards, my mouth tasted like pennies, my throat closed up. The leaves on the trees blurred together so they could carry me.

I sat on a swivel chair practicing handwritings. The backwards slant, the loopy up-and-down. Who would I ever be? My mother was inside the lawyer's office signing papers about the business. That waiting room, with its dull wooden side tables and gloomy magazines, had absolutely nothing to do with me. Never for a second was I drawn toward the world of the dreary professional. I would be a violinist with the Zurich symphony. I would play percussion in a traveling band. I would bake zucchini muffins in Yarmouth, Nova Scotia.

In the car traveling slowly home under a thick gray sky, I worked up courage. Rain, rain, the intimacy of cars. At a stoplight, staring hard at my mother, I asked, "What really happens between men and women to make babies?"

She jumped as if I'd thrown ice at her.

"Not *that!* Not *now!*" From red to green, the light, the light. "There is *oh so much you do not know.*"

It was all she ever told me. The weight of my ignorance pressed upon us both.

Later she slipped me a book, *Little Me, Big Me.* One of the more incomprehensible documents of any childhood: "When a man and a woman love one another enough, he puts his arms around her and part of him goes into part of her and the greatness of their love for one another causes this to feel pleasurable."

On my twelfth birthday, my father came home with our first tape recorder. My mother produced a bouquet of shiny boxes, including a long, slim one. My Lutheran grandparents sat neatly on the couch as the heavy reels wound up our words. "Do you like it? Is it just what you've been waiting for?"

They wanted me to hold it up to my body, the way I would when I put it on. My mother shushing, "Oh, I guess it's private!"

Later the tape would play someone's giggles in the background. My brother? Or the gangs of little girl angels that congregate around our heads, chanting, "Don't grow up, don't grow up!"

I never liked wearing it as much as I did thinking about it.

1996

Mimi Schwartz (B. 1940)

Memoir? Fiction? Where's the Line?

"It was very cold the night my mother died . . ."
Anna Quindlen

I don't remember what my second grade teacher wore! How can I recall the dialogue when my Dad left 10 years ago? All my summers in Maine blur together. That's what my students will say tomorrow when I return their first efforts at turning memories into memoir. They are mostly 21- and 22-year-old college seniors, plus a few retirees and second careerists, all eager to explore their lives on paper for themselves, friends and the world. No one is famous, although one woman said she won the lottery.

The memory worries will come mainly from marine biologists, psychology and history majors who deal in term papers and lab reports, rarely from poets and fiction writers who have taken enough creative writing workshops to understand, as V. S. Pritchett once wrote about memoir, "It's all in the art. You get no credit for living."

Some of these "creative" writers assume such advice excludes their boring lives, and so I have written "Great detail!" in many margins of first essays only to find out that the date rape or house burning down didn't happen. No, no, you can't do that, I say. That's fiction, not memoir. You have to play by the rules; there's a line you can't cross. And where is that? they ask. I don't know, only that if you make up too much, you've crossed it. The murkiness makes writer Anna Quindlen choose fiction over memoir. In "How Dark? How Stormy? I Can't Recall!" (*New York Times Book Review*), she says that the newspaper reporter in her made her check old weather charts before she could publish the line, "It was very cold the night my mother died." Like my fact-conscious students, she worries: "Was it very cold or was that just the trick memory played on a girl who was sick and shivering, at least metaphorically?"

and this worry, combined with a lousy memory, makes Quindlen avoid memoir, "a terrain too murky for me to tread." She says she can't, like Frank McCourt in *Angela's Ashes*, "remember half a century later the raw, itching sore that erupted between his eyebrows when he was a boy." So she writes fiction, preferring to create a world "from the ground up, the imagined minutiae of the lives of characters I invent from my knowledge of characters."

"But what about your *true* stories?" I would ask, if Anna were in my class. Don't you tell your friends, family, especially your children, about who you were, who your family was once upon a time? And do you want those stories to last more than one minute? If we stick only to facts, our past is as skeletal as black-and-white line drawings in a coloring book. We must color it in.

I tell the Annas in my class what I tell myself as memoir writer: Go for the emotional truth, that's what matters. Yes, gather the facts by all means. Look at old photos, return to old places, ask family members what they remember, look up time-line books for the correct songs and fashion styles, read old newspapers, encyclopedias, whatever—and then use the imagination to fill in the remembered experience. You don't need a tape recording of what your parents said to "remember" what they said that day. You don't need a photo of your kindergarten teacher to describe her; the clothes you imagine will match your feeling about her. Maybe you see a red, mini-suited girl; maybe you see a woman in a thick, long black dress with white cuffs. Either way, we see the teacher as you saw her. And who knows? She might even have worn those white cuffs! The subconscious is remembering.

That's also what I told my mother last week when she called to tell me that an essay I'd sent her about my love affair with horses was wrong. "I picked you up that day you fell off that horse, Sultan."

"You did not. I still remember everyone staring because my pants were ripped, my knee all bloody on the bus ride home."

"You were crying in the Pontiac."

"I was not."

It was her memory against mine with no one else to ask, so I wasn't changing my story. It was true for me—the humiliation following my glory riding Sultan—and she could tell her version, I said. That's what Rosemary Wolff threatened when her two sons, Geoffrey and Tobias, wrote separate and conflicting memoirs of their youth. (Or so Geoffrey Wolff said once in a workshop I took in Aspen.)

How subjective can you be in memoir, accidentally or on purpose? That is a central question, and different writers have different solutions. I teach the possibilities. You might start with a disclaimer the way John Irving did in "Trying to Save Piggy Sneed." He warns readers up front to "Please remember that all memoir is fiction," and then tells a wonderful story about how a retarded garbage man started him on his career as a writer. You might hint a disclaimer in your title, as Mary Carr does in *The Liar's Club*, and leave the reader wondering. You might tip off the reader with phrases such as "I imagine her . . . " or "Perhaps he said . . . ", the way Jane Bernstein does in her retelling of her sister's murder 2,000 miles away and 20 years before. You might use exaggeration as Russell Baker does in *Growing Up*, so that the dialogue of his interview to become a paperboy sounds as if he were being interviewed to head up IBM.

You might even give a lament that you don't remember, as Bret Lott does in his book, *Fathers, Sons, and Brothers*, before he gives a rich description of the morning that his son stopped calling him Mommy:

> The sad thing, though, is that I can't recall the first day he called me Daddy when I went into his room. I could make up a story about it, here and now; I could tell you how it was on a Tuesday—Melanie's morning—and how there seemed something different in his voice as I came up from sleep. . . .

Whatever else, there's always Joan Didion's wonderful permission in "On Reading a Notebook"—that if you remember it, it's true. I use it often.

> Perhaps it never did snow that August in Vermont; perhaps there never were flurries in the night wind, and maybe no one else felt the ground hardening and summer already dead even as we pretended to bask in it, but that was how it felt to me, and it might as well have snowed, could have snowed, did snow.

How it felt to me! What a relief to memoir writers who want to explore the emotional truth of memory. It may be "murky terrain," you may cross the line into fiction and have to step back reluctantly into what really happened—the struggle creates the tension that makes memoir either powerfully true or hopelessly phony. The challenge of this genre is that it hands you characters, plot and setting, and says, "Go figure them out!"—using fact, memory and imagination to recreate the complexity of real moments, big and small, with no invented rapes or houses burning down. If the challenge intrigues you, imaginatively and emotionally, and you find the right voice—one savvy and appealing enough to make the reader say, "Yes. I've been there. I know what you mean!"—you have something good. But if the voice you adopt annoys, embarrasses or bores because of lack of insight, then beware. The reader will say, "So what? I don't care about you!" often in anger.[1]

It's that personal, the judgment. It's YOU, not some anonymous character they are talking about. Like a smile at a cocktail party, the voice of memoir—far more than in fiction—can evoke a quick response. Phony or real. I like this person. I hate this person. Nothing lukewarm or impersonal about it.

That vulnerability—more than a bad memory, I suspect—makes many agree with writer Pam Houston: "I write fiction to tell the truth." The seeming anonymity of fiction, even autobiographical fiction, can be creatively freeing, as Jamaica Kincaid shows in *Annie John*. She makes her real-life, older brothers disappear so that the emotional focus is on a girl and her mother, and she calls the story fiction—even though other basics are true.

---

[1] James Woolcott's recent article, "Me, Myself and I," in *Vanity Fair* is a good example of that anger. He attacks Anne Roiphe as "the true queen of the daytime soaps," creative nonfiction as "civic journalism for the soul," and others like Laurie Stone as "navel gazers"—as if the person, genre and subject ("no detail is too mundane to share") and not the art sinks the "I" of true stories.

(Kincaid, like the main character, Annie, grew up on the island of Antigua and left at 17.) But if your story is really about Mom in Iowa, why turn her into a half-sister in New York—unless in the transformation, you, like Kincaid, tap into the real story you need to tell?

One essay, out of the 25 I just finished reading, does hook me with its savvy. This young woman of 22, Nicole Ross, already knows what it has taken me years to figure out: that the ambiguity of memoir, its shifting planes of truth and memory, can take you somewhere important:

> I want to remember a childhood brimming with sunlight, with just enough suffering to make it seem real. Each Christmas becomes bleaker than the last; it always seems as if there are fewer presents under the tree, and less laughter as my grandparents grow older. Ironically, the Christmases of my childhood have become lavish feasts of endless caroling because I don't remember them any more. I think that my collection of memories is nothing more than a soothing deception; many details have been supplied by a fertile imagination. It can't be all bad, though, because my parents still smile at me the way they do in my memories of those early Christmases.

Unlike Anna, Nicole is comfortable with how memory, fact and imagination mix up her Christmases; she trusts the process. I wrote "Great!" in every margin of her six pages. I believed every word, heard the caroling, saw her parents smile.

There *is* one reason not to write memoir, aside from worries about memory and the restraints on creative freedom: Mom may not speak to you again if you write her story, and you care. Frank McCourt waited to publish his memoir until after his mother died because he didn't want to hurt her. Others don't wait and call their story fiction, so they can tell Mom, family, friends, anyone real who appears on the page: "Of course that isn't you. I made that part up." No one is fooled, but you save face, maybe a lawsuit.

A writer does have some fictive leeway even in memoir, I believe—*if* you are cautious (and not too famous). Tomorrow I will tell the student who wrote about her bulimic roommate that her profile could be just as powerful and less hurtful if she moved the girl next door, changed her hair color and did not call her Kimmie.[2] I will tell the class that in a memoir about six months in my marriage, I made a few composite characters of minor characters and wrote this disclaimer in my introduction: "The story is 90 percent factual; the rest is made up to protect those who didn't ask to be in this book." The problem was not my husband and my children (I was willing to take my chances with them); it was my friends, like the one who was leaving her husband just as I was deciding to stay with mine. In fact, I had three friends who were thinking about divorce, so in the book, I made a composite character and we met for cappuccino.

Depending on the story's focus, you sometimes collapse time and characters as well, I will tell my students, and still are "true" on my truth scale.

---

[2]This anonymity is essential if, like me, you have students share their work in progress in class. Why should the roommate's problems become public knowledge?

Writer Jack Connor, in a personal essay about a weekend of watching eagles, collapsed three days into one morning and mentioned only two of the four students who accompanied him on that trip. He wanted to capture how young people reawakened in him the simple pleasure of birding even in a mid-January freeze, and the number of days, the number of people, didn't matter—although in a scientific field report they would. I will show my students how his original journal entry of facts and private observations evolved many drafts later into a published story ("A Lesson from Mott's Creek") with a voice and a point of view.

Journal Entry:

1/11/94—eagle weekend—
one of the best birding experiences of the last year this weekend—the eagle survey with Jerry Liguori, Brian Sullivan, two folks from Ocean City (modermotts?), and on Sunday with Joe Mangion and Bil Seng.
. . . both days cold—and windy, temp in teens, with wind chill, probably below 10, maybe even bordering on zero, but blue sky, growing cloudy on saturday around one and then mostly cloudy. Sunday, blue until 2 or so and only partly cloudy after that. . . .

Essay Opening:

"Binoculars in my fingers, tears in my eyes from the January glare, face stiff from the hard wind, I am standing between Brian Sullivan and Jerry Liguori and wonder, "Why don't I come out here every single day?"

I will also tell my students about a friend who is writing about her aunt who had a lobotomy 50 years ago. My friend visited the mental institution where it happened, looked up records, talked to a nurse and doctor who remembered her aunt and tried writing what her aunt's life was like. But those "facts" weren't enough to recreate the story. She must take an imaginative leap, our writing group told her, imagine herself as her aunt and what would it feel like, maybe write in first person. Draft in hand, my friend can then check with a psychiatrist—"Does this ring true?"—and with relatives, before revising for more accuracy.

The Joan Didions and John Irvings in tomorrow's class will nod their heads in agreement. The Anna Quindlens will not. They want clear-cut boundaries and would side with my writer friend, Andrea Herrmann, who warns me: "If the writer can make a composite character, what prevents her from making up scenes, blending parts of places together, switching historical time frames?" Making up anything, for them, is crossing the line into fiction and should be called that. But I disagree. If the main plot, characters, and setting are true, if the intent is to make honest sense of "how it felt to me" and tell that true story well (with disclaimers as needed), it's memoir to me.

In "Why Memoir Now?" Vivian Gornick writes, "What happened to the writer is not what matters; what matters is the larger sense that the writer is able to make of what happened. For that the power of a writing imagination is required." Use that imagination in memoir, I tell myself and my students, to find the language and complexity of real lives, not imagined ones. It's OK to trust yourself (with a bit of Quindlen's and Herrmann's wariness)—even if you can't remember the temperature on the night Mom died.

1999

Leslie Marmon Silko (B. 1948)

Landscape, History, and the Pueblo Imagination

From a High Arid Plateau in New Mexico

You see that after a thing is dead, it dries up. It might take weeks or years, but eventually if you touch the thing, it crumbles under your fingers. It goes back to dust. The soul of the thing has long since departed. With the plants and wild game the soul may have already been borne back into bones and blood or thick green stalk and leaves. Nothing is wasted. What cannot be eaten by people or in some way used must then be left where other living creatures may benefit. What domestic animals or wild scavengers can't eat will be fed to the plants. The plants feed on the dust of these few remains.

The ancient Pueblo people buried the dead in vacant rooms or partially collapsed rooms adjacent to the main living quarters. Sand and clay used to construct the roof make layers many inches deep once the roof has collapsed. The layers of sand and clay make for easy gravedigging. The vacant room fills with cast-off objects and debris. When a vacant room has filled deep enough, a shallow but adequate grave can be scooped in a far corner. Archaeologists have remarked over formal burials complete with elaborate funerary objects excavated in trash middens of abandoned rooms. But the rocks and adobe mortar of collapsed walls were valued by the ancient people. Because each rock had been carefully selected for size and shape, then chiseled to an even face. Even the pink clay adobe melting with each rainstorm had to be prayed over, then dug and carried some distance. Corn cobs and husks, the rinds and stalks and animal bones were not regarded by the ancient people as filth or garbage. The remains were merely resting at a mid-point in their journey back to dust. Human remains are not so different. They should rest with the bones and rinds where they all may benefit living creatures—small rodents and insects—until their return is completed. The remains of things—animals and plants, the clay and the stones—were treated with respect. Because for the ancient people all these things had spirit and being. The antelope merely consents to return home with the hunter. All phases of the hunt are conducted with love. The love the hunter and the people have for the Antelope People. And the love of the antelope who agree to give up their meat and blood so that human beings will not starve. Waste of meat or even the thoughtless handling of bones cooked bare will offend the antelope spirits. Next year the hunters will vainly search the dry plains for antelope. Thus it is necessary to return carefully the bones and hair, and the stalks and leaves to the earth who first created them. The spirits remain close by. They do not leave us.

The dead become dust, and in this becoming they are once more joined with the Mother. The ancient Pueblo People called the earth the Mother Creator of all things in this world. Her sister, the Corn Mother, occasionally merges with her because all succulent green life rises out of the depths of the earth.

Rocks and clay are part of the Mother. They emerge in various forms, but at some time before, they were smaller particles or great boulders. At a later time they may again become what they once were. Dust.

A rock shares this fate with us and with animals and plants as well. A rock has being or spirit, although we may not understand it. The spirit may differ from the spirit we know in animals or plants or in ourselves. In the end we all originate from the depths of the earth. Perhaps this is how all beings share in the spirit of the Creator. We do not know.

From the Emergence Place

Pueblo potters, the creators of petroglyphs and oral narratives, never conceived of removing themselves from the earth and sky. So long as the human consciousness remains within the hills, canyons, cliffs, and the plants, clouds, and sky, the term landscape, as it has entered the English language, is misleading. "A portion of territory the eye can comprehend in a single view" does not correctly describe the relationship between the human being and his or her surroundings. This assumes the viewer is somehow outside or separate from the territory he or she surveys. Viewers are as much a part of the landscape as the boulders they stand on. There is no high mesa edge or mountain peak where one can stand and not immediately be part of all that surrounds. Human identity is linked with all the elements of Creation through the clan: you might belong to the Sun Clan or the Lizard Clan or the Corn Clan or the Clay Clan.[1] Standing deep within the natural world, the ancient Pueblo understood the thing as it was—the squash blossom, grasshopper, or rabbit itself could never be created by the human hand. Ancient Pueblos took the modest view that the thing itself (the landscape) could not be improved upon. The ancients did not presume to tamper with what had already been created. Thus *realism*, as we now recognize it in painting and sculpture, did not catch the imaginations of Pueblo people until recently.

---

[1]*Clan*—A social unit composed of families sharing common ancestors who trace their lineage back to the Emergence where their ancestors allied themselves with certain plants or animals or elements. (*Silko's note*)

The squash blossom is *one thing:* itself. So the ancient Pueblo potter abstracted what she saw to be the key elements of the squash blossom—the four symmetrical petals, with four symmetrical stamens in the center. These key elements, while suggesting the squash flower, also link it with the four cardinal directions. By representing only its intrinsic form, the squash flower is released from a limited meaning or restricted identity. Even in the most sophisticated abstract form, a squash flower or a cloud or a lightning bolt became intricately connected with a complex system of relationships which the ancient Pueblo people maintained with each other, and with the populous natural world they lived within. A bolt of lightning is itself, but at the same time it may mean much more. It may be a messenger of good fortune when summer rains are needed. It may deliver death, perhaps the result of manipulations by the Gunnadeyahs, destructive necromancers. Lightning may strike down an evil-doer. Or lightning may strike a person of good will. If the person survives, lightning endows him or her with heightened power.

Pictographs and petroglyphs of constellations or elk or antelope draw their magic in part from the process wherein the focus of all prayer and concentration is upon the thing itself, which, in its turn, guides the hunter's hand. Connection with the spirit dimensions requires a figure or form which is all-inclusive. A "lifelike" rendering of an elk is too restrictive. Only the elk *is* itself. A *realistic* rendering of an elk would be only one particular elk anyway. The purpose of the hunt rituals and magic is to make contact with *all* the spirits of the Elk.

The land, the sky, and all that is within them—the landscape—includes human beings. Interrelationships in the Pueblo landscape are complex and fragile. The unpredictability of the weather, the aridity and harshness of much of the terrain in the high plateau country explain in large part the relentless attention the ancient Pueblo people gave the sky and the earth around them. Survival depended upon harmony and cooperation not only among human beings, but among all things—the animate and the less animate, since rocks and mountains were known to move, to travel occasionally.

The ancient Pueblos believed the Earth and the Sky were sisters (or sister and brother in the post-Christian version). As long as good family relations are maintained, then the Sky will continue to bless her sister, the Earth, with rain, and the Earth's children will continue to survive. But the old stories recall incidents in which troublesome spirits or beings threaten the earth. In one story, a malicious ka'tsina, called the Gambler, seizes the Shiwana, or Rainclouds, the Sun's beloved children.[2] The Shiwana are snared in magical power late one afternoon on a high mountain top. The Gambler takes the Rainclouds to his mountain stronghold where he locks them in the north room of his house. What was his idea? The Shiwana were beyond value. They brought life to all things on earth. The Gambler wanted a big stake to wager in his games of chance. But such greed, even

---

[2]*Ka'tsina*—Ka'tsinas are spirit beings who roam the earth and who inhabit kachina masks worn in Pueblo ceremonial dances. (*Silko's note*)

on the part of only one being, had the effect of threatening the survival of all life on earth. Sun Youth, aided by old Grandmother Spider, outsmarts the Gambler and the rigged game, and the Rainclouds are set free. The drought ends, and once more life thrives on earth.

Through the Stories We Hear Who We Are

All summer the people watch the west horizon, scanning the sky from south to north for rain clouds. Corn must have moisture at the time the tassels form. Otherwise pollination will be incomplete, and the ears will be stunted and shriveled. An inadequate harvest may bring disaster. Stories told at Hopi, Zuni, and at Acoma and Laguna describe drought and starvation as recently as 1900. Precipitation in west-central New Mexico averages fourteen inches annually. The western pueblos are located at altitudes over 5,600 feet above sea level, where winter temperatures at night fall below freezing. Yet evidence of their presence in the high desert plateau country goes back ten thousand years. The ancient Pueblo people not only survived in this environment, but many years they thrived. In A.D. 1100 the people at Chaco Canyon had built cities with apartment buildings of stone five stories high. Their sophistication as skywatchers was surpassed only by Mayan and Inca astronomers. Yet this vast complex of knowledge and belief, amassed for thousands of years, was never recorded in writing.

Instead, the ancient Pueblo people depended upon collective memory through successive generations to maintain and transmit an entire culture, a world view complete with proven strategies for survival. The oral narrative, or "story," became the medium in which the complex of Pueblo knowledge and belief was maintained. Whatever the event or the subject, the ancient people perceived the world and themselves within that world as part of an ancient continuous story composed of innumerable bundles of other stories.

The ancient Pueblo vision of the world was inclusive. The impulse was to leave nothing out. Pueblo oral tradition necessarily embraced all levels of human experience. Otherwise, the collective knowledge and beliefs comprising ancient Pueblo culture would have been incomplete. Thus stories about the Creation and Emergence of human beings and animals into this World continue to be retold each year for four days and four nights during the winter solstice. The "humma-hah" stories related events from the time long ago when human beings were still able to communicate with animals and other living things. But, beyond these two preceding categories, the Pueblo oral tradition knew no boundaries. Accounts of the appearance of the first Europeans in Pueblo country or of the tragic encounters between Pueblo people and Apache raiders were no more and no less important than stories about the biggest mule deer ever taken or adulterous couples surprised in cornfields and chicken coops. Whatever happened, the ancient people instinctively sorted events and details into a loose narrative structure. Everything became a story.

Traditionally everyone, from the youngest child to the oldest person, was expected to listen and to be able to recall or tell a portion, if only a small detail, from a narrative account or story. Thus the remembering and retelling were a communal process. Even if a key figure, an elder who knew much more than others, were to die unexpectedly, the system would remain intact. Through the efforts of a great many people, the community was able to piece together valuable accounts and crucial information that might otherwise have died with an individual.

Communal storytelling was a self-correcting process in which listeners were encouraged to speak up if they noted an important fact or detail omitted. The people were happy to listen to two or three different versions of the same event or the same humma-hah story. Even conflicting versions of an incident were welcomed for the entertainment they provided. Defenders of each version might joke and tease one another, but seldom were there any direct confrontations. Implicit in the Pueblo oral tradition was the awareness that loyalties, grudges, and kinship must always influence the narrator's choices as she emphasizes to listeners this is the way *she* has always heard the story told. The ancient Pueblo people sought a communal truth, not an absolute. For them this truth lived somewhere within the web of differing versions, disputes over minor points, outright contradictions tangling with old feuds and village rivalries.

A dinner-table conversation, recalling a deer hunt forty years ago when the largest mule deer ever was taken, inevitably stimulates similar memories in listeners. But hunting stories were not merely after-dinner entertainment. These accounts contained information of critical importance about behavior and migration patterns of mule deer. Hunting stories carefully described key landmarks and locations of fresh water. Thus a deer-hunt story might also serve as a "map." Lost travelers, and lost piñon-nut gathers, have been saved by sighting a rock formation they recognize only because they once heard a hunting story describing this rock formation.

The importance of cliff formations and water holes does not end with hunting stories. As offspring of the Mother Earth, the ancient Pueblo people could not conceive of themselves within a specific landscape. Location, or "place," nearly always plays a central role in the Pueblo oral narratives. Indeed, stories are most frequently recalled as people are passing by a specific geographical feature or the exact place where a story takes place. The precise date of the incident often is less important than the place or location of the happening. "Long, long ago," "a long time ago," "not too long ago," and "recently" are usually how stories are classified in terms of time. But the places where the stories occur are precisely located, and prominent geographical details recalled, even if the landscape is well-known to listeners. Often because the turning point in the narrative involved a peculiarity or special quality of a rock or tree or plant found only at that place. Thus, in the case of many of the Pueblo narratives, it is impossible to determine which came first: the incident or the geographical feature which begs to be brought alive in a story that features some unusual aspect of this location.

There is a giant sandstone boulder about a mile north of Old Laguna, on the road to Paguate. It is ten feet tall and twenty feet in circumference. When I was a child, and we would pass this boulder driving to Paguate village, someone usually made reference to the story about Kochininako, Yellow Woman, and the Estrucuyo, a monstrous giant who nearly ate her. The Twin Hero Brothers saved Kochininako, who had been out hunting rabbits to take home to feed her mother and sisters. The Hero Brothers had heard her cries just in time. The Estrucuyo had cornered her in a cave too small to fit its monstrous head. Kochininako had already thrown to the Estrucuyo all her rabbits, as well as her moccasins and most of her clothing. Still the creature had not been satisfied. After killing the Estrucuyo with their bows and arrows, the Twin Hero Brothers slit open the Estrucuyo and cut out its heart. They threw the heart as far as they could. The monster's heart landed there, beside the old trail to Paguate village, where the sandstone boulder rests now.

It may be argued that the existence of the boulder precipitated the creation of a story to explain it. But sandstone boulders and sandstone formations of strange shapes abound in the Laguna Pueblo area. Yet most of them do not have stories. Often the crucial element in a narrative is the terrain—some specific detail of the setting.

A high dark mesa rises dramatically from a grassy plain fifteen miles southeast of Laguna, in an area known as Swanee. On the grassy plain one hundred and forty years ago, my great-grandmother's uncle and his brother-in-law were grazing their herd of sheep. Because visibility on the plain extends for over twenty miles, it wasn't until the two sheepherders came near the high dark mesa that the Apaches were able to stalk them. Using the mesa to obscure their approach, the raiders swept around from both ends of the mesa. My great-grandmother's relatives were killed, and the herd lost. The high dark mesa played a critical role: the mesa had compromised the safety which the openness of the plains had seemed to assure. Pueblo and Apache alike relied upon the terrain, the very earth herself, to give them protection and aid. Human activities or needs were maneuvered to fit the existing surroundings and conditions. I imagine the last afternoon of my distant ancestors as warm and sunny for late September. They might have been traveling slowly, bringing the sheep closer to Laguna in preparation for the approach of colder weather. The grass was tall and only beginning to change from green to a yellow which matched the late-afternoon sun shining off it. There might have been comfort in the warmth and the sight of the sheep fattening on good pasture which lulled my ancestors into their fatal inattention. They might have had a rifle whereas the Apaches had only bows and arrows. But there would have been four or five Apache raiders, and the surprise attack would have canceled any advantage the rifles gave them.

Survival in any landscape comes down to making the best use of all available resources. On that particular September afternoon, the raiders made better use of the Swanee terrain than my poor ancestors did. Thus the high dark mesa and the story of the two lost Laguna herders became inextricably linked. The memory of them and their story resides in part with the high black mesa. For as long as the mesa stands, people within the family and clan will be reminded of the story of that afternoon long ago. Thus the continuity and accuracy of the oral narratives are reinforced by the landscape—and the Pueblo interpretation of that landscape is *maintained*.

The Migration Story: An Interior Journey

The Laguna Pueblo migration stories refer to specific places—mesas, springs, or cottonwood trees—not only locations which can be visited still, but also locations which lie directly on the state highway route linking Paguate village with Laguna village. In traveling this road as a child with older Laguna people I first heard a few of the stories from that much larger body of stories linked with the Emergence and Migration.[3] It may be coincidental that Laguna people continue to follow the same route which, according to the Migration story, the ancestors followed south from the Emergence Place. It may be that the route is merely the shortest and best route for car, horse, or foot traffic between Laguna and Paguate villages. But if the stories about boulders, springs, and hills are actually remnants from a ritual that retraces the creation and emergence of the Laguna Pueblo people as a culture, as the people they became, then continued use of that route creates a unique relationship between the ritual-mythic world and the actual, everyday world. A journey from Paguate to Laguna down the long incline of Paguate Hill retraces the original journey from the Emergence Place, which is located slightly north of the Paguate village. Thus the landscape between Paguate and Laguna takes on a deeper significance: the landscape resonates the spiritual or mythic dimension of the Pueblo world even today.

Although each Pueblo culture designates a specific Emergence Place—usually a small natural spring edged with mossy sandstone and full of cat-tails and wild watercress—it is clear that they do not agree on any single location or natural spring as the one and only true Emergence Place. Each Pueblo group recounts its own stories about Creation, Emergence, and Migration, although they all believe that all human beings, with all the animals and plants, emerged at the same place and at the same time.[4]

Natural springs are crucial sources of water for all life in the high desert plateau country. So the small spring near Paguate village is literally the source and continuance of life for the people in the area. The spring also

---

[3]*The Emergence*—All the human beings, animals, and life which had been created emerged from the four worlds below when the earth became habitable. The *Migration*—The Pueblo people emerged into the Fifth World, but they had already been warned they would have to travel and search before they found the place they were meant to live. (*Silko's note*)

[4]*Creation*—Tse'itsi'nako, Thought Woman, the Spider, thought about it, and everything she thought came into being. First she thought of three sisters for herself, and they helped her think of the rest of the Universe, including the Fifth World and the Four worlds below. *The Fifth World* is the world we are living in today. There are four previous worlds below this world. (*Silko's note*)

functions on a spiritual level, recalling the original Emergence Place and linking the people and the spring water to all other people and to that moment when the Pueblo people became aware of themselves as they are even now. The Emergence was an emergence into a precise cultural identity. Thus the Pueblo stories about the Emergence and Migration are not to be taken as literally as the anthropologists might wish. Prominent geographical features and landmarks which are mentioned in the narratives exist for ritual purposes, not because the Laguna people actually journeyed south for hundreds of years from Chaco Canyon or Mesa Verde, as the archaeologists say, or eight miles from the site of the natural springs at Paguate to the sandstone hilltop at Laguna.

The eight miles, marked with boulders, mesas, springs, and river crossings, are actually a ritual circuit or path which marks the interior journey the Laguna people made: a journey of awareness and imagination in which they emerged from being within the earth and from everything included in earth to the culture and people they became, differentiating themselves for the first time from all that had surrounded them, always aware that interior distances cannot be reckoned in physical miles or in calendar years.

The narratives linked with prominent features of the landscape between Paguate and Laguna delineate the complexities of the relationship which human beings must maintain with the surrounding natural world if they hope to survive in this place. Thus the journey was an interior process of the imagination, a growing awareness that being human is somehow different from all other life—animal, plant, and inanimate. Yet we are all from the same source: the awareness never deteriorated into Cartesian duality, cutting off the human from the natural world.

The people found the opening into the Fifth World too small to allow them or any of the animals to escape. They had sent a fly out through the small hole to tell them if it was the world which the Mother Creator had promised. It was, but there was the problem of getting out. The antelope tried to butt the opening to enlarge it, but the antelope enlarged it only a little. It was necessary for the badger with her long claws to assist the antelope, and at last the opening was enlarged enough so that all the people and animals were able to emerge up into the Fifth World. The human beings could not have emerged without the aid of antelope and badger. The human beings depended upon the aid and charity of the animals. Only through interdependence could the human beings survive. Families belonged to clans, and it was by clan that the human being joined with the animal and plant world. Life on the high arid plateau became viable when the human beings were able to imagine themselves as sisters and brothers to the badger, antelope, clay, yucca, and sun. Not until they could find a viable relationship to the terrain, the landscape they found themselves in, could they *emerge*. Only at the moment the requisite balance between human and *other* was realized could the Pueblo people become a culture, a distinct group whose population and survival remained stable despite the vicissitudes of climate and terrain.

Landscape thus has similarities with dreams. Both have the power to seize terrifying feelings and deep instincts and translate them into images—visual, aural, tactile—into the concrete where human beings may more readily confront and channel the terrifying instincts or powerful emotions into rituals and narratives which reassure the individual while reaffirming cherished values of the group. The identity of the individual as a part of the group and the greater Whole is strengthened, and the terror of facing the world alone is extinguished.

Even now, the people at Laguna Pueblo spend the greater portion of social occasions recounting recent incidents or events which have *occurred in the Laguna area*. Nearly always, the discussion will precipitate the retelling of older stories about similar incidents or other stories connected with a specific place. The stories often contain disturbing or provocative material, but are nonetheless told in the presence of children and women. The effect of these inter-family or inter-clan exchanges is the reassurance for each person that she or he will never be separated or apart from the clan, no matter what might happen. Neither the worst blunders or disasters nor the greatest financial prosperity and joy will ever be permitted to isolate anyone from the rest of the group. In the ancient times, cohesiveness was all that stood between extinction and survival, and, while the individual certainly was recognized, it was always as an individual simultaneously bonded to family and clan by a complex bundle of custom and ritual. You are never the first to suffer a grave loss or profound humiliation. You are never the first, and you understand that you will probably not be the last to commit or be victimized by a repugnant act. Your family and clan are able to go on at length about others now passed on, others older or more experienced than you who suffered similar losses.

The wide deep arroyo near the Kings Bar (located across the reservation borderline) has over the years claimed many vehicles. A few years ago, when a Viet Nam veteran's new red Volkswagen rolled backwards into the arroyo while he was inside buying a six-pack of beer, the story of his loss joined the lively and large collection of stories already connected with that big arroyo. I do not know whether the Viet Nam veteran was consoled when he was told the stories about the other cars claimed by the ravenous arroyo. All his savings of combat pay had gone for the red Volkswagen. But this man could not have felt any worse than the man who, some years before, had left his children and mother-in-law in his station wagon with the engine running. When he came out of the liquor store his station wagon was gone. He found it and its passengers upside down in the big arroyo. Broken bones, cuts and bruises, and a total wreck of the car. The big arroyo has a wide mouth. Its existence needs no explanation. People in the area regard the arroyo much as they might regard a living being, which has a certain character and personality. I seldom drive past that wide deep arroyo without feeling a familiarity with and even a strange affection for this arroyo. Because as treacherous as it may be, the arroyo maintains a strong connection between human beings and the earth. The arroyo demands from us the caution and attention that constitute respect. It is this sort of respect the old believers have in mind when they tell us we must respect and love the earth.

Hopi Pueblo elders have said that the austere and, to some eyes, barren plains and hills surrounding their mesa-top villages actually help to nurture the spirituality of the Hopi *way*. The Hopi elders say the Hopi people might have settled in locations far more lush where daily life would not have been so grueling. But there on the high silent sandstone mesas that overlook the sandy arid expanses stretching to all horizons, the Hopi elders say the Hopi people must "live by their prayers" if they are to survive. The Hopi way cherishes the intangible: the riches realized from interaction and interrelationships with all beings above all else. Great abundances of material things, even food, the Hopi elders believe, tend to lure human attention away from what is most valuable and important. The views of the Hopi elders are not much different from those elders in all the Pueblos.

The bare vastness of the Hopi landscape emphasizes the visual impact of every plant, every rock, every arroyo. Nothing is overlooked or taken for granted. Each ant, each lizard, each lark is imbued with great value simply because the creature is there, simply because the creature is alive in a place where any life at all is precious. Stand on the mesa edge at Walpai and look west over the bare distances toward the pale blue outlines of the San Francisco peaks where the ka'tsina spirits reside. So little lies between you and the sky. So little lies between you and the earth. One look and you know that simply to survive is a great triumph, that every possible resource is needed, every possibly ally—even the most humble insect or reptile. You realize you will be speaking with all of them if you intend to last out the year. Thus it is that the Hopi elders are grateful to the landscape for aiding them in their quest as spiritual people.

1986

Jonathan Swift (1667–1745)

A Modest Proposal

For Preventing the Children of Poor People in Ireland from Being a Burden to Their Parents or Country, and for Making Them Beneficial to the Public

It is a melancholy object to those who walk through this great town or travel in the country, when they see the streets, the roads, and cabin doors, crowded with beggars of the female sex, followed by three, four, or six children, all in rags and importuning every passenger for an alms. These mothers, instead of being able to work for their honest livelihood, are forced to employ all their time in strolling to beg sustenance for their helpless infants, who, as they grow up, either turn thieves for want of work, or leave their dear native country to fight for the Pretender in Spain, or sell themselves to the Barbadoes.

I think it is agreed by all parties that this prodigious number of children in the arms, or on the backs, or at the heels of their mothers, and frequently of their fathers, is in the present deplorable state of the kingdom a very great additional grievance; and therefore whoever could find out a fair, cheap, and easy method of making these children sound, useful members of the commonwealth would deserve so well of the public as to have his statue set up for a preserver of the nation.

But my intention is very far from being confined to provide only for the children of professed beggars; it is of a much greater extent, and shall take in the whole number of infants at a certain age who are born of parents in effect as little able to support them as those who demand our charity in the streets.

As to my own part, having turned my thoughts for many years upon this important subject, and maturely weighed the several schemes of other projectors, I have always found them grossly mistaken in their computation. It is true, a child just dropped from its dam may be supported by her milk for a solar year, with little other nourishment; at most not above the value of two shillings, which the mother may certainly get, or the value in scraps, by her lawful occupation of begging; and it is exactly at one year old that I propose to provide for them in such a manner as instead of being a charge upon their parents or the parish, or wanting food and raiment for the rest of their lives, they shall on the contrary contribute to the feeding, and partly to the clothing, of many thousands.

There is likewise another great advantage in my scheme, that it will prevent those voluntary abortions, and that horrid practice of women murdering their bastard children, alas, too frequent among us, sacrificing the poor innocent babes, I doubt, more to avoid the expense than the shame, which would move tears and pity in the most savage and inhuman breast.

The number of souls in this kingdom being usually reckoned one million and a half, of these I calculate there may be about two hundred thousand couple whose wives are breeders; from which number I subtract thirty thousand couples who are able to maintain their own children, although I apprehend there cannot be so many under the present distresses of the kingdom; but this being granted, there will remain an hundred and seventy thousand breeders. I again subtract fifty thousand for those women who miscarry, or whose children die by accident or disease within the year. There only remain an hundred and twenty thousand children of poor parents annually born. The question therefore is, how this number shall be reared and provided for, which, as I have already said, under the present situation of affairs, is utterly impossible by all the methods hitherto proposed. For we can neither employ them in handicraft or agriculture; we neither build houses (I mean in the country) nor cultivate land. They can very seldom pick up a livelihood by stealing till they arrive at six years old, except where they are of towardly parts; although

I confess they learn the rudiments much earlier, during which time they can however be looked upon only as probationers, as I have been informed by a principal gentleman in the county of Cavan, who protested to me that he never knew above one or two instances under the age of six, even in a part of the kingdom so renowned for the quickest proficiency in that art.

I am assured by our merchants that a boy or a girl before twelve years old is no salable commodity; and even when they come to this age they will not yield above three pounds, or three pounds and half a crown at most on the Exchange; which cannot turn to account either to the parents or the kingdom, the charge of nutriment and rags having been at least four times that value.

I shall now therefore humbly propose my own thoughts, which I hope will not be liable to the least objection.

I have been assured by a very knowing American of my acquaintance in London, that a young healthy child well nursed is at a year old a most delicious, nourishing, and wholesome food, whether stewed, roasted, baked, or boiled; and I make no doubt that it will equally serve in a fricassee or a ragout.

I do therefore humbly offer it to public consideration that of the hundred and twenty thousand children, already computed, twenty thousand may be reserved for breed, whereof only one fourth part to be males, which is more than we allow to sheep, black cattle, or swine; and my reason is that these children are seldom the fruits of marriage, a circumstance not much regarded by our savages, therefore one male will be sufficient to serve four females. That the remaining hundred thousand may at a year old be offered in sale to the persons of quality and fortune through the kingdom, always advising the mother to let them suck plentifully in the last month, so as to render them plump and fat for a good table. A child will make two dishes at an entertainment for friends; and when the family dines alone, the fore or hind quarter will make a reasonable dish, and seasoned with a little pepper or salt will be very good boiled on the fourth day, especially in winter.

I have reckoned upon a medium that a child just born will weigh twelve pounds, and in a solar year if tolerably nursed increaseth to twenty-eight pounds.

I grant this food will be somewhat dear, and therefore very proper for landlords, who, as they have already devoured most of the parents, seem to have the best title to the children.

Infant's flesh will be in season throughout the year, but more plentiful in March, and a little before and after. For we are told by a grave author, an eminent French physician, that fish being a prolific diet, there are more children born in Roman Catholic countries about nine months after Lent than at any other season; therefore, reckoning a year after Lent, the markets will be more glutted than usual, because the number of popish infants is at least three to one in this kingdom; and therefore it will have one other collateral advantage, by lessening the number of Papists among us.

I have already computed the charge of nursing a beggar's child (in which list I reckon all cottagers, laborers, and four fifths of the farmers) to be about two shillings per annum, rags included; and I believe no gentleman would repine to give ten shillings for the carcass of a good fat child, which, as I have said, will make four dishes of excellent nutritive meat, when he hath only some particular friend or his own family to dine with him. Thus the squire will learn to be a good landlord, and grow popular among the tenants; the mother will have eight shillings net profit, and be fit for work till she produces another child.

Those who are more thrifty (as I must confess the times require) may flay the carcass; the skin of which artificially dressed will make admirable gloves for ladies, and summer boots for fine gentlemen.

As to our city of Dublin, shambles may be appointed for this purpose in the most convenient parts of it, and butchers we may be assured will not be wanting; although I rather recommend buying the children alive, and dressing them hot from the knife as we do roasting pigs.

A very worthy person, a true lover of his country, and whose virtues I highly esteem, was lately pleased in discoursing on this matter to offer a refinement upon my scheme. He said that many gentlemen of this kingdom, having of late destroyed their deer, he conceived that the want of venison might be well supplied by the bodies of young lads and maidens, not exceeding fourteen years of age nor under twelve, so great a number of both sexes in every county being now ready to starve for want of work and service; and these to be disposed of by their parents, if alive, or otherwise by their nearest relations. But with due deference to so excellent a friend and so deserving a patriot, I cannot be altogether in his sentiments; for as to the males, my American acquaintance assured me from frequent experience that their flesh was generally tough and lean, like that of our schoolboys, by continual exercise, and their taste disagreeable; and to fatten them would not answer the charge. Then as to the females, it would, I think with humble submission, be a loss to the public, because they soon would become breeders themselves: and besides, it is not improbable that some scrupulous people might be apt to censure such a practice (although indeed very unjustly) as a little bordering upon cruelty; which, I confess, hath always been with me the strongest objection against any project, how well soever intended.

But in order to justify my friend, he confessed that this expedient was put into his head by the famous Psalmanazar, a native of the island Formosa, who came from thence to London above twenty years ago, and in conversation told my friend that in his country when any young person happened to be put to death, the executioner sold the carcass to persons of quality as a prime dainty; and that in his time the body of a plump girl of fifteen, who was crucified for an attempt to poison the emperor, was sold to his Imperial Majesty's prime minister of state, and other great mandarins of the court, in joints from the gibbet, at four hundred crowns. Neither indeed can I deny that if the same use were made of several plump young girls in this town, who without one single groat to their fortunes cannot stir abroad without a chair, and appear at the play-house and assemblies in foreign fineries which they never will pay for, the kingdom would not be the worse.

Some persons of a desponding spirit are in great concern about that vast number of poor people who are aged, diseased, or maimed, and I have been desired to employ my thoughts what course may be taken to ease the nation of so grievous an encumbrance. But I am not in the least pain upon that matter, because it is very well known that they are every day dying and rotting by cold and famine, and filth and vermin, as fast as can be reasonably expected. And as to the younger laborers, they are now in almost as hopeful a condition. They cannot get work, and consequently pine away for want of nourishment to a degree that if at any time they are accidentally hired to common labor, they have not strength to perform it; and thus the country and themselves are happily delivered from the evils to come.

I have too long digressed, and therefore shall return to my subject. I think the advantages by the proposal which I have made are obvious and many, as well as of the highest importance.

For first, as I have already observed, it would greatly lessen the number of Papists, with whom we are yearly overrun, being the principal breeders of the nation as well as our most dangerous enemies; and who stay at home on purpose to deliver the kingdom to the Pretender, hoping to take their advantage by the absence of so many good Protestants, who have chosen rather to leave their country than stay at home and pay tithes against their conscience to an Episcopal curate.

Secondly, the poorer tenants will have something valuable of their own, which by law may be made liable to distress, and help to pay their landlord's rent, their corn and cattle being already seized and money a thing unknown.

Thirdly, whereas the maintenance of an hundred thousand children, from two years old and upwards, cannot be computed at less than ten shillings a piece per annum, the nation's stock will be thereby increased fifty thousand pounds per annum, besides the profit of a new dish introduced to the tables of all gentlemen of fortune in the kingdom who have any refinement in taste. And the money will circulate among ourselves, the goods being entirely of our own growth and manufacture.

Fourthly, the constant breeders, besides the gain of eight shillings sterling per annum by the sale of their children, will be rid of the charge of maintaining them after the first year.

Fifthly, this food would likewise bring great custom to taverns, where the vintners will certainly be so prudent as to procure the best receipts for dressing it to perfection, and consequently have their houses frequented by all the fine gentlemen, who justly value themselves upon their knowledge in good eating; and a skillful cook, who understands how to oblige his guests, will contrive to make it as expensive as they please.

Sixthly, this would be a great inducement to marriage, which all wise nations have either encouraged by rewards or enforced by laws and penalties. It would increase the care and tenderness of mothers toward their children, when they were sure of a settlement for life to the poor babes, provided in some sort by the public, to their annual profit instead of expense. We should see an honest emulation among the married women, which of them could bring the fattest child to the market. Men would become as fond of their wives during the time of their pregnancy as they are now of their mares in foal, their cows in calf, or sows when they are ready to farrow; nor offer to beat or kick them (as is too frequent a practice) for fear of a miscarriage.

Many other advantages might be enumerated. For instance, the addition of some thousand carcasses in our exportation of barreled beef, the propagation of swine's flesh, and improvement in the art of making good bacon, so much wanted among us by the great destruction of pigs, too frequent at our tables, which are no way comparable in taste or magnificence to a well-grown, fat, yearling child, which roasted whole will make a considerable figure at a lord mayor's feast or any other public entertainment. But this and many others I omit, being studious of brevity.

Supposing that one thousand families in this city would be constant customers for infants' flesh, besides others who might have it at merry meetings, particularly weddings and christenings, I compute that Dublin would take off annually about twenty thousand carcasses, and the rest of the kingdom (where probably they will be sold somewhat cheaper) the remaining eighty thousand.

I can think of no one objection that will possibly be raised against this proposal, unless it should be urged that the number of people will be thereby much lessened in the kingdom. This I freely own, and it was indeed one principal design in offering it to the world. I desire the reader will observe, that I calculate my remedy for this one individual kingdom of Ireland and for no other that ever was, is, or I think ever can be upon earth. Therefore let no man talk to me of other expedients: of taxing our absentees at five shillings a pound: of using neither clothes nor household furniture except what is of our own growth and manufacture: of utterly rejecting the materials and instruments that promote foreign luxury: of curing the expensiveness of pride, vanity, idleness, and gaming in our women: of introducing a vein of parsimony, prudence, and temperance: of learning to love our country, in the want of which we differ even from Laplanders and the inhabitants of Topinamboo: of quitting our animosities and factions, nor acting any longer like the Jews, who were murdering one another at the very moment their city was taken: of being a little cautious not to sell our country and conscience for nothing: of teaching landlords to have at least one degree of mercy toward their tenants: lastly, of putting a spirit of honesty, industry, and skill into our shopkeepers; who, if a resolution could now be taken to buy only our native goods, would immediately unite to cheat and exact upon us in the price, the measure, and the goodness, nor could ever yet be brought to make one fair proposal of just dealing, though often and earnestly invited to it.

Therefore I repeat, let no man talk to me of these and the like expedients, till he hath at least some glimpse of hope that there will ever be some hearty and sincere attempt to put them in practice.

But as to myself, having been wearied out for many years with offering vain, idle, visionary thoughts, and at length utterly despairing of success, I fortunately fell upon this proposal, which, as it is wholly new, so it hath something solid and real, of no expense and little trouble, full in our own power, and whereby we can incur no danger in disobliging England. For this kind of commodity will not bear exportation, the flesh being of too tender a consistence to admit a long continuance in salt, although perhaps I could name a country which would be glad to eat up our whole nation without it.

After all, I am not so violently bent upon my own opinion as to reject any offer proposed by wise men, which shall be found equally innocent, cheap, easy, and effectual. But before something of that kind shall be advanced in contradiction to my scheme, and offering a better, I desire the author or authors will be pleased maturely to consider two points. First, as things now stand, how they will be able to find food and raiment for an hundred thousand useless mouths and backs. And secondly, there being a round million of creatures in human figure throughout this kingdom, whose sole subsistence put into a common stock would leave them in debt two millions of pounds sterling, adding those who are beggars by profession to the bulk of farmers, cottagers, and laborers, with their wives and children who are beggars in effect; I desire those politicians who dislike my overture, and may perhaps be so bold to attempt an answer, that they will first ask the parents of these mortals whether they would not at this day think it a great happiness to have been sold for food at a year old in the manner I prescribe, and thereby have avoided such a perpetual scene of misfortunes as they have since gone through by the oppression of landlords, the impossibility of paying rent without money or trade, the want of common sustenance, with neither house nor clothes to cover them from the inclemencies of the weather, and the most inevitable prospect of entailing the like or greater miseries upon their breed forever.

I profess, in the sincerity of my heart, that I have not the least personal interest in endeavoring to promote this necessary work, having no other motive than the public good of my country, by advancing our trade, providing for infants, relieving the poor, and giving some pleasure to the rich. I have no children by which I can propose to get a single penny; the youngest being nine years old, and my wife past childbearing.

1729

Alice Walker (B. 1944)

Am I Blue?

"Ain't these tears in these eyes tellin' you?"

For about three years my companion and I rented a small house in the country that stood on the edge of a large meadow that appeared to run from the end of our deck straight into the mountains. The mountains, however, were quite far away, and between us and them there was, in fact, a town. It was one of the many pleasant aspects of the house that you never really were aware of this.

It was a house of many windows, low, wide, nearly floor to ceiling in the living room, which faced the meadow, and it was from one of these that I first saw our closest neighbor, a large white horse, cropping grass, flipping its mane, and ambling about—not over the entire meadow, which stretched well out of sight of the house, but over the five or so fenced-in acres that were next to the twenty-odd that we had rented. I soon learned that the horse, whose name was Blue, belonged to a man who lived in another town, but was boarded by our neighbors next door. Occasionally, one of the children, usually a stocky teen-ager, but sometimes a much younger girl or boy, could be seen riding Blue. They would appear in the meadow, climb up on his back, ride furiously for ten or fifteen minutes, then get off, slap Blue on the flanks, and not be seen again for a month or more.

There were many apple trees in our yard, and one by the fence that Blue could almost reach. We were soon in the habit of feeding him apples, which he relished, especially because by the middle of summer the meadow grasses—so green and succulent since January—had dried out from lack of rain, and Blue stumbled about munching the dried stalks half-heartedly. Sometimes he would stand very still just by the apple tree, and when one of us came out he would whinny, snort loudly, or stamp the ground. This meant, of course: I want an apple.

It was quite wonderful to pick a few apples, or collect those that had fallen to the ground overnight, and patiently hold them, one by one, up to his large, toothy mouth. I remained as thrilled as a child by his flexible dark lips, huge, cubelike teeth that crunched the apples, core and all, with such finality, and his high, broad-breasted *enormity*; beside which, I felt small indeed. When I was a child, I used to ride horses, and was especially friendly with one named Nan until the day I was riding and my brother deliberately spooked her and I was thrown, head first, against the trunk of a tree. When I came to, I was in bed and my mother was bending worriedly over me; we silently agreed that perhaps horseback riding was not the safest sport for me. Since then I have walked, and prefer walking to horseback riding—but I had forgotten the depth of feeling one could see in horses' eyes.

I was therefore unprepared for the expression in Blue's. Blue was lonely. Blue was horribly lonely and bored. I was not shocked that this should be the case; five acres to tramp by yourself, endlessly, even in the most beautiful of meadows—and his was—cannot provide many interesting events, and once rainy season turned to dry that was about it. No, I was shocked that I had forgotten that human animals and nonhuman animals can communicate quite well; if we are brought up around animals as children we take this for granted. By the time we are adults we no longer remember. However, the animals have not changed. They are in fact *completed* creations (at least they seem to be, so much more than we) who are not likely *to* change; it is their nature to express themselves. What else are they going to express? And they do. And, generally speaking, they are ignored.

After giving Blue the apples, I would wander back to the house, aware that he was observing me. Were more apples not forthcoming then? Was that to be his sole entertainment for the day? My partner's small son had decided he wanted to learn how to piece a quilt; we worked in silence on our respective squares as I thought . . .

Well, about slavery: about white children, who were raised by black people, who knew their first all-accepting love from black women, and then, when they were twelve or so, were told they must "forget" the deep levels of communication between themselves and "mammy" that they knew. Later they would be able to relate quite calmly, "My old mammy was sold to another good family." "My old mammy was _____." Fill in the blank. Many more years later a white woman would say: "I can't understand these Negroes, these blacks. What do they want? They're so different from us."

And about the Indians, considered to be "like animals" by the "settlers" (a very benign euphemism for what they actually were), who did not understand their description as a compliment.

And about the thousands of American men who marry Japanese, Korean, Filipina, and other non-English-speaking women and of how happy they report they are, "*blissfully*," until their brides learn to speak English, at which point the marriages tend to fall apart. What then did the men see, when they looked into the eyes of the women they married, before they could speak English? Apparently only their own reflections.

I thought of society's impatience with the young. "Why are they playing the music so loud?" Perhaps the children have listened to much of the music of oppressed people their parents danced to before they were born, with its passionate but soft cries for acceptance and love, and they have wondered why their parents failed to hear.

I do not know how long Blue had inhabited his five beautiful, boring acres before we moved into our house; a year after we had arrived—and had also traveled to other valleys, other cities, other worlds—he was still there.

But then, in our second year at the house, something happened in Blue's life. One morning, looking out the window at the fog that lay like a ribbon over the meadow, I saw another horse, a brown one, at the other end of Blue's field. Blue appeared to be afraid of it, and for several days made no attempt to go near. We went away for a week. When we returned, Blue had decided to make friends and the two horses ambled or galloped along together, and Blue did not come nearly as often to the fence underneath the apple tree.

When he did, bringing his new friend with him, there was a different look in his eyes. A look of independence, of self-possession, of inalienable *horse*ness. His friend eventually became pregnant. For months and months there was, it seemed to me, a mutual feeling between me and the horses of justice, of peace. I fed apples to them both. The look in Blue's eyes was one of unabashed "this is itness."

It did not, however, last forever. One day, after a visit to the city, I went out to give Blue some apples. He stood waiting, or so I thought, though not beneath the tree. When I shook the tree and jumped back from the shower of apples, he made no move. I carried some over to him. He managed to half-crunch one. The rest he let fall to the ground. I dreaded looking into his eyes—because I had of course noticed that Brown, his partner, had gone—but I did look. If I had been born into slavery, and my partner had been sold or killed, my eyes would have looked like that. The children next door explained that Blue's partner had been "put with him' (the same expression that old people used, I had noticed, when speaking of an ancestor during slavery who had been impregnated by her owner) so that they could mate and she conceive. Since that was accomplished, she had been taken back by her owner, who lived somewhere else.

Will she be back? I asked.

They didn't know.

Blue was like a crazed person. Blue *was*, to me, a crazed person. He galloped furiously, as if he were being ridden, around and around his five beautiful acres. He whinnied until he couldn't. He tore at the ground with his hooves. He butted himself against his single shade tree. He looked always and always toward the road down which his partner had gone. And then, occasionally, when he came up for apples, or I took apples to him, he looked at me. It was a look so piercing, so full of grief, a look so *human*, I almost laughed (I felt too sad to cry) to think there are people who do not know that animals suffer. People like me who have forgotten, and daily forget, all that animals try to tell us. "Everything you do to us will happen to you; we are your teachers, as you are ours. We are one lesson" is essentially it, I think. There are those who never once have even considered animals' rights: those who have been taught that animals actually want to be used and abused by us, as small children "love" to be frightened, or women "love" to be mutilated and raped. . . . They are the great-grandchildren of those who honestly thought, because someone taught them this: "Women can't think," and "niggers can't faint." But most disturbing of all, in Blue's large brown eyes was a new look, more painful than the look of despair: the look of disgust with human beings, with life; the look of hatred. And it was odd what the look of hatred did. It gave him, for the first time, the look of a beast. And what that meant was that he had put up a barrier within to protect himself from further violence; all the apples in the world wouldn't change that fact.

And so Blue remained, a beautiful part of our landscape, very peaceful to look at from the window, white against the grass. Once a friend came to visit and said, looking out on the soothing view: "And it *would* have to be a *white* horse; the very image of freedom." And I thought, yes, the animals are forced to become for us merely "images" of what they once so beautifully expressed. And we are used to drinking milk from containers showing "contented" cows, whose real lives we want to hear nothing about, eating eggs and drumsticks from "happy" hens, and munching hamburgers advertised by bulls of integrity who seem to command their fate.

As we talked of freedom and justice one day for all, we sat down to steaks. I am eating misery, I thought, as I took the first bite. And spit it out.

1986

Fiction

Anton Chekhov (1860–1904)

Misery

Translated by Constance Garnett

"To Whom Shall I Tell My Grief?"
A line from a Russian folksong

The twilight of evening. Big flakes of wet snow are whirling lazily about the street lamps, which have just been lighted, and lying in a thin soft layer on roofs, horses' backs, shoulders, caps. Iona Potapov, the sledge-driver, is all white like a ghost. He sits on the box without stirring, bent as double as the living body can be bent. If a regular snowdrift fell on him it seems as though even then he would not think it necessary to shake it off. . . . His little mare is white and motionless too. Her stillness, the angularity of her lines, and the stick-like straightness of her legs make her look like a halfpenny gingerbread horse. She is probably lost in thought. Anyone who has been torn away from the plough, from the familiar gray landscapes, and cast into this slough, full of monstrous lights, of unceasing uproar and hurrying people, is bound to think.

It is a long time since Iona and his nag have budged. They came out of the yard before dinner-time and not a single fare yet. But now the shades of evening are falling on the town. The pale light of the street lamps changes to a vivid color, and the bustle of the street grows noisier.

"Sledge to Vyborgskaya!" Iona hears. "Sledge!"

Iona starts, and through his snow-plastered eyelashes sees an officer in a military overcoat with a hood over his head.

"To Vyborgskaya," repeats the officer. "Are you asleep? To Vyborgskaya!"

In token of assent Iona gives a tug at the reins which sends cakes of snow flying from the horse's back and shoulders. The officer gets into the sledge. The sledge-driver clicks to the horse, cranes his neck like a swan, rises in his seat, and more from habit than necessity brandishes his whip. The mare cranes her neck, too, crooks her stick-like legs, and hesitatingly sets off. . . .

"Where are you shoving, you devil?" Iona immediately hears shouts from the dark mass shifting to and fro before him. "Where the devil are you going? Keep to the r-right!"

"You don't know how to drive! Keep to the right," says the officer angrily.

A coachman driving a carriage swears at him; a pedestrian crossing the road and brushing the horse's nose with his shoulder looks at him angrily and shakes the snow off his sleeve. Iona fidgets on the box as though he were sitting on thorns, jerks his elbows, and turns his eyes about like one possessed, as though he did not know where he was or why he was there.

"What rascals they all are!" says the officer jocosely. "They are simply doing their best to run up against you or fall under the horse's feet. They must be doing it on purpose."

Iona looks at his fare and moves his lips. . . . Apparently he means to say something, but nothing comes out but a sniff.

"What?" inquires the officer.

Iona gives a wry smile, and straining his throat, brings out huskily: "My son . . . , er . . . my son died this week, sir."

"H'm! What did he die of?"

Iona turns his whole body round to his fare, and says:

"Who can tell! It must have been from fever. . . . He lay three days in the hospital and then he died. . . . God's will."

"Turn round, you devil!" comes out of the darkness. "Have you gone cracked, you old dog? Look where you are going!"

"Drive on! drive on! . . . " says the officer. "We shan't get there till tomorrow going on like this. Hurry up!"

The sledge-driver cranes his neck again, rises in his seat, and with heavy grace swings his whip. Several times he looks round at the officer, but the latter keeps his eyes shut and is apparently disinclined to listen. Putting his fare down at Vyborgskaya, Iona stops by a restaurant, and again sits huddled up on the box. . . . Again the wet snow paints him and his horse white. One hour passes, and then another. . . .

Three young men, two tall and thin, one short and hunchbacked, come up, railing at each other and loudly stamping on the pavement with their galoshes.

"Cabby, to the Police Bridge!" the hunchback cries in a cracked voice. "The three of us, . . . twenty kopecks!"

Iona tugs at the reins and clicks to his horse. Twenty kopecks is not a fair price, but he has no thoughts for that. Whether it is a rouble or whether it is five kopecks does not matter to him now so long as he has a fare. . . . The three young men, shoving each other and using bad language, go up to the sledge, and all three try to sit down at once. The question remains to be settled: Which are to sit down and which one is to stand? After a long altercation, ill-temper, and abuse, they come to the conclusion that the hunchback must stand because he is the shortest.

"Well, drive on," says the hunchback in his cracked voice, settling himself and breathing down Iona's neck. "Cut along! What a cap you've got, my friend! You wouldn't find a worse one in all Petersburg. . . . "

"He-he! . . . he-he! . . . " laughs Iona. "It's nothing to boast of!"

"Well, then, nothing to boast of, drive on! Are you going to drive like this all the way? Eh? Shall I give you one in the neck?"

"My head aches," says one of the tall ones. "At the Dukmasovs' yesterday Vaska and I drank four bottles of brandy between us."

"I can't make out why you talk such stuff," says the other tall one angrily. "You lie like a brute."

"Strike me dead, it's the truth! . . . "

"It's about as true as that a louse coughs."

"He-he!" grins Iona. "Me-er-ry gentlemen!"

"Tfoo! the devil take you!" cries the hunchback indignantly. "Will you get on, you old plague, or won't you? Is that the way to drive? Give her one with the whip. Hang it all, give it her well."

Iona feels behind his back the jolting person and quivering voice of the hunchback. He hears abuse addressed to him, he sees people, and the feeling of loneliness begins little by little to be less heavy on his heart. The hunchback swears at him, till he chokes over some elaborately whimsical string of epithets and is overpowered by his cough. His tall companions begin talking of a certain Nadyezhda Petrovna. Iona looks round at them. Waiting till there is a brief pause, he looks round once more and says:

"This week . . . er . . . my . . . er . . . son died!"

"We shall all die, . . . " says the hunchback with a sigh, wiping his lips after coughing. "Come, drive on! drive on! My friends, I simply cannot stand crawling like this! When will he get us there?"

"Well, you give him a little encouragement . . . one in the neck!"

"Do you hear, you old plague? I'll make you smart. If one stands on ceremony with fellows like you one may as well walk. Do you hear, you old dragon? Or don't you care a hang what we say?"

And Iona hears rather than feels a slap on the back of his neck.

"He-he! . . . " he laughs. "Merry gentlemen . . . God give you health!"

"Cabman, are you married?" asks one of the tall ones.

"I? He-he! Me-er-ry gentlemen. The only wife for me now is the damp earth. . . . He-ho-ho! . . . The grave that is! . . . Here my son's dead and I am alive. . . . It's a strange thing, death has come in at the wrong door. . . . Instead of coming for me it went for my son. . . . "

And Iona turns round to tell them how his son died, but at that point the hunchback gives a faint sigh and announces that, thank God! they have arrived at last. After taking his twenty kopecks, Iona gazes for a long while after the revelers, who disappear into a dark entry. Again he is alone and again there is silence for him. . . . The misery which has been for a brief space eased comes back again and tears his heart more cruelly than ever. With a look of anxiety and suffering Iona's eyes stray restlessly among the crowds moving to and fro on both sides of the street: can he not find among those thousands someone who will listen to him? But the crowds flit by heedless of him and his misery. . . . His misery is immense, beyond all bounds. If Iona's heart were to burst and his misery to flow out, it would flood the whole world, it seems, but yet it is not seen. It has found a hiding-place in such an insignificant shell that one would not have found it with a candle by daylight. . . .

Iona sees a house-porter with a parcel and makes up his mind to address him.

"What time will it be, friend?" he asks.

"Going on for ten. . . . Why have you stopped here? Drive on!"

Iona drives a few paces away, bends himself double, and gives himself up to his misery. He feels it is no good to appeal to people. But before five minutes have passed he draws himself up, shakes his head as though he feels a sharp pain, and tugs at the reins. . . . He can bear it no longer.

"Back to the yard!" he thinks. "To the yard!"

And his little mare, as though she knew his thoughts, falls to trotting. An hour and a half later Iona is sitting by a big dirty stove. On the stove, on the floor, and on the benches are people snoring. The air is full of smells and stuffiness. Iona looks at the sleeping figures, scratches himself, and regrets that he has come home so early. . . .

"I have not earned enough to pay for the oats, even," he thinks. "That's why I am so miserable. A man who knows how to do his work, . . . who has had enough to eat, and whose horse has had enough to eat, is always at ease. . . . "

In one of the corners a young cabman gets up, clears his throat sleepily, and makes for the waterbucket.

"Want a drink?" Iona asks him.

"Seems so."

"May it do you good. . . . But my son is dead, mate. . . . Do you hear? This week in the hospital. . . . It's queer business. . . . "

Iona looks to see the effect produced by his words, but he sees nothing. The young man has covered his head over and is already asleep. The old man sighs and scratches himself. . . . Just as the young man had been thirsty for water, he thirsts for speech. His son will soon have been dead a week, and he has not really talked to anybody yet. . . . He wants to talk of it properly, with deliberation. . . . He wants to tell how his son was taken ill, how he suffered, what he said before he died, how he died. . . . He wants to describe the funeral, and how he went to the hospital to get his son's clothes. He still has his daughter Anisya in the country. . . . And he wants to talk about her too. . . . Yes, he has plenty to talk about now. His listener ought to sigh and exclaim and lament. . . . It would be even better to talk to women. Though they are silly creatures, they blubber at the first word.

"Let's go out and have a look at the mare," Iona thinks. "There is always time for sleep. . . . You'll have sleep enough, no fear. . . . "

He puts on his coat and goes into the stables where his mare is standing. He thinks about oats, about hay, about the weather. . . . He cannot think about his son when he is alone. . . . To talk about him with someone is possible, but to think of him and picture him is insufferable anguish. . . .

"Are you munching?" Iona asks his mare, seeing her shining eyes. "There, munch away, munch away. . . . Since we have not earned enough for oats, we will eat hay. . . . Yes, . . . I have grown too old to drive. . . . My son ought to be driving, not I. . . . He was a real coachman. . . . He ought to have lived. . . . "

Iona is silent for a while, and then he goes on:

"That's how it is, old girl. . . . Kuzma Ionitch is gone. . . . He said good-by to me. . . . He went and died for no reason. . . . Now, suppose you had a little colt, and you were mother to that little colt. . . . And all at once that same little colt went and died. . . . You'd be sorry, wouldn't you? . . . "

The little mare munches, listens, and breathes on her master's hands. Iona is carried away and tells her all about it.

1886

Evan Connell (B. 1924)

From *Mrs. Bridge*

3 Preliminary Training

She brought up her children very much as she herself had been brought up, and she hoped that when they were spoken of it would be in connection with their nice manners, their pleasant dispositions, and their cleanliness, for these were qualities she valued above all others.

With Ruth and later with Carolyn, because they were girls, she felt sure of her guidance; but with the boy she was at times obliged to guess and to hope, and as it turned out—not only with Douglas but with his two sisters—what she stressed was not at all what they remembered as they grew older.

What Ruth was to recall most vividly about childhood was an incident which Mrs. Bridge had virtually forgotten an hour after it occurred. One summer afternoon the entire family, with the exception of Mr. Bridge who was working, had gone to the neighborhood swimming pool; Douglas lay on a rubber sheet in the shade of an umbrella, kicking his thin bowed legs and gurgling, and Carolyn was splashing around in the wading pool. The day was exceptionally hot. Ruth took off her bathing suit and began walking across the terrace. This much she could hardly remember, but she was never to forget what happened next. Mrs. Bridge, having suddenly discovered Ruth was naked, snatched up the bathing suit and hurried after her. Ruth began to run, and being wet and slippery she squirmed out of the arms that reached for her from every direction. She thought it was a new game. Then she noticed the expression on her mother's face. Ruth became bewildered and then alarmed, and when she was finally caught she was screaming hysterically.

24 Advanced Training

Appearances were an abiding concern of Mrs. Bridge, which was the reason that one evening as she saw Ruth preparing to go out she inquired, "Aren't you taking a purse, dear?"

Ruth answered in a husky voice that whatever she needed she could carry in her pockets.

Said Mrs. Bridge, "Carolyn always takes a purse."

Ruth was standing in front of the hall mirror, standing in a way that disturbed Mrs. Bridge, though she did not know precisely why, unless it could be that Ruth's feet were too far apart and her hips a little too forward. Mrs. Bridge had been trying to cure her of this habit by making her walk around the house with a book balanced on her head, but as soon as the book was removed Ruth resumed sauntering and standing in that unseemly posture.

"And you're older than Corky," Mrs. Bridge went on with a frown; and yet, looking at her elder daughter, she could not continue frowning. Ruth really was quite lovely, just as Gladys Schmidt's husband had said; if only she were not so conscious of it, not so aware of people turning to look at her, for they did stop to look—men and women both—so deliberately sometimes that Mrs. Bridge grew uneasy, and could not get over the idea that Ruth, by her posture and her challenging walk, was encouraging people to stare.

"Is somebody coming by for you?"

"I'm only going to the drugstore."

"What on earth do you do in the drugstore?" asked Mrs. Bridge after a pause. "Madge Arlen told me she saw you there one evening sitting all by yourself in a booth. She said she supposed you were waiting for someone."

At this Ruth stiffened noticeably, and Mrs. Bridge wanted to ask, "Were you?"

"I really don't approve of you sitting around in drugstores," she went on, for she was afraid to ask directly if Ruth was going there to meet a boy—not afraid of asking the question, but of the answer. "And I don't believe your father would approve of it either," she continued, feeling helpless and querulous in the knowledge that her daughter was hardly listening. "Goodness, I should think you could find something else to do. What about playing with Carolyn and her friends?"

Ruth didn't bother to answer.

"I'll lend you my blue suede purse, if you like," said Mrs. Bridge hopefully, but again there was no response. Ruth was still admiring herself in the mirror.

"I shouldn't think you could carry much in those pockets."

Ruth stepped backward, narrowed her eyes, and unfastened the top button of her blouse.

"Really, you *need* some things," Mrs. Bridge remarked a trifle sharply. "And button yourself up, for goodness sake. You look like a chorus girl."

"Good night," said Ruth flatly and started for the door.

"But, dear, a lady always carries a purse!" Mrs. Bridge was saying when the door closed.

30 The Search for Love

It seemed to Mrs. Bridge that she had done the necessary thing, and therefore the right thing, in regard to the monstrous tower. Again and again she thought about it, and the reason she thought about it so intensively was that she perceived a change in Douglas's attitude toward her. He was more withdrawn.

As time went on she felt an increasing need for reassurance. Her husband had never been a demonstrative man, not even when they were first married; consequently she did not expect too much from him. Yet there were moments when she was overwhelmed by a terrifying, inarticulate need. One evening as she and he were finishing supper together, alone, the children having gone out, she inquired rather sharply if he loved her. She was surprised by her own bluntness and by the almost shrewish tone of her voice, because that was not the way she actually felt. She saw him gazing at her in astonishment; his expression said very clearly: Why on earth do you think I'm here if I don't love you? Why aren't I somewhere else? What in the world has got into you?

Mrs. Bridge smiled across the floral centerpiece—and it occurred to her that these flowers she had so carefully arranged on the table were what separated her from her husband—and said, a little wretchedly, "I know it's silly, but it's been such a long time since you told me."

Mr. Bridge grunted and finished his coffee. She knew it was not that he was annoyed, only that he was incapable of the kind of declaration she needed. It was so little, and yet so much. While they sat across from each other, neither knowing quite what to do next, she became embarrassed; and in her embarrassment she moved her feet and she inadvertently stepped on the buzzer, concealed beneath the carpet, that connected with the kitchen, with the result that Harriet soon appeared in the doorway to see what it was that Mrs. Bridge desired.

1959

Charlotte Perkins Gilman (1860–1935)

The Yellow Wallpaper

It is very seldom that mere ordinary people like John and myself secure ancestral halls for the summer.

A colonial mansion, a hereditary estate, I would say a haunted house and reach the height of romantic felicity—but that would be asking too much of fate!

Still I will proudly declare that there is something queer about it.

Else, why should it be let so cheaply? And why have stood so long untenanted?

John laughs at me, of course, but one expects that.

John is practical in the extreme. He has no patience with faith, an intense horror of superstition, and he scoffs openly at any talk of things not to be felt and seen and put down in figures.

John is a physician, and *perhaps*—(I would not say it to a living soul, of course, but this is dead paper and a great relief to my mind)—*perhaps* that is one reason I do not get well faster.

You see, he does not believe I am sick! And what can one do?

If a physician of high standing, and one's own husband, assures friends and relatives that there is really nothing the matter with one but temporary nervous depression—a slight hysterical tendency—what is one to do?

My brother is also a physician, and also of high standing, and he says the same thing.

So I take phosphates or phosphites—whichever it is—and tonics, and air and exercise, and journeys, and am absolutely forbidden to "work" until I am well again.

Personally, I disagree with their ideas.

Personally, I believe that congenial work, with excitement and change, would do me good.

But what is one to do?

I did write for a while in spite of them; but it *does* exhaust me a good deal—having to be so sly about it, or else meet with heavy opposition.

I sometimes fancy that in my condition, if I had less opposition and more society and stimulus—but John says the very worst thing I can do is to think about my condition, and I confess it always makes me feel bad.

So I will let it alone and talk about the house.

The most beautiful place! It is quite alone, standing well back from the road, quite three miles from the village. It makes me think of English places that you read about, for there are hedges and walls and gates that lock, and lots of separate little houses for the gardeners and people.

There is a *delicious* garden! I never saw such a garden—large and shady, full of box-bordered paths, and lined with long grape-covered arbors with seats under them.

There were greenhouses, but they are all broken now.

There was some legal trouble, I believe, something about the heirs and coheirs; anyhow, the place has been empty for years.

That spoils my ghostliness, I am afraid, but I don't care—there is something strange about the house—I can feel it.

I even said so to John one moonlight evening, but he said what I felt was a *draught,* and shut the window.

I get unreasonably angry with John sometimes. I'm sure I never used to be so sensitive. I think it is due to this nervous condition.

But John says if I feel so I shall neglect proper self-control; so I take pains to control myself—before him, at least, and that makes me very tired.

I don't like our room a bit. I wanted one downstairs that opened onto the piazza and had roses all over the window, and such pretty old-fashioned chintz hangings! But John would not hear of it.

He said there was only one window and not room for two beds, and no near room for him if he took another.

He is very careful and loving, and hardly lets me stir without special direction.

I have a schedule prescription for each hour in the day; he takes all care from me, and so I feel basely ungrateful not to value it more.

He said he came here solely on my account, that I was to have perfect rest and all the air I could get. "Your exercise depends on your strength, my dear," said he, "and your food somewhat on your appetite; but air you can absorb all the time." So we took the nursery at the top of the house.

It is a big, airy room, the whole floor nearly, with windows that look all ways, and air and sunshine galore. It was a nursery first, and then playroom and gymnasium, I should judge, for the windows are barred for little children, and there are rings and things in the walls.

The paint and paper look as if a boys' school had used it. It is stripped off—the paper—in great patches all around the head of my bed, about as far as I can reach, and in a great place on the other side of the room low down. I never saw a worse paper in my life. One of those sprawling, flamboyant patterns committing every artistic sin.

It is dull enough to confuse the eye in following, pronounced enough constantly to irritate and provoke study, and when you follow the lame uncertain curves for a little distance they suddenly commit suicide—plunge off at outrageous angles, destroy themselves in unheard-of contradictions.

The color is repellent, almost revolting: a smouldering unclean yellow, strangely faded by the slow-turning sunlight. It is a dull yet lurid orange in some places, a sickly sulphur tint in others.

No wonder the children hated it! I should hate it myself if I had to live in this room long.

There comes John, and I must put this away—he hates to have me write a word.

We have been here two weeks, and I haven't felt like writing before, since that first day.

I am sitting by the window now, up in this atrocious nursery, and there is nothing to hinder my writing as much as I please, save lack of strength.

John is away all day, and even some nights when his cases are serious.

I am glad my case is not serious!

But these nervous troubles are dreadfully depressing.

John does not know how much I really suffer. He knows there is no *reason* to suffer, and that satisfies him.

Of course it is only nervousness. It does weigh on me so not to do my duty in any way!

I meant to be such a help to John, such a real rest and comfort, and here I am a comparative burden already!

Nobody would believe what an effort it is to do what little I am able— to dress and entertain, and order things.

It is fortunate Mary is so good with the baby. Such a dear baby!

And yet I *cannot* be with him, it makes me so nervous.

I suppose John never was nervous in his life. He laughs at me so about this wallpaper!

At first he meant to repaper the room, but afterward he said that I was letting it get the better of me, and that nothing was worse for a nervous patient than to give way to such fancies.

He said that after the wallpaper was changed it would be the heavy bedstead, and then the barred windows, and then that gate at the head of the stairs, and so on.

"You know the place is doing you good," he said, "and really, dear, I don't care to renovate the house just for a three months' rental."

"Then do let us go downstairs," I said. "There are such pretty rooms there."

Then he took me in his arms and called me a blessed little goose, and said he would go down to the cellar, if I wished, and have it whitewashed into the bargain.

But he is right enough about the beds and windows and things.

It is as airy and comfortable a room as anyone need wish, and, of course, I would not be so silly as to make him uncomfortable just for a whim.

I'm really getting quite fond of the big room, all but that horrid paper.

Out of one window I can see the garden—those mysterious deepshaded arbors, the riotous old-fashioned flowers, and bushes and gnarly trees.

Out of another I get a lovely view of the bay and a little private wharf belonging to the estate. There is a beautiful shaded lane that runs down there from the house. I always fancy I see people walking in these numerous paths and arbors, but John has cautioned me not to give way to fancy in the least. He says that with my imaginative power and habit of storymaking, a nervous weakness like mine is sure to lead to all manner of excited fancies, and that I ought to use my will and good sense to check the tendency. So I try.

I think sometimes that if I were only well enough to write a little it would relieve the press of ideas and rest me.

But I find I get pretty tired when I try.

It is so discouraging not to have any advice and companionship about my work. When I get really well, John says we will ask Cousin Henry and Julia down for a long visit; but he says he would as soon put fireworks in my pillowcase as to let me have those stimulating people about now.

I wish I could get well faster.

But I must not think about that. This paper looks to me as if it *knew* what a vicious influence it had!

There is a recurrent spot where the pattern lolls like a broken neck and two bulbous eyes stare at you upside down.

I get positively angry with the impertinence of it and the everlastingness. Up and down and sideways they crawl, and those absurd unblinking eyes are everywhere. There is one place where two breadths didn't match, and the eyes go all up and down the line, one a little higher than the other.

I never saw so much expression in an inanimate thing before, and we all know how much expression they have! I used to lie awake as a child and get more entertainment and terror out of blank walls and plain furniture than most children could find in a toy-store.

I remember what a kindly wink the knobs of our big old bureau used to have, and there was one chair that always seemed like a strong friend.

I used to feel that if any of the other things looked too fierce I could always hop into that chair and be safe.

The furniture in this room is no worse than inharmonious, however, for we had to bring it all from downstairs. I suppose when this was used as a playroom they had to take the nursery things out, and no wonder! I never saw such ravages as the children have made here.

The wallpaper, as I said before, is torn off in spots, and it sticketh closer than a brother—they must have had perseverance as well as hatred.

Then the floor is scratched and gouged and splintered, the plaster itself is dug out here and there, and this great heavy bed, which is all we found in the room, looks as if it had been through the wars.

But I don't mind it a bit—only the paper.

There comes John's sister. Such a dear girl as she is, and so careful of me! I must not let her find me writing.

She is a perfect and enthusiastic housekeeper, and hopes for no better profession. I verily believe she thinks it is the writing which made me sick!

But I can write when she is out, and see her a long way off from these windows.

There is one that commands the road, a lovely shaded winding road, and one that just looks off over the country. A lovely country, too, full of great elms and velvet meadows.

This wallpaper has a kind of subpattern in a different shade, a particularly irritating one, for you can only see it in certain lights, and not clearly then.

But in the places where it isn't faded and where the sun is just so—I can see a strange, provoking, formless sort of figure that seems to skulk about behind that silly and conspicuous front design.

There's sister on the stairs!

Well, the Fourth of July is over! The people are all gone, and I am tired out. John thought it might do me good to see a little company, so we just had Mother and Nellie and the children down for a week.

Of course I didn't do a thing. Jennie sees to everything now.

But it tired me all the same.

John says if I don't pick up faster he shall send me to Weir Mitchell[1] in the fall.

But I don't want to go there at all. I had a friend who was in his hands once, and she says he is just like John and my brother, only more so!

Besides, it is such an undertaking to go so far.

I don't feel as if it was worthwhile to turn my hand over for anything, and I'm getting dreadfully fretful and querulous.

I cry at nothing, and cry most of the time.

Of course I don't when John is here, or anybody else, but when I am alone.

And I am alone a good deal just now. John is kept in town very often by serious cases, and Jennie is good and lets me alone when I want her to.

So I walk a little in the garden or down that lovely lane, sit on the porch under the roses, and lie down up here a good deal.

I'm getting really fond of the room in spite of the wallpaper. Perhaps *because* of the wallpaper.

It dwells in my mind so!

I lie here on this great immovable bed—it is nailed down, I believe—and follow that pattern about by the hour. It is as good as gymnastics, I assure you. I start, we'll say, at the bottom, down in the corner over there where it has not been touched, and I determine for the thousandth time that I *will* follow that pointless pattern to some sort of a conclusion.

I know a little of the principle of design, and I know this thing was not arranged on any laws of radiation,[2] or alternation, or repetition, or symmetry, or anything else that I ever heard of.

It is repeated, of course, by the breadths, but not otherwise.

Looked at in one way, each breadth stands alone; the bloated curves and flourishes—a kind of "debased Romanesque" with *delirium tremens*—go waddling up and down in isolated columns of fatuity.

But, on the other hand, they connect diagonally, and the sprawling outlines run off in great slanting waves of optic horror, like a lot of wallowing seaweeds in full chase.

The whole thing goes horizontally, too, at least it seems so, and I exhaust myself trying to distinguish the order of its going in that direction.

They have used a horizontal breadth for a frieze, and that adds wonderfully to the confusion.

There is one end of the room where it is almost intact, and there, when the crosslights fade and the low sun shines directly upon it, I can almost

---

[1] *Weir Mitchell* (1829–1914): famed nerve specialist who actually treated the author, Charlotte Perkins Gilman, for nervous prostration with his well-known "rest cure." (The cure was not successful.) Also the author of *Diseases of the Nervous System, Especially of Women* (1881).

[2] *Laws of radiation*: a principle of design in which all elements are arranged in some circular pattern around a center.

fancy radiation after all—the interminable grotesque seems to form around a common center and rush off in headlong plunges of equal distraction.

It makes me tired to follow it. I will take a nap, I guess.

I don't know why I should write this.

I don't want to.

I don't feel able.

And I know John would think it absurd. But I *must* say what I feel and think in some way—it is such a relief!

But the effort is getting to be greater than the relief.

Half the time now I am awfully lazy, and lie down ever so much. John says I mustn't lose my strength, and has me take cod liver oil and lots of tonics and things, to say nothing of ale and wines and rare meat.

Dear John! He loves me very dearly, and hates to have me sick. I tried to have a real earnest reasonable talk with him the other day, and tell him how I wish he would let me go and make a visit to Cousin Henry and Julia.

But he said I wasn't able to go, nor able to stand it after I got there; and I did not make out a very good case for myself, for I was crying before I had finished.

It is getting to be a great effort for me to think straight. Just this nervous weakness, I suppose.

And dear John gathered me up in his arms, and just carried me upstairs and laid me on the bed, and sat by me and read to me till it tired my head.

He said I was his darling and his comfort and all he had, and that I must take care of myself for his sake, and keep well.

He says no one but myself can help me out of it, that I must use my will and self-control and not let any silly fancies run away with me.

There's one comfort—the baby is well and happy, and does not have to occupy this nursery with the horrid wallpaper.

If we had not used it, that blessed child would have! What a fortunate escape! Why, I wouldn't have a child of mine, an impressionable little thing, live in such a room for worlds.

I never thought of it before, but it is lucky that John kept me here after all; I can stand it so much easier than a baby, you see.

Of course I never mention it to them any more—I am too wise—but I keep watch for it all the same.

There are things in the wallpaper that nobody knows about but me, or ever will.

Behind that outside pattern the dim shapes get clearer every day.

It is always the same shape, only very numerous.

And it is like a woman stooping down and creeping about behind that pattern. I don't like it a bit. I wonder—I begin to think—I wish John would take me away from here!

It is so hard to talk with John about my case, because he is so wise, and because he loves me so.

But I tried it last night.

It was moonlight. The moon shines in all around just as the sun does.

I hate to see it sometimes, it creeps so slowly, and always comes in by one window or another.

John was asleep and I hated to waken him, so I kept still and watched the moonlight on that undulating wallpaper till I felt creepy.

The faint figure behind seemed to shake the pattern, just as if she wanted to get out.

I got up softly and went to feel and see if the paper *did* move, and when I came back John was awake.

"What is it, little girl?" he said. "Don't go walking about like that— you'll get cold."

I thought it was a good time to talk, so I told him that I really was not gaining here, and that I wished he would take me away.

"Why, darling!" said he. "Our lease will be up in three weeks, and I can't see how to leave before.

"The repairs are not done at home, and I cannot possibly leave town just now. Of course, if you were in any danger, I could and would, but you really are better, dear, whether you can see it or not. I am a doctor, dear, and I know. You are gaining flesh and color, your appetite is better, I feel really much easier about you."

"I don't weigh a bit more," said I, "nor as much; and my appetite may be better in the evening when you are here but it is worse in the morning when you are away!"

"Bless her little heart!" said he with a big hug. "She shall be as sick as she pleases! But now let's improve the shining hours by going to sleep, and talk about it in the morning!"

"And you won't go away?" I asked gloomily.

"Why, how can I, dear? It is only three weeks more and then we will take a nice little trip for a few days while Jennie is getting the house ready. Really, dear, you are better!"

"Better in body perhaps—" I began, and stopped short, for he sat up straight and looked at me with such a stern, reproachful look that I could not say another word.

"My darling," said he, "I beg you, for my sake and for our child's sake, as well as for your own, that you will never for one instant let that idea enter your mind! There is nothing so dangerous, so fascinating, to a temperament like yours. It is a false and foolish fancy. Can you trust me as a physician when I tell you so?"

So of course I said no more on that score, and we went to sleep before long. He thought I was asleep first, but I wasn't, and lay there for hours trying to decide whether that front pattern and the back pattern really did move together or separately.

On a pattern like this, by daylight, there is a lack of sequence, a defiance of law, that is a constant irritant to a normal mind.

The color is hideous enough, and unreliable enough, and infuriating enough, but the pattern is torturing.

You think you have mastered it, but just as you get well under way in following, it turns a back-somersault and there you are. It slaps you in the face, knocks you down, and tramples upon you. It is like a bad dream.

The outside pattern is a florid arabesque,[3] reminding one of a fungus. If you can imagine a toadstool in joints, an interminable string of toadstools, budding and sprouting in endless convolutions—why, that is something like it.

That is, sometimes!

There is one marked peculiarity about this paper, a thing nobody seems to notice but myself, and that is that it changes as the light changes.

When the sun shoots in through the east window—I always watch for that first long, straight ray—it changes so quickly that I never can quite believe it.

That is why I watch it always.

By moonlight—the moon shines in all night when there is a moon—I wouldn't know it was the same paper.

At night in any kind of light, in twilight, candlelight, lamplight, and worst of all by moonlight, it becomes bars! The outside pattern, I mean, and the woman behind it is as plain as can be.

I didn't realize for a long time what the thing was that showed behind, that dim subpattern, but now I am quite sure it is a woman.

By daylight she is subdued, quiet. I fancy it is the pattern that keeps her so still. It is so puzzling. It keeps me quiet by the hour.

I lie down ever so much now. John says it is good for me, and to sleep all I can.

Indeed he started the habit by making me lie down for an hour after each meal.

It is a very bad habit, I am convinced, for you see, I don't sleep.

And that cultivates deceit, for I don't tell them I'm awake—oh, no!

The fact is I am getting a little afraid of John.

He seems very queer sometimes, and even Jennie has an inexplicable look.

It strikes me occasionally, just as a scientific hypothesis, that perhaps it is the paper!

I have watched John when he did not know I was looking, and come into the room suddenly on the most innocent excuses, and I've caught him several times *looking at the paper!* And Jennie too. I caught Jennie with her hand on it once.

She didn't know I was in the room, and when I asked her in a quiet, a very quiet voice, with the most restrained manner possible, what she was

---

[3]*Arabesque*: a type of ornamental style (Arabic in origin) that uses flowers, foliage, fruit, or other figures to create an intricate pattern of interlocking shapes and lines.

doing with the paper, she turned around as if she had been caught stealing, and looked quite angry—asked me why I should frighten her so!

Then she said that the paper stained everything it touched, that she had found yellow smooches[4] on all my clothes and John's and she wished we would be more careful!

Did not that sound innocent? But I know she was studying that pattern, and I am determined that nobody shall find it out but myself!

Life is very much more exciting now than it used to be. You see, I have something more to expect, to look forward to, to watch. I really do eat better, and am more quiet than I was.

John is so pleased to see me improve! He laughed a little the other day, and said I seemed to be flourishing in spite of my wallpaper.

I turned it off with a laugh. I had no intention of telling him it was *because* of the wallpaper—he would make fun of me. He might even want to take me away.

I don't want to leave now until I have found it out. There is a week more, and I think that will be enough.

I'm feeling so much better!

I don't sleep much at night, for it is so interesting to watch developments; but I sleep a good deal during the daytime.

In the daytime it is tiresome and perplexing.

There are always new shoots on the fungus, and new shades of yellow all over it. I cannot keep count of them, though I have tried conscientiously.

It is the strangest yellow, that wallpaper! It makes me think of all the yellow things I ever saw—not beautiful ones like buttercups, but old, foul, bad yellow things.

But there is something else about that paper—the smell! I noticed it the moment we came into the room, but with so much air and sun it was not bad. Now we have had a week of fog and rain, and whether the windows are open or not, the smell is here.

It creeps all over the house.

I find it hovering in the dining-room, skulking in the parlor, hiding in the hall, lying in wait for me on the stairs.

It gets into my hair.

Even when I go to ride, if I turn my head suddenly and surprise it—there is that smell!

Such a peculiar odor, too! I have spent hours in trying to analyze it, to find what it smelled like.

It is not bad—at first—and very gentle, but quite the subtlest, most enduring odor I ever met.

In this damp weather it is awful. I wake up in the night and find it hanging over me.

---

[4]*Smooches:* smudges or smears.

It used to disturb me at first. I thought seriously of burning the house—to reach the smell.

But now I am used to it. The only thing I can think of that it is like is the *color* of the paper! A yellow smell.

There is a very funny mark on this wall, low down, near the mopboard. A streak that runs round the room. It goes behind every piece of furniture, except the bed, a long, straight, even *smooch*, as if it had been rubbed over and over.

I wonder how it was done and who did it, and what they did it for. Round and round and round—round and round and round—it makes me dizzy!

I really have discovered something at last.

Through watching so much at night, when it changes so, I have finally found out.

The front pattern *does* move—and no wonder! The woman behind shakes it!

Sometimes I think there are a great many women behind, and sometimes only one, and she crawls around fast, and her crawling shakes it all over.

Then in the very bright spots she keeps still, and in the very shady spots she just takes hold of the bars and shakes them hard.

And she is all the time trying to climb through. But nobody could climb through that pattern—it strangles so; I think that is why it has so many heads.

They get through and then the pattern strangles them off and turns them upside down, and makes their eyes white!

If those heads were covered or taken off it would not be half so bad.

I think that woman gets out in the daytime!

And I'll tell you why—privately—I've seen her!

I can see her out of every one of my windows!

It is the same woman, I know, for she is always creeping, and most women do not creep by daylight.

I see her in that long shaded lane, creeping up and down. I see her in those dark grape arbors, creeping all round the garden.

I see her on that long road under the trees, creeping along, and when a carriage comes she hides under the blackberry vines.

I don't blame her a bit. It must be very humiliating to be caught creeping by daylight!

I always lock the door when I creep by daylight. I can't do it at night, for I know John would suspect something at once.

And John is so queer now that I don't want to irritate him. I wish he would take another room! Besides, I don't want anybody to get that woman out at night but myself.

I often wonder if I could see her out of all the windows at once.

But, turn as fast as I can, I can only see out of one at one time.

And though I always see her, she *may* be able to creep faster than I can turn! I have watched her sometimes away off in the open country, creeping as fast as a cloud shadow in a wind.

If only that top pattern could be gotten off from the under one! I mean to try it, little by little.

I have found out another funny thing, but I shan't tell it this time! It does not do to trust people too much.

There are only two more days to get this paper off, and I believe John is beginning to notice. I don't like the look in his eyes.

And I heard him ask Jennie a lot of professional questions about me. She had a very good report to give.

She said I slept a good deal in the daytime.

John knows I don't sleep very well at night, for all I'm so quiet!

He asked me all sorts of questions too, and pretended to be very loving and kind.

As if I couldn't see through him!

Still, I don't wonder he acts so, sleeping under this paper for three months.

It only interests me, but I feel sure John and Jennie are affected by it.

Hurrah! This is the last day, but it is enough. John is to stay in town over night, and won't be out until this evening.

Jennie wanted to sleep with me—the sly thing; but I told her I should undoubtedly rest better for a night all alone.

That was clever, for really I wasn't alone a bit! As soon as it was moonlight and that poor thing began to crawl and shake the pattern, I got up and ran to help her.

I pulled and she shook. I shook and she pulled, and before morning we had peeled off yards of that paper.

A strip about as high as my head and half around the room.

And then when the sun came and that awful pattern began to laugh at me, I declared I would finish it today!

We go away tomorrow, and they are moving all my furniture down again to leave things as they were before.

Jennie looked at the wall in amazement, but I told her merrily that I did it out of pure spite at the vicious thing.

She laughed and said she wouldn't mind doing it herself, but I must not get tired.

How she betrayed herself that time!

But I am here, and no person touches this paper but Me—not *alive!*

She tried to get me out of the room—it was too patent! But I said it was so quiet and empty and clean now that I believed I would lie down again and sleep all I could, and not to wake me even for dinner—I would call when I woke.

So now she is gone, and the servants are gone, and the things are gone, and there is nothing left but that great bedstead nailed down, with the canvas mattress we found on it.

We shall sleep downstairs tonight, and take the boat home tomorrow.

I quite enjoy the room, now it is bare again.

How those children did tear about here!

This bedstead is fairly gnawed!

But I must get to work.

I have locked the door and thrown the key down into the front path.

I don't want to go out, and I don't want to have anybody come in, till John comes.

I want to astonish him.

I've got a rope up here that even Jennie did not find. If that woman does get out, and tries to get away, I can tie her!

But I forgot I could not reach far without anything to stand on!

This bed will *not* move!

I tried to lift and push it until I was lame, and then I got so angry I bit off a little piece at one corner—but it hurt my teeth.

Then I peeled off all the paper I could reach standing on the floor. It sticks horribly and the pattern just enjoys it! All those strangled heads and bulbous eyes and waddling fungus growths just shriek with derision!

I am getting angry enough to do something desperate. To jump out of the window would be admirable exercise, but the bars are too strong even to try.

Besides I wouldn't do it. Of course not. I know well enough that a step like that is improper and might be misconstrued.

I don't like to *look* out of the windows even—there are so many of those creeping women, and they creep so fast.

I wonder if they all come out of that wallpaper as I did!

But I am securely fastened now by my well-hidden rope—you don't get *me* out in the road there!

I suppose I shall have to get back behind the pattern when it comes night, and that is hard!

It is so pleasant to be out in this great room and creep around as I please!

I don't want to go outside. I won't, even if Jennie asks me to.

For outside you have to creep on the ground, and everything is green instead of yellow.

But here I can creep smoothly on the floor, and my shoulder just fits in that long smooch around the wall, so I cannot lose my way.

Why, there's John at the door!

It is no use, young man, you can't open it!

How he does call and pound!

Now he's crying to Jennie for an axe.

It would be a shame to break down that beautiful door!

"John, dear!" said I in the gentlest voice. "The key is down by the front steps, under a plantain leaf!"

That silenced him for a few moments.

Then he said, very quietly indeed, "Open the door, my darling!"

"I can't," said I. "The key is down by the front door under a plantain leaf!" And then I said it again, several times, very gently and slowly, and said it so often that he had to go and see, and he got it of course, and came in. He stopped short by the door.

"What is the matter?" he cried. "For God's sake, what are you doing!"

I kept on creeping just the same, but I looked at him over my shoulder.

"I've got out at last," said I, "in spite of you and Jane.[5] And I've pulled off most of the paper, so you can't put me back!"

Now why should that man have fainted? But he did, and right across my path by the wall, so that I had to creep over him every time!

1892

James Joyce (1882–1941)

From *A Portrait of the Artist as a Young Man*

Chapter 1

Once upon a time and a very good time it was there was a moocow coming down along the road and this moocow that was down along the road met a nicens little boy named baby tuckoo. . . .

His father told him that story: his father looked at him through a glass: he had a hairy face.

He was baby tuckoo. The moocow came down the road where Betty Byrne lived: she sold lemon platt.

> *O, the wild rose blossoms*
> *On the little green place.*

He sang that song. That was his song.

> *O, the green wothe botheth.*

When you wet the bed, first it is warm then it gets cold. His mother put on the oilsheet. That had the queer smell.

His mother had a nicer smell than his father. She played on the piano the sailor's hornpipe for him to dance. He danced:

> *Tralala lala,*
> *Tralala tralaladdy,*
> *Tralala lala,*
> *Tralala lala.*

---

[5] *Jane:* presumably the given name of her housekeeper, Jennie.

Uncle Charles and Dante clapped. They were older than his father and mother but Uncle Charles was older than Dante.

Dante had two brushes in her press. The brush with the maroon velvet back was for Michael Davitt and the brush with the green velvet back was for Parnell. Dante gave him a cachou every time he brought her a piece of tissue paper.

The Vances lived in number seven. They had a different father and mother. They were Eileen's father and mother. When they were grown up he was going to marry Eileen. He hid under the table. His mother said:

—O, Stephen will apologise.

Dante said:

—O, if not, the eagles will come and pull out his eyes—

> Pull out his eyes,
> Apologise,
> Apologise,
> Pull out his eyes.
> Apologise,
> Pull out his eyes,
> Pull out his eyes,
> Apologise.

★ ★ ★

The wide playgrounds were swarming with boys. All were shouting and the prefects urged them on with strong cries. The evening air was pale and chilly and after every charge and thud of the footballers the greasy leather orb flew like a heavy bird through the grey light. He kept on the fringe of his line, out of sight of his prefect, out of the reach of the rude feet, feigning to run now and then. He felt his body small and weak amid the throng of players and his eyes were weak and watery. Rody Kickham was not like that: he would be captain of the third line all the fellows said.

Rody Kickham was a decent fellow but Nasty Roche was a stink. Rody Kickham had greaves in his number and a hamper in the refectory. Nasty Roche had big hands. He called the Friday pudding dog-in-the-blanket. And one day he had asked:

—What is your name?

Stephen had answered: Stephen Dedalus.

Then Nasty Roche had said:

—What kind of a name is that?

And when Stephen had not been able to answer Nasty Roche had asked:

—What is your father?

Stephen had answered:

—A gentleman.

Then Nasty Roche had asked:

—Is he a magistrate?

He crept about from point to point on the fringe of his line, making little runs now and then. But his hands were bluish with cold. He kept his hands in the side pockets of his belted grey suit. That was a belt round his pocket. And belt was also to give a fellow a belt. One day a fellow had said to Cantwell:

—I'd give you such a belt in a second.

Cantwell had answered:

—Go and fight your match. Give Cecil Thunder a belt. I'd like to see you. He'd give you a toe in the rump for yourself.

That was not a nice expression. His mother had told him not to speak with the rough boys in the college. Nice mother! The first day in the hall of the castle when she had said goodbye she had put up her veil double to her nose to kiss him: and her nose and eyes were red. But he had pretended not to see that she was going to cry. She was a nice mother but she was not so nice when she cried. And his father had given him two five-shilling pieces for pocket money. And his father had told him if he wanted anything to write home to him and, whatever he did, never to peach on a fellow. Then at the door of the castle the rector had shaken hands with his father and mother, his soutane fluttering in the breeze, and the car had driven off with his father and mother on it. They had cried to him from the car, waving their hands:

—Good-bye, Stephen, goodbye!

—Good-bye, Stephen, goodbye!

He was caught in the whirl of a scrimmage and, fearful of the flashing eyes and muddy boots, bent down to look through the legs. The fellows were struggling and groaning and their legs were rubbing and kicking and stamping. Then Jack Lawton's yellow boots dodged out the ball and all the other boots and legs ran after. He ran after them a little way and then stopped. It was useless to run on. Soon they would be going home for the holidays. After supper in the study hall he would change the number pasted up inside his desk from seventy-seven to seventy-six.

It would be better to be in the study hall than out there in the cold. The sky was pale and cold but there were lights in the castle. He wondered from which window Hamilton Rowan had thrown his hat on the haha and had there been flowerbeds at that time under the windows. One day when he had been called to the castle the butler had shown him the marks of the soldiers' slugs in the wood of the door and had given him a piece of shortbread that the community ate. It was nice and warm to see the lights in the castle. It was like something in a book. Perhaps Leicester Abbey was like that. And there were nice sentences in Doctor Cornwell's Spelling Book. They were like poetry but they were only sentences to learn the spelling from.

> *Wolsey died in Leicester Abbey*
> *Where the abbots buried him.*
> *Canker is a disease of plants,*
> *Cancer one of animals.*

It would be nice to lie on the hearthrug before the fire, leaning his head upon his hands, and think on those sentences. He shivered as if he had cold slimy water next his skin. That was mean of Wells to shoulder him into the square ditch because he would not swop his little snuffbox for Wells's seasoned hacking chestnut, the conqueror of forty. How cold and slimy the water had been! A fellow had once seen a big rat jump into the scum. Mother was sitting at the fire with Dante waiting for Brigid to bring in the tea. She had her feet on the fender and her jewelly slippers were so hot and they had such a lovely warm smell! Dante knew a lot of things. She had taught him where the Mozambique Channel was and what was the longest river in America and what was the name of the highest mountain in the moon. Father Arnall knew more than Dante because he was a priest but both his father and Uncle Charles said that Dante was a clever woman and a wellread woman. And when Dante made that noise after dinner and then put up her hand to her mouth: that was heartburn.

A voice cried far out on the playground:

—All in!

Then other voices cried from the lower and third lines:

—All in! All in!

The players closed around, flushed and muddy, and he went among them, glad to go in. Rody Kickham held the ball by its greasy lace. A fellow asked him to give it one last: but he walked on without even answering the fellow. Simon Moonan told him not to because the prefect was looking. The fellow turned to Simon Moonan and said:

—We all know why you speak. You are McGlade's suck.

Suck was a queer word. The fellow called Simon Moonan that name because Simon Moonan used to tie the prefect's false sleeves behind his back and the prefect used to let on to be angry. But the sound was ugly. Once he had washed his hands in the lavatory of the Wicklow Hotel and his father pulled the stopper up by the chain after and the dirty water went down through the hole in the basin. And when it had all gone down slowly the hole in the basin had made a sound like that: suck. Only louder.

To remember that and the white look of the lavatory made him feel cold and then hot. There were two cocks that you turned and water came out: cold and hot. He felt cold and then a little hot: and he could see the names printed on the cocks. That was a very queer thing.

And the air in the corridor chilled him too. It was queer and wettish. But soon the gas would be lit and in burning it made a light noise like a little song. Always the same; and when the fellows stopped talking in the playroom you could hear it.

It was the hour for sums. Father Arnall wrote a hard sum on the board and then said:

—Now then, who will win? Go ahead, York! Go ahead, Lancaster!

Stephen tried his best but the sum was too hard and he felt confused. The little silk badge with the white rose on it that was pinned on the breast of his jacket began to flutter. He was no good at sums but he tried his best so that York might not lose. Father Arnall's face looked very black but he was not in a wax: he was laughing. Then Jack Lawton cracked his fingers and Father Arnall looked at his copybook and said:

—Right. Bravo Lancaster! The red rose wins. Come on now, York! Forge ahead!

Jack Lawton looked over from his side. The little silk badge with the red rose on it looked very rich because he had a blue sailor top on. Stephen felt his own face red too, thinking of all the bets about who would get first place in Elements, Jack Lawton or he. Some weeks Jack Lawton got the card for first and some weeks he got the card for first. His white silk badge fluttered and fluttered as he worked at the next sum and heard Father Arnall's voice. Then all his eagerness passed away and he felt his face quite cool. He thought his face must be white because it felt so cool. He could not get out the answer for the sum but it did not matter. White roses and red roses: those were beautiful colours to think of. And the cards for first place and third place were beautiful colours too: pink and cream and lavender. Lavender and cream and pink roses were beautiful to think of. Perhaps a wild rose might be like those colours and he remembered the song about the wild rose blossoms on the little green place. But you could not have a green rose. But perhaps somewhere in the world you could.

The bell rang and then the classes began to file out of the rooms and along the corridors towards the refectory. He sat looking at the two prints of butter on his plate but could not eat the damp bread. The tablecloth was damp and limp. But he drank off the hot weak tea which the clumsy scullion, girt with a white apron, poured into his cup. He wondered whether the scullion's apron was damp too or whether all white things were cold and damp. Nasty Roche and Saurin drank cocoa that their people sent them in tins. They said they could not drink the tea; that it was hogwash. Their fathers were magistrates, the fellows said.

All the boys seemed to him very strange. They had all fathers and mothers and different clothes and voices. He longed to be at home and lay his head on his mother's lap. But he could not: and so he longed for the play and study and prayers to be over and to be in bed.

He drank another cup of hot tea and Fleming said:

—What's up? Have you a pain or what's up with you?

—I don't know, Stephen said.

—Sick in your bread basket, Fleming said, because your face looks white. It will go away.

—O yes, Stephen said.

But he was not sick there. He thought that he was sick in his heart if you could be sick in that place. Fleming was very decent to ask him. He wanted to cry. He leaned his elbows on the table and shut and opened the flaps of his ears. Then he heard the noise of the refectory every time he opened the flaps of his ears. It made a roar like a train at night. And when he closed the flaps the roar was shut off like a train going into a tunnel. That night at Dalkey the train had roared like that and then, when it went into the tunnel, the roar stopped. He closed his eyes and the train went on, roaring and then stopping; roaring again, stopping. It was nice to hear it roar and stop and then roar out of the tunnel again and then stop.

Then the higher line fellows began to come down along the matting in the middle of the refectory, Paddy Rath and Jimmy Magee and the Spaniard who was allowed to smoke cigars and the little Portuguese who wore the woolly cap. And then the lower line tables and the tables of the third line. And every single fellow had a different way of walking.

He sat in a corner of the playroom pretending to watch a game of dominos and once or twice he was able to hear for an instant the little song of the gas. The prefect was at the door with some boys and Simon Moonan was knotting his false sleeves. He was telling them something about Tullabeg.

Then he went away from the door and Wells came over to Stephen and said:

—Tell us, Dedalus, do you kiss your mother before you go to bed?

Stephen answered:

—I do.

Wells turned to the other fellows and said:

—O, I say, here's a fellow says he kisses his mother every night before he goes to bed.

The other fellows stopped their game and turned round, laughing. Stephen blushed under their eyes and said:

—I do not.

Wells said:

—O, I say, here's a fellow says he doesn't kiss his mother before he goes to bed.

They all laughed again. Stephen tried to laugh with them. He felt his whole body hot and confused in a moment. What was the right answer to the question? He had given two and still Wells laughed. But Wells must know the right answer for he was in third of grammar. He tried to think of Wells's mother but he did not dare to raise his eyes to Wells's face. He did not like Wells's face. It was Wells who had shouldered him into the square ditch the day before because he would not swop his little snuffbox for Wells's seasoned hacking chestnut, the conqueror of forty. It was a mean thing to do; all the fellows said it was. And how cold and slimy the water had been! And a fellow had once seen a big rat jump plop into the scum.

The cold slime of the ditch covered his whole body; and, when the bell rang for study and the lines filed out of the playrooms, he felt the cold air of the corridor and staircase inside his clothes. He still tried to think what was the right answer. Was it right to kiss his mother or wrong to kiss his mother? What did that mean, to kiss? You put your face up like that to say goodnight and then his mother put her face down. That was to kiss. His mother put her lips on his cheek; her lips were soft and they wetted his cheek; and they made a tiny little noise: kiss. Why did people do that with their two faces?

Sitting in the study hall he opened the lid of his desk and changed the number pasted up inside from seventy-seven to seventy-six. But the

Christmas vacation was very far away: but one time it would come because the earth moved round always.

There was a picture of the earth on the first page of his geography: a big ball in the middle of clouds. Fleming had a box of crayons and one night during free study he had coloured the earth green and the clouds maroon. That was like the two brushes in Dante's press, the brush with the green velvet back for Parnell and the brush with the maroon velvet back for Michael Davitt. But he had not told Fleming to colour them those colours. Fleming had done it himself.

He opened the geography to study the lesson; but he could not learn the names of places in America. Still they were all different places that had different names. They were all in different countries and the countries were in continents and the continents were in the world and the world was in the universe.

He turned to the flyleaf of the geography and read what he had written there: himself, his name and where he was.

> *Stephen Dedalus*
> *Class of Elements*
> *Clongowes Wood College*
> *Sallins*
> *County Kildare*
> *Ireland*
> *Europe*
> *The World*
> *The Universe*

That was in his writing: and Fleming one night for a cod had written on the opposite page:

> *Stephen Dedalus is my name,*
> *Ireland is my nation.*
> *Clongowes is my dwellingplace*
> *And heaven my expectation.*

He read the verses backwards but then they were not poetry. Then he read the flyleaf from the bottom to the top till he came to his own name. That was he: and he read down the page again. What was after the universe? Nothing. But was there anything round the universe to show where it stopped before the nothing place began? It could not be a wall but there could be a thin thin line there all round everything. It was very big to think about everything and everywhere. Only God could do that. He tried to think what a big thought that must be but he could think only of God. God was God's name just as his name was Stephen. *Dieu* was the French for God and that was God's name too; and when anyone prayed to God and said *Dieu* then God knew at once that it was a French person that was praying. But though there were different names for God in all the different languages in the world and God understood what all the people who prayed said in their different languages still God remained always the same God and God's real name was God.

1941

Jamaica Kincaid (B. 1949)

Girl

Wash the white clothes on Monday and put them on the stone heap; wash the color clothes on Tuesday and put them on the clothes-line to dry; don't walk barehead in the hot sun; cook pumpkin fritters in very hot sweet oil; soak your little cloths right after you take them off; when buying cotton to make yourself a nice blouse, be sure that it doesn't have gum on it, because that way it won't hold up well after a wash; soak salt fish overnight before you cook it; is it true that you sing benna[1] in Sunday school?; always eat your food in such a way that it won't turn someone else's stomach; on Sundays try to walk like a lady and not like the slut you are so bent on becoming; don't sing benna in Sunday school; you mustn't speak to wharf-rat boys, not even to give directions; don't eat fruits on the street—flies will follow you; *but I don't sing benna on Sundays at all and never in Sunday school;* this is how to sew on a button; this is how to make a buttonhole for the button you have just sewed on; this is how to hem a dress when you see the hem coming down and so to prevent yourself from looking like the slut I know you are so bent on becoming; this is how you iron your father's khaki shirt so that it doesn't have a crease; this is how you iron your father's khaki pants so that they don't have a crease; this is how you grow okra—far from the house, because okra tree harbors red ants; when you are growing dasheen, make sure it gets plenty of water or else it makes your throat itch when you are eating it; this is how you sweep a corner; this is how you sweep a whole house; this is how you sweep a yard; this is how you smile to someone you don't like too much; this is how you smile to someone you don't like at all; this is how you smile to someone you like completely; this is how you set a table for tea; this is how you set a table for dinner; this is how you set a table for dinner with an important guest; this is how you set a table for lunch; this is how you set a table for breakfast; this is how to behave in the presence of men who don't know you very well, and this way they won't recognize immediately the slut I have warned you against becoming; be sure to wash

---

[1]*Benna:* Kincaid defined this word, for two editors who inquired, as meaning "songs of the sort your parents didn't want you to sing, at first calypso and later rock and roll" (quoted by Sylvan Barnet and Marcia Stubbs, *The Little Brown Reader*, 2nd ed. Boston: Little Brown, 1980, p. 74).

every day, even if it is with your own spit; don't squat down to play mar-
bles—you are not a boy, you know; don't pick people's flowers—you might
catch something; don't throw stones at blackbirds, because it might not be
a blackbird at all; this is how to make a bread pudding; this is how to make
doukona; this is how to make pepper pot; this is how to make a good medicine for a cold; this is how to make a good medicine to throw away a child
before it even becomes a child; this is how to catch a fish; this is how to throw
back a fish you don't like, and that way something bad won't fall on you; this
is how to bully a man; this is how a man bullies you; this is how to love a
man, and if this doesn't work there are other ways, and if they don't work
don't feel too bad about giving up; this is how to spit up in the air if you
feel like it, and this is how to move quick so that it doesn't fall on you; this
is how to make ends meet; always squeeze bread to make sure it's fresh;
but what if the baker won't let me feel the bread?; you mean to say that after
all you are really going to be the kind of woman who the baker won't let near
the bread?

1983

Ursula K. Le Guin (B. 1929)

The Wife's Story

He was a good husband, a good father. I don't understand it. I don't believe
in it. I don't believe that it happened. I saw it happen but it isn't true. It
can't be. He was always gentle. If you'd have seen him playing with the children, anybody who saw him with the children would have known that there
wasn't any bad in him, not one mean bone. When I first met him he was
still living with his mother, over near Spring Lake, and I used to see them
together, the mother and the sons, and think that any young fellow that was
that nice with his family must be one worth knowing. Then one time when
I was walking in the woods I met him by himself coming back from a hunting trip. He hadn't got any game at all, not so much as a field mouse, but
he wasn't cast down about it. He was just larking along enjoying the morning air. That's one of the things I first loved about him. He didn't take things
hard, he didn't grouch and whine when things didn't go his way. So we
got to talking that day. And I guess things moved right along after that,
because pretty soon he was over here pretty near all the time. And my sister said—see, my parents had moved out the year before and gone south,
leaving us the place—my sister said, kind of teasing but serious, "Well! If
he's going to be here every day and half the night, I guess there isn't room
for me!" And she moved out—just down the way. We've always been real
close, her and me. That's the sort of thing doesn't ever change. I couldn't
ever have got through this bad time without my sis.

Well, so he come to live here. And all I can say is, it was the happy year of my life. He was just purely good to me. A hard worker and never lazy, and so big and fine-looking. Everybody looked up to him, you know, young as he was. Lodge Meeting nights, more and more often they had him to lead the singing. He had such a beautiful voice, and he'd lead off strong, and the others following and joining in, high voices and low. It brings the shivers on me now to think of it, hearing it, nights when I'd stayed home from meeting when the children was babies—the singing coming up through the trees there, and the moonlight, summer nights, the full moon shining. I'll never hear anything so beautiful. I'll never know a joy like that again.

It was the moon, that's what they say. It's the moon's fault, and the blood. It was in his father's blood. I never knew his father, and now I wonder what become of him. He was from up Whitewater way, and had no kin around here. I always thought he went back there, but now I don't know. There was some talk about him, tales, that come out after what happened to my husband. It's something runs in the blood, they say, and it may never come out, but if it does, it's the change of the moon that does it. Always it happens in the dark of the moon. When everybody's home and asleep. Something comes over the one that's got the curse in his blood, they say, and he gets up because he can't sleep, and goes out into the glaring sun, and goes off all alone—drawn to find those like him.

And it may be so, because my husband would do that. I'd half rouse and say, "Where you going to?" and he'd say, "Oh, hunting, be back this evening," and it wasn't like him, even his voice was different. But I'd be so sleepy, and not wanting to wake the kids, and he was so good and responsible, it was no call of mine to go asking "Why?" and "Where?" and all like that.

So it happened that way maybe three times or four. He'd come back late, and worn out, and pretty near cross for one so sweet-tempered—not wanting to talk about it. I figured everybody got to bust out now and then, and nagging never helped anything. But it did begin to worry me. Not so much that he went, but that he come back so tired and strange. Even, he smelled strange. It made my hair stand up on end. I could not endure it and I said, "What is that—those smells on you? All over you!" And he said, "I don't know," real short, and made like he was sleeping. But he went down when he thought I wasn't noticing, and washed and washed himself. But those smells stayed in his hair, and in our bed, for days.

And then the awful thing. I don't find it easy to tell about this. I want to cry when I have to bring it to my mind. Our youngest, the little one, my baby, she turned from her father. Just overnight. He come in and she got scared-looking, stiff, with her eyes wide, and then she begun to cry and try to hide behind me. She didn't yet talk plain but she was saying over and over, "Make it go away! Make it go away!"

The look in his eyes, just for one moment, when he heard that. That's what I don't want ever to remember. That's what I can't forget. The look in his eyes looking at his own child.

I said to the child, "Shame on you, what's got into you!"—scolding, but keeping her right up close to me at the same time, because I was frightened too. Frightened to shaking.

He looked away then and said something like, "Guess she just waked up dreaming," and passed it off that way. Or tried to. And so did I. And I got real mad with my baby when she kept on acting crazy scared of her own dad. But she couldn't help it and I couldn't change it.

He kept away that whole day. Because he knew, I guess. It was just beginning dark of the moon.

It was hot and close inside, and dark, and we'd all been asleep some while, when something woke me up. He wasn't there beside me. I heard a little stir in the passage, when I listened. So I got up, because I could bear it no longer. I went out into the passage, and it was light there, hard sunlight coming in from the door. And I saw him standing just outside, in the tall grass by the entrance. His head was hanging. Presently he sat down, like he felt weary, and looked down at his feet. I held still, inside, and watched—I didn't know what for.

And I saw what he saw. I saw the changing. In his feet, it was, first. They got long, each foot got longer, stretching out, the toes stretching out and the foot getting long, and fleshy, and white. And no hair on them.

The hair begun to come away all over his body. It was like his hair fried away in the sunlight and was gone. He was white all over, then, like a worm's skin. And he turned his face. It was changing while I looked. It got flatter and flatter, the mouth flat and wide, and the teeth grinning flat and dull, and the nose just a knob of flesh with nostril holes, and the ears gone, and the eyes gone blue—blue, with white rims around the blue—staring at me out of that flat, soft, white face.

He stood up then on two legs.

I saw him, I had to see him, my own dear love, turned into the hateful one.

I couldn't move, but as I crouched there in the passage staring out into the day I was trembling and shaking with a growl that burst out into a crazy, awful howling. A grief howl and a terror howl and a calling howl. And the others heard it, even sleeping, and woke up.

It stared and peered, that thing my husband had turned into, and shoved its face up to the entrance of our house. I was still bound by mortal fear, but behind me the children had waked up, and the baby was whimpering. The mother anger come into me then, and I snarled and crept forward.

The man thing looked around. It had no gun, like the ones from the man places do. But it picked up a heavy fallen tree branch in its long white foot, and shoved the end of that down into our house, at me. I snapped the end of it in my teeth and started to force my way out, because I knew the man would kill our children if it could. But my sister was already coming. I saw her running at the man with her head low and her mane high and her eyes yellow as the winter sun. It turned on her and raised up that branch to hit her. But I come out of the doorway, mad with the mother anger, and the others all were coming answering my call, the whole pack gathering, there in that blind glare and heat of the sun at noon.

The man looked round at us and yelled out loud, and brandished the branch it held. Then it broke and ran, heading for the cleared fields and plowlands, down the mountainside. It ran, on two legs, leaping and weaving, and we followed it.

I was last, because love still bound the anger and the fear in me. I was running when I saw them pull it down. My sister's teeth were in its throat. I got there and it was dead. The others were drawing back from the kill, because of the taste of the blood, and the smell. The younger ones were cowering and some crying, and my sister rubbed her mouth against her forelegs over and over to get rid of the taste. I went up close because I thought if the thing was dead the spell, the curse must be done, and my husband could come back—alive, or even dead, if I could only see him, my true love, in his true form, beautiful. But only the dead man lay there white and bloody. We drew back and back from it, and turned and ran, back up into the hills, back to the woods of the shadows and the twilight and the blessed dark.

1982

Doris Lessing (B. 1919)

A Woman on a Roof

It was during the week of hot sun, that June.

Three men were at work on the roof, where the leads got so hot they had the idea of throwing water on to cool them. But the water steamed, then sizzled; and they made jokes about getting an egg from some woman in the flats under them, to poach it for their dinner. By two it was not possible to touch the guttering they were replacing, and they speculated about what workmen did in regularly hot countries. Perhaps they should borrow kitchen gloves with the egg? They were all a bit dizzy, not used to the heat; and they shed their coats and stood side by side squeezing themselves into a foot-wide patch of shade against a chimney, careful to keep their feet in the thick socks and boots out of the sun. There was a fine view across several acres of roofs. Not far off a man sat in a deck chair reading the newspapers. Then they saw her, between chimneys, about fifty yards away. She lay face down on a brown blanket. They could see the top part of her: black hair, a flushed solid back, arms spread out.

"She's stark naked," said Stanley, sounding annoyed.

Harry, the oldest, a man of about forty-five, said: "Looks like it."

Young Tom, seventeen, said nothing, but he was excited and grinning.

Stanley said: "Someone'll report her if she doesn't watch out."

"She thinks no one can see," said Tom, craning his head all ways to see more.

At this point the woman, still lying prone, brought her two hands up behind her shoulders with the ends of a scarf in them, tied it behind her back, and sat up. She wore a red scarf tied around her breasts and brief red bikini pants. This being the first day of the sun she was white, flushing red. She sat smoking, and did not look up when Stanley let out a wolf whistle. Harry said: "Small things amuse small minds," leading the way back to their part of the roof, but it was scorching. Harry said: "Wait, I'm going to rig up some shade," and disappeared down the skylight into the building. Now that he'd gone, Stanley and Tom went to the farthest point they could to peer at the woman. She had moved, and all they could see were two pink legs stretched on the blanket. They whistled and shouted but the legs did not move. Harry came back with a blanket and shouted: "Come on, then." He sounded irritated with them. They clambered back to him and he said to Stanley: "What about your missus?" Stanley was newly married, about three months. Stanley said, jeering: "What about my missus?"— preserving his independence. Tom said nothing, but his mind was full of the nearly naked woman. Harry slung the blanket, which he had borrowed from a friendly woman downstairs, from the stem of a television aerial to a row of chimney-pots.[1] This shade fell across the piece of gutter they had to replace. But the shade kept moving, they had to adjust the blanket, and not much progress was made. At last some of the heat left the roof, and they worked fast, making up for lost time. First Stanley, then Tom, made a trip to the end of the roof to see the woman. "She's on her back," Stanley said, adding a jest which made Tom snicker, and the older man smile tolerantly. Tom's report was that she hadn't moved, but it was a lie. He wanted to keep what he had seen to himself: he had caught her in the act of rolling down the little red pants over her hips, till they were no more than a small triangle. She was on her back, fully visible, glistening with oil.

Next morning, as soon as they came up, they went to look. She was already there, face down, arms spread out, naked except for the little red pants. She had turned brown in the night. Yesterday she was a scarlet-and-white woman, today she was a brown woman. Stanley let out a whistle. She lifted her head, startled, as if she'd been asleep, and looked straight over at him. The sun was in her eyes, she blinked and stared, then she dropped her head again. At this gesture of indifference, they all three, Stanley, Tom and old Harry, let out whistles and yells. Harry was doing it in parody of the younger men, making fun of them, but he was also angry. They were all angry because of her utter indifference to the three men watching her.

"Bitch," said Stanley.

"She should ask us over," said Tom, snickering.

---

[1]*Chimney-pots:* the pipe, usually of earthenware or metal, fitted on a roof to the top of a chimney.

Harry recovered himself and reminded Stanley: "If she's married, her old man wouldn't like that."

"Christ," said Stanley virtuously, "if my wife lay about like that, for everyone to see, I'd soon stop her."

Harry said, smiling: "How do you know, perhaps she's sunning herself at this very moment?"

"Not a chance, not on our roof." The safety of his wife put Stanley into a good humor, and they went to work. But today it was hotter than yesterday; and several times one or the other suggested they should tell Matthew, the foreman, and ask to leave the roof until the heat wave was over. But they didn't. There was work to be done in the basement of the big block of flats, but up here they felt free, on a different level from ordinary humanity shut in the streets or the buildings. A lot more people came out on to the roofs that day, for an hour at midday. Some married couples sat side by side in deck chairs, the women's legs stockingless and scarlet, the men in vests with reddening shoulders.

The woman stayed on her blanket, turning herself over and over. She ignored them, no matter what they did. When Harry went off to fetch more screws, Stanley said: "Come on." Her roof belonged to a different system of roofs, separated from theirs at one point by about twenty feet. It meant a scrambling climb from one level to another, edging along parapets,[2] clinging to chimneys, while their big boots slipped and slithered, but at last they stood on a small square projecting roof looking straight down at her, close. She sat smoking, reading a book. Tom thought she looked like a poster, or a magazine cover, with the blue sky behind her and her legs stretched out. Behind her a great crane at work on a new building in Oxford Street[3] swung its black arm across roofs in a great arc. Tom imagined himself at work on the crane, adjusting the arm to swing over and pick her up and swing her back across the sky to drop her near him.

They whistled. She looked up at them, cool and remote, then went on reading. Again, they were furious. Or, rather, Stanley was. His sun-heated face was screwed into a rage as he whistled again and again, trying to make her look up. Young Tom stopped whistling. He stood beside Stanley, excited, grinning; but he felt as if he were saying to the woman: Don't associate me with *him*, for his grin was apologetic. Last night he had thought of the unknown woman before he slept, and she had been tender with him. This tenderness he was remembering as he shifted his feet by the jeering, whistling Stanley, and watched the indifferent, healthy brown woman a few feet off, with the gap that plunged to the street between them. Tom thought it was romantic, it was like being high on two hilltops. But there was a shout from Harry, and they clambered back. Stanley's face was hard, really angry. The boy kept looking at him and wondered why he hated the woman so much, for by now he loved her.

---

[2]*Parapets:* generally a rampart, in this case, the low railing around the edge of a roof.
[3]*Oxford Street:* busy shopping street in central London.

They played their little games with the blanket, trying to trap shade to work under; but again it was not until nearly four that they could work seriously, and they were exhausted, all three of them. They were grumbling about the weather by now. Stanley was in a thoroughly bad humor. When they made their routine trip to see the woman before they packed up for the day, she was apparently asleep, face down, her back all naked save for the scarlet triangle on her buttocks. "I've got a good mind to report her to the police," said Stanley, and Harry said: "What's eating you? What harm's she doing?"

"I tell you, if she was my wife!"

"But she isn't, is she?" Tom knew that Harry, like himself, was uneasy at Stanley's reaction. He was normally a sharp young man, quick at his work, making a lot of jokes, good company.

"Perhaps it will be cooler tomorrow," said Harry.

But it wasn't; it was hotter, if anything, and the weather forecast said the good weather would last. As soon as they were on the roof, Harry went over to see if the woman was there, and Tom knew it was to prevent Stanley going, to put off his bad humor. Harry had grownup children, a boy the same age as Tom, and the youth trusted and looked up to him.

Harry came back and said: "She's not there."

"I bet her old man has put his foot down," said Stanley, and Harry and Tom caught each other's eyes and smiled behind the young married man's back.

Harry suggested they should get permission to work in the basement, and they did, that day. But before packing up Stanley said: "Let's have a breath of fresh air." Again Harry and Tom smiled at each other as they followed Stanley up to the roof, Tom in the devout conviction that he was there to protect the woman from Stanley. It was about five-thirty, and a calm, full sunlight lay over the roofs. The great crane still swung its black arm from Oxford Street to above their heads. She was not there. Then there was a flutter of white from behind a parapet, and she stood up, in a belted, white dressing gown. She had been there all day, probably, but on a different patch of roof, to hide from them. Stanley did not whistle; he said nothing, but watched the woman bend to collect papers, books, cigarettes, then fold the blanket over her arm. Tom was thinking: If they weren't here, I'd go over and say . . . what? But he knew from his nightly dreams of her that she was kind and friendly. Perhaps she would ask him down to her flat? Perhaps . . . He stood watching her disappear down the skylight. As she went, Stanley let out a shrill derisive yell; she started, and it seemed as if she nearly fell. She clutched to save herself, they could hear things falling. She looked straight at them, angry. Harry said, facetiously: "Better be careful on those slippery ladders, love." Tom knew he said it to save her from Stanley, but she could not know it. She vanished, frowning. Tom was full of a secret delight, because he knew her anger was for the others, not for him.

"Roll on some rain," said Stanley, bitter, looking at the blue evening sky.

Next day was cloudless, and they decided to finish the work in the basement. They felt excluded, shut in the gray cement basement fitting pipes, from the holiday atmosphere in London in a heat wave. At lunchtime they came up for some air, but while the married couples, and the men in shirt-sleeves or vests, were there, she was not there, either on her usual patch of roof or where she had been yesterday. They all, even Harry, clambered about, between chimney-pots, over parapets, the hot leads stinging their fingers. There was not a sign of her. They took off their shirts and vests and exposed their chests, feeling their feet sweaty and hot. They did not mention the woman. But Tom felt alone again. Last night she had him into her flat: it was big and had fitted white carpets and a bed with a padded white leather headboard. She wore a black filmy negligée and her kindness to Tom thickened his throat as he remembered it. He felt she had betrayed him by not being there.

And again after work they climbed up, but still there was nothing to be seen of her. Stanley kept repeating that if it was as hot as this tomorrow he wasn't going to work and that's all there was to it. But they were all there next day. By ten the temperature was in the middle seventies, and it was eighty long before noon. Harry went to the foreman to say it was impossible to work on the leads in that heat; but the foreman said there was nothing else he could put them on, and they'd have to. At midday they stood, silent, watching the skylight on her roof open, and then she slowly emerged in her white gown, holding a bundle of blanket. She looked at them, gravely, then went to the part of the roof where she was hidden from them. Tom was pleased. He felt she was more his when the other men couldn't see her. They had taken off their shirts and vests, but now they put them back again, for they felt the sun bruising their flesh. "She must have the hide of a rhino," said Stanley, tugging at guttering and swearing. They stopped work, and sat in the shade, moving around behind chimney stacks. A woman came to water a yellow window box opposite them. She was middle-aged, wearing a flowered summer dress. Stanley said to her: "We need a drink more than them." She smiled and said: "Better drop down to the pub quick, it'll be closing in a minute." They exchanged pleasantries, and she left them with a smile and a wave.

"Not like Lady Godiva,"[4] said Stanley. "She can give us a bit of a chat and a smile."

"You didn't whistle at *her*," said Tom, reproving.

"Listen to him," said Stanley, "you didn't whistle, then?"

But the boy felt as if he hadn't whistled, as if only Harry and Stanley had. He was making plans, when it was time to knock off work, to get left behind and somehow make his way over to the woman. The weather report said the hot spell was due to break, so he had to move quickly. But there was no chance of being left.

---

[4]*Lady Godiva:* the eleventh-century noblewoman who rode naked through the streets of Coventry, England, to save the common people from crippling taxes. Out of respect the townspeople did not look at her, except for one young man named Tom, who legend claims was struck blind. Posterity remembers him as "Peeping Tom."

The other two decided to knock off work at four, because they were exhausted. As they went down, Tom quickly climbed a parapet and hoisted himself higher by pulling his weight up a chimney. He caught a glimpse of her lying on her back, her knees up, eyes closed, a brown woman lolling in the sun. He slipped and clattered down, as Stanley looked for information: "She's gone down," he said. He felt as if he had protected her from Stanley, and that she must be grateful to him. He could feel the bond between the woman and himself.

Next day, they stood around on the landing below the roof, reluctant to climb up into the heat. The woman who had lent Harry the blanket came out and offered them a cup of tea. They accepted gratefully, and sat around Mrs. Pritchett's kitchen an hour or so, chatting. She was married to an airline pilot. A smart blonde, of about thirty, she had an eye for the handsome sharp-eyed Stanley; and the two teased each other while Harry sat in a corner, watching, indulgent, though his expression reminded Stanley that he was married. And young Tom felt envious of Stanley's ease in badinage;[5] felt, too, that Stanley's getting off with Mrs. Pritchett left his romance with the woman on the roof safe and intact.

"I thought they said the heat wave'd break," said Stanley, sullen, as the time approached when they really would have to climb up into the sunlight.

"You don't like it, then?" asked Mrs. Pritchett.

"All right for some," said Stanley. "Nothing to do but lie about as if it was a beach up there. Do you ever go up?"

"Went up once," said Mrs. Pritchett. "But it's a dirty place up there, and it's too hot."

"Quite right too," said Stanley.

Then they went up, leaving the cool near little flat and the friendly Mrs. Pritchett.

As soon as they were up they saw her. The three men looked at her, resentful at her ease in this punishing sun. Then Harry said, because of the expression on Stanley's face: "Come on, we've got to pretend to work, at least."

They had to wrench another length of guttering that ran beside a parapet out of its bed, so that they could replace it. Stanley took it in his two hands, tugged, swore, stood up. "Fuck it," he said, and sat down under a chimney. He lit a cigarette. "Fuck them," he said. "What do they think we are, lizards? I've got blisters all over my hands." Then he jumped up and climbed over the roofs and stood with his back to them. He put his fingers either side of his mouth and let out a shrill whistle. Tom and Harry squatted, not looking at each other, watching him. They could just see the woman's head, the beginnings of her brown shoulders. Stanley whistled again. Then he began stamping with his feet, and whistled and yelled and screamed at the woman, his face getting scarlet. He seemed

---

[5]*Badinage:* (French) teasing, playful conversation.

quite mad, as he stamped and whistled, while the woman did not move, she did not move a muscle.

"Barmy," said Tom.

"Yes," said Harry, disapproving.

Suddenly the older man came to a decision. It was, Tom knew, to save some sort of scandal or real trouble over the woman. Harry stood up and began packing tools into a length of oily cloth. "Stanley," he said, commanding. At first Stanley took no notice, but Harry said: "Stanley, we're packing it in, I'll tell Matthew."

Stanley came back, cheeks mottled, eyes glaring.

"Can't go on like this," said Harry. "It'll break in a day or so. I'm going to tell Matthew we've got sunstroke, and if he doesn't like it, it's too bad." Even Harry sounded aggrieved, Tom noted. The small, competent man, the family man with his gray hair, who was never at a loss, sounded really off balance. "Come on," he said, angry. He fitted himself into the open square in the roof, and went down, watching his feet on the ladder. Then Stanley went, with not a glance at the woman. Then Tom, who, his throat beating with excitement, silently promised her on a backward glance: Wait for me, wait, I'm coming.

On the pavement Stanley said: "I'm going home." He looked white now, so perhaps he really did have sunstroke. Harry went off to find the foreman who was at work on the plumbing of some flats down the street. Tom slipped back, not into the building they had been working on, but the building on whose roof the woman lay. He went straight up, no one stopping him. The skylight stood open, with an iron ladder leading up. He emerged on to the roof a couple of yards from her. She sat up, pushing back her black hair with both hands. The scarf across her breasts bound them tight, and brown flesh bulged around it. Her legs were brown and smooth. She stared at him in silence. The boy stood grinning, foolish, claiming the tenderness he expected from her.

"What do you want?" she asked.

"I . . . I came to . . . make your acquaintance," he stammered, grinning, pleading with her.

They looked at each other, the slight, scarlet-faced excited boy, and the serious, nearly naked woman. Then, without a word, she lay down on her brown blanket, ignoring him.

"You like the sun, do you?" he enquired of her glistening back.

Not a word. He felt panic, thinking of how she had held him in her arms, stroked his hair, brought him where he sat, lordly, in her bed, a glass of some exhilarating liquor he had never tasted in life. He felt that if he knelt down, stroked her shoulders, her hair, she would turn and clasp him in her arms.

He said: "The sun's all right for you, isn't it?"

She raised her head, set her chin on two small fists: "Go away," she said. He did not move. "Listen," she said, in a slow reasonable voice, where anger was kept in check, though with difficulty; looking at him, her face weary with anger, "if you get a kick out of seeing women in bikinis, why don't you take a sixpenny bus ride to the Lido?[6] You'd see dozens of them, without all this mountaineering."

She hadn't understood him. He felt her unfairness pale him. He stammered: "But I like you, I've been watching you and . . . "

"Thanks," she said, and dropped her face again, turned away from him.

She lay there. He stood there. She said nothing. She had simply shut him out. He stood, saying nothing at all, for some minutes. He thought: She'll have to say something if I stay. But the minutes went past, with no sign of them in her, except in the tension of her back, her thighs, her arms— the tension of waiting for him to go.

He looked up at the sky, where the sun seemed to spin in heat; and over the roofs where he and his mates had been earlier. He could see the heat quivering where they had worked. And they expect us to work in these conditions! he thought, filled with righteous indignation. The woman hadn't moved. A bit of hot wind blew her black hair softly; it shone, and was iridescent. He remembered how he had stroked it last night.

Resentment of her at last moved him off and away down the ladder, through the building, into the street. He got drunk then, in hatred of her.

Next day when he woke the sky was gray. He looked at the wet gray and thought, vicious: Well, that's fixed you, hasn't it now? That's fixed you good and proper.

The three men were at work early on the cool leads, surrounded by damp drizzling roofs where no one came to sun themselves, black roofs, slimy with rain. Because it was cool now, they would finish the job that day, if they hurried.

1963

Alice Munro (B. 1931)

How I Met My Husband

We heard the plane come over at noon, roaring through the radio news, and we were sure it was going to hit the house, so we all ran out into the yard. We saw it come in over the treetops, all red and silver, the first close-up plane I ever saw. Mrs. Peebles screamed.

"Crash landing," their little boy said. Joey was his name.

"It's okay," said Dr. Peebles. "He knows what he's doing." Dr. Peebles was only an animal doctor, but had a calming way of talking, like any doctor.

---

[6]*Lido:* an outdoor swimming spot with sunbathing facilities in London's Hyde Park.

This was my first job—working for Dr. and Mrs. Peebles, who had bought an old house out on the Fifth Line, about five miles out of town. It was just when the trend was starting of town people buying up old farms, not to work them but to live on them.

We watched the plane land across the road, where the fairgrounds used to be. It did make a good landing field, nice and level for the old race track, and the barns and display sheds torn down now for scrap lumber so there was nothing in the way. Even the old grandstand bays had burned.

"All right," said Mrs. Peebles, snappy as she always was when she got over her nerves. "Let's go back in the house. Let's not stand here gawking like a set of farmers."

She didn't say that to hurt my feelings. It never occurred to her.

I was just setting the dessert down when Loretta Bird arrived, out of breath, at the screen door.

"I thought it was going to crash into the house and kill youse all!"

She lived on the next place and the Peebleses thought she was a country-woman, they didn't know the difference. She and her husband didn't farm, he worked on the roads and had a bad name for drinking. They had seven children and couldn't get credit at the HiWay Grocery. The Peebleses made her welcome, not knowing any better, as I say, and offered her dessert.

Dessert was never anything to write home about, at their place. A dish of Jell-O or sliced bananas or fruit out of a tin. "Have a house without a pie, be ashamed until you die," my mother used to say, but Mrs. Peebles operated differently.

Loretta Bird saw me getting the can of peaches.

"Oh, never mind," she said. "I haven't got the right kind of a stomach to trust what comes out of those tins, I can only eat home canning."

I could have slapped her. I bet she never put down fruit in her life.

"I know what he's landed here for," she said. "He's got permission to use the fairgrounds and take people up for rides. It costs a dollar. It's the same fellow who was over at Palmerston[1] last week and was up the lakeshore before that. I wouldn't go up, if you paid me."

"I'd jump at the chance," Dr. Peebles said. "I'd like to see this neighborhood from the air."

Mrs. Peebles said she would just as soon see it from the ground. Joey said he wanted to go and Heather did, too. Joey was nine and Heather was seven.

"Would you, Edie?" Heather said.

I said I didn't know. I was scared, but I never admitted that, especially in front of children I was taking care of.

"People are going to be coming out here in their cars raising dust and trampling your property, if I was you I would complain," Loretta said. She hooked her legs around the chair rung and I knew we were in for a lengthy

---

[1]*Palmerston:* a town in southern Ontario, Canada.

visit. After Dr. Peebles went back to his office or out on his next call and Mrs. Peebles went for her nap, she would hang around me while I was trying to do the dishes. She would pass remarks about the Peebleses in their own house.

"She wouldn't find time to lay down in the middle of the day, if she had seven kids like I got."

She asked me did they fight and did they keep things in the dresser drawer not to have babies with. She said it was a sin if they did. I pretended I didn't know what she was talking about.

I was fifteen and away from home for the first time. My parents had made the effort and sent me to high school for a year, but I didn't like it. I was shy of strangers and the work was hard, they didn't make it nice for you or explain the way they do now. At the end of the year the averages were published in the paper, and mine came out at the very bottom, 37 percent. My father said that's enough and I didn't blame him. The last thing I wanted, anyway, was to go on and end up teaching school. It happened the very day the paper came out with my disgrace in it, Dr. Peebles was staying at our place for dinner, having just helped one of the cows have twins, and he said I looked smart to him and his wife was looking for a girl to help. He said she felt tied down, with the two children, out in the country. I guess she would, my mother said, being polite, though I could tell from her face she was wondering what on earth it would be like to have only two children and no barn work, and then to be complaining.

When I went home I would describe to them the work I had to do, and it made everybody laugh. Mrs. Peebles had an automatic washer and dryer, the first I ever saw. I have had those in my own home for such a long time now it's hard to remember how much of a miracle it was to me, not having to struggle with the wringer and hang up and haul down. Let alone not having to heat water. Then there was practically no baking. Mrs. Peebles said she couldn't make pie crust, the most amazing thing I ever heard a woman admit. I could, of course, and I could make light biscuits and a white cake and dark cake, but they didn't want it, she said they watched their figures. The only thing I didn't like about working there, in fact, was feeling half hungry a lot of the time. I used to bring back a box of doughnuts made out at home, and hide them under my bed. The children found out, and I didn't mind sharing, but I thought I better bind them to secrecy.

The day after the plane landed Mrs. Peebles put both children in the car and drove over to Chesley, to get their hair cut. There was a good woman then at Chesley for doing hair. She got hers done at the same place, Mrs. Peebles did, and that meant they would be gone a good while. She had to pick a day Dr. Peebles wasn't going out into the country, she didn't have her own car. Cars were still in short supply then, after the war.

I loved being left in the house alone, to do my work at leisure. The kitchen was all white and bright yellow, with fluorescent lights. That was before they ever thought of making the appliances all different colors and doing the cupboards like dark old wood and hiding the lighting. I loved light. I loved the double sink. So would anybody new-come from washing dishes in a dishpan with a rag-plugged hole on an oilcloth-covered table by light of a coal-oil lamp. I kept everything shining.

The bathroom too. I had a bath in there once a week. They wouldn't have minded if I took one oftener, but to me it seemed like asking too much, or maybe risking making it less wonderful. The basin and the tub and the toilet were all pink, and there were glass doors with flamingoes painted on them, to shut off the tub. The light had a rosy cast and the mat sank under your feet like snow, except that it was warm. The mirror was three-way. With the mirror all steamed up and the air like a perfume cloud, from things I was allowed to use, I stood up on the side of the tub and admired myself naked, from three directions. Sometimes I thought about the way we lived out at home and the way we lived here and how one way was so hard to imagine when you were living the other way. But I thought it was still a lot easier, living the way we lived at home, to picture something like this, the painted flamingoes and the warmth and the soft mat, than it was anybody knowing only things like this to picture how it was the other way. And why was that?

I was through my jobs in no time, and had the vegetables peeled for supper and sitting in cold water besides. Then I went into Mrs. Peebles' bedroom. I had been in there plenty of times, cleaning, and I always took a good look in her closet, at the clothes she had hanging there. I wouldn't have looked in her drawers, but a closet is open to anybody. That's a lie. I would have looked in drawers, but I would have felt worse doing it and been more scared she could tell.

Some clothes in her closet she wore all the time, I was quite familiar with them. Others she never put on, they were pushed to the back. I was disappointed to see no wedding dress. But there was one long dress I could just see the skirt of, and I was hungering to see the rest. Now I took note of where it hung and lifted it out. It was satin, a lovely weight on my arm, light bluishgreen in color, almost silvery. It had a fitted, pointed waist and a full skirt and an off-the-shoulder fold hiding the little sleeves.

Next thing was easy. I got out of my own things and slipped it on. I was slimmer at fifteen than anybody would believe who knows me now and the fit was beautiful. I didn't, of course, have a strapless bra on, which was what it needed, I just had to slide my straps down my arms under the material. Then I tried pinning up my hair, to get the effect. One thing led to another. I put on rouge and lipstick and eyebrow pencil from her dresser. The heat of the day and the weight of the satin and all the excitement made me thirsty, and I went out to the kitchen, got-up as I was, to get a glass of ginger ale with ice cubes from the refrigerator. The Peebleses drank ginger ale, or fruit drinks, all day, like water, and I was getting so I did too. Also there was no limit on ice cubes, which I was so fond of I would even put them in a glass of milk.

I turned from putting the ice tray back and saw a man watching me through the screen. It was the luckiest thing in the world I didn't spill the ginger ale down the front of me then and there.

"I never meant to scare you. I knocked but you were getting the ice out, you didn't hear me."

I couldn't see what he looked like, he was dark the way somebody is pressed up against a screen door with the bright daylight behind them. I only knew he wasn't from around here.

"I'm from the plane over there. My name is Chris Watters and what I was wondering was if I could use that pump."

There was a pump in the yard. That was the way the people used to get their water. Now I noticed he was carrying a pail.

"You're welcome," I said. "I can get it from the tap and save you pumping." I guess I wanted him to know we had piped water, didn't pump ourselves.

"I don't mind the exercise." He didn't move, though, and finally he said, "Were you going to a dance?"

Seeing a stranger there had made me entirely forget how I was dressed.

"Or is that the way ladies around here generally get dressed up in the afternoon?"

I didn't know how to joke back then. I was too embarrassed.

"You live here? Are you the lady of the house?"

"I'm the hired girl."

Some people change when they find that out, their whole way of looking at you and speaking to you changes, but his didn't.

"Well, I just wanted to tell you you look very nice. I was so surprised when I looked in the door and saw you. Just because you looked so nice and beautiful."

I wasn't even old enough then to realize how out of the common it is, for a man to say something like that to a woman, or somebody he is treating like a woman. For a man to say a word like *beautiful*. I wasn't old enough to realize or to say anything back, or in fact to do anything but wish he would go away. Not that I didn't like him, but just that it upset me so, having him look at me, and me trying to think of something to say.

He must have understood. He said good-bye, and thanked me, and went and started filling his pail from the pump. I stood behind the Venetian blinds in the dining room, watching him. When he had gone, I went into the bedroom and took the dress off and put it back in the same place. I dressed in my own clothes and took my hair down and washed my face, wiping it on Kleenex, which I threw in the wastebasket.

The Peebleses asked me what kind of man he was. Young, middle-aged, short, tall? I couldn't say.

"Good-looking?" Dr. Peebles teased me.

I couldn't think a thing but that he would be coming to get his water again, he would be talking to Dr. or Mrs. Peebles, making friends with them, and he would mention seeing me that first afternoon, dressed up. Why not mention it? He would think it was funny. And no idea of the trouble it would get me into.

After supper the Peebleses drove into town to go to a movie. She wanted to go somewhere with her hair fresh done. I sat in my bright kitchen wondering what to do, knowing I would never sleep. Mrs. Peebles might not fire me, when she found out, but it would give her a different feeling about me altogether. This was the first place I ever worked but I already had picked up things about the way people feel when you are working for them. They like to think you aren't curious. Not just that you aren't dishonest, that isn't enough. They like to feel you don't notice things, that you don't think or wonder about anything but what they liked to eat and how they liked things ironed, and so on. I don't mean they weren't kind to me, because they were. They had me eat my meals with them (to tell the truth I expected to, I didn't know there were families who don't) and sometimes they took me along in the car. But all the same.

I went up and checked on the children being asleep and then I went out. I had to do it. I crossed the road and went in the old fairgrounds gate. The plane looked unnatural sitting there, and shining with the moon. Off at the far side of the fairgrounds where the bush was taking over, I saw his tent.

He was sitting outside it smoking a cigarette. He saw me coming.

"Hello, were you looking for a plane ride? I don't start taking people up till tomorrow." Then he looked again and said, "Oh, it's you. I didn't know you without your long dress on."

My heart was knocking away, my tongue was dried up. I had to say something. But I couldn't. My throat was closed and I was like a deaf-and-dumb.

"Did you want a ride? Sit down. Have a cigarette."

I couldn't even shake my head to say no, so he gave me one.

"Put it in your mouth or I can't light it. It's a good thing I'm used to shy ladies."

I did. It wasn't the first time I had smoked a cigarette, actually. My girl-friend out home, Muriel Lowe, used to steal them from her brother.

"Look at your hand shaking. Did you just want to have a chat, or what?"

In one burst I said, "I wisht you wouldn't say anything about that dress."

"What dress? Oh, the long dress."

"It's Mrs. Peebles'."

"Whose? Oh, the lady you work for? She wasn't home so you got dressed up in her dress, eh? You got dressed up and played queen. I don't blame you. You're not smoking the cigarette right. Don't just puff. Draw it in. Did anybody ever show you how to inhale? Are you scared I'll tell on you? Is that it?"

I was so ashamed at having to ask him to connive this way I couldn't nod. I just looked at him and he saw *yes*.

"Well I won't. I won't in the slightest way mention it or embarrass you. I give you my word of honor."

Then he changed the subject, to help me out, seeing I couldn't even thank him.

"What do you think of this sign?"

It was a board sign lying practically at my feet.

SEE THE WORLD FROM THE SKY. ADULTS $1.00, CHILDREN 50¢. QUALIFIED PILOT.

"My old sign was getting pretty beat up, I thought I'd make a new one. That's what I've been doing with my time today."

The lettering wasn't all that handsome, I thought. I could have done a better one in half an hour.

"I'm not an expert at sign making."

"It's very good," I said.

"I don't need it for publicity, word of mouth is usually enough. I turned away two carloads tonight. I felt like taking it easy. I didn't tell them ladies were dropping in to visit me."

Now I remembered the children and I was scared again, in case one of them had waked up and called me and I wasn't there.

"Do you have to go so soon?"

I remembered some manners. "Thank you for the cigarette."

"Don't forget. You have my word of honor."

I tore off across the fairgrounds, scared I'd see the car heading home from town. My sense of time was mixed up, I didn't know how long I'd been out of the house. But it was all right, it wasn't late, the children were asleep. I got in my bed myself and lay thinking what a lucky end to the day, after all, and among things to be grateful for I could be grateful Loretta Bird hadn't been the one who caught me.

The yard and borders didn't get trampled, it wasn't as bad as that. All the same it seemed very public, around the house. The sign was on the fairgrounds gate. People came mostly after supper but a good many in the afternoon, too. The Bird children all came without fifty cents between them and hung on the gate. We got used to the excitement of the plane coming in and taking off, it wasn't excitement anymore. I never went over, after that one time, but would see him when he came to get his water. I would be out on the steps doing sitting-down work, like preparing vegetables, if I could.

"Why don't you come over? I'll take you up in my plane."

"I'm saving my money," I said, because I couldn't think of anything else.

"For what? For getting married?"

I shook my head.

"I'll take you up for free if you come sometime when it's slack. I thought you would come, and have another cigarette."

I made a face to hush him, because you never could tell when the children would be sneaking around the porch, or Mrs. Peebles herself listening in the house. Sometimes she came out and had a conversation with him. He told her things he hadn't bothered to tell me. But then I hadn't thought to ask. He told her he had been in the war, that was where he learned to fly a plane, and how he couldn't settle down to ordinary life, this was what he liked. She said she couldn't imagine anybody liking such a thing. Though sometimes, she said, she was almost bored enough to try anything herself, she wasn't brought up to living in the country. It's all my husband's idea, she said. This was news to me.

"Maybe you ought to give flying lessons," she said.

"Would you take them?"

She just laughed.

Sunday was a busy flying day in spite of it being preached against from two pulpits. We were all sitting out watching. Joey and Heather were over on the fence with the Bird kids. Their father had said they could go, after their mother saying all week they couldn't.

A car came down the road past the parked cars and pulled up right in the drive. It was Loretta Bird who got out, all importance, and on the driver's side another woman got out, more sedately. She was wearing sunglasses.

"This is a lady looking for the man that flies the plane," Loretta Bird said. "I heard her inquire in the hotel coffee shop where I was having a Coke and I brought her out."

"I'm sorry to bother you," the lady said. "I'm Alice Kelling, Mr. Watters' fiancée."

This Alice Kelling had on a pair of brown and white checked slacks and a yellow top. Her bust looked to me rather low and bumpy. She had a worried face. Her hair had had a permanent, but had grown out, and she wore a yellow band to keep it off her face. Nothing in the least pretty or even young-looking about her. But you could tell from how she talked she was from the city, or educated, or both.

Dr. Peebles stood up and introduced himself and his wife and me and asked her to be seated.

"He's up in the air right now, but you're welcome to sit and wait. He gets his water here and he hasn't been yet. He'll probably take his break about five."

"That is him, then?" said Alice Kelling, wrinkling and straining at the sky.

"He's not in the habit of running out on you, taking a different name?" Dr. Peebles laughed. He was the one, not his wife, to offer iced tea. Then she sent me into the kitchen to fix it. She smiled. She was wearing sunglasses too.

"He never mentioned his fiancée," she said.

I loved fixing iced tea with lots of ice and slices of lemon in tall glasses. I ought to have mentioned before, Dr. Peebles was an abstainer, at least around the house, or I wouldn't have been allowed to take the place. I had to fix a glass for Loretta Bird too, though it galled me, and when I went out she had settled in my lawn chair, leaving me the steps.

"I knew you was a nurse when I first heard you in that coffee shop."

"How would you know a thing like that?"

"I get my hunches about people. Was that how you met him, nursing?"

"Chris? Well yes. Yes, it was."

"Oh, were you overseas?" said Mrs. Peebles.

"No, it was before he went overseas. I nursed him when he was stationed at Centralia and had a ruptured appendix. We got engaged and then he went overseas. My, this is refreshing, after a long drive."

"He'll be glad to see you," Dr. Peebles said. "It's a rackety kind of life, isn't it, not staying one place long enough to really make friends."

"Youse've had a long engagement," Loretta Bird said.

Alice Kelling passed that over. "I was going to get a room at the hotel, but when I was offered directions I came on out. Do you think I could phone them?"

"No need," Dr. Peebles said. "You're five miles away from him if you stay at the hotel. Here, you're right across the road. Stay with us. We've got rooms on rooms, look at this big house."

Asking people to stay, just like that, is certainly a country thing, and maybe seemed natural to him now, but not to Mrs. Peebles, from the way she said, oh yes, we have plenty of room. Or to Alice Kelling, who kept protesting, but let herself be worn down. I got the feeling it was a temptation to her, to be that close. I was trying for a look at her ring. Her nails were painted red, her fingers were freckled and wrinkled. It was a tiny stone. Muriel Lowe's cousin had one twice as big.

Chris came to get his water, late in the afternoon just as Dr. Peebles had predicted. He must have recognized the car from a way off. He came smiling.

"Here I am chasing after you to see what you're up to," called Alice Kelling. She got up and went to meet him and they kissed, just touched, in front of us.

"You're going to spend a lot on gas that way," Chris said.

Dr. Peebles invited Chris to stay for supper, since he had already put up the sign that said: NO MORE RIDES TILL 7 P.M. Mrs. Peebles wanted it served in the yard, in spite of the bugs. One thing strange to anybody from the country is this eating outside. I had made a potato salad earlier and she had made a jellied salad, that was one thing she could do, so it was just a matter of getting those out, and some sliced meat and cucumbers and fresh leaf lettuce. Loretta Bird hung around for some time saying, "Oh, well, I guess I better get home to those yappers," and, "It's so nice just sitting here, I sure hate to get up," but nobody invited her, I was relieved to see, and finally she had to go.

That night after rides were finished Alice Kelling and Chris went off somewhere in her car. I lay awake till they got back. When I saw the car lights sweep my ceiling I got up to look down on them through the slats of my blind. I don't know what I thought I was going to see. Muriel Lowe and I used to sleep on her front veranda and watch her sister and her sister's boy friend saying good night. Afterward we couldn't get to sleep, for longing for somebody to kiss us and rub against us and we would talk about suppose you were out in a boat with a boy and he wouldn't bring you in to shore unless you did it, or what if somebody got you trapped in a barn, you would have to, wouldn't you, it wouldn't be your fault. Muriel said her two girl cousins used to try with a toilet paper roll that one of them was a boy. We wouldn't do anything like that; just lay and wondered.

All that happened was that Chris got out of the car on one side and she got out on the other and they walked off separately—him toward the fairgrounds and her toward the house. I got back in bed and imagined about me coming home with him, not like that.

Next morning Alice Kelling got up late and I fixed a grapefruit for her the way I had learned and Mrs. Peebles sat down with her to visit and have another cup of coffee. Mrs. Peebles seemed pleased enough now, having company. Alice Kelling said she guessed she better get used to putting in a day just watching Chris take off and come down, and Mrs. Peebles said she didn't know if she should suggest it because Alice Kelling was the one with the car, but the lake was only twenty-five miles away and what a good day for a picnic.

Alice Kelling took her up on the idea and by eleven o'clock they were in the car, with Joey and Heather and a sandwich lunch I had made. The only thing was that Chris hadn't come down, and she wanted to tell him where they were going.

"Edie'll go over and tell him," Mrs. Peebles said. "There's no problem."

Alice Kelling wrinkled her face and agreed.

"Be sure and tell him we'll be back by five!"

I didn't see that he would be concerned about knowing this right away, and I thought of him eating whatever he ate over there, alone, cooking on his camp stove, so I got to work and mixed up a crumb cake and baked it, in between the other work I had to do; then, when it was a bit cooled, wrapped it in a tea towel. I didn't do anything to myself but take off my apron and comb my hair. I would like to have put some makeup on, but I was too afraid it would remind him of the way he first saw me, and that would humiliate me all over again.

He had come and put another sign on the gate: NO RIDES THIS P.M. APOLOGIES. I worried that he wasn't feeling well. No sign of him outside and the tent flap was down. I knocked on the pole.

"Come in," he said, in a voice that would just as soon have said *Stay out*.

I lifted the flap.

"Oh, it's you. I'm sorry. I didn't know it was you."

He had been just sitting on the side of the bed, smoking. Why not at least sit and smoke in the fresh air?

"I brought a cake and hope you're not sick," I said.

"Why would I be sick? Oh—that sign. That's all right. I'm just tired of talking to people. I don't mean you. Have a seat." He pinned back the tent flap. "Get some fresh air in here."

I sat on the edge of the bed, there was no place else. It was one of those foldup cots, really: I remembered and gave him his fiancée's message.

He ate some of the cake. "Good."

"Put the rest away for when you're hungry later."

"I'll tell you a secret. I won't be around here much longer."

"Are you getting married?"

"Ha ha. What time did you say they'd be back?"

"Five o'clock."

"Well, by that time this place will have seen the last of me. A plane can get further than a car." He unwrapped the cake and ate another piece of it, absentmindedly.

"Now you'll be thirsty."

"There's some water in the pail."

"It won't be very cold. I could bring some fresh. I could bring some ice from the refrigerator."

"No," he said. "I don't want you to go. I want a nice long time of saying good-bye to you."

He put the cake away carefully and sat beside me and started those little kisses, so soft, I can't ever let myself think about them, such kindness in his face and lovely kisses, all over my eyelids and neck and ears, all over, then me kissing back as well as I could (I had only kissed a boy on a dare before, and kissed my own arms for practice) and we lay back on the cot and pressed together, just gently, and he did some other things, not bad things or not in a bad way. It was lovely in the tent, that smell of grass and hot tent cloth with the sun beating down on it, and he said, "I wouldn't do you any harm for the world." Once, when he had rolled on top of me and we were sort of rocking together on the cot, he said softly, "Oh, no," and freed himself and jumped up and got the water pail. He splashed some of it on his neck and face, and the little bit left, on me lying there.

"That's to cool us off, miss."

When we said good-bye I wasn't at all sad, because he held my face and said, "I'm going to write you a letter. I'll tell you where I am and maybe you can come and see me. Would you like that? Okay then. You wait." I was really glad I think to get away from him, it was like he was piling presents on me I couldn't get the pleasure of till I considered them alone.

No consternation at first about the plane being gone. They thought he had taken somebody up, and I didn't enlighten them. Dr. Peebles had phoned he had to go to the country, so there was just us having supper, and then Loretta Bird thrusting her head in the door and saying, "I see he's took off."

"What?" said Alice Kelling, and pushed back her chair.

"The kids come and told me this afternoon he was taking down his tent. Did he think he'd run through all the business there was around here? He didn't take off without letting you know, did he?"

"He'll send me word," Alice Kelling said. "He'll probably phone tonight. He's terribly restless, since the war."

"Edie, he didn't mention it to you, did he?" Mrs. Peebles said. "When you took over the message?"

"Yes," I said. So far so true.

"Well why didn't you say?" All of them were looking at me. "Did he say where he was going?"

"He said he might try Bayfield," I said. What made me tell such a lie? I didn't intend it.

"Bayfield, how far is that?" said Alice Kelling.

Mrs. Peebles said, "Thirty, thirty-five miles."

"That's not far. Oh, well, that's really not far at all. It's on the lake, isn't it?"

You'd think I'd be ashamed of myself, setting her on the wrong track. I did it to give him more time, whatever time he needed. I lied for him, and also, I have to admit, for me. Women should stick together and not do things like that. I see that now, but didn't then. I never thought of myself as being in any way like her, or coming to the same troubles, ever.

She hadn't taken her eyes off me. I thought she suspected my lie.

"When did he mention this to you?"

"Earlier."

"When you were over at the plane?"

"Yes."

"You must've stayed and had a chat." She smiled at me, not a nice smile. "You must've stayed and had a little visit with him."

"I took a cake," I said, thinking that telling some truth would spare me telling the rest.

"We didn't have a cake," said Mrs. Peebles rather sharply.

"I baked one."

Alice Kelling said, "That was very friendly of you."

"Did you get permission," said Loretta Bird. "You never know what these girls'll do next," she said. "It's not they mean harm so much, as they're ignorant."

"The cake is neither here nor there," Mrs. Peebles broke in. "Edie, I wasn't aware you knew Chris that well."

I didn't know what to say.

"I'm not surprised," Alice Kelling said in a high voice. "I knew by the look of her as soon as I saw her. We get them at the hospital all the time." She looked hard at me with her stretched smile. "Having their babies. We have to put them in a special ward because of their diseases. Little country tramps. Fourteen and fifteen years old. You should see the babies they have, too."

"There was a bad woman here in town had a baby that pus was running out of its eyes," Loretta Bird put in.

"Wait a minute," said Mrs. Peebles. "What is this talk? Edie. What about you and Mr. Watters? Were you intimate with him?"

"Yes," I said. I was thinking of us lying on the cot and kissing, wasn't that intimate? And I would never deny it.

They were all one minute quiet, even Loretta Bird.

"Well," said Mrs. Peebles. "I am surprised. I think I need a cigarette. This is the first of any such tendencies I've seen in her," she said, speaking to Alice Kelling, but Alice Kelling was looking at me.

"Loose little bitch." Tears ran down her face. "Loose little bitch, aren't you? I knew as soon as I saw you. Men despise girls like you. He just made use of you and went off, you know that, don't you? Girls like you are just nothing, they're just public conveniences, just filthy little rags!"

"Oh, now," said Mrs. Peebles.

"Filthy," Alice Kelling sobbed. "Filthy little rags!"

"Don't get yourself upset," Loretta Bird said. She was swollen up with pleasure at being in on this scene. "Men are all the same."

"Edie, I'm very surprised," Mrs. Pebbles said. "I thought your parents were so strict. You don't want to have a baby, do you?"

I'm still ashamed of what happened next. I lost control, just like a six-year-old, I started howling. "You don't get a baby from just doing that!"

"You see. Some of them are that ignorant," Loretta Bird said.

But Mrs. Peebles jumped up and caught my arms and shook me.

"Calm down. Don't get hysterical. Calm down. Stop crying. Listen to me. Listen I'm wondering, if you know what being intimate means. Now tell me. What did you think it meant?"

"Kissing," I howled.

She let go. "Oh, Edie. Stop it. Don't be silly. It's all right. It's all a misunderstanding. Being intimate means a lot more than that. Oh, I *wondered*."

"She's trying to cover up, now," said Alice Kelling. "Yes. She's not so stupid. She sees she got herself in trouble."

"I believe her," Mrs. Peebles said. "This is an awful scene."

"Well there is one way to find out," said Alice Kelling, getting up. "After all, I am a nurse."

Mrs. Peebles drew a breath and said, "No. No. Go to your room, Edie. And stop that noise. This is too disgusting."

I heard the car start in a little while. I tried to stop crying, pulling back each wave as it started over me. Finally I succeeded, and lay heaving on the bed.

Mrs. Peebles came and stood in the doorway.

"She's gone," she said. "That Bird woman too. Of course, you know you should never have gone near that man and that is the cause of all this trouble. I have a headache. As soon as you can, go and wash your face in cold water and get at the dishes and we will not say any more about this."

Nor we didn't. I didn't figure out till years later the extent of what I had been saved from. Mrs. Peebles was not very friendly to me afterward, but she was fair. Not very friendly is the wrong way of describing what she was. She had never been very friendly. It was just that now she had to see me all the time and it got on her nerves, a little.

As for me, I put it all out of my mind like a bad dream and concentrated on waiting for my letter. The mail came every day except Sunday, between one-thirty and two in the afternoon, a good time for me because Mrs. Peebles was always having her nap. I would get the kitchen all cleaned and then go up to the mailbox and sit in the grass, waiting. I was perfectly happy, waiting. I forgot all about Alice Kelling and her misery and awful talk and Mrs. Peebles and her chilliness and the embarrassment of whether she told Dr. Peebles and the face of Loretta Bird, getting her fill of other people's troubles. I was always smiling when the mailman got there, and continued smiling even after he gave me the mail and I saw today wasn't the day. The mailman was a Carmichael. I knew by his face because there are a lot of Carmichaels living out by us and so many of them have a sort of sticking-out top lip. So I asked his name (he was a young man, shy, but good-humored, anybody could ask him anything) and then I said, "I knew by your face!" He was pleased by that and always glad to see me and got a little less shy. "You've got the smile I've been waiting for all day!" he used to holler out the car window.

It never crossed my mind for a long time a letter might not come. I believed in it coming just like I believed the sun would rise in the morning. I just put off my hope from day to day, and there was the goldenrod out around the mailbox and the children gone back to school, and the leaves turning, and I was wearing a sweater when I went to wait. One day walking back with the hydro bill stuck in my hand, that was all, looking across at the fairgrounds with the full-blown milkweed and dark teasels, so much like fall, it just struck me: *No letter was ever going to come.* It was an impossible idea to get used to. No, not impossible. If I thought about Chris's face when he said he was going to write me, it was impossible, but if I forgot that and thought about the actual tin mailbox, empty, it was plain and true. I kept on going to meet the mail, but my heart was heavy now like a lump of lead. I only smiled because I thought of the mailman counting on it, and he didn't have an easy life, with the winter driving ahead.

Till it came to me one day there were women doing this with their lives, all over. There were women just waiting and waiting by mailboxes for one letter or another. I imagined me making this journey day after day and year after year, and my hair starting to get gray, and I thought, I was never made to go on like that. So I stopped meeting the mail. If there were women all through life waiting, and women busy and not waiting, I knew which I had to be. Even though there might be things the second kind of women have to pass up and never know about, it still is better.

I was surprised when the mailman phoned the Peebleses' place in the evening and asked for me. He said he missed me. He asked if I would like to go to Goderich, where some well-known movie was on, I forget now what. So I said yes, and I went out with him for two years and he asked me to marry him, and we were engaged a year more while I got my things together, and then we did marry. He always tells the children the story of how I went after him by sitting by the mailbox every day, and naturally I laugh and let him, because I like for people to think what pleases them and makes them happy.

1974

Tim O'Brien (B. 1946)

The Things They Carried

First Lieutenant Jimmy Cross carried letters from a girl named Martha, a junior at Mount Sebastian College in New Jersey. They were not love letters, but Lieutenant Cross was hoping, so he kept them folded in plastic at the bottom of his rucksack. In the late afternoon, after a day's march, he would dig his foxhole, wash his hands under a canteen, unwrap the letters, hold them with the tips of his fingers, and spend the last hour of light pretending. He would imagine romantic camping trips into the White Mountains in New Hampshire. He would sometimes taste the envelope flaps, knowing her tongue had been there. More than anything, he wanted Martha to love him as he loved her, but the letters were mostly chatty, elusive on the matter of love. She was a virgin, he was almost sure. She was an English major at Mount Sebastian, and she wrote beautifully about her professors and roommates and midterm exams, about her respect for Chaucer and her great affection for Virginia Woolf. She often quoted lines of poetry; she never mentioned the war, except to say, Jimmy, take care of yourself. The letters weighed 10 ounces. They were signed Love, Martha, but Lieutenant Cross understood that Love was only a way of signing and did not mean what he sometimes pretended it meant. At dusk, he would carefully return the letters to his rucksack. Slowly, a bit distracted, he would get up and move among his men, checking the perimeter; then at full dark he would return to his hole and watch the night and wonder if Martha was a virgin.

The things they carried were largely determined by necessity. Among the necessities or near-necessities were P-38 can openers, pocket knives, heat tabs, wristwatches, dog tags, mosquito repellent, chewing gum, candy, cigarettes, salt tablets, packets of Kool-Aid, lighters, matches, sewing kits, Military Payment Certificates, C rations, and two or three canteens of water. Together, these items weighed between 15 and 20 pounds, depending upon a man's habits or rate of metabolism. Henry Dobbins, who was a big man, carried extra rations; he was especially fond of canned peaches in heavy syrup over pound cake. Dave Jensen, who practiced field hygiene, carried a toothbrush, dental floss, and several hotel-sized bars of soap he'd stolen on R&R[1] in Sydney, Australia. Ted Lavender who was scared, carried tranquilizers until he was shot in the head outside the village of Than Khe in mid-April. By necessity, and because it was SOP,[2] they all carried steel helmets that weighed 5 pounds including the liner and camouflage cover. They carried the standard fatigue jackets and trousers. Very few car-

---

[1]*R&R:* the military abbreviation for "rest and rehabilitation," a brief vacation from active service.
[2]*SOP:* standard operating procedure.

ried underwear. On their feet they carried jungle boots—2.1 pounds—
and Dave Jensen carried three pairs of socks and a can of Dr. Scholl's foot
powder as a precaution against trench foot. Until he was shot, Ted Lavender carried six or seven ounces of premium dope, which for him was a
necessity. Mitchell Sanders, the RTO,[3] carried condoms. Norman Bowker
carried a diary. Rat Kiley carried comic books. Kiowa, a devout Baptist, carried an illustrated New Testament that had been presented to him by his
father, who taught Sunday school in Oklahoma City, Oklahoma. As a hedge
against bad times, however, Kiowa also carried his grandmother's distrust
of the white man, his grandfather's old hunting hatchet. Necessity dictated.
Because the land was mined and booby-tapped, it was SOP for each man
to carry a steel-centered, nylon-covered flak jacket, which weighed 6.7
pounds, but which on hot days seemed much heavier. Because you could
die so quickly, each man carried at least one large compress bandage, usually in the helmet band for easy access. Because the nights were cold, and
because the monsoons were wet, each carried a green plastic poncho that
could be used as a raincoat or groundsheet or makeshift tent. With its
quilted liner, the poncho weighed almost two pounds, but it was worth
every ounce. In April, for instance, when Ted Lavender was shot, they used
his poncho to wrap him up, then to carry him across the paddy, then to
lift him into the chopper that took him away.

They were called legs or grunts.
To carry something was to hump it, as when Lieutenant Jimmy Cross
humped his love for Martha up the hills and through the swamps. In its
intransitive form, to hump meant to walk, or to march, but it implied burdens far beyond the intransitive.
Almost everyone humped photographs. In his wallet, Lieutenant Cross
carried two photographs of Martha. The first was a Kodacolor snapshot
signed Love, though he knew better. She stood against a brick wall. Her
eyes were gray and neutral, her lips slightly open as she stared straight-on
at the camera. At night, sometimes, Lieutenant Cross wondered who had
taken the picture, because he knew she had boyfriends, because he loved
her so much, and because he could see the shadow of the picture-taker
spreading out against the brick wall. The second photograph had been
clipped from the 1968 Mount Sebastian yearbook. It was an action shot—
women's volleyball—and Martha was bent horizontal to the floor, reaching, the palms of her hands in sharp focus, the tongue taut, the expression
frank and competitive. There was no visible sweat. She wore white gym
shorts. Her legs, he thought, were almost certainly the legs of a virgin, dry
and without hair, the left knee cocked and carrying her entire weight, which
was just over one hundred pounds. Lieutenant Cross remembered touching that left knee. A dark theater, he remembered, and the movie was *Bonnie
and Clyde*, and Martha wore a tweed skirt, and during the final scene, when

[3]*RTO:* radio and telephone operator.

he touched her knee, she turned and looked at him in a sad, sober way that made him pull his hand back, but he would always remember the feel of the tweed skirt and the knee beneath it and the sound of the gunfire that killed Bonnie and Clyde, how embarrassing it was, how slow and oppressive. He remembered kissing her good night at the dorm door. Right then, he thought, he should've done something brave. He should've carried her up the stairs to her room and tied her to the bed and touched that left knee all night long. He should've risked it. Whenever he looked at the photographs, he thought of new things he should've done.

What they carried was partly a function of rank, partly of field specialty.

As a first lieutenant and platoon leader, Jimmy Cross carried a compass, maps, code books, binoculars, and a .45-caliber pistol that weighed 2.9 pounds fully loaded. He carried a strobe light and the responsibility for the lives of his men.

As an RTO, Mitchell Sanders carried the PRC-25 radio, a killer, 26 pounds with its battery.

As a medic, Rat Kiley carried a canvas satchel filled with morphine and plasma and malaria tablets and surgical tape and comic books and all the things a medic must carry, including M&M's[4] for especially bad wounds, for a total weight of nearly 20 pounds.

As a big man, therefore a machine gunner, Henry Dobbins carried the M-60, which weighed 23 pounds unloaded, but which was almost always loaded. In addition, Dobbins carried between 10 and 15 pounds of ammunition draped in belts across his chest and shoulders.

As PFCs or Spec 4s, most of them were common grunts and carried the standard M-16 gas-operated assault rifle. The weapon weighed 7.5 pounds unloaded, 8.2 pounds with its full 20-round magazine. Depending on numerous factors, such as topography and psychology, the riflemen carried anywhere from 12 to 20 magazines, usually in cloth bandoliers, adding on another 8.4 pounds at minimum, 14 pounds at maximum. When it was available, they also carried M-16 maintenance gear—rods and steel brushes and swabs and tubes of LSA oil—all of which weighed about a pound. Among the grunts, some carried the M-79 grenade launcher, 5.9 pounds unloaded, a reasonably light weapon except for the ammunition, which was heavy. A single round weighed 10 ounces. The typical load was 25 rounds. But Ted Lavender, who was scared, carried 34 rounds when he was shot and killed outside Than Khe, and he went down under an exceptional burden, more than 20 pounds of ammunition, plus the flak jacket and helmet and rations and water and toilet paper and tranquilizers and all the rest, plus the unweighed fear. He was dead weight. There was no twitching or flopping. Kiowa, who saw it happen, said it was like watching a rock fall, or a big sandbag or something—just boom, then down—not like the movies where the dead guy rolls around and does fancy spins

---

[4]*M&M's:* comic slang for medical supplies.

and goes ass over teakettle—not like that, Kiowa said, the poor bastard just flat-fuck fell. Boom. Down. Nothing else. It was a bright morning in mid-April. Lieutenant Cross felt the pain. He blamed himself. They stripped off Lavender's canteens and ammo, all the heavy things, and Rat Kiley said the obvious, the guy's dead, and Mitchell Sanders used his radio to report one U.S. KIA[5] and to request a chopper. Then they wrapped Lavender in his poncho. They carried him out to a dry paddy, established security, and sat smoking the dead man's dope until the chopper came. Lieutenant Cross kept to himself. He pictured Martha's smooth young face, thinking he loved her more than anything, more than his men, and now Ted Lavender was dead because he loved her so much and could not stop thinking about her. When the dustoff arrived, they carried Lavender aboard. Afterward they burned Than Khe. They marched until dusk, then dug their holes, and that night Kiowa kept explaining how you had to be there, how fast it was, how the poor guy just dropped like so much concrete. Boom-down, he said. Like cement.

In addition to the three standard weapons—the M-60, M-16, and M-79—they carried whatever presented itself, or whatever seemed appropriate as a means of killing or staying alive. They carried catch-as-catch-can. At various times, in various situations, they carried M-14s and CAR-15s and Swedish Ks and grease guns and captured AK-47s and Chi-Coms and RPGs and Simonov carbines and black market Uzis and .38-caliber Smith & Wesson handguns and 66 mm LAWs and shotguns and silencers and blackjacks and bayonets and C-4 plastic explosives. Lee Strunk carried a slingshot; a weapon of last resort, he called it. Mitchell Sanders carried brass knuckles. Kiowa carried his grandfather's feathered hatchet. Every third or fourth man carried a Claymore antipersonnel mine—3.5 pounds with its firing device. They all carried fragmentation grenades—14 ounces each. They all carried at least one M-18 colored smoke grenade—24 ounces. Some carried CS or tear gas grenades. Some carried white phosphorus grenades. They carried all they could bear, and then some, including a silent awe for the terrible power of the things they carried.

In the first week of April, before Lavender died, Lieutenant Jimmy Cross received a good-luck charm from Martha. It was a simple pebble, an ounce at most. Smooth to the touch, it was a milky white color with flecks of orange and violet, oval-shaped, like a miniature egg. In the accompanying letter, Martha wrote that she had found the pebble on the Jersey shoreline, precisely where the land touched water at high tide, where things came together but also separated. It was this separate-but-together quality, she wrote, that had inspired her to pick up the pebble and to carry it in her breast pocket for several days, where it seemed weightless, and then to send it through the mail, by air, as a token of her truest feelings for

---

[5] *KIA:* killed in action.

him. Lieutenant Cross found this romantic. But he wondered what her truest feelings were, exactly, and what she meant by separate-but-together. He wondered how the tides and waves had come into play on that afternoon along the Jersey shoreline when Martha saw the pebble and bent down to rescue it from geology. He imagined bare feet. Martha was a poet, with the poet's sensibilities, and her feet would be brown and bare, the toenails unpainted, the eyes chilly and somber like the ocean in March, and though it was painful, he wondered who had been with her that afternoon. He imagined a pair of shadows moving along the strip of sand where things came together but also separated. It was phantom jealousy, he knew, but he couldn't help himself. He loved her so much. On the march, through the hot days of early April, he carried the pebble in his mouth, turning it with his tongue, tasting sea salt and moisture. His mind wandered. He had difficulty keeping his attention on the war. On occasion he would yell at his men to spread out the column, to keep their eyes open, but then he would slip away into daydreams, just pretending, walking barefoot along the Jersey shore, with Martha, carrying nothing. He would feel himself rising. Sun and waves and gentle winds, all love and lightness.

What they carried varied by mission.

When a mission took them to the mountains, they carried mosquito netting, machetes, canvas tarps, and extra bug juice.

If a mission seemed especially hazardous, or if it involved a place they knew to be bad, they carried everything they could. In certain heavily mined AOs,[6] where the land was dense with Toe Poppers and Bouncing Betties, they took turns humping a 28-pound mine detector. With its headphones and big sensing plate, the equipment was a stress on the lower back and shoulders, awkward to handle, often useless because of the shrapnel in the earth, but they carried it anyway, partly for safety, partly for the illusion of safety.

On ambush, or other night missions, they carried peculiar little odds and ends. Kiowa always took along his New Testament and a pair of moccasins for silence. Dave Jensen carried night-sight vitamins high in carotene. Lee Strunk carried his slingshot; ammo, he claimed, would never be a problem. Rat Kiley carried brandy and M&M's candy. Until he was shot, Ted Lavender carried the starlight scope, which weighed 6.3 pounds with its aluminum carrying case. Henry Dobbins carried his girlfriend's pantyhose wrapped around his neck as a comforter. *They all carried ghosts.* When dark came, they would move out single file across the meadows and paddies to their ambush coordinates, where they would quietly set up the Claymores and lie down and spend the night waiting.

Other missions were more complicated and required special equipment. In mid-April, it was their mission to search out and destroy the elaborate tunnel complexes in the Than Khe area south of Chu Lai. To blow

---

[6]*AOs:* areas of operation.

the tunnels, they carried one-pound blocks of pentrite high explosives, four blocks to a man, 68 pounds in all. They carried wiring, detonators, and battery-powered clackers. Dave Jensen carried earplugs. Most often, before blowing the tunnels, they were ordered by higher command to search them, which was considered bad news, but by and large they just shrugged and carried out orders. Because he was a big man, Henry Dobbins was excused from tunnel duty. The others would draw numbers. Before Lavender died there were 17 men in the platoon, and whoever drew the number 17 would strip off his gear and crawl in headfirst with a flashlight and Lieutenant Cross's .45-caliber pistol. The rest of them would fan out as security. They would sit down or kneel, not facing the hole, listening to the ground beneath them, imagining cobwebs and ghosts, whatever was down there—the tunnel walls squeezing in—how the flashlight seemed impossibly heavy in the hand and how it was tunnel vision in the very strictest sense, compression in all ways, even time, and how you had to wiggle in—ass and elbows—a swallowed-up feeling—and how you found yourself worrying about odd things: Will your flashlight go dead? Do rats carry rabies? If you screamed, how far would the sound carry? Would your buddies hear it? Would they have the courage to drag you out? In some respects, though not many, the waiting was worse than the tunnel itself. Imagination was a killer.

On April 16, when Lee Strunk drew the number 17, he laughed and muttered something and went down quickly. The morning was hot and very still. Not good, Kiowa said. He looked at the tunnel opening, then out across a dry paddy toward the village of Than Khe. Nothing moved. No clouds or birds or people. As they waited, the men smoked and drank Kool-Aid, not talking much, feeling sympathy for Lee Strunk but also feeling the luck of the draw. You win some, you lose some, said Mitchell Sanders, and sometimes you settle for a rain check. It was a tired line and no one laughed.

Henry Dobbins ate a tropical chocolate bar. Ted Lavender popped a tranquilizer and went off to pee.

After five minutes, Lieutenant Jimmy Cross moved to the tunnel, leaned down, and examined the darkness. Trouble, he thought—a cave-in maybe. And then suddenly, without willing it, he was thinking about Martha. The stresses and fractures, the quick collapse, the two of them buried alive under all that weight. Dense, crushing love. Kneeling, watching the hole, he tried to concentrate on Lee Strunk and the war, all the dangers, but his love was too much for him, he felt paralyzed, he wanted to sleep inside her lungs and breathe her blood and be smothered. He wanted her to be a virgin and not a virgin, all at once. He wanted to know her. Intimate secrets: Why poetry? Why so sad? Why that grayness in her eyes? Why so alone? Not lonely, just alone—riding her bike across campus or sitting off by herself in the cafeteria—even dancing, she danced alone—and it was the aloneness that filled him with love. He remembered telling her that one evening. How she nodded and looked away. And how, later, when he kissed her, she received the kiss without returning it, her eyes wide open, not afraid, not a virgin's eyes, just flat and uninvolved.

Lieutenant Cross gazed at the tunnel. But he was not there. He was buried with Martha under the white sand at the Jersey shore. They were pressed together, and the pebble in his mouth was her tongue. He was smiling. Vaguely, he was aware of how quiet the day was, the sullen paddies, yet he could not bring himself to worry about matters of security. He was beyond that. He was just a kid at war, in love. He was twenty-four years old. He couldn't help it.

A few moments later Lee Strunk crawled out of the tunnel. He came up grinning, filthy but alive. Lieutenant Cross nodded and closed his eyes while the others clapped Strunk on the back and made jokes about rising from the dead.

Worms, Rat Kiley said. Right out of the grave. Fuckin' zombie.

The men laughed. They all felt great relief.

Spook city, said Mitchell Sanders.

Lee Strunk made a funny ghost sound, a kind of moaning, yet very happy, and right then, when Strunk made that high happy moaning sound, when he went *Ahhooooo*, right then Ted Lavender was shot in the head on his way back from peeing. He lay with his mouth open. The teeth were broken. There was a swollen black bruise under his left eye. The cheekbone was gone. Oh shit, Rat Kiley said, the guy's dead. The guy's dead, he kept saying, which seemed profound—the guy's dead. I mean really.

The things they carried were determined to some extent by superstition. Lieutenant Cross carried his good-luck pebble. Dave Jensen carried a rabbit's foot. Norman Bowker, otherwise a very gentle person, carried a thumb that had been presented to him as a gift by Mitchell Sanders. The thumb was dark brown, rubbery to the touch, and weighed four ounces at most. It had been cut from a VC corpse, a boy of fifteen or sixteen. They'd found him at the bottom of an irrigation ditch, badly burned, flies in his mouth and eyes. The boy wore black shorts and sandals. At the time of his death he had been carrying a pouch of rice, a rifle, and three magazines of ammunition.

You want my opinion, Mitchell Sanders said, there's a definite moral here.

He put his hand on the dead boy's wrist. He was quiet for a time, as if counting a pulse, then he patted the stomach, almost affectionately, and used Kiowa's hunting hatchet to remove the thumb.

Henry Dobbins asked what the moral was.

Moral?

You know. *Moral.*

Sanders wrapped the thumb in toilet paper and handed it across to Norman Bowker. There was no blood. Smiling, he kicked the boy's head, watched the flies scatter, and said, It's like with that old TV show—Paladin. Have gun, will travel.

Henry Dobbins thought about it.

Yeah, well, he finally said. I don't see no moral.

There it *is*, man.

Fuck off.

They carried USO stationery and pencils and pens. They carried Sterno, safety pins, trip flares, signal flares, spools of wire, razor blades, chewing tobacco, liberated joss sticks and statuettes of the smiling Buddha, candles, grease pencils, *The Stars and Stripes*, fingernail clippers, Psy Ops leaflets, bush hats, bolos, and much more. Twice a week, when the resupply choppers came in, they carried hot chow in green mermite cans and large canvas bags filled with iced beer and soda pop. They carried plastic water containers, each with a two-gallon capacity. Mitchell Sanders carried a set of starched tiger fatigues for special occasions. Henry Dobbins carried Black Flag insecticide. Dave Jensen carried empty sandbags that could be filled at night for added protection. Lee Strunk carried tanning lotion. Some things they carried in common. Taking turns, they carried the big PRC-77 scrambler radio, which weighed 30 pounds with its battery. They shared the weight of memory. They took up what others could no longer bear. Often, they carried each other, the wounded or weak. They carried infections. They carried chess sets, basketballs, Vietnamese-English dictionaries, insignia of rank, Bronze Stars and Purple Hearts, plastic cards imprinted with the Code of Conduct. They carried diseases, among them malaria and dysentery. They carried lice and ringworm and leeches and paddy algae and various rots and molds. They carried the land itself—Vietnam, the place, the soil—a powdery orange-red dust that covered their boots and fatigues and faces. They carried the sky. The whole atmosphere, they carried it, the humidity, the monsoons, the stink of fungus and decay, all of it, they carried gravity. They moved like mules. By daylight they took sniper fire, at night they were mortared, but it was not battle, it was just the endless march, village to village, without purpose, nothing won or lost. They marched for the sake of the march. They plodded along slowly, dumbly, leaning forward against the heat, unthinking, all blood and bone, simple grunts, soldiering with their legs, toiling up the hills and down into the paddies and across the rivers and up again and down, just humping, one step and then the next and then another, but no volition, no will, because it was automatic, it was anatomy, and the war was entirely a matter of posture and carriage, the hump was everything, a kind of inertia, a kind of emptiness, a dullness of desire and intellect and conscience and hope and human sensibility. Their principles were in their feet. Their calculations were biological. They had no sense of strategy or mission. They searched the villages without knowing what to look for, not caring, kicking over jars of rice, frisking children and old men, blowing tunnels, sometimes setting fires and sometimes not, then forming up and moving on to the next village, then other villages, where it would always be the same. They carried their own lives. The pressures were enormous. In the heat of early afternoon, they would remove their helmets and flak jackets, walking bare, which was dangerous but which helped ease the strain. They would often discard things along the route of march. Purely for comfort, they would throw away rations, blow their Claymores and grenades, no matter, because by night-fall the resupply choppers would arrive with more of the same, then a day or two later still more, fresh watermelons and crates of ammunition and sunglasses and woolen sweaters—the resources were stunning—sparklers for the Fourth of July, colored eggs for Easter—it was the great American war chest—the fruits of science, the smokestacks, the canneries, the arse-nals at Hartford, the Minnesota forests, the machine shops, the vast fields of corn and wheat—they carried like freight trains; they carried it on their backs and shoulders—and for all the ambiguities of Vietnam, all the mys-teries and unknowns, there was at least the single abiding certainty that they would never be at a loss for things to carry.

After the chopper took Lavender away, Lieutenant Jimmy Cross led his men into the village of Than Khe. They burned everything. They shot chick-ens and dogs, they trashed the village well, they called in artillery and watched the wreckage, then they marched for several hours through the hot afternoon, and then at dusk, while Kiowa explained how Lavender died, Lieutenant Cross found himself trembling.

He tried not to cry. With his entrenching tool, which weighed five pounds, he began digging a hole in the earth.

He felt shame. He hated himself. He had loved Martha more than his men, and as a consequence Lavender was now dead, and this was some-thing he would have to carry like a stone in his stomach for the rest of the war.

All he could do was dig. He used his entrenching tool like an ax, slash-ing, feeling both love and hate, and then later, when it was full dark, he sat at the bottom of his foxhole and wept. It went on for a long while. In part, he was grieving for Ted Lavender, but mostly it was for Martha, and for himself, because she belonged to another world, which was not quite real, and because she was a junior at Mount Sebastian College in New Jersey, a poet and a virgin and uninvolved, and because he realized she did not love him and never would.

Like cement, Kiowa whispered in the dark. I swear to God—boom, down. Not a word.

I've heard this, said Norman Bowker.

A pisser, you know? Still zipping himself up. Zapped while zipping.

All right, fine. That's enough.

Yeah, but you had to see it, the guy just—

I *heard*, man. Cement. So why not shut the fuck *up?*

Kiowa shook his head sadly and glanced over at the hole where Lieu-tenant Jimmy Cross sat watching the night. The air was thick and wet. A warm dense fog had settled over the paddies and there was the stillness that precedes rain.

After a time Kiowa sighed.

One thing for sure, he said. The lieutenant's in some deep hurt. I mean that crying jag—the way he was carrying on—it wasn't fake or anything, it was real heavy-duty hurt. The man cares.

Sure, Norman Bowker said.

Say what you want, the man does care.

We all got problems.

Not Lavender.

No, I guess not, Bowker said. Do me a favor, though.

Shut up?

That's a smart Indian. Shut up.

Shrugging, Kiowa pulled off his boots. He wanted to say more, just to lighten up his sleep, but instead he opened his New Testament and arranged it beneath his head as a pillow. The fog made things seem hollow and unattached. He tried not to think about Ted Lavender, but then he was thinking how fast it was, no drama, down and dead, and how it was hard to feel anything except surprise. It seemed unchristian. He wished he could find some great sadness, or even anger, but the emotion wasn't there and he couldn't make it happen. Mostly he felt pleased to be alive. He liked the smell of the New Testament under his cheek, the leather and ink and paper and glue, whatever the chemicals were. He liked hearing the sounds of night. Even his fatigue, it felt fine, the stiff muscles and the prickly awareness of his own body, a floating feeling. He enjoyed not being dead. Lying there, Kiowa admired Lieutenant Jimmy Cross's capacity for grief. He wanted to share the man's pain, he wanted to care as Jimmy Cross cared. And yet when he closed his eyes, all he could think was Boom-down, and all he could feel was the pleasure of having his boots off and the fog curling in around him and the damp soil and the Bible smells and the plush comfort of night.

After a moment Norman Bowker sat up in the dark.

What the hell, he said. You want to talk, *talk*. Tell it to me.

Forget it.

No, man, go on. One thing I hate, it's a silent Indian.

For the most part they carried themselves with poise, a kind of dignity. Now and then, however, there were times of panic, when they squealed or wanted to squeal but couldn't, when they twitched and made moaning sounds and covered their heads and said Dear Jesus and flopped around on the earth and fired their weapons blindly and cringed and sobbed and begged for the noise to stop and went wild and made stupid promises to themselves and to God and to their mothers and fathers, hoping not to die. In different ways, it happened to all of them. Afterward, when the firing ended, they would blink and peek up. They would touch their bodies, feeling shame, then quickly hiding it. They would force themselves to stand. As if in slow motion, frame by frame, the world would take on the old logic—absolute silence, then the wind, then sunlight, then voices. It was the burden of being alive. Awkwardly, the men would reassemble themselves, first in private, then in groups, becoming soldiers again. They would repair the leaks in their eyes. They would check for casualties, call in dustoffs, light cigarettes, try to smile, clear their throats and spit and begin cleaning their weapons. After a time someone would shake his head and say, No lie, I almost shit my pants, and someone else would laugh, which meant it was bad, yes, but the guy had obviously not shit his pants, it wasn't that bad, and in any case nobody would ever do such a thing and then go ahead and talk about it. They would squint into the dense, oppressive sunlight. For a few moments, perhaps, they would fall silent, lighting a joint and tracking its passage from man to man, inhaling, holding in the humiliation. Scary stuff, one of them might say. But then someone else would grin or flick his eyebrows and say, Roger-dodger, almost cut me a new asshole, *almost*.

There were numerous such poses. Some carried themselves with a sort of wistful resignation, others with pride or stiff soldierly discipline or good humor or macho zeal. They were afraid of dying but they were even more afraid to show it.

They found jokes to tell.

They used a hard vocabulary to contain the terrible softness. *Greased* they'd say. *Offed, lit up, zapped while zipping.* It wasn't cruelty, just stage presence. They were actors. When someone died, it wasn't quite dying, because in a curious way it seemed scripted, and because they had their lines mostly memorized, irony mixed with tragedy, and because they called it by other names, as if to encyst and destroy the reality of death itself. They kicked corpses. They cut off thumbs. They talked grunt lingo. They told stories about Ted Lavender's supply of tranquilizers, how the poor guy didn't feel a thing, how incredibly tranquil he was.

There's a moral here, said Mitchell Sanders.

They were waiting for Lavender's chopper, smoking the dead man's dope.

The moral's pretty obvious, Sanders said, and winked. Stay away from drugs. No joke, they'll ruin your day every time.

Cute, said Henry Dobbins.

Mind blower, get it? Talk about wiggy. Nothing left, just blood and brains.

They made themselves laugh.

There it is, they'd say. Over and over—there it is, my friend, there it is—as if the repetition itself were an act of poise, a balance between crazy and almost crazy, knowing without going, there it is, which meant be cool, let it ride, because Oh yeah, man, you can't change what can't be changed, there it is, there it absolutely and positively and fucking well *is*.

They were tough.

They carried all the emotional baggage of men who might die. Grief, terror, love, longing—these were intangibles, but the intangibles had their own mass and specific gravity, they had tangible weight. They carried shameful memories. They carried the common secret of cowardice barely restrained, the instinct to run or freeze or hide, and in many respects this was the heaviest burden of all, for it could never be put down, it required perfect balance and perfect posture. They carried their reputations. They carried the soldier's greatest fear, which was the fear of blushing. Men killed, and died, because they were embarrassed not to. It was what had brought them to the war in the first place, nothing positive, no dreams of glory or honor, just to avoid the blush of dishonor. They died so as not to die of embarrassment. They crawled into tunnels and walked point and advanced under fire. Each morning, despite the unknowns, they made their legs move. They endured. They kept humping. They did not submit to the obvious alternative, which was simply to close the eyes and fall. So easy, really. Go limp and tumble to the ground and let the muscles unwind and not speak and not budge until your buddies picked you up and lifted you into the chopper that would roar and dip its nose and carry you off to the world. A mere matter of falling, yet no one ever fell. It was not courage, exactly; the object was not valor. Rather, they were too frightened to be cowards.

By and large they carried these things inside, maintaining the masks of composure. They sneered at sick call. They spoke bitterly about guys who had found release by shooting off their own toes or fingers. Pussies, they'd say. Candy-asses. It was fierce, mocking talk, with only a trace of envy or awe, but even so the image played itself out behind their eyes.

They imagined the muzzle against flesh. So easy: squeeze the trigger and blow away a toe. They imagined it. They imagined the quick, sweet pain, then the evacuation to Japan, then a hospital with warm beds and cute geisha nurses.

And they dreamed of freedom birds.

At night, on guard, staring into the dark, they were carried away by jumbo jets. They felt the rush of takeoff. *Gone!* they yelled. And then velocity—wings and engines—a smiling stewardess—but it was more than a plane, it was a real bird, a big sleek silver bird with feathers and talons and high screeching. They were flying. The weights fell off; there was nothing to bear. They laughed and held on tight, feeling the cold slap of wind and altitude, soaring, thinking *It's over, I'm gone!*—they were naked, they were light and free—it was all lightness, bright and fast and buoyant, light as light, a helium buzz in the brain, a giddy bubbling in the lungs as they were taken up over the clouds and the war, beyond duty, beyond gravity and mortification and global entanglements—*Sin loi![7]* they yelled. *I'm sorry, mother-fuckers, but I'm out of it, I'm goofed, I'm on a space cruise, I'm gone!*—and it was a restful, unencumbered sensation, just riding the light waves, sailing that big silver freedom bird over the mountains and oceans, over America, over the farms and great sleeping cities and cemeteries and highways and the golden arches of McDonald's, it was flight, a kind of fleeing, a kind of falling, falling higher and higher, spinning off the edge of the earth and beyond the sun and through the vast, silent vacuum where

---

[7] *Sin loi:* Vietnamese for sorry.

there were no burdens and where everything weighed exactly nothing—
Gone! they screamed. *I'm sorry but I'm gone!*—and so at night, not quite
dreaming, they gave themselves over to lightness, they were carried, they
were purely borne.

On the morning after Ted Lavender died, First Lieutenant Jimmy Cross
crouched at the bottom of his foxhole and burned Martha's letters. Then
he burned the two photographs. There was a steady rain falling, which made
it difficult, but he used heat tabs and Sterno to build a small fire, screen-
ing it with his body, holding the photographs over the tight blue flame
with the tips of his fingers.

He realized it was only a gesture. Stupid, he thought. Sentimental,
too, but mostly just stupid.

Lavender was dead. You couldn't burn the blame.

Besides, the letters were in his head. And even now, without photographs, Lieutenant Cross could see Martha playing volleyball in her white
gym shorts and yellow T-shirt. He could see her moving in the rain.

When the fire died out, Lieutenant Cross pulled his poncho over his
shoulders and ate breakfast from a can.

There was no great mystery, he decided.

In those burned letters Martha had never mentioned the war, except to
say, Jimmy, take care of yourself. She wasn't involved. She signed the letters Love, but it wasn't love, and all the fine lines and technicalities did
not matter. Virginity was no longer an issue. He hated her. Yes, he did. He
hated her. Love, too, but it was a hard, hating kind of love.

The morning came up wet and blurry. Everything seemed part of everything else, the fog and Martha and the deepening rain.

He was a soldier, after all.

Half smiling, Lieutenant Jimmy Cross took out his maps. He shook
his head hard, as if to clear it, then bent forward and began planning the
day's march. In ten minutes, or maybe twenty, he would rouse the men and
they would pack up and head west, where the maps showed the country
to be green and inviting. They would do what they had always done. The
rain might add some weight, but otherwise it would be one more day layered upon all the other days.

He was realistic about it. There was that new hardness in his stomach. He loved her but he hated her.

No more fantasies, he told himself.

Henceforth, when he thought about Martha, it would be only to think
that she belonged elsewhere. He would shut down the daydreams. This was
not Mount Sebastian, it was another world, where there were no pretty
poems or midterm exams, a place where men died because of careless-
ness and gross stupidity. Kiowa was right. Boom-down, and you were dead,
never partly dead.

Briefly, in the rain, Lieutenant Cross saw Martha's gray eyes gazing
back at him.

He understood.

It was very sad, he thought. The things men carried inside. The things men did or felt they had to do.

He almost nodded at her, but didn't.

Instead he went back to his maps. He was now determined to perform his duties firmly and without negligence. It wouldn't help Lavender, he knew that, but from this point on he would comport himself as an officer. He would dispose of his good-luck pebble. Swallow it, maybe, or use Lee Strunk's slingshot, or just drop it along the trail. On the march he would impose strict field discipline. He would be careful to send out flank security, to prevent straggling or bunching up, to keep his troops moving at the proper pace and at the proper interval. He would insist on clean weapons. He would confiscate the remainder of Lavender's dope. Later in the day, perhaps, he would call the men together and speak to them plainly. He would accept the blame for what had happened to Ted Lavender. He would be a man about it. He would look them in the eyes, keeping his chin level, and he would issue the new SOPs in a calm, impersonal tone of voice, a lieutenant's voice, leaving no room for argument or discussion. Commencing immediately, he'd tell them, they would no longer abandon equipment along the route of march. They would police up their acts. They would get their shit together, and keep it together, and maintain it neatly and in good working order.

He would not tolerate laxity. He would show strength, distancing himself.

Among the men there would be grumbling, of course, and maybe worse, because their days would seem longer and their loads heavier, but Lieutenant Jimmy Cross reminded himself that his obligation was not to be loved but to lead. *He would dispense with love*; it was not now a factor. And if anyone quarreled or complained, he would simply tighten his lips and arrange his shoulders in the correct command posture. He might give a curt little nod. Or he might not. He might just shrug and say, Carry on, then they would saddle up and form into a column and move out toward the villages west of Than Khe.

1990

Edgar Allan Poe (1809–1849)

The Tell-Tale Heart

True!—nervous—very, very dreadfully nervous I had been and am; but why *will* you say that I am mad? The disease had sharpened my senses—not destroyed—not dulled them. Above all was the sense of hearing acute. I heard all things in the heaven and in the earth. I heard many things in hell. How, then, am I mad? Hearken! and observe how healthily—how calmly I can tell you the whole story.

It is impossible to say how first the idea entered my brain; but once conceived, it haunted me day and night. Object there was none. Passion there was none. I loved the old man. He had never wronged me. He had never given me insult. For his gold I had no desire. I think it was his eye! yes, it was this! One of his eyes resembled that of a vulture—a pale blue eye, with a film over it. Whenever it fell upon me, my blood ran cold; and so by degrees—very gradually—I made up my mind to take the life of the old man, and thus rid myself of the eye for ever.

Now this is the point. You fancy me mad. Madmen know nothing. But you should have seen *me*. You should have seen how wisely I proceeded—with what caution—with what foresight—with what dissimulation I went to work! I was never kinder to the old man than during the whole week before I killed him. And every night, about midnight, I turned the latch of his door and opened it—oh, so gently! And then, when I had made an opening sufficient for my head, I put in a dark lantern, all closed, closed, so that no light shone out, and then I thrust in my head. Oh, you would have laughed to see how cunningly I thrust it in! I moved it slowly—very, very slowly, so that I might not disturb the old man's sleep. It took me an hour to place my whole head within the opening so far that I could see him as he lay upon his bed. Ha!—would a madman have been so wise as this? And then, when my head was well in the room, I undid the lantern cautiously—oh, so cautiously—cautiously (for the hinges creaked)—I undid it just so much that a single thin ray fell upon the vulture eye. And this I did for seven long nights—every night just at midnight—but I found the eye always closed; and so it was impossible to do the work; for it was not the old man who vexed me, but his Evil Eye. And every morning, when the day broke, I went boldly into the chamber, and spoke courageously to him, calling him by name in a hearty tone, and inquiring how he had passed the night. So you see he would have been a very profound old man, indeed, to suspect that every night, just at twelve, I looked in upon him while he slept.

Upon the eighth night I was more than usually cautious in opening the door. A watch's minute hand moves more quickly than did mine. Never before that night had I *felt* the extent of my own powers—of my sagacity. I could scarcely contain my feelings of triumph. To think that there I was, opening the door, little by little, and he not even to dream of my secret deeds or thoughts. I fairly chuckled at the idea; and perhaps he heard me; for he moved on the bed suddenly, as if startled. Now you may think that I drew back—but no. His room was as black as pitch with the thick darkness, (for the shutters were close fastened, through fear of robbers), and so I knew that he could not see the opening of the door, and I kept pushing it on steadily, steadily.

I had my head in, and was about to open the lantern, when my thumb slipped upon the tin fastening, and the old man sprang up in the bed, crying out—"Who's there?"

I kept quite still and said nothing. For a whole hour I did not move a muscle, and in the meantime I did not hear him lie down. He was still sitting up in the bed, listening;—just as I have done, night after night, hearkening to the death watches[1] in the wall.

Presently I heard a slight groan, and I knew it was the groan of mortal terror. It was not a groan of pain or of grief—oh, no!—it was the low stifled sound that arises from the bottom of the soul when overcharged with awe. I knew the sound very well. Many a night, just at midnight, when all the world slept, it has welled up from my own bosom, deepening, with its dreadful echo, the terrors that distracted me. I say I knew it well. I knew what the old man felt, and pitied him, although I chuckled at heart. I knew that he had been lying awake ever since the first slight noise, when he had turned in the bed. His fears had been ever since growing upon him. He had been trying to fancy them causeless, but could not. He had been saying to himself—"It is nothing but the wind in the chimney—it is only a mouse crossing the floor," or "it is merely a cricket which has made a single chirp." Yes, he had been trying to comfort himself with these suppositions; but he had found all in vain. *All in vain;* because Death, in approaching him, had stalked with his black shadow before him, and enveloped the victim. And it was the mournful influence of the unperceived shadow that caused him to feel—although he neither saw nor heard—to *feel* the presence of my head within the room.

When I had waited a long time, very patiently, without hearing him lie down, I resolved to open a little—a very, very little crevice in the lantern. So I opened it—you cannot imagine how stealthily, stealthily—until, at length, a single dim ray, like the thread of the spider, shot from out the crevice and fell upon the vulture eye.

It was open—wide, wide open—and I grew furious as I gazed upon it. I saw it with perfect distinctness—all a dull blue, with a hideous veil over it that chilled the very marrow in my bones; but I could see nothing else of the old man's face or person: for I had directed the ray as if by instinct, precisely upon the damned spot.

And now have I not told you that what you mistake for madness is but over-acuteness of the senses?—now, I say, there came to my ears a low, dull, quick sound, such as a watch makes when enveloped in cotton. I knew *that* sound well, too. It was the beating of the old man's heart. It increased my fury, as the beating of a drum stimulates the soldier into courage.

But even yet I refrained and kept still. I scarcely breathed. I held the lantern motionless. I tried how steadily I could maintain the ray upon the eye. Meantime the hellish tattoo of the heart increased. It grew quicker and quicker, and louder and louder every instant. The old man's terror *must* have been extreme! It grew louder, I say, louder every moment!—do you mark me well? I have told you that I am nervous: so I am. And now at the dead hour of the night, amid the dreadful silence of that old house, so strange a noise as this excited me to uncontrollable terror. Yet, for some minutes longer I refrained and stood still. But the beating grew louder, louder! I thought the heart must burst. And now a new anxiety seized me—

---

[1]*Death watches:* beetles that infest timbers. Their clicking sound was thought to be an omen of death.

the sound would be heard by a neighbor! The old man's hour had come! With a loud yell, I threw open the lantern and leaped into the room. He shrieked once—once only. In an instant I dragged him to the floor, and pulled the heavy bed over him. I then smiled gaily, to find the deed so far done. But, for many minutes, the heart beat on with a muffled sound. This, however, did not vex me; it would not be heard through the wall. At length it ceased. The old man was dead. I removed the bed and examined the corpse. Yes, he was stone, stone dead. I placed my hand upon the heart and held it there many minutes. There was no pulsation. He was stone dead. His eye would trouble me no more.

If still you think me mad, you will think so no longer when I describe the wise precautions I took for the concealment of the body. The night waned, and I worked hastily, but in silence. First of all I dismembered the corpse. I cut off the head and the arms and the legs.

I then took up three planks from the flooring of the chamber, and deposited all between the scantlings. I then replaced the boards so cleverly, so cunningly, that no human eye—not even *his*—could have detected anything wrong. There was nothing to wash out—no stain of any kind—no bloodspot whatever. I had been too wary for that. A tub had caught all—ha! ha!

When I had made an end of these labors, it was four o'clock—still dark as midnight. As the bell sounded the hour, there came a knocking at the street door. I went down to open it with a light heart,—for what had I *now* to fear? There entered three men, who introduced themselves, with perfect suavity, as officers of the police. A shriek had been heard by a neighbor during the night; suspicion of foul play had been aroused; information had been lodged at the police office, and they (the officers) had been deputed to search the premises.

I smiled,—for *what* had I to fear? I bade the gentlemen welcome. The shriek, I said, was my own in a dream. The old man, I mentioned, was absent in the country. I took my visitors all over the house. I bade them search— search *well*. I led them, at length, to *his* chamber. I showed them his treasures, secure, undisturbed. In the enthusiasm of my confidence, I brought chairs into the room, and desired them *here* to rest from their fatigues, while I myself, in the wild audacity of my perfect triumph, placed my own seat upon the very spot beneath which reposed the corpse of the victim.

The officers were satisfied. My *manner* had convinced them. I was singularly at ease. They sat, and while I answered cheerily, they chatted of familiar things. But, ere long, I felt myself getting pale and wished them gone. My head ached, and I fancied a ringing in my ears: but still they sat and still chatted. The ringing became more distinct:—it continued and became more distinct: I talked more freely to get rid of the feeling: but it continued and gained definitiveness—until, at length, I found that the noise was *not* within my ears.

No doubt I now grew *very* pale:—but I talked more fluently, and with a heightened voice. Yet the sound increased—and what could I do? It was *a low, dull, quick sound—much such a sound as a watch makes when enveloped in cotton*. I gasped for breath—and yet the officers heard it not. I talked more quickly—more vehemently; but the noise steadily increased. I arose and argued about trifles, in a high key and with violent gesticulations; but the noise steadily increased. Why *would* they not be gone? I paced the floor to and fro with heavy strides, as if excited to fury by the observations of the men—but the noise steadily increased. Oh God! what *could* I do? I foamed—I raved—I swore! I swung the chair upon which I had been sitting, and grated it upon the boards, but the noise arose over all and continually increased. It grew louder—louder—*louder!* And still the men chatted pleasantly, and smiled. Was it possible they heard not? Almighty God!—no, no! They heard!—they suspected!—they *knew!*—they were making a mockery of my horror!—this I thought, and this I think. But any thing was better than this agony! Anything was more tolerable than this derision! I could bear those hypocritical smiles no longer! I felt that I must scream or die!—and now—again!—hark! louder! louder! louder! *louder!*—"Villains!" I shrieked, "dissemble no more! I admit the deed!—tear up the planks!—here, here!—it is the beating of his hideous heart!"

[1843] 1850

Sharon Oard Warner (B. 1952)

A Simple Matter of Hunger

Last night Paul told me that loving Jancey will have to be my job. "I can't do it, Eleanor," he said. "Every time I go in and look at her, see how beautiful she is, how special, a cold wind rushes around inside me." We were in bed, and the room was so dark that I couldn't see his face. He was a voice speaking, and I was a body listening. Silent, I stared into the darkness, tried to see right through it, but the harder I looked, the thicker it got, until the darkness itself seemed to have texture, like the furry back of an enormous black bear.

In the thin hours of morning, I woke and heard Jancey rolling around in her crib. She wasn't crying, so I waited, thinking she might go back to sleep. Tiny as she is, she can make that crib creak. It's an old thing, plenty used when we bought it. Joel slept in it for nearly three years and now Jancey. Good thing she's so small, I told myself, but it's not a good thing at all.

In another minute, her crying wafted ghostlike down the hall, and before I could convince myself to throw off the covers, Paul nudged me with his knuckles. He's one of those people who can only go to sleep once each night, so he does what he can to keep from waking. Used to be, people would call in the middle of the night—broken pipes and such—and after saying hello, he'd stuff the receiver under the pillow and go right on sleeping. Eventually, we switched places. Now, I sleep closest to the phone.

The house was chilly, but Jancey's room glowed warmly. Two nightlights burned, one under the bed, and the other, a china cat, on her dresser. She wakes often, and I like to be able to change her, take her temperature even, without turning on an overhead light. Both of us stay sleepier that way. Her eyes were closed, but she was moaning and pitching from one side to the other, as though she were in the midst of a sea dream.

"Jancey," I whispered. At the sound of my voice, she opened her eyes and stared up at me, clearly awake. I hated to think of her like that, fully conscious but eyes closed. "Oh, Jancey," I said, picking her up. She was damp with sweat and so hot that I carried her across the room and switched on the light without thinking, blinding us both for an instant. I wanted to hurry her down the hall to Paul, press her close to him, wake him for good and all. Instead, I closed the door and did the only things I knew to do: I took off her sleeper and diaper, wrapped her in a blanket, coated the rectal thermometer with Vaseline, inserted it gently and sang to her while we waited.

It read 105. Drawing a deep breath, I took her into the kitchen, dribbled red liquid down her throat, and made a pact with myself. If her fever wasn't down in half an hour, I would call Dr. Kesl and have Paul drive me over to the hospital, to hell with them. As I carried her back to her room, I wondered if she could feel the pounding of my heart.

Most of her clothes were piled on the floor by the washing machine, so I put her in one of Joel's old sleepers, blue of course, but heavy and warm. She kicked her legs and stared up at me while I worked. Ordinarily, her thick black hair stands out all over her head, but last night it was slick with sweat, and after I'd dressed her, I combed the wet strands and clipped them into place with a blue barrette. "There now," I said. "You're pretty enough to go out on the town." With her dark coloring, she looks better in blue than Joel ever did.

He was a pasty little bald-headed thing, no hair on his head to speak of for over a year. "Please, God, let him have hair for a few good years," my husband Paul had prayed at the dinner table, one of those jokes that's no laughing matter. Paul's hairline has receded to the edges of his head now, nothing left but fringe around his ears and neck. He's not a vain man, but it bothers him when my hand strays to the top of his head while we make love. I like to rub the smooth skin there; something in me responds to the warm pulse beneath my fingers. I used to rub Joel's head while he nursed, my palm cupped around his skull. Love is never a pure emotion, is it? Sometimes Paul's hug brings back that sinking sensation I used to feel in the arms of my father, and once, kissing Joel goodnight, I was surprised by the same wash of tenderness that had come over me those last days with my mother in the hospital.

Jancey and I rocked for a good hour, and slowly her temperature fell. She relaxed and settled against me, her eyes opening and closing, opening again to find my face. I kept mine on her, smiled my reassurance. Once the medicine began to work, she drifted off, but as soon as I reached for the remote control to flip on the TV, she looked up at me, alert and interested. I muted the sound, but turned the chair so she could watch. She likes television—the motion and lights, the peculiar sounds. For a five-month-old, Jancey is attentive and obliging. When smiled at, she smiles; when given a toy, she holds on, waving it about with an expression that's downright grateful. If she senses she is supposed to sleep, she closes her eyes and nuzzles against me; her breathing slows. She could fool Dr. Spock with her act. We sat together and watched a couple dance across the screen, maybe Fred Astaire and Ginger Rogers. I couldn't tell for sure because I didn't have my glasses on. Their fuzzy forms swished back and forth, so graceful in the dark silence of my living room. The movie was in black and white, and it occurred to me that the dancers were probably dead, gone now except for these bits of celluloid. I went on watching until the movie was over and Jancey was deep into sleep.

★ ★ ★

Paul's side of the bed was already cold by the time the alarm went off. Up-before-he-has-to-get-up is a bad sign. When he's worried he doesn't sleep. Sometimes I find him out in the garage sweeping the cement floor, or in the back filling the bird feeder, or leaning over the fence feeding last night's bones to the neighbor's dog. This morning I found him in Jancey's room, his hands gripping the slats of her bed.

I came up behind him and rested a hand on his shoulder. "What's wrong?" I whispered. All of his muscles were strung tight, and I knew that he'd have a headache in an hour or so. Believe it or not, taking in Jancey had been his idea. His brother David is a social worker for one of the state agencies here in Des Moines, and he told us all about these babies, how there's no one to take care of them. It hurt my heart to think of them. I've always been partial to babies. One night Paul told me he'd been thinking. "Don't you see?" he'd explained. "You'd have an income, and we could do a little good in this world." Doing-a-little-good runs in Paul's family. He's a plumber, but his father was a missionary, his brother's a social worker, and his mother, old as she is, volunteers three days a week at the nursing home. She told me last week she'd started a knitting group. Just yesterday she brought over three pairs of booties for Jancey. They resemble tiny Christmas stockings in odd shades of green and gold.

Jancey was sleeping, still covered with the receiving blanket I'd draped over her. She looked peaceful, but her hair was damp again. The fever was returning.

"She's getting worse, Eleanor," he said as we filed out and I closed her door.

"I'm taking her to the doctor this morning," I told him, then followed him down the hall, scuffing my big pink house slippers against the carpet. One toe was stained yellow from Jancey's vomit. I'd washed the shoe in the sink, but the worst things, the things you don't want to be reminded of, those never come out. While I watched my slippers take one step at a time, I thought of those dancers, the way they'd seemed to float, the woman's dress billowing, nothing in the world to hold her down.

Paul put on the coffee and kept his back to me. First thing in the morning he walks around the house in boxer shorts. The material flaps around his spindly legs, and his long pale feet slap at the floor. He's a strong man in most ways, but what drew me to him, what keeps me close now, are his weaknesses. While he waited for the water, he went down the hall to give Joel his first shaking. Five or six times each morning Paul or I pull off the covers and shake Joel's foot, each time harder than the last. Joel is six years old now, but he still hasn't discovered anything he likes better than sleeping. This morning Paul tried tickling, and it seemed to work. I could hear Joel's desperate little giggle, then a breathless "Stop, Dad, stop."

The coffee was ready by the time he got back. "A new technique?" I asked, trying to keep my voice light. He filled his cup slowly then turned to me. His skin was still baggy from sleep, and he looked old. He'd been in there tickling Joel, but there was no trace of a smile on his face. "You knew it was going to be like this, didn't you?" I asked. His hand trembled a little as he replaced the pot.

"God knows I didn't," he said simply. Then he carried his coffee away down the long hall to the bathroom.

★ ★ ★

The pediatric waiting room is divided into two unequal sections by a length of Plexiglass that juts out into the middle of the room. A table at one end keeps people from walking into the flat edge. Orange and brown upholstered chairs line both sides of this transparent wall, back to back, as though some enormous game of musical chairs is about to begin. The smaller section of the room is reserved for well patients, and a prominent sign directs the rest of us to the other side.

When I carried Jancey in this morning, I stopped in the entranceway, momentarily confused. Some redecorating had gone on since our last visit. A large oval braided rug covered an expanse of institutional carpet in the unwell section, and a baby not much older than Jancey was seated in the big middle of it. While I watched, he crawled to the edge then back again, as though the rug were an island and he were marooned.

"Come on in," one of the receptionists called to me, waving and smiling in that way teachers and nurses and social workers do, professional encouragers.

I had Jancey in her big plastic carseat. It's shaped something like a bucket or a scoop and is perfectly portable if you're big and strong. The inside was lined with receiving blankets, and Jancey was asleep among them. She'd slept straight through her morning feeding, and when I'd lifted her from the crib into the seat she hadn't so much as stirred. More than once this morning I'd passed my hand before her face to feel her breath. When I got to the counter, I heaved the seat onto it and sighed in relief. The three receptionists who work the desk dress in nurses' uniforms, but to assert their individuality, they also wear sweater vests or buttondowns in bright primary colors. They're trim and efficient and seem always to have gotten enough sleep the night before.

The blonde curly-haired one ran a finger down a list of appointments until she found the name then glanced up at me and smiled brightly.

"Jancey Hernandez," she said, her voice much louder than it needed to be. Instantly, the other two looked up. One was on the phone, the receiver cradled on her shoulder, and the other was seated in front of the computer, watching as one screen after another clicked past. The one at the computer abandoned her post to come over.

"I never pass up a chance to coo at a baby," she explained to no one in particular. Her red hair was clipped short around her ears and neck but had been left fluffy on top; little tendrils curled prettily. On her blue sweater she wore a puffy plastic heart pin, red as Snow White's apple. Last month she'd sported a snowman with a tiny top hat, and the month before that a fat Jack O'Lantern. I'd seen her many times in the last few months, watched her fingers moving over the keys of the computer, her small perfectly shaped head bent to the task. She'd never taken notice of me or my baby.

"What a darling," she cried, peering into the bucket from a safe distance. I stared back and said nothing.

"Dr. Kesl will be with you shortly, Mrs. Wilson," the blonde told me as she, too, moved closer to get a look at my baby. I was grateful Jancey was sleeping; otherwise, I knew she would smile back at them, betraying us both. Grabbing up the bucket, I turned and made my way across the brief expanse of carpet to the first available seat. I sat down just as my arms began to shake.

Of course, a baby with AIDS is the sort of thing people talk about, but I hadn't expected it from the people at the Clinic. Up until now, we'd kept the secret fairly well, I'd thought, the doctors, Paul, and I. By some sort of unspoken agreement, we rarely use identifying terms, referring only occasionally to "the disease." Otherwise, we talked about the same illnesses that worry other parents: ear infections, staph infections, urinary infections. For Jancey though, these diseases are only symptoms, not the real thing. Sometimes, I think of AIDS as a monster, the kind that lives in closets in children's books, a horrifying creature with five heads, a scaley body, and horns growing out of his tail. The more frightened I become, the bigger and uglier he gets, until I am sure that he will burst out of the closet and kill us all.

After I'd recovered, I settled Jancey's seat into the chair next to mine and pulled the covers from around her so she wouldn't get too hot. Revived by the cool air of the waiting room, she began the slow process of waking, a series of stretches, blinks, and yawns. Like Joel, she is more at home in her dream world than in this one.

The receptionists made a pretense of returning to work, but again and again their eyes strayed to Jancey. While they watched, I raised her from the bucket and into my arms, bent my face to hers and kissed the round apple of her cheek. When I felt the warmth of her skin against my lips, my heart shrank back. I've never been afraid of Jancey before, not even that first time I held her in the hospital, when the nurse had lifted her into my arms and said, "She's yours now. God bless you." To stop it, to reprimand us all, I spoke aloud: "She's just a baby, damn it."

Only the curly-haired receptionist seemed to hear. She looked over at me as though I were a new arrival, someone she hardly recognized. "Is Jancey here today for a routine checkup, Mrs. Wilson?" she asked, her eyes flitting to a spot on the wall just above my head and then back to my face again. Obligingly, I craned my head to read the sign: THIS SECTION RESERVED FOR WELL PATIENTS ONLY. YOUR COOPERATION IS APPRECIATED. Smiling, I turned back to her. "Yes," I lied, suddenly myself again.

Jancey and I sat and played pat-a-cake for five minutes or so, until she wet her diaper. While we were off in the restroom changing it, another mother arrived with her baby, a red and shriveled newborn. Though the room was full of empty chairs, the mother took the seat right next to mine. Perhaps she noticed Jancey's empty baby bucket and imagined we might have a chat.

No big deal, really, her sitting next to us. Such a thing might have happened anywhere else, and I wouldn't have given it a thought. Jancey couldn't give her illness to either the mother or her child—even the receptionists knew as much. Still, their foreheads furrowed with concern. "All right," their expressions said. "You've made your point. Now get back to the sick section where you belong." And I considered doing just that—gathering my things, and murmuring some sort of excuse, something about a sneeze or a cough. But I couldn't do it. People who've lost control of life are a superstitious lot: they look for signs, indulge in rituals, refuse to backtrack or take peeks into the future. They huddle in the present and hold on for dear life. It seemed a bad move to go from the well section to the sick section, hasty and unnecessary. So I stayed put and smiled graciously at the new mother, dressed just as I was in the housewife uniform of blue jeans and plain-front sweatshirt, hers powder blue and mine Christmas green.

Jancey rested on my chest, her head on my shoulder. The waving and cooing she'd done while I changed her diaper were over. She seemed spent, her limbs slack, as though she were sleeping. Periodically, though, I felt the brush of her lashes against my neck. I sighed deeply, prompting the new mother to touch my arm. "It's tough, isn't it?" she said.

Her baby was tucked into the small valley between her legs, swaddled hospital fashion. Seeing him reminded me of the day I'd brought Joel home from the hospital. Anxiously, I'd unwrapped him to check his diaper then been unable to rewrap him again. Poor thing, he'd spent an hour or more on the kitchen table wailing and kicking, so angry and frightened that he finally lay gasping for breath while I rolled him up first one way, then another. By the time I gave up, I'd been crying, too. I remembered it now as though it had happened to someone else.

"Yes, it is," I replied, and while I watched, the little being in the blue blanket began to struggle, rocking himself in his mother's lap like an upended and legless caterpillar, helpless, entirely so.

"Hungry again?" his mother asked him, as though all unhappiness were a simple matter of hunger. Already an old hand, she leaned over her diaper bag, drew forth a crocheted blanket, draped it over one shoulder, and lifting the sweatshirt beneath it, readied herself to nurse. Her baby had just opened his mouth to wail when she turned his body and gently nudged his head beneath the green and yellow crochet. I watched him latch on then relax against her.

"Are you nursing?" the new mother asked, ready now for our chat. I had already decided to say yes. After all, I had nursed Joel for nearly a year. Just watching her brought back the ache of the milk followed by the pull of the baby's mouth, pain that passed into pleasure.

"Jancey Hernandez," the nurse called out. I lurched to my feet, jerking Jancey so that her head banged against my shoulder. She responded with a one syllable scream, a sound like someone falling down a well. The new mother looked up at me, surprised. Her baby lay nestled against her, both of them in exactly the right place. For them, this visit to the doctor would be nothing more than an exchange of smiles and compliments. Afterwards, they'd go home and nap together, still nearly one.

★ ★ ★

I'd been home from the clinic for maybe fifteen minutes when I spotted Joel from the kitchen window, on his way home for lunch. He trudged slowly up the sidewalk, hands in his pockets, a red wool cap pulled low over his forehead. As I watched, he smiled to himself, and my heart lifted, but the smile faded quickly. As he approached the house, Joel seemed to grow smaller instead of larger. I turned away from the window and set his place for lunch, resisting the impulse to rush out and hug him tight. I'd whipped up a box of macaroni and cheese, opened a couple of cans—green beans and fruit cocktail. I arranged several spoons of each on a plastic plate and stored the rest in the refrigerator.

"Where's your lunch?" he asked when he came into the kitchen. Usually, we sit down to lunch together.

"Shh," I said, "Jancey's sleeping."

The doctor's office had sapped whatever energy she had left. The mere sight of someone in white terrifies her. To Dr. Kesl and the others, she's a tiny hostile being, stiff and red-faced. Her rage, though I've seen it many times, surprises even me. In the car on the way home from these visits, she wails, gathers her breath, then wails again. To calm her, I sing lullabies as I drive, my voice so loud that by the time we turn into the driveway, both of us are hoarse. Once, Paul rode along, and was shocked by the din we created. "Eleanor," he cried, "you're screaming, too." On the way home today, I gave up the pretense of singing and simply screamed along with her. At a red light, I paused for breath, and turning my head, looked out the window. In the car next to me an elderly woman sat watching, one hand over her mouth. Snapping my own mouth closed, I tried to compose my features, to reassure her with a smile, but she wouldn't look my way again. She sat stiffly in her bucket seat, staring through her windshield. When the light changed, she pulled away fast, as though leaving the scene of a crime.

"What did the doctor say?" Joel asked. He sat down and picked up his fork.

"Oh, not much new," I sighed, striking that delicate balance between near-truth and outright lie. Joel knows a little about Jancey, but not as much as he should know.

"Jancey's sick, you know," I said, sitting down next to him.

He turned to me with those gentle eyes of his, my mother's eyes. "Don't worry, Momma," he said, patting my knee. "She'll get better." My words, he consoled me with them now.

"Do you think so?" I asked. Then, I got up to fix him a glass of milk.

★ ★ ★

"Be prepared," Dr. Kesl had told me. "She may take a turn for the worse." He'd examined her slowly—pressing, tapping, prodding—his big hands passing over her again and again. I stood by silently, my eyes on his face, trying to guess his thoughts. No point in asking questions. Jancey's piercing cry drowned out everything, even the ringing telephone. The nurse, who slipped in and out of the room while Dr. Kesl worked, stuck her hand in the door at one point and waved a slip of paper. ANSWER THE PHONE, it said in large red letters.

Dr. Kesl had seemed distracted in a way I couldn't interpret. Something was worrying him, but it might have been something other than Jancey. "Everything doesn't have to do with you," my mother used to remind me.

"Listen," I said when he'd finished the exam, shouted his directions, and passed on a new sheaf of prescriptions. He was stripping off the gloves while his nurse ripped the paper from the examining table. Both of them wore masks and paper gowns; I felt like a naked person on a spaceship. Dr. Kesl glanced over at me and moved to the sink, thrust his hands beneath the faucet and began to wash in that way they all learn in medical school. "Don't adoptive mothers nurse sometimes?" I asked him. I was dressing Jancey, pushing her thin brown arms into the sleeves of a yellow playsuit. Because Dr. Kesl no longer loomed over her, she screamed intermittently. We talked in the silent spaces she left us.

"They do, yes," he replied, half-turned away, clean and ready to go. Dr. Kesl is a tall man with permanently hunched shoulders and a small bald patch on the back of the head that should make him look older but somehow doesn't. Seeing it made me think of the little bald spot newborns get from rubbing their heads against the sheet. I used to like Dr. Kesl very much. "Don't know much about it, though," he finished and went out the door. As soon as he was gone, Jancey quieted, a momentary lull. I could feel her eyes on my face, but I didn't look back at her just yet. Instead, my gaze slipped from the dark wood of the closed door over to a matted and framed photo of a waterfall that hung between the door and one corner of the wall. Dr. Kesl had snapped it himself while vacationing in Hawaii. I remembered the day he'd pointed it out to me, a better day for both of us. "You ought to go sometime," he'd suggested, his smile warm on me. I'd nodded and cradled newborn Jancey, who still trusted doctors and lay quietly in my arms.

This afternoon, the photograph seemed changed; I no longer recognized its contours. I blinked and stared, blinked and stared, but what I saw made no sense to me. It might have been abstract art. Backing up to a chair, I sank into it and turned my eyes to Jancey. She waited for me in her bucket, intent on a mobile that hung over the examining table. Little lambs, pigs, and rabbits turned slowly above our heads. When the nurse looked in, we were both watching the animals. "Are you all right, Eleanor?" she asked. I noticed for the first time that she, too, was wearing a puffy heart pin. Coincidence, I told myself, though I no longer believe in it.

★ ★ ★

After Joel returned to school, I flipped on the TV and sat down to watch my soap. I remember nothing of what I saw, though I stared at the screen, my hands folded in my lap. Halfway through the program, I got up and hurried back to the bedroom to Paul's desk. One of the drawers is reserved for my things—old letters, Joel's baby book, a box so full of Mother's costume jewelry that I keep it closed with rubber bands. In the manila folder marked JANCEY I found the letter I received a few weeks ago. The envelope is lavender, postmarked San Antonio, Texas. Holding it, I thought of pictures I've seen of the Alamo, a small fort surrounded by palm trees, the hot sun beating down on people wearing big straw hats.

Jancey's mother is a young woman, hardly more than a teenager. If the picture she sent favors, she is pretty. Her dark hair waves over her shoulders, full and soft looking, but her bangs are teased and sprayed, so that she looks as if she's just come in out of the wind. Her features are arranged nearly on her face; nothing calls attention to itself. The photo she sent, which was taken in one of those arcade booths, is actually a series of three photos. She must have sat very still while the camera clicked because all three look remarkably the same. On the back, she scrawled, TO ELEANOR, WITH LOVE FROM MARY ELIZABETH. You'd think I were her aunt or some school friend. Actually, Mary Elizabeth and I have never met. In some ways, she is no more real to me than the characters on my show. None of them has AIDS, but several have drug problems. They prick their arms with needles and take hideous chances in dark corners.

Like her, these characters are young and carry their problems home to their parents. When Mary Elizabeth got sick, she moved back to her mother's house in San Antonio. In her letter, she described cramped quarters and her mother's habit of cooking more food than the two of them can possibly eat. "P.S." she wrote, "Please call me sometime," but she didn't include her phone number.

"She doesn't really want you to call," Paul told me when I wondered about it out loud.

"Maybe she just forgot," I said.

She had printed her address in the upper left-hand corner of the envelope, so it was a simple matter of calling directory assistance. Someone answered on the fourth ring.

"Hello," I chirped, my voice falsely cheerful, like some salesperson's. "This is Eleanor Wilson. Is Mary Elizabeth there?"

"No, she's not." A mixture of accents gave the words a rich, rounded sound, but I heard the hesitancy behind them. This was Mary Elizabeth's mother, Jancey's grandmother. I tried to think what she might look like. Dark hair and dark eyes was as far as I could get.

"Mrs. Hernandez," I went on. "I'm Eleanor Wilson, Jancey's foster mother. Mary Elizabeth sent me a letter a few weeks ago. She asked me to call."

All I heard was her breath, then mine, then hers again. "My baby Jancey?" she finally murmured.

"Yes." I said.

"Do you know I've never seen her, Mrs. Wilson? Only photos and those are months old."

"Well, I could send . . . "

"No, don't," she interrupted. "It's good of you, but sometimes it's easier not to believe in her, not to believe in any of it."

"She's real, Mrs. Hernandez," I said quietly.

"To you she's real," the rich voice came back. "To me, Mary Elizabeth is real. When you called, I was putting on my sweater, going out the door. She's in the hospital. They don't say when she might come out."

"Oh," I sighed.

"I pray for you every day," Mrs. Hernandez told me. Her voice was suddenly thin. It hardly reached my ear before it was gone.

I thanked her. In the other room, the crib creaked as Jancey shifted and stretched. In another minute or so, I knew she would begin to sob.

"Do you believe in God, Mrs. Wilson?" Mary Elizabeth's mother asked. My own mother had asked the same question of me the day before she died.

"I try." It was the answer I'd given Mother, though not the one she'd hoped for. The last time I'd bent to kiss her, she'd thrown her arms around me, clutched at me as though she expected us to be separated for eternity. "Listen," I said, then stretched my arm overhead, holding the receiver into the air. Jancey was wailing; her indignant scream grew louder each time she took a breath.

"Oh, my little baby," I heard Mrs. Hernandez say.

★ ★ ★

By the time I hung up, Jancey had soaked herself, her blankets, the sheet. While I cleaned up the mess, I spoke to her in that funny, high-pitched voice she likes.

"Guess who was on the phone?" I asked. She gazed up at me intently. As usual, I had her undivided attention. "Your grandmother," I went on. "You didn't even know you had a grandmother, did you? And she loves you. We all love you."

When she was clean, I carried Jancey into my bedroom, sat down with her in the rocker by the window and put her to my breast. She seemed to know what to do. She sucked for a moment, looked up at me, then returned to the task. She will get nothing today, I know, but if we keep it up, my body may respond.

The view from this window is the best in the house. From my chair, I can see a line of farmland—tan in winter and green in summer—and above that, a wide swatch of sky. Birds glide by, soaring then dipping out of sight. When I was a little girl someone told me that birds house the souls of the dead. I don't know who would tell a child a thing like that, but the idea has stuck with me. I remember being eight years old and standing stock still in the fields, shading my eyes with one hand so I could watch those birds move back and forth between heaven and earth. It seemed to me then that they couldn't quite decide which place they liked best. Sometimes, I tried to sneak up on them while they pecked at the ground. "It's all right," I'd whisper when I got close. "I just want to know your name." Of course, the sound of my voice sent them straight back to the skies. Startled souls, they have always been just out of my reach.

1992

Sherman Alexie (B. 1966)

Indian Education

Crazy Horse came back to life
in a storage room of the Smithsonian,
his body rising from a wooden crate
mistakenly marked ANONYMOUS HOPI MALE.

Crazy Horse wandered the halls, found   5
the surface of the moon, Judy Garland
and her red shoes, a stuffed horse named
Comanche, the only surviving

member of the Seventh Cavalry
at Little Big Horn. Crazy Horse was found   10
in the morning by a security guard
who took him home and left him alone

in a room with cable television. Crazy Horse
watched a basketball game, every black and white
western, a documentary about a scientist   15
who travelled the Great Plains in the 1800s

measuring Indians and settlers, discovering
that the Indians were two inches taller
on average, and in some areas, the difference
in height exceeded a foot, which proved nothing   20

although Crazy Horse measured himself
against the fact of a mirror, traded faces
with a taxi driver and memorized the city,
folding, unfolding, his mapped heart.

                                          1996

W. H. Auden (1907–1973)

Musée des Beaux Arts

About suffering they were never wrong,
The Old Masters: how well they understood
Its human position; how it takes place
While someone else is eating or opening a window or just walking
    dully along;
How, when the aged are reverently, passionately waiting   5
For the miraculous birth, there always must be
Children who did not specially want it to happen, skating
On a pond at the edge of the wood:
They never forgot
That even the dreadful martyrdom must run its course   10
Anyhow in a corner, some untidy spot
Where the dogs go on with their doggy life and the torturer's horse
Scratches its innocent behind on a tree.

In Brueghel's *Icarus*, for instance: how everything turns away
Quite leisurely from the disaster; the ploughman may   15
Have heard the splash, the forsaken cry,
But for him it was not an important failure; the sun shone
As it had to on the white legs disappearing into the green
Water; and the expensive delicate ship that must have seen
Something amazing, a boy falling out of the sky,   20
Had somewhere to get to and sailed calmly on.

                                    1940

Elizabeth Bishop (1911–1979)

One Art

The art of losing isn't hard to master;
so many things seem filled with the intent
to be lost that their loss is no disaster.

Lose something every day. Accept the fluster
of lost door keys, the hour badly spent.   5
The art of losing isn't hard to master.

Then practice losing farther, losing faster:
places, and names, and where it was you meant
to travel. None of these will bring disaster.

I lost my mother's watch. And look! my last, or   10
next-to-last, of three loved houses went.
The art of losing isn't hard to master.

I lost two cities, lovely ones. And, vaster,
some realms I owned, two rivers, a continent.
I miss them, but it wasn't a disaster.   15

—Even losing you (the joking voice, a gesture
I love) I shan't have lied. It's evident
the art of losing's not too hard to master
though it may look like (*Write* it!) like disaster.

1976

Robert Browning (1812–1889)

My Last Duchess

Ferrara

That's my last Duchess painted on the wall,
Looking as if she were alive. I call
That piece a wonder, now; Frà Pandolf's hands
Worked busily a day, and there she stands.
Will't please you sit and look at her? I said   5
"Frà Pandolf" by design, for never read
Strangers like you that pictured countenance,
The depth and passion of its earnest glance,
But to myself they turned (since none puts by
The curtain I have drawn for you, but I)   10
And seemed as they would ask me, if they durst,
How such a glance came there; so, not the first
Are you to turn and ask thus. Sir, 'twas not
Her husband's presence only, called that spot
Of joy into the Duchess' cheek: perhaps   15
Frà Pandolf chanced to say, "Her mantle laps
Over my lady's wrist too much," or "Paint
Must never hope to reproduce the faint
Half-flush that dies along her throat." Such stuff
Was courtesy, she thought, and cause enough   20
For calling up that spot of joy. She had
A heart—how shall I say?—too soon made glad,
Too easily impressed; she liked whate'er
She looked on, and her looks went everywhere.
Sir, 'twas all one! My favor at her breast,   25
The dropping of the daylight in the West,

The bough of cherries some officious fool
Broke in the orchard for her, the white mule
She rode with round the terrace—all and each
Would draw from her alike the approving speech,   30
Or blush, at least. She thanked men,—good! but thanked
Somehow—I know not how—as if she ranked
My gift of a nine-hundred-years-old name
With anybody's gift. Who'd stoop to blame
This sort of trifling? Even had you skill   35
In speech—which I have not—to make your will
Quite clear to such an one, and say "Just this
Or that in you disgusts me; here you miss,
Or there exceed the mark"—and if she let
Herself be lessoned so, nor plainly set   40
Her wits to yours, forsooth, and made excuse—
E'en then would be some stooping; and I choose
Never to stoop. Oh, sir, she smiled, no doubt,
Whene'er I passed her; but who passed without
Much the same smile? This grew; I gave commands;   45
Then all smiles stopped together. There she stands
As if alive. Will't please you rise? We'll meet
The company below, then. I repeat,
The Count your master's known munificence
Is ample warrant that no just pretense   50
Of mine for dowry will be disallowed;
Though his fair daughter's self, as I avowed
At starting, is my object. Nay, we'll go
Together down, sir. Notice Neptune, though,
Taming a sea-horse, thought a rarity,   55
Which Claus of Innsbruck cast in bronze for me!

1842

My Last Duchess. Ferrara, a city in northern Italy, is the scene. Browning may have modeled his speaker after Alonzo, Duke of Ferrara (1533–1598). 3 *Frà Pandolf* and 56 *Claus of Innsbruck*: fictitious names of artists.

Gerry Cambridge (B. 1959)

Goldfinch in Spring

That finch which sings above my head,
Last year's speckled egg, is now
A partner in some nest instead,
That finch which sings above my head,

Buff-gold dandy masked with read,   5
    And hen on eggs upon some swaying bough
That finch which sings. Above my head
    Last year's speckled egg is now.

                                    1995

Lewis Carroll
(Charles Lutwidge Dodgson) (1832–1898)

Jabberwocky

'Twas brillig, and the slithy toves
    Did gyre and gimble in the wabe:
All mimsy were the borogoves,
    And the mome raths outgrabe.

"Beware the Jabberwock, my son!   5
    The jaws that bite, the claws that catch!
Beware the Jubjub bird, and shun
    The frumious Bandersnatch!"

He took his vorpal sword in hand;
    Long time the manxome foe he sought—   10
So rested he by the Tumtum tree
    And stood awhile in thought.

And, as in uffish thought he stood,
    The Jabberwock, with eyes of flame,
Came whiffling through the tulgey wood,   15
    And burbled as it came!

One, two! One, two! And through and through
    The vorpal blade went snicker-snack!
He left it dead, and with its head
    He went galumphing back.   20

"And hast thou slain the Jabberwock?
    Come to my arms, my beamish boy!
O frabjous day! Callooh, Callay!"
    He chortled in his joy.

'Twas brillig, and the slithy toves   25
    Did gyre and gimble in the wabe:
All mimsy were the borogoves,
    And the mome raths outgrabe.

                                    1871

Jabberwocky. Fussy about pronunciation, Carroll in his preface to *The Hunting of the Snark* declares: "The first 'o' in 'borogoves' is pronounced like the 'o' in 'borrow.' I have heard people try to give it the sound of the 'o' in 'worry.' Such is Human Perversity." *Toves*, he adds, rimes with *groves*.

Wendy Cope (B. 1945)

Lonely Hearts

Can someone make my simple wish come true?
Male biker seeks female for touring fun.
Do you live in North London? Is it you?

Gay vegetarian whose friends are few,
I'm into music, Shakespeare and the sun.   5
Can someone make my simple wish come true?

Executive in search of something new—
Perhaps bisexual woman, arty, young.
Do you live in North London? Is it you?

Successful, straight and solvent? I am too—   10
Attractive Jewish lady with a son.
Can someone make my simple wish come true?

I'm Libran, inexperienced and blue—
Need slim non-smoker, under twenty-one.
Do you live in North London? Is it you?   15

Please write (with photo) to Box 152.
Who knows where it may lead once we've begun?
Can someone make my simple wish come true?
Do you live in North London? Is it you?

1986

Hart Crane (1899–1932)

My Grandmother's Love Letters

There are no stars tonight
But those of memory.
Yet how much room for memory there is
In the loose girdle of soft rain.

There is even room enough   5
For the letters of my mother's mother,
Elizabeth,
That have been pressed so long
Into a corner of the roof
That they are brown and soft,   10
And liable to melt as snow.

Over the greatness of such space
Steps must be gentle.
It is all hung by an invisible white hair.
It trembles as birch limbs webbing the air.   15

And I ask myself:

"Are your fingers long enough to play
Old keys that are but echoes:
Is the silence strong enough
To carry back the music to its source   20
And back to you again
As though to her?"

Yet I would lead my grandmother by the hand
Through much of what she would not understand;
And so I stumble. And the rain continues on the roof   25
With such a sound of gently pitying laughter.

                                                 1926

Paul Laurence Dunbar (1872–1906)

We Wear the Mask

We wear the mask that grins and lies,
It hides our cheeks and shades our eyes—
This debt we pay to human guile;
With torn and bleeding hearts we smile,
And mouth with myriad subtleties.   5

Why should the world be over-wise,
In counting all our tears and sighs?
Nay, let them only see us, while
     We wear the mask.

We smile, but O great Christ, our cries   10
To thee from tortured souls arise.
We sing, but oh the clay is vile

Beneath our feel, and long the mile;
But let the world dream otherwise,
    We wear the mask! 15

                        1896

Rhina P. Espaillat (B. 1932)

Bilingual/Bilingüe

My father liked them separate, one there,
one here (allá y aquí), as if aware

that words might cut in two his daughter's heart
(el corazón) and lock the alien part

to what he was—his memory, his name 5
(su nombre)—with a key he could not claim.

"English outside this door, Spanish inside,"
he said, "y basta." But who can divide

the world, the word (mundo y palabra) from
any child? I knew how to be dumb 10

and stubborn (testaruda); late, in bed,
I hoarded secret syllables I read

until my tongue (mi lengua) learned to run
where his stumbled. And still the heart was one.

I like to think he knew that, even when, 15
proud (orgulloso) of his daughter's pen,

he stood outside mis versos, half in fear
of words he loved but wanted not to hear.

                        1998

Robert Frost (1874–1963)

The Road Not Taken

Two roads diverged in a yellow wood,
And sorry I could not travel both
And be one traveler, long I stood

And looked down one as far as I could
To where it bent in the undergrowth; 5
Then took the other, as just as fair,
And having perhaps the better claim,
Because it was grassy and wanted wear;
Though as for that the passing there
Had worn them really about the same, 10
And both that morning equally lay
In leaves no step had trodden black.
Oh, I kept the first for another day!
Yet knowing how way leads on to way,
I doubted if I should ever come back. 15
I shall be telling this with a sigh
Somewhere ages and ages hence:
Two roads diverged in a wood, and I—
I took the one less traveled by,
And that has made all the difference. 20

1916

Out, Out—

The buzz-saw snarled and rattled in the yard
And made dust and dropped stove-length sticks of wood,
Sweet-scented stuff when the breeze drew across it.
And from there those that lifted eyes could count
Five mountain ranges one behind the other 5
Under the sunset far into Vermont.
And the saw snarled and rattled, snarled and rattled,
As it ran light, or had to bear a load.
And nothing happened: day was all but done.
Call it a day, I wish they might have said 10
To please the boy by giving him the half hour
That a boy counts so much when saved from work.
His sister stood beside them in her apron
To tell them "Supper." At the word, the saw,
As if to prove saws knew what supper meant, 15
Leaped out at the boy's hand, or seemed to leap—
He must have given the hand. However it was,
Neither refused the meeting. But the hand!
The boy's first outcry was a rueful laugh,
As he swung toward them holding up the hand 20
Half in appeal, but half as if to keep
The life from spilling. Then the boy saw all—
Since he was old enough to know, big boy
Doing a man's work, though a child at heart—
He saw all spoiled. "Don't let him cut my hand off— 25

The doctor, when he comes. Don't let him, sister!"
So. But the hand was gone already.
The doctor put him in the dark of ether.
He lay and puffed his lips out with his breath.
And then—the watcher at his pulse took fright.   30
No one believed. They listened at his heart.
Little—less—nothing!—and that ended it.
No more to build on there. And they, since they
Were not the one dead, turned to their affairs.

                                                 1916

Dana Gioia (B. 1950)

My Confessional Sestina

Let me confess. I'm sick of these sestinas
written by youngsters in poetry workshops
for the delectation of their fellow students,
and then published in little magazines
that no one reads, not even the contributors   5
who at least in this omission show some taste.

Is this merely a matter of personal taste?
I don't think so. Most sestinas
are such dull affairs. Just ask the contributors
the last time they finished one outside of a workshop,   10
even the poignant one on herpes in that new little magazine
edited by their most brilliant fellow student.

Let's be honest. It has become a form for students,
an exercise to build technique rather than taste
and the official entry blank into the little magazines—   15
because despite its reputation, a passable sestina
isn't very hard to write, even for kids in workshops
who care less about being poets than contributors.

Granted nowadays everyone is a contributor.
My barber is currently a student   20
in a rigorous correspondence school workshop.
At lesson six he can already taste
success having just placed his own sestina
in a national tonsorial magazine.

Who really cares about most little magazines?   25
Eventually not even their own contributors
who having published a few preliminary sestinas

send their work East to prove they're no longer students.
They need to be recognized as the new arbiters of taste
so they can teach their own graduate workshops.   30

Where will it end? This grim cycle of workshops
churning out poems for little magazines
no one honestly finds to their taste?
This ever-lengthening column of contributors
scavenging the land for more students   35
teaching them to write their boot-camp sestinas?

Perhaps there is an afterlife where all contributors
have two workshops, a tasteful little magazine, and sexy students
who worshipfully memorize their every sestina.

                                                        1991

R. S. Gwynn (B. 1948)

Shakespearean Sonnet

(With a first line taken from the tv listings)

A man is haunted by his father's ghost.
Boy meets girl while feuding families fight.
A Scottish king is murdered by his host.
Two couples get lost on a summer night.
A hunchback murders all who block his way.   5
A ruler's rivals plot against his life.
A fat man and a prince make rebels pay.
A noble Moor has doubts about his wife.
An English king decides to conquer France.
A duke learns that his best friend is a she.   10
A forest sets the scene for this romance.
An old man and his daughters disagree.
A Roman leader makes a big mistake.
A sexy queen is bitten by a snake.

                                                        2001

Joy Harjo (B. 1951)

She Had Some Horses

She had some horses.

She had horses who were bodies of sand.
She had horses who were maps drawn of blood.
She had horses who were skins of ocean water.
She had horses who were the blue air of sky.   5
She had horses who were fur and teeth.
She had horses who were clay and would break.
She had horses who were splintered red cliff.

She had some horses.

She had horses with long, pointed breasts.   10
She had horses with full, brown thighs.
She had horses who laughed too much.
She had horses who threw rocks at glass houses.
She had horses who licked razor blades.

She had some horses.   15

She had horses who danced in their mothers' arms.
She had horses who thought they were the sun and their
bodies shone and burned like stars.
She had horses who waltzed nightly on the moon.
She had horses who were much too shy, and kept quiet   20
in stalls of their own making.

She had some horses.

She had horses who liked Creek Stomp Dance songs.
She had horses who cried in their beer.
She had horses who spit at male queens who made   25
them afraid of themselves.
She had horses who said they weren't afraid.
She had horses who lied.
She had horses who told the truth, who were stripped
bare of their tongues.   30

She had some horses.

She had horses who called themselves, "horse".
She had horses who called themselves, "spirit", and kept
their voices secret and to themselves.
She had horses who had no names.   35
She had horses who had books of names.

She had some horses.

She had horses who whispered in the dark, who were afraid to speak.
She had horses who screamed out of fear of the silence, who
carried knives to protect themselves from ghosts.   40
She had horses who waited for destruction.
She had horses who waited for resurrection.

She had some horses.

She had horses who got down on their knees for any saviour.
She had horses who thought their high price had saved them. 45
She had horses who tried to save her, who climbed in her
bed at night and prayed as they raped her.

She had some horses.

She had some horses she loved.
She had some horses she hated. 50

These were the same horses.

1983

Nikos Kavadias (1913–1975)

A Knife

I always carry, tight on my belt,
a small African knife I've had for years—
the kind that are commonly seen in the North,
which I bought from an old merchant in Algiers.

I remember, as if it were now, the old dealer 5
who looked like a Goya oil painting,
standing next to long swords and torn
uniforms—in a hoarse voice, saying,

"This knife, here, which you want to buy—
legend surrounds it. Everyone knows 10
that those who have owned it, one after another
have all, at some time, killed someone close.

Don Basilio used it to kill
Donna Giulia, his unfaithful wife.
And Count Antonio, one night, secretly 15
murdered his brother with this knife.

Some Italian sailor—a Greek boatswain.
An African, in a jealous rage, his lover.
Hand to hand, it fell into mine.
I've seen many things, but this brings me terror. 20

Bend down. Look. Here, hold it. It's light.
And see here, the anchor and coat of arms.
But I would advise you to buy something else.

How much? Seven francs. Since you want it, it's yours."

This dagger now tight in my belt—my strangeness   25
made me take it off that shelf.
Since there's no one I hate enough to kill,
I fear someday I'll turn it on myself.

1936; trans. 2003
Translated by Diane Thiel

Shirley Geok-Lin Lim (B. 1944)

Pantoum for Chinese Women

*"At present, the phenomenon of butchering, drowning, and
leaving to die female infants has been very serious."*

(PEOPLE'S DAILY OF BEIJING, MARCH 3, 1983)

They say a child with two mouths is no good.
In the slippery wet, a hollow space
Smooth gumming, echoing wide for food.
No wonder my man is not here at his place.

In the slippery wet, a hollow space,   5
a slit narrowly sheathed within its hood.
No wonder my man is not here at his place:
He is digging for the dragon jar of soot,

that slit, narrowly sheathed within its hood!
His mother, squatting, coughs by the fire's blaze   10
while he digs for the dragon jar of soot.
We had saved ashes for a hundred days.

His mother, squatting, coughs by the fire's blaze.
The child kicks against me, mewing like a flute.
We had saved ashes for a hundred days,   15
knowing, if the time came, that we would.

The child kicks against me, crying like a flute
Through its two weak mouths. His mother prays,
Knowing when the time comes, that we would,
For broken clay is never set in glaze.   20

Through her two weak mouths his mother prays.
She will not pluck the rooster, nor serve its blood,
For broken clay is never set in glaze:

Women are made of river sand and wood.

She will not pluck the rooster nor serve its blood.   25
My husband frowns, pretending in his haste
Women are made of river sand and wood.
Milk soaks the bedding. I cannot bear the waste.

My husband frowns, pretending in his haste.
Oh clean the girl, dress her in ashy soot!   30
Milk soaks our bedding. I cannot bear the waste.
They say a child with two mouths is no good.

                                                              1994

April Lindner (B. 1962)

Spice

I save jars for the transparent hope
of what they'll hold, and later I save
what's in those jars past pungency,

lug them from one city to the next.
My pantry's bottom shelf recalls   5
an Indian grocery, bolts of silvered cloth,

sitar on eight-track tapes. The homesick owner
fussed over his only Anglo customer,
guiding me through the dusty shelves out back

past lentils, yellow, pink, and black,   10
past burlap sacks of *basmati*, to the spices
whose names I loved, whose perfumes I had to own:

garam masala, amchoor, fenugreek,
even *asafetida,* the fetid root
whose musk seeps through mason glass   15

to fog the air with gold. Saffron filaments,
cardamom pods, black and green.
Here's a souvenir mailed from Barbados,

nutmegs ground to slivers, impossible
to grate without shredding finger skin,   20
and from an Asian market in Toledo

this powder I bought for its pretty bottle
and licked from my palm on the drive home—
orange peel? red pepper? poppy seed?—

conjuring cool tatami floors, rice paper,   25
a tea ceremony's slow unfolding. Now I linger
at this small glass skyline in the shadows,

this shrine to continents I planned to reach
and haven't yet, my fingertips burnished,
the air a billowing veil of coriander.   30

2002

David Mason (B. 1954)

Acrostic from Aegina

Anemones you brought back from the path
Nod in a glass beside our rumpled bed.
Now you are far away. In the aftermath
Even these flowers arouse my sleepy head.

Love, when I think of the ready look in your eyes,   5
Erotas that would make these stone walls blush
Nerves me to write away the morning's hush.
Nadir of longing, and the red anemones
Over the lucent rim—my poor designs,
X-rated praise I've hidden between these lines.   10

2004

Marianne Moore (1887–1972)

Poetry

I too, dislike it: there are things that are important beyond all this fiddle.
    Reading it, however, with a perfect contempt for it, one discovers
    that there is in
    it after all, a place for the genuine.
            Hands that can grasp, eyes
            that can dilate, hair that can rise
                if it must, these things are important not because a   5

high sounding interpretation can be put upon them but because they are
    useful; when they become so derivative as to become unintelligible,
                        the
        same thing may be said for all of us—that we

do not admire what   10
    we cannot understand. The bat,
        holding on upside down or in quest of something to

eat, elephants pushing, a wild horse taking a roll, a tireless wolf under
    a tree, the immovable critic twinkling his skin like a horse that feels a
        flea, the base-
ball fan, the statistician—case after case   15
    could be cited did
    one wish it; nor is it valid
        to discriminate against "business documents and

school-books"; all these phenomena are important. One must make a
        distinction
    however: when dragged into prominence by half poets, the result is
        not poetry,   20
    nor till the autocrats among us can be
        "literalists of
    the imagination"—above
        insolence and triviality and can present

for inspection, imaginary gardens with real toads in them, shall we
        have   25
    it. In the meantime, if you demand on one hand, in defiance of their
        opinion—
the raw material of poetry in
    all its rawness and
    that which is, on the other hand,
        genuine then you are interested in poetry.   30

                1921

Frederick Morgan (B. 1922)

1904

The things they did together, no one knew
It was late June. Behind the old wood-shed
wild iris was in blossom, white and blue,
but what those proud ones did there, no one knew,
though some suspected there were one or two   5
who led the others where they would be led.
Years passed—but what they did there, no one knew,
those summer children long since safely dead.

                1987

Marilyn Nelson (B. 1946)

Chosen

Diverne wanted to die, that August night
his face hung over hers, a sweating moon.
She wished so hard, she killed part of her heart.

If she had died, her one begotten son,
her life's one light, would never have been born.   5
Pomp Atwood might have been another man:

born with a single race, another name.
Diverne might not have known the starburst joy
her son would give her. And the man who came

out of a twelve-room house and ran to her   10
close shack across three yards that night, to leap
onto her cornshuck pallet. Pomp was their

share of the future. And it wasn't rape.
In spite of her raw terror. And his whip.

1990

Naomi Shihab Nye (B. 1952)

Famous

The river is famous to the fish.

The loud voice is famous to silence,
which knew it would inherit the earth
before anybody said so.

The cat sleeping on the fence is famous to the birds   5
watching him from the birdhouse.

The tear is famous, briefly, to the cheek.

The idea you carry close to your bosom
is famous to your bosom.

The boot is famous to the earth,   10
more famous than the dress shoe,
which is famous only to floors.

The bent photograph is famous to the one who carries it

and not at all famous to the one who is pictured.

I want to be famous to shuffling men   15
who smile while crossing streets,
sticky children in grocery lines,
famous as the one who smiled back.

I want to be famous in the way a pulley is famous,
or a buttonhole, not because it did anything spectacular,   20
but because it never forgot what it could do.

                                                          1982

Craig Raine (B. 1944)

A Martian Sends
a Postcard Home

Caxtons are mechanical birds with many wings
and some are treasured for their markings—

they cause the eyes to melt
or the body to shriek without pain.

I have never seen one fly, but   5
sometimes they perch on the hand.

Mist is when the sky is tired of flight
and rests its soft machine on ground:

then the world is dim and bookish
like engravings under tissue paper.   10

Rain is when the earth is television.
It has the property of making colours darker.

Model T is a room with the lock inside—
a key is turned to free the world

for movement, so quick there is a film   15
to watch for anything missed.

But time is tied to the wrist
or kept in a box, ticking with impatience.

In homes, a haunted apparatus sleeps,
that snores when you pick it up.   20

If the ghost cries, they carry it
to their lips and soothe it to sleep

with sounds. And yet, they wake it up
deliberately, by tickling with a finger.

Only the young are allowed to suffer
openly. Adults go to a punishment room

with water but nothing to eat.
They lock the door and suffer the noises

alone. No one is exempt
and everyone's pain has a different smell.

At night, when all the colours die,
they hide in pairs

and read about themselves—
in colour, with their eyelids shut.

1979

Dudley Randall (1914–2000)

Ballad of Birmingham

(On the Bombing of a Church in Birmingham,
Alabama, 1963)

"Mother dear, may I go downtown
Instead of out to play,
And march the streets of Birmingham
In a Freedom March today?"

"No, baby, no; you may not go,
For the dogs are fierce and wild,
And clubs and hoses, guns and jail
Aren't good for a little child."

"But, mother, I won't be alone.
Other children will go with me,
And march the streets of Birmingham
To make our country free."

"No, baby, no, you may not go,
For I fear those guns will fire.
But you may go to church instead
And sing in the children's choir."

She has combed and brushed her night-dark hair,
And bathed rose petal sweet,

And drawn white gloves on her small brown hands,
And white shoes on her feet.   20

The mother smiled to know her child
Was in the sacred place,
But that smile was the last smile
To come upon her face.

For when she heard the explosion,   25
Her eyes grew wet and wild.
She raced through the streets of Birmingham
Calling for her child.

She clawed through bits of glass and brick,
Then lifted out a shoe.   30
"O here's the shoe my baby wore,
But, baby, where are you!"

1966

Edwin Arlington Robinson (1869–1935)

Richard Cory

Whenever Richard Cory went down town,
We people on the pavement looked at him:
He was a gentleman from sole to crown,
Clean favored, and imperially slim.

And he was always quietly arrayed,   5
And he was always human when he talked;
But still he fluttered pulses when he said,
"Good-morning," and he glittered when he walked.

And he was rich—yes, richer than a king—
And admirably schooled in every grace: 10
In fine, we thought that he was everything
To make us wish that we were in his place.

So on we worked, and waited for the light,
And went without the meat, and cursed the bread;
And Richard Cory, one calm summer night,   15
Went home and put a bullet through his head.

1897

William Shakespeare (1564–1616)

When, in Disgrace with Fortune and Men's Eyes

When, in disgrace with fortune and men's eyes,
I all alone beweep my outcast state,
And trouble deaf heaven with my bootless cries,
And look upon myself and curse my fate,
Wishing me like to one more rich in hope,   5
Featured like him, like him with friends possessed,
Desiring this man's art, and that man's scope,
With what I most enjoy contented least,
Yet in these thoughts myself almost despising,
Haply I think on thee, and then my state,   10
Like to the lark at break of day arising
From sullen earth, sings hymns at heaven's gate;
For thy sweet love rememb'red such wealth brings
That then I scorn to change my state with kings.

1609

Sor Juana Inés de la Cruz (1648?–1695)

She Promises to Hold a Secret in Confidence

This page, discreetly, will convey
how, on the moment that I read it,
I tore apart your secret
not to let it be torn away
from me—and I will further say   5
what firm insurance followed:
those paper fragments, I also swallowed.
This secret, so dearly read—
I wouldn't want one shred
out of my chest, to be hollowed.   10

1689; trans. 2004
Translated by Diane Thiel

William Stafford (1914–1993)

Traveling through the Dark

Traveling through the dark I found a deer
dead on the edge of the Wilson River road.
It is usually best to roll them into the canyon:
that road is narrow; to swerve might make more dead.

By glow of the tail-light I stumbled back of the car   5
and stood by the heap, a doe, a recent killing;
she had stiffened already, almost cold.
I dragged her off; she was large in the belly.

My fingers touching her side brought me the reason—
her side was warm; her fawn lay there waiting,   10
alive, still, never to be born.
Beside that mountain road I hesitated.

The car aimed ahead its lowered parking lights;
under the hood purred the steady engine.
I stood in the glare of the warm exhaust turning red;   15
around our group I could hear the wilderness listen.

I thought hard for us all—my only swerving—
then pushed her over the edge into the river.

                                                                    1962

Alfonsina Storni (1892–1938)

Ancestral Burden

You told me my father never cried
You told me my grandfather never cried.
The men of my lineage never cried
They were steel inside.

As you were saying this, you dropped a tear   5
that fell into my mouth—such poison
I have never drunk from any other cup
than this small one.

Weak woman, poor woman who understands
the ache of centuries I knew as I swallowed.   10
Oh, my spirit cannot carry
all of its load.

                                                    1919; trans. 2004
                                                  Translated by Diane Thiel

Diane Thiel (B. 1967)

Memento Mori in Middle School

When I was twelve, I chose Dante's *Inferno*
in gifted class—an oral presentation
with visual aids. My brother, *il miglior fabbro*,

said he would draw the tortures. We used ten
red posterboards. That day, for school, I dressed   5
in pilgrim black, left earlier to hang them

around the class. The students were impressed.
The teacher, too. She acted quite amused
and peered too long at all the punishments.

We knew by reputation she was cruel.   10
The class could see a hint of twisted forms
and asked to be allowed to round the room

as I went through my final presentation.
We passed the first one, full of poets cut
out of a special issue of *Horizon*.   15

The class thought these were such a boring set,
they probably deserved their tedious fates.
They liked the next, though—bodies blown about,

the lovers kept outside the tinfoil gates.
We had a new boy in our class named Paolo   20
and when I noted Paolo's wind-blown state

and pointed out Francesca, people howled.
I knew that more than one of us not-so-
covertly liked him. It seemed like hours

before we moved on to the gluttons, though,   25
where they could hold the cool fistfuls of slime
I brought from home. An extra touch. It sold

in canisters at toy stores at the time.
The students recognized the River Styx,
the logo of a favorite band of mine.   30

We moved downriver to the town of Dis,
which someone loudly re-named Dis and Dat.
And for the looming harpies and the furies,

who shrieked and tore things up, I had clipped out
the shrillest, most deserving teacher's heads   35
from our school paper, then thought better of it.

At the wood of suicides, we quieted.
Though no one in the room would say a word,
I know we couldn't help but think of Fred.

His name was in the news, though we had heard   40
he might have just been playing with the gun.
We moved on quickly by that huge, dark bird

and rode the flying monster, Geryon,
to reach the counselors, each wicked face,
again, I had resisted pasting in.   45

To represent the ice in that last place,
where Satan chewed the traitors' frozen heads,
my mother had insisted that I take

an ice-chest full of popsicles—to end
my gruesome project on a lighter note.   50
"It is a comedy, isn't it," she said.

She hadn't read the poem, or seen our art,
but asked me what had happened to the sweet,
angelic poems I once read and wrote.

The class, though, was delighted by the treat,   55
and at the last round, they all pushed to choose
their colors quickly, so they wouldn't melt.

The bell rang. Everyone ran out of school,
as always, yelling at the top of their lungs,
The *Inferno* fast forgotten, but their howls   60

showed off their darkened red and purple tongues.

                                                    2000

Memento Mori in Middle School. *Memento Mori:* Latin for "Remember you must die," the phrase now means any reminder of human mortality and the need to lead a virtuous life. 1 *Dante's* Inferno: The late medieval epic poem by the Italian poet Dante Alighieri describes a Christian soul's journey through hell. (*Inferno* means "hell" in Italian.) 3 *il miglior fabbro*: the better craftsman—Dante's term for fellow poet Daniel Arnaut, which T. S. Eliot later famously quoted to praise Ezra Pound. 15 *Horizon*: a magazine of art and culture. 20–23: *Paolo . . . Francesca*: two lovers in Dante's *Inferno* who have been damned for their adultery. 29 *River Styx*: the sacred river that flows around hell to mark its boundary. 31 *Dis*: the main city of hell named after its ruler, Dis (Pluto). 43 Geryon: a mythical three-headed, three-bodied monster Dante places in his *Inferno*.

César Vallejo (1892?–1938)

To My Brother Miguel
(in memoriam)

Brother, today I am on the bench by the house
where you leave a bottomless loss.
I remember how we would play
at this time of the day and how Mama
would lovingly chide us, "Now children."   5

Now I hide
as before, from all these evening
prayers and hope you will not find me
in the living room, the entryway, the corridors.
Later you hide, and I can't find you.   10
I remember how we made each other cry
brother—in that game.

Miguel, you disappeared
one night in August, nearly at dawn
but instead of laughing as you hid yourself,   15
you were anguished
And your twin heart of these extinguished
afternoons is weary of not finding you. Already
shadow falls on the spirit.

Listen, brother, don't be too late   20
showing up. Or Mama will fret.

1918; trans. 2004
Translated by Diane Thiel

Carolyn Beard Whitlow (B. 1945)

Rockin' a Man, Stone Blind

Cake in the oven, clothes out on the line,
Night wind blowin' against sweet, yellow thighs,
Two-eyed woman rockin' a man stone blind.

Man smell of honey, dark like coffee grind;
Countin' on his fingers since last July.   5
Cake in the oven, clothes out on the line.

Mister Jacobs say he be colorblind,
But got to tighten belts and loosen ties.
Two-eyed woman rockin' a man stone blind.

Winter becoming angry, rent behind.   10
Strapping spring sun needed to make mud pies.
Cake in the oven, clothes out on the line.

Looked in the mirror, Bessie's face I find.
I be so down low, my man be so high.
Two-eyed woman rockin' a man stone blind.   15

Policemans found him; damn near lost my mind.
Can't afford no flowers; can't even cry.
Cake in the oven, clothes out on the line.
Two-eyed woman rockin' a man stone blind.

                                                                  1986

Walt Whitman (1819–1892)

When I Heard the Learn'd Astronomer

When I heard the learn'd astronomer,
When the proofs, the figures, were ranged in columns before me,
When I was shown the charts and diagrams, to add, divide, and measure
    them,
When I sitting heard the astronomer where he lectured with much
    applause in the lecture-room,
How soon unaccountable I became tired and sick,   5
Till rising and gliding out I wandered off by myself,
In the mystical moist night-air, and from time to time,
Looked up in perfect silence at the stars.

                                                                  1865

Richard Wilbur (B. 1921)

The Writer

In her room at the prow of the house
Where light breaks, and the windows are tossed with linden,
My daughter is writing a story.

I pause in the stairwell, hearing
From her shut door a commotion of typewriter-keys   5
Like a chain hauled over a gunwale.

Young as she is, the stuff
Of her life is a great cargo, and some of it heavy:

I wish her a lucky passage.

But now it is she who pauses,   10
As if to reject my thought and its easy figure.
A stillness greatens, in which

The whole house seems to be thinking,
And then she is at it again with a bunched clamor
Of strokes, and again is silent.   15

I remember the dazed starling
Which was trapped in that very room, two years ago;
How we stole in, lifted a sash

And retreated, not to affright it;
And how for a helpless hour, through the crack of the door,   20
We watched the sleek, wild, dark

And iridescent creature
Batter against the brilliance, drop like a glove
To the hard floor, or the desk-top.

And wait then, humped and bloody,   25
For the wits to try it again; and how our spirits
Rose when, suddenly sure,

It lifted off from a chair-back,
Beating a smooth course for the right window
And clearing the sill of the world.   30

It is always a matter, my darling,
Of life or death, as I had forgotten. I wish
What I wished you before, but harder.

                                                          1976

Miller Williams (B. 1930)

The Curator

We thought it would come, we thought the Germans would come,
were almost certain they would. I was thirty-two,
the youngest assistant curator in the country.
I had some good ideas in those days.

Well, what we did was this. We had boxes   5
precisely built to every size of canvas.
We put the boxes in the basement and waited.

When word came that the Germans were coming in,
we got each painting put in the proper box
and out of Leningrad in less than a week.   10

They were stored somewhere in southern Russia.

But what we did, you see, besides the boxes
waiting in the basement, which was fine,
a grand idea, you'll agree, and it saved the art—
but what we did was leave the frames hanging,   15
so after the war it would be a simple thing
to put the paintings back where they belonged.

Nothing will seem surprised or sad again
compared to those imperious, vacant frames.

Well, the staff stayed on to clean the rubble   20
after the daily bombardments. We didn't dream—
You know it lasted nine hundred days.
Much of the roof was lost and snow would lie
sometimes a foot deep on this very floor,
but the walls stood firm and hardly a frame fell.   25

Here is the story, now, that I want to tell you.
Early one day, a dark December morning,
we came on three young soldiers waiting outside,
pacing and swinging their arms against the cold.
They told us this: in three homes far from here   30
all dreamed of one day coming to Leningrad
to see the Hermitage, as they supposed
every Soviet citizen dreamed of doing.
Now they had been sent to defend the city,
a turn of fortune the three could hardly believe.   35

I had to tell them there was nothing to see
but hundreds and hundreds of frames where the paintings had hung.

"Please, sir," one of them said, "let us see them."

And so we did. It didn't seem any stranger
than all of us being here in the first place,   40
inside such a building, strolling in snow.

We led them around most of the major rooms,
what they could take the time for, wall by wall.
Now and then we stopped and tried to tell them
part of what they would see if they saw the paintings.   45
I told them how those colors would come together,
described a brushstroke here, a dollop there,
mentioned a model and why she seemed to pout
and why this painter got the roses wrong.

The next day a dozen waited for us,   50
then thirty or more, gathered in twos and threes.
Each of us took a group in a different direction:
Castagno, Caravaggio, Brueghel, Cézanne, Matisse,

Orozco, Manet, da Vinci, Goya, Vermeer,
Picasso, Uccello, your Whistler, Wood, and Gropper.   55
We pointed to more details about the paintings,
I venture to say, than if we had had them there,
some unexpected use of line or light,
balance or movement, facing the cluster of faces
the same way we'd done it every morning   60
before the war, but then we didn't pay
so much attention to what we talked about.
People could see for themselves. As a matter of fact
we'd sometimes said our lines as if they were learned
out of a book, with hardly a look at the paintings.   65

But now the guide and the listeners paid attention
to everything—the simple differences
between the first and post-impressionists,
romantic and heroic, shade and shadow.

Maybe this was a way to forget the war ·   70
a little while. Maybe more than that.
Whatever it was, the people continued to come.
It came to be called The Unseen Collection.

Here. Here is the story I want to tell you.

Slowly, blind people began to come.   75
A few at first then more of them every morning,
some led and some alone, some swaying a little.
They leaned and listened hard, they screwed their faces,
they seemed to shift their eyes, those that had them,
to see better what was being said.   80
And a cock of the head. My God, they paid attention.

After the siege was lifted and the Germans left
and the roof was fixed and the paintings were in their places,
the blind never came again. Not like before.
This seems strange, but what I think it was,   85
they couldn't see the paintings anymore.
They could still have listened, but the lectures became
a little matter-of-fact. What can I say?
Confluences come when they will and they go away.

                                        1992

William Carlos Williams (1883–1963)

The Dance

In Brueghel's great picture, The Kermess,
the dancers go round, they go round and

around, the squeal and the blare and the
tweedle of bagpipes, a bugle and fiddles
tipping their bellies (round as the thick-   5
sided glasses whose wash they impound)
their hips and their bellies off balance
to turn them. Kicking and rolling about
the Fair Grounds, swinging their butts, those
shanks must be sound to bear up under such   10
rollicking measures, prance as they dance
in Brueghel's great picture, The Kermess.

1944

William Butler Yeats (1865–1939)

The Stolen Child

Where dips the rocky highland
Of Sleuth Wood in the lake,
There lies a leafy island
Where flapping herons wake
The drowsy water-rats;   5
There we've hid our fairy vats,
Full of berries
And of reddest stolen cherries.
Come away, O human child!
To the waters and the wild   10
With a faery hand in hand,
For the world's more full of weeping than you can understand.

Where the wave of moonlight glosses
The dim grey sands with light,
Far off by furthest Rosses   15
We foot it all the night,
Weaving olden dances,
Mingling hands and mingling glances
Till the moon has taken flight;
To and fro we leap   20
And chase the frothy bubbles,
While the world is full of troubles
And is anxious in its sleep.
Come away, O human child!
To the waters and the wild   25
With a faery hand in hand,
For the world's more full of weeping than you can understand.

Where the wandering water gushes
From the hills above Glen-Car,

In pools among the rushes   30
That scarce could bathe a star,
We seek for slumbering trout
And whispering in their ears
Give them unquiet dreams;
Leaning softly out   35
From ferns that drop their tears
Over the young streams.
Come away, O human child!
To the waters and the wild
With a faery hand in hand,   40
For the world's more full of weeping than you can understand.

Away with us he's going,
The solemn-eyed:
He'll hear no more the lowing
Of the calves on the warm hillside   45
Or the kettle on the hob
Sing peace into his breast,
Or see the brown mice bob
Round and round the oatmeal-chest.
For he comes, the human child,   50
To the waters and the wild
With a faery hand in hand,
From a world more full of weeping than you can understand.

                                                    1889

The Lake Isle of Innisfree

I will arise and go now, and go to Innisfree,
And a small cabin build there, of clay and wattles made:
Nine bean-rows will I have there, a hive for the honey-bee,
And live alone in the bee-loud glade.

And I shall have some peace there, for peace comes dropping slow,   5
Dropping from the veils of the morning to where the cricket sings;
There midnight's all a glimmer, and noon a purple glow,
And evening full of the linnet's wings.

I will arise and go now, for always night and day
I hear lake water lapping with low sounds by the shore;   10
While I stand on the roadway, or on the pavements gray,
I hear it in the deep heart's core.

                                                    1892

Drama

Sherman Alexie (B. 1966)*

From *Smoke Signals*

Screenplay

We HEAR the last few moments of an instrumental synthe-sized disco dance song and the first few words of a female disc jockey.

FEMALE DISC JOCKEY:
(V.O.) Good morning to all you insomniac disco lovers out there. It's 2:45 a.m. on a hot Bicentennial Fourth of July in 1976. I hope you're all curled up with a patriotic lover. I'm sending this next song out to all of you. And just remember, sweethearts, when you get that disco fever, it burns.

fade in:

1 ext. house—night

We are looking into a pitch-dark room through an open doorway.
We can only SEE shadows of shadows.
But then a flicker of flames, just a spark, and then the fire begins to grow.
As the flames grow, CAMERA PULLS AWAY and reveals more and more of house.

2 ext. dirt road—night

CLOSE ANGLE ON ARNOLD JOSEPH, a large Coeur d'Alene Indian man in his thirties.
He is watching the house burn.
His face is illuminated by flames.
He is silent and still for a moment, then makes his decision and runs toward the burning house.

3 ext. dirt road—night

CAMERA FOLLOWS Arnold Joseph as he is running down a dirt road toward the house that is now engulfed by flames.

We also SEE for the first time other INDIANS stumbling around the burning house.

They are coughing, crying, and screaming.

4 ext. burning house—night

Arnold runs up to the burning house.
INDIANS are stumbling around the house.
They are coughing and gagging from the smoke.
Arnold stops a COUGHING INDIAN MAN.

ARNOLD JOSEPH: Where's Arlene? Where's Arlene? Where's my wife?

The coughing Indian man cannot speak. He shakes his head and runs away.

ANGLE ON Arnold trying to get in the front door, but the flames and smoke drive him back.

ARLENE JOSEPH is carrying the BABY VICTOR JOSEPH, just a few months old, in her arms when she stumbles up to Arnold.

She had already exited the house.

ARNOLD JOSEPH: Arlene, are you okay? Are you okay?
ARLENE JOSEPH: There are people still in there!

We HEAR a scream coming from inside the house.

There is no way Arnold can make it into the house.

ANGLE ON Arnold Joseph as he runs around the house looking for a way to get inside.

ARNOLD'S POV on a pair of hands hanging outside a second-story window.

The hands hold a baby.

The baby is quiet.

The hands thrust the baby upward into the sky.

The baby is BABY THOMAS BUILDS-THE-FIRE, also just a few months old.

Baby Thomas, wrapped in a blanket, is drifting freely upward toward the night stars . . .

Arnold Joseph looks up, his eyes widen, his mouth falls open . . .

Arnold runs across the wet grass, slipping and sliding . . .

Arnold running, his hands outstretched as if he were trying to catch a football . . .

Baby Thomas falling, blanket on fire now, with the burning house behind him . . .

The crowd of Indians, their heads turning to follow Arnold's race to catch Baby Thomas . . .

Arnold diving to make the catch . . .

Baby Thomas hits Arnold's hands and falls through . . .

The crowd of Indians staring with flames dancing on their faces . . .
Arnold stands with Baby Thomas, rips the smoldering blanket off his little body . . .
Arnold stares down at Baby Thomas . . .
ARNOLD'S POV down on Baby Thomas, who is oddly conscious and silent, staring back at Arnold.

5 int. burning house—night

CLOSE ANGLE ON the radio as the flames engulf it.
We HEAR the music crackle and fade out under the weight and heat of the flames.

6 ext. burned house—morning

The house has burned down to its frame.
Arnold and Arlene Joseph are standing beside each other.
Arnold still holds Baby Thomas.
Arlene holds Baby Victor.
ANGLE ON GRANDMA BUILDS-THE-FIRE, an Indian woman in her fifties, as she comes running up to Arnold.

GRANDMA: Arnold, what happened? What happened?

Arnold hands Baby Thomas over to his grandmother.
Grandma looks down at her grandson.

GRANDMA *(cont'd)*: Where's his mother? And father?

Arnold doesn't know what to say. He looks back toward the burned-out house.
Grandma understands. She wails. She brings down the sky with her grief.

7 ext. burned house—morning

A few hours have passed.
People are sifting through the ashes.
We SEE white sheets over two bodies.
There is now only smoke and grief.
Grandma Builds-the-Fire, still weeping a little, is rocking Baby Thomas.
Arlene, holding Baby Victor, is standing near her.
Arnold stands between Grandma and Arlene.
ANGLE ON Grandma, with Baby Thomas in her arms, as she looks at Arnold, then at Arlene and Baby Victor.

GRANDMA *(to Arlene)*: Arlene, your son? His name is Victor, enit?
ARLENE JOSEPH: Yes, it is.

GRANDMA: A good name. It means he's going to win, enit?

ARLENE JOSEPH *(to Grandma):* I guess. And your grandson's name is Thomas, enit? What does it mean?

GRANDMA: I don't know.

Grandma turns her attention to Arnold.

GRANDMA *(to Arnold):* You saved my grandson's life.

ARNOLD JOSEPH: It was nothing. I didn't even think about it . . . I just . . .

GRANDMA *(firmly):* You saved him. You saved Thomas. You did a good thing.

ARNOLD JOSEPH: I didn't mean to.

> *ANGLE ON Grandma Builds-the-Fire holding Baby Thomas on the left side of FRAME and Arlene holding Baby Victor on the right side of FRAME with Arnold standing between them.*
>
> *AN INDIAN FIREFIGHTER races between the CAMERA and the Josephs and Builds-the-Fires for a:*

SWIPE CUT TO:

8 ext. baseball diamond (1988)—day

> *ANGLE ON YOUNG THOMAS BUILDS-THE-FIRE, twelve years old, standing on the left side of the FRAME and YOUNG VICTOR JOSEPH, twelve years old, standing on the right side of the FRAME with a burning barrel sitting between them.*
>
> *Young Thomas is wearing a thirdhand sport coat with blue jeans and T-shirt.*
>
> *He also wears very traditionally braided hair and thick glasses.*
>
> *He is very much an Indian nerd.*
>
> *Young Victor is wearing a red T-shirt and blue jeans.*
>
> *He is a very handsome and confident boy.*

YOUNG THOMAS: Hey, Victor, what do you know about fire?

YOUNG VICTOR: Thomas, I don't know what you're talking about.

YOUNG THOMAS: No, really, Victor. I mean, did you know that things burn in colors? I mean, sodium burns yellow and carbon burns orange. Just like that. You can tell what's in a fire by the color of the flames.

> *(beat)*

Hey, Victor, I heard your dad is living in Phoenix, Arizona, now.

YOUNG VICTOR: Yeah, Thomas, what about it?

YOUNG THOMAS: Man, he's lived everywhere since he left you, huh?

> *Victor ignores Thomas.*

YOUNG THOMAS *(cont'd):* I mean, he lived in Neah Bay, and then in Eureka, and then in Riverside, and then in Tijuana, and now in Phoenix, Arizona.

(beat)

    Man, Phoenix is like a million miles away from here, enit?

YOUNG VICTOR: Is that so, Thomas?

(beat)

    You know, I was wondering. What color do you think your mom and dad were when they burned up?

Young Thomas is hurt by this. He is silent for a moment.

YOUNG THOMAS: You know, your dad ain't coming back.

YOUNG VICTOR: Yes, he is.

YOUNG THOMAS: No, he's gone. When Indians go away, they don't come back. Last of the Mohicans, last of the Sioux, last of the Navajo. last of the Winnebago, last of the Coeur d'Alene people . . .

YOUNG VICTOR *(interrupting Thomas):* Shut up, Thomas. Or I'll beat you up again.

Long beat.

YOUNG THOMAS: What does it mean?

YOUNG VICTOR: What does what mean?

YOUNG THOMAS: What does Phoenix, Arizona, mean?

CUT TO:

    OPENING CREDITS ROLL

CUT TO:

title card: "phoenix, arizona, 1998"

CUT TO:

9 ext. silver mobile home—day

    ANGLE ON a shiny silver mobile home sitting quietly beside a dirt road.

    This is Arnold Joseph's Phoenix home.

    A small white dog lies in the dirt in front of the trailer.

    A makeshift basketball hoop and backboard are nailed to a post that is in turn sunk into the ground.

    A worn, incredibly battered yellow pickup truck sits beside the trailer.

    Beneath the burning Arizona sun, the trailer seems to be very isolated in this lunar landscape of red dust and red rock.

    WIDE ANGLE ON the same silver mobile home, but now we can also SEE another more contemporary trailer home sitting a short distance farther down the dirt road.

It is fairly small.
We then SEE a blue car approaching on the road.
As the car draws closer, we HEAR the white dog begin to howl.
ANGLE ON SUZY SONG, an Indian woman in her mid-twenties, who is driving the car.
She is wearing a nice business suit.
She has long black hair, brown skin and eyes, and is very attractive.
She is singing along to a song on the car radio.
WIDE ANGLE ON Suzy's car as it pulls up in front of her trailer.
Her car is much nicer than her small trailer.
She steps out of the car, stops briefly as she hears the dog howling.
She listens for a moment then opens her car trunk and pulls out a large suitcase.
She has obviously been on a vacation or business trip.
She lifts the suitcase and a laptop computer bag out of the trunk and sets them on the ground.
The dog continues to howl.
Suzy listens for a moment and then walks toward Arnold Joseph's trailer.
ANGLE ON Suzy as she is walking.

SUZY SONG *(to dog):* Kafka? Hey, Kafka? What's the matter, boy?

ANGLE ON Suzy as she kneels down beside Kafka, the white dog, who is now whimpering.
She pets him but he doesn't respond.

SUZY SONG: What is it, boy? Where's your master, huh? Where's Arnold?

ANGLE ON Suzy as she walks toward Arnold's trailer.
She picks up a basketball and shoots at the outdoor hoop.
She MISSES the shot.
As she walks toward Arnold's trailer, she smells something terrible.
She covers her mouth and nose with one hand.
She tries to open the front door of the trailer, but it is locked.
She then walks around the side of the trailer to the kitchen window.

10 int. silver mobile home—day

CAMERA POV out the trailer's kitchen window as we see Suzy looking inside.

Throughout Arnold's trailer, we SEE that maps and travel posters cover the walls.

There is a bare amount of furniture and an old-fashioned turntable and albums in the living room.

There is a table and chairs in the kitchen, along with a couple sets of plates and glasses.

The bedroom and bathroom are clean and mostly bare.

Other than that, there is a conspicuous lack of possessions, as if Arnold had just moved in, even though he'd been there for years.

FROM CAMERA POV, Suzy disappears from kitchen window and CAMERA MOVES through trailer to living room window, where Suzy appears, peering inside.

She disappears from living room window. CAMERA MOVES back through trailer, down hallway into bathroom, and to the window.

Suzy is peering through the bathroom window.

She disappears from bathroom window.

CAMERA MOVES away from bathroom window, out of bathroom, down the hall toward the bedroom, then into bedroom.

We SEE a body, obviously dead and very decomposed, lying facedown on the bed.

This is Arnold Joseph.

He is wearing only a pair of boxer shorts.

We SEE that a red shirt and a pair of blue jeans are draped over a chair.

Black boots on the floor.

CAMERA MOVES across bedroom to a CLOSE ANGLE on a blank television set.

CAMERA MOVES UP to empty window above television.

The window is empty for a beat, then Suzy's face appears.

She peers in, sees what is inside.

Shock on her face, then pain and grief, horror.

She disappears from the window.

CUT TO:

title card: "coeur d'alene indian reservation, idaho, 1998"

CUT TO:

11 ext. isolated landscape—coeur d'alene reservation—day

WIDE ANGLE ON a basketball hoop and half-court set in the middle of an isolated landscape, a flat valley surrounded by pine trees and rolling hills.

Very green and beautiful.

We can also SEE THREE INDIAN MEN playing basketball.

The basket clearly does not belong in such a beautiful and remote place, but there it is.

CAMERA MOVES in on the basketball court and we can more clearly SEE that two of the Indian men, JUNIOR and BOO, are wearing white T-shirts and black shorts while the third, the ADULT VICTOR JOSEPH, twenty-two years old, wears a bright red T-shirt and cutoff blue jeans.

We can HEAR the sounds of their exertion: grunting, heavy breathing, squeaking of basketball shoes on the cement, ball bouncing, curses.

CAMERA MOVES closer and closer to the players, onto the court itself, until we are in the middle of their game.

The game is very loud and passionate now.

We HEAR shouts of encouragement, insults, curses, etc.

We continue to HEAR the basketball players as the CAMERA MOVES through the game, off the court on the opposite side, leaving the court behind.

At this point, we notice, in the distance, a LONE FIGURE walking toward the game.

We also notice that this lone figure, who is the ADULT THOMAS BUILDS-THE-FIRE, twenty-two years old, is engaged in some sort of mysteriously repetitive behavior as he walks toward the court.

Thomas is a short, slight Indian man with very traditional braids.

He wears a three-piece suit and tennis shoes.

He is constantly smiling.

As the CAMERA MOVES closer and closer to Thomas, we begin to understand what he is doing.

As he walks toward the game, Thomas is transporting, in an assembly line fashion, a plastic chair, a small end table, and a portable radio.

He has all three items set in a line: the radio in front, then the end table, and the chair at the rear.

Thomas picks up the last item in line, the chair, walks it to the front and sets it down.

Then he walks to the back of the line and picks up the end table, walks to the front of the line, and sets it in front of the chair.

Then he walks to the back of the line, picks up the radio, and then walks to the front of the line again and sets it down in front of the end table.

He repeats this process again and again, making sure, steady, and slightly crazy progress toward the court.

The CAMERA MOVES BACKWARD away from Thomas, onto the basketball court, through the middle of the game again, and just off the court, where it STOPS for a:

WIDE ANGLE ON the basketball court, as Victor Joseph, who is obviously the most talented player on the court, scores at will and plays tenacious defense.

Victor has long, black, unbraided hair. He is a tall, very handsome man.

As the following exchange happens, we SEE Thomas, in the background, as he finally arrives at courtside.

He sets his chair and end table closer to one another, and then sets his radio on the end table.

He fiddles with the dials trying to find a signal.

VICTOR *(to Junior, who is guarding him):* Game point, cousin, game point.
JUNIOR POLATKIN: Bring it on, Victor, bring it on.

Junior Polatkin smiles at Victor, who is completely serious.

Victor fakes left, drives right, hesitates, then spins around Junior and Boo for the winning lay-in, which Victor somehow misses.

VICTOR: Foul!

Junior picks up the loose ball, advances on Victor.

JUNIOR POLATKIN: Bullshit! There wasn't no one near you, Victor!
VICTOR *(taking the ball from Junior):* If I say it's a foul, then it's a foul.

Junior knocks the ball away from Victor.
It bounces off the court and rolls to a stop at Thomas's feet.
Thomas looks down at it as if it were a dead animal.

VICTOR: Hey, Thomas, give us some help, huh?

Thomas hesitates, but then picks up the basketball, and throws it weakly back toward Victor.

Thomas is extremely clumsy and awkward, so the ball only makes it halfway to Victor.

Victor looks at the other players, who are laughing at Thomas's weakness.

Victor walks over to the ball, picks it up, and looks at Thomas.
Thomas is embarrassed and intimidated by Victor.
VICTOR *(shaking his head):* Nice suit, Thomas.

Laughing, Victor turns back to his game.

As he dribbles the ball into play, the CAMERA MOVES above the court, focuses on the wooden basketball backboard, which has a bright red sun painted on it.

MATCH DISSOLVE TO:
12 ext. silver mobile home—phoenix, arizona—day

ANGLE ON the flashing red lights of a police car.

WIDE ANGLE ON the police car and an ambulance parked in front of the silver mobile home.

Suzy Song, still wearing her nice business suit, is talking to a WHITE POLICEMAN, who is taking notes.

TWO WHITE AMBULANCE MEN, wearing surgical masks against the smell, carry Arnold Joseph's body out of the trailer.

SUZY SONG: His name is Arnold Joseph.

13 ext. basketball court—coeur d'alene reservation—day

ANGLE ON Victor Joseph and his basketball buddies, Junior and Boo, as they sit on the court.

In the background we SEE Thomas is still sitting with his radio, chair, and little plastic table.

JUNIOR POLATKIN: Hey, Victor, who do you think is the best basketball player ever?

VICTOR: That's easy. Geronimo.

JUNIOR POLATKIN: Geronimo? He couldn't play basketball, man. He was Apache, man. Those suckers are about three feet tall.

VICTOR: It's Geronimo, man. He was lean, mean, and bloody. Would have dunked on your flat Indian ass and then cut it off.

JUNIOR POLATKIN: Yeah, sometimes it's a good day to die. Sometimes, it's a good day to play basketball.

BOO: What about Sitting Bull?

VICTOR: A veteran player. Would have used those old-man moves. Stepping on your foot so you can't jump. Holding your shirt when you tried to run by him. Poke you in the belly when you take a shot.

JUNIOR POLATKIN: Yeah, he played in the Six-Feet-and-Under, Forty-Years-and-Older, Indian Spiritual Leader Basketball League.

VICTOR: Kind of a slow league, though, enit? All those old guys running up and down the court with their drums and medicine bundles and singing and shit.

(pounding his leg in rhythm and singing a makeshift powwow song)
Oh, I took the ball to the hoop and what did I see? Oh, I took the ball to the hoop and what did I see? General George Armstrong Custer was a-guarding me! Way, ya, hi, ye! Way, ya, hi, ye!
(Junior and Boo join in)
Oh, I took the ball to the hoop and what did I see? Oh, I took the ball to the hoop and what did I see. General George Armstrong Custer was a-guarding me! Way, ya, hi, ye! Way, ya, hi, ye!

JUNIOR POLATKIN: What about Chief Joseph? He had to be good.

VICTOR: He retired young, man. He will play basketball no more forever.

BOO: What about Pocahontas? Was she a cheerleader or what?

VICTOR: Shit, old Pokey was a point guard. Strapped on a rawhide athletic bra to cover up those big ol' Technicolor Disney boobs and kicked some white boys' asses.

JUNIOR POLATKIN: What about Thomas?

VICTOR: What about him?

> *ANGLE ON Thomas sitting alone in his chair.*

14 ext. suzy song's trailer house—phoenix, arizona—day

> *ANGLE ON Suzy Song as she sits alone on her porch.*
> *She is still wearing her business suit, though she holds her jacket in her arms.*
> *She holds it up to her face and breathes in the terrible smell of Arnold's death.*
> *Disgusted, she throws the jacket to the ground.*
> *She stares into the distance.*

15 ext. outdoor basketball court—day

> *ANGLE ON Victor, Junior, and Boo leaving the outdoor basketball court.*
> *Victor is dribbling the basketball.*
> *Thomas is still sitting on his chair beside the court.*
> *He stands and watches Victor and his pals walk away.*

THOMAS: Hey, Victor!

> *Victor ignores Thomas.*
> *He continues to dribble the basketball.*

JUNIOR POLATKIN: Hey, Victor, how come you don't hello Thomas when you know him so easy.

> *Victor ignores Junior.*
> *Junior and Boo laugh together as if sharing some secret joke.*

JUNIOR POLATKIN *(to Victor)*: Jeez, look at you, leaving your *se-sen-sah*[1] behind.

VICTOR: He's not my brother!

> *Junior and Boo laugh harder.*
> *They are having a good time at Victor's expense.*
> *The three continue to walk away from Thomas.*

THOMAS: Hey, Victor!

---

[1]little brother.

Victor continues to ignore Thomas.
> *Victor dribbles the basketball.*
> *He fakes left, right, dribbles past an imaginary defender.*
> *ANGLE ON Thomas standing all alone.*

16 int. suzy's mobile-home living room—day

ANGLE ON Suzy Song sitting on her couch.
> *She is now wearing a T-shirt and blue jeans.*
> *The room is simple and neat.*
> *A recliner, couch, coffee table, television.*
> *There are many books of all kinds stacked in piles everywhere.*
> *She must be quite a reader.*
> *She picks up a beaded wallet, completely beaded with an eagle design, Arnold's wallet.*
> *Suzy opens it and pulls out a photograph.*
> *INSERT SHOT of the photograph of Arnold, Arlene, and Baby Victor.*
> *A happy family photograph.*
> *Suzy looks at the back side of the photograph.*
> *There is nothing.*
> *ANGLE ON Suzy as she picks up the phone and dials a phone number.*

17 int. josephs' house—day

ANGLE ON Arlene Joseph.
> *We HEAR the phone ringing.*
> *She picks it up and holds the phone to her ear.*
> *We SEE the shock, then grief on her face as Suzy gives her the news.*
> *ANGLE ON Victor as he comes through the front door.*
> *Arlene turns to face him.*
> *They share a long look.*
> *Victor is standing very still.*

18 int. coeur d'alene indian trading post—day

ANGLE ON Victor as he stands very still in line at the checkout counter, looking down at a forty-dollar check from his mom.
> *He looks up to see the CASHIER, a large Indian woman.*

VICTOR: Can you cash this? It's from my mom.

The Cashier takes the check, throws it in her register, gives Victor forty dollars.
> *He looks at the money, knowing it isn't very much.*

THOMAS: Hey, Victor.

Victor turns to face Thomas Builds-the-Fire.

THOMAS: I'm sorry about your father.

VICTOR: How'd you hear about it?

THOMAS: I heard it on the wind. I heard it from the birds. I felt it in the sunlight. And your mother was just in here crying.

Victor is suddenly very uncomfortable.

VICTOR: Listen, Thomas. I got to go. I've got things to take care of.

Victor turns to leave again, but Thomas grabs his arm.

THOMAS: Victor, your mom said she only had forty bucks. That ain't enough money to get you to Phoenix.

(beat)

I can help, you know?

VICTOR: Help what?

THOMAS: I can help you get to Phoenix. I have some money.

(pleading, Thomas holds up a glass jar, his piggy bank, filled with paper money and coins)

I can help.

VICTOR: Listen, Thomas, I can't take your money. Why don't you go buy a car or something. Go find a woman. Anything. But leave me alone, okay?

THOMAS: I can get you to Phoenix.

VICTOR: Okay, so you can get me to Phoenix. But what do you get out of the deal?

THOMAS: You have to take me with you.

VICTOR *(laughing, dismissive):* Sure, Thomas, whatever.

Thomas watches as the adult Victor walks out the trading post door, which is covered with red handbills advertising The Last Goodbye Powwow . . .

MATCH CUT TO:

19 ext. coeur d'alene indian trading post (july 4, 1988)— day

. . . and then we SEE the YOUNG VICTOR walk out of the trading post into the parking lot.

A few beat-up cars are there, as are a few Indians standing around, laughing and talking.

Young Victor is wearing a red T-shirt and blue jeans.

From behind him, out of the trading post door, the YOUNG THOMAS comes racing out.

He is wearing his typical three-piece suit.
He is also holding a burning sparkler firework.

YOUNG THOMAS: Hey, Victor, happy Fourth of July! Look at this. Ain't it cool?

Victor walks over to Thomas.
Together, they both stare at the sparkler.
Thomas is grinning like crazy.
His happiness is infectious.
Victor has to smile too.

YOUNG THOMAS *(cont'd):* Hey, Victor, you want to hold it?
YOUNG VICTOR: Nah, Thomas, it's yours. You hang on to it.

ANGLE ON Young Victor as he is suddenly picked up from behind.
He is scared at first but then we SEE it is Arnold Joseph who has picked up his son.

ARNOLD JOSEPH: Hey, little Thomas, you better get home. Your grandma is looking for you.

Young Thomas smiles and runs away.
Arnold Joseph carries Young Victor over his shoulder to his pickup and deposits him inside.
Young Victor is giggling like crazy.
Arnold gets inside the pickup.

20 int. pickup (july 4, 1988)—day

Arnold and Young Victor sit in the pickup.
Arnold reaches into a cooler sitting on the seat between them and pulls out a beer.
He opens it, takes a big drink, hands it to Young Victor.
Young Victor is holding it tightly.
He looks up at his father and smiles.
Arnold smiles at his son.
He shows empty hands and then magically pulls a coin from behind Young Victor's ear.
Arnold starts the car and pulls out of the trading post parking lot, heading for home.
As he drives, he talks.
Arnold is not drunk.
He is just beginning to catch a buzz.
As he talks, Young Victor listens with rapt attention.

ARNOLD JOSEPH: Happy Independence Day, Victor. You feeling independent? I'm feeling independent. I'm feeling extra magical today, Victor. Like I could make anything disappear. Houdini with braids, you know? Wave my hand and poof! The white people are gone, sent back to where they belong. Poof! Paris, London, Moscow. Poof! Berlin, Rome, Athens. Poof! Poof! Poof! Wave my hand and the reservation is gone. The trading post and the post office, the tribal school and the pine trees, the dogs and cats, the drunks and the Catholics, and the drunk Catholics. Poof! And all the little Indian boys named Victor.

Arnold looks at his son with a big smile, musses his hair.

ARNOLD JOSEPH: I'm magic. I'm magic. I just wave my hand and make it disappear, send it somewhere else. I can make you disappear. Where do you want to go, Victor? You want to go to Disneyland? The moon? The North Pole? I'm so good, I can make myself disappear. Poof! And I'm gone.

Arnold focuses on the road, dreaming of places he'd go.
He pulls the truck up in front of their house.
Young Victor looks up at him.

ARNOLD JOSEPH: Here, give me that beer.

Young Victor holds the beer out to his father.
But the beer slips from Young Victor's hand and falls to the seat.
Beer spills.
Angrily, Arnold slaps his son across the face.

ARNOLD JOSEPH: Look what you did!

Young Victor is crying.
Arnold cleans up the mess, drinks the rest of the beer from the bottle.
He grabs a new beer.

ARNOLD JOSEPH: Ah, quit your crying. I didn't hit you that hard.

(beat)

Now, go see your mom. Tell her I'll be right in.

ANGLE ON Young Victor, still crying, as he climbs out of the pickup.
ARNOLD'S POV ON Young Victor as he runs toward the Josephs' house.
ANGLE ON Arnold as he takes a big drink of beer. He looks out the window.
ANGLE ON Young Victor as he runs onto the porch, opens the front door, and walks inside . . .

MATCH CUT TO:
21 int. josephs' house (present day)—night

. . . and we see the Adult Victor walk into the house.
He walks through the living room into kitchen.

Arlene Joseph is making fry bread.
She looks up when Victor walks into the room.

ARLENE JOSEPH: Did you cash the check?
VICTOR: Yeah.
ARLENE JOSEPH: That's all the money I got.
VICTOR: I know.
ARLENE JOSEPH: Is it enough?
VICTOR: No.

Arlene drops a piece of fry bread to the floor.
She smiles and rubs her hands.

ARLENE JOSEPH: Damn arthritis.
VICTOR: Hurting bad today, enit?

Arlene shrugs her shoulders.
Victor walks over to his mother, takes her hands in his, and gently rubs them.

22 int. builds-the-fires' house—night

ANGLE ON Grandma and Thomas standing in their kitchen.
Defying gender expectations, Thomas is making the fry bread.
He kneads the dough and drops it into hot oil.

GRANDMA: Do you think Victor is going to take your money?

ANGLE ON Thomas as he shrugs his shoulders.

GRANDMA: I don't trust him, you know. He's mean to you.
THOMAS: He wasn't always mean.

ANGLE ON the fry bread sizzling in the pan.

23 int. josephs' house—night

ANGLE ON fry bread sizzling in a different pan.
WIDE ANGLE ON Arlene and Victor standing in their kitchen.
Arlene pulls a piece of hot fry bread from the grease and drops it into a basket.
Victor leans against the refrigerator, drinking a Coke.

VICTOR: Thomas says he'll give me the money. But he wants to go with me.

Victor reaches over and grabs a piece of fry bread from the basket.
It's hot, so he bounces it from hand to hand to cool it off.
He takes a bite, swallows some Coke to wash it down.
He looks at his mother.
She looks up at him.

ARLENE JOSEPH: You know, people always tell me I make the best fry bread in the world. Maybe it's true. But I don't make it by myself, you know? I got the recipe from your grandmother, who got it from her grandmother. And I listen to people when they eat my bread, too. Sometimes, they might say, "Arlene, there's too much flour," or "Arlene, you should knead the dough a little more." I listen to them. And I watch that Julia Child all the time.

(beat)

She's a pretty good cook, too. But she's got lots of help.

VICTOR: So, do you think I should go with Thomas?

ARLENE JOSEPH: That's your decision.

(beat)

But if you go, I want you to promise me you'll come back.

VICTOR: Come on, Mom.

ARLENE JOSEPH: Promise me

VICTOR: Jeez, Mom. You want me to sign something?

ARLENE JOSEPH: No way. You know how Indians feel about signing papers.

ANGLE ON Arlene as she picks a piece of fry bread from the pan.
CLOSE ANGLE ON that piece of fry bread being dropped onto a plate.

24 int. builds-the-fires' house—night

CLOSE ANGLE ON a different piece of fry bread dropping onto a different plate.
WIDE ANGLE ON Grandma and Thomas sitting at the kitchen table, silently eating dinner.
Both look up as they HEAR a knock on the door.
They look at each other and smile.
We HEAR Victor's voice over this.

VICTOR: (V.O.) Okay, Thomas, I need the money and you can come with me. But I have a few rules. First of all, you can't wear that stupid suit.

1998

Susan Glaspell (1882–1948)

Trifles

Characters

GEORGE HENDERSON, county attorney
HENRY PETERS, sheriff
LEWIS HALE, a neighboring farmer
MRS. PETERS
MRS. HALE

Scene. The kitchen in the now abandoned farmhouse of John Wright, a gloomy kitchen, and left without having been put in order—unwashed pans under the sink, a loaf of bread outside the breadbox, a dish towel on the table—other signs of incompleted work. At the rear the outer door opens and the Sheriff comes in followed by the County Attorney and Hale. The Sheriff and Hale are men in middle life, the County Attorney is a young man; all are much bundled up and go at once to the stove. They are followed by two women—the Sheriff's wife first; she is a slight wiry woman, a thin nervous face. Mrs. Hale is larger and would ordinarily be called more comfortable looking, but she is disturbed now and looks fearfully about as she enters. The women have come in slowly, and stand close together near the door.

COUNTY ATTORNEY: [*Rubbing his hands.*] This feels good. Come up to the fire, ladies.
MRS. PETERS: [*After taking a step forward.*] I'm not—cold.
SHERIFF: [*Unbuttoning his overcoat and stepping away from the stove as if to mark the beginning of official business.*] Now, Mr. Hale, before we move things about, you explain to Mr. Henderson just what you saw when you came here yesterday morning.
COUNTY ATTORNEY: By the way, has anything been moved? Are things just as you left them yesterday?
SHERIFF: [*Looking about.*] It's just the same. When it dropped below zero last night I thought I'd better send Frank out this morning to make a fire for us—no use getting pneumonia with a big case on, but I told him not to touch anything except the stove—and you know Frank.
COUNTY ATTORNEY: Somebody should have been left here yesterday.
SHERIFF: Oh—yesterday. When I had to send Frank to Morris Center for that man who went crazy—I want you to know I had my hands full yesterday, I knew you could get back from Omaha by today and as long as I went over everything here myself—

COUNTY ATTORNEY: Well, Mr. Hale, tell just what happened when you came here yesterday morning.

HALE: Harry and I had started to town with a load of potatoes. We came along the road from my place and as I got here I said, "I'm going to see if I can't get John Wright to go in with me on a party telephone." I spoke to Wright about it once before and he put me off, saying folks talked too much anyway, and all he asked was peace and quiet—I guess you know about how much he talked himself; but I thought maybe if I went to the house and talked about it before his wife, though I said to Harry that I didn't know as what his wife wanted made much difference to John—

COUNTY ATTORNEY: Let's talk about that later, Mr. Hale. I do want to talk about that, but tell now just what happened when you got to the house.

HALE: I didn't hear or see anything; I knocked at the door, and still it was all quiet inside. I knew they must be up, it was past eight o'clock. So I knocked again, and I thought I heard somebody say, "Come in." I wasn't sure, I'm not sure yet, but I opened the door—this door [*Indicating the door by which the two women are still standing*] and there in that rocker—[*Pointing to it*] sat Mrs. Wright.

[They all look at the rocker.]

COUNTY ATTORNEY: What—was she doing?

HALE: She was rockin' back and forth. She had her apron in her hand and was kind of—pleating it.

COUNTY ATTORNEY: And how did she—look?

HALE: Well, she looked queer.

COUNTY ATTORNEY: How do you mean—queer?

HALE: Well, as if she didn't know what she was going to do next. And kind of done up.

COUNTY ATTORNEY: How did she seem to feel about your coming?

HALE: Why, I don't think she minded—one way or other. She didn't pay much attention. I said, "How do, Mrs. Wright, it's cold, ain't it?" And she said, "Is it?"—and went on kind of pleating at her apron. Well, I was surprised; she didn't ask me to come up to the stove, or to set down, but just sat there, not even looking at me, so I said, "I want to see John." And then she—laughed. I guess you would call it a laugh. I thought of Harry and the team outside, so I said a little sharp: "Can't I see John?" "No," she says, kind o' dull like. "Ain't he home?" says I. "Yes," says she, "he's home." "Then why can't I see him?" I asked her, out of patience. "Cause he's dead," says she. "*Dead?*" says I. She just nodded her head, not getting a bit excited, but rockin' back and forth. "Why—where is he?" says I, not knowing what to say. She just pointed upstairs—like that [*Himself pointing to the room above.*] I got up, with the idea of going up there. I walked from there to here—then I says, "Why, what did he die of?" "He died of a rope round his neck," says she, and just went on pleatin' at her apron. Well, I went out and called Harry. I thought I might—need help. We went upstairs and there he was lyin'—

COUNTY ATTORNEY: I think I'd rather have you go into that upstairs, where you can point it all out. Just go on now with the rest of the story.

HALE: Well, my first thought was to get that rope off. It looked . . . [*Stops, his face twitches*] . . . but Harry, he went up to him, and he said, "No, he's dead all right, and we'd better not touch anything." So we went back down stairs. She was still sitting that same way. "Has anybody been notified?" I asked. "No," says she, unconcerned. "Who did this, Mrs. Wright?" said Harry. He said it businesslike—and she stopped pleatin' of her apron. "I don't know," she says. "You don't *know?*" says Harry. "No," says she. "Weren't you sleepin' in the bed with him?" says Harry. "Yes," says she, "but I was on the inside." "Somebody slipped a rope round his neck and strangled him and you didn't wake up?" says Harry. "I didn't wake up," she said after him. We must a looked as if we didn't see how that could be, for after a minute she said, "I sleep sound." Harry was going to ask her more questions but I said maybe we ought to let her tell her story first to the coroner, or the sheriff, so Harry went fast as he could to Rivers' place, where there's a telephone.

COUNTY ATTORNEY: And what did Mrs. Wright do when she knew that you had gone for the coroner?

HALE: She moved from that chair to this one over here [*Pointing to a small chair in the corner*] and just sat there with her hands held together and looking down. I got a feeling that I ought to make some conversation, so I said I had come in to see if John wanted to put in a telephone, and at that she started to laugh, and then she stopped and looked at me—scared. [*The County Attorney, who has had his notebook out, makes a note.*] I dunno, maybe it wasn't scared. I wouldn't like to say it was. Soon Harry got back, and then Dr. Lloyd came, and you, Mr. Peters, and so I guess that's all I know that you don't.

COUNTY ATTORNEY: [*Looking around.*] I guess we'll go upstairs first—and then out to the barn and around there. [*To the Sheriff*] You're convinced that there was nothing important here—nothing that would point to any motive.

SHERIFF: Nothing here but kitchen things.

[*The County Attorney, after again looking around the kitchen, opens the door of a cupboard closet. He gets up on a chair and looks on a shelf. Pulls his hand away sticky.*]

COUNTY ATTORNEY: Here's a nice mess.

[*The women draw nearer.*]

MRS. PETERS: [*To the other woman.*] Oh, her fruit; it did freeze. [*To the County Attorney*] She worried about that when it turned so cold. She said the fire'd go out and her jars would break.

SHERIFF: Well, can you beat the women! Held for murder and worryin' about her preserves.

COUNTY ATTORNEY: I guess before we're through she may have something more serious than preserves to worry about.

HALE: Well, women are used to worrying over trifles.

[The two women move a little closer together.]

COUNTY ATTORNEY: [*With the gallantry of a young politician.*] And yet, for all their worries, what would we do without the ladies? [*The women do not unbend. He goes to the sink, takes a dipperful of water from the pail and pouring it into a basin, washes his hands. Starts to wipe them on the roller towel, turns it for a cleaner place.*] Dirty towels! [*Kicks his foot against the pans under the sink.*] Not much of a housekeeper, would you say, ladies?

MRS. HALE: [*Stiffly.*] There's a great deal of work to be done on a farm.

COUNTY ATTORNEY: To be sure. And yet [*With a little bow to her*] I know there are some Dickson county farmhouses which do not have such roller towels.

[He gives it a pull to expose its full length again.]

MRS. HALE: Those towels get dirty awful quick. Men's hands aren't always as clean as they might be.

COUNTY ATTORNEY: Ah, loyal to your sex, I see. But you and Mrs. Wright were neighbors. I suppose you were friends, too.

MRS. HALE: [*Shaking her head.*] I've not seen much of her of late years. I've not been in this house—it's more than a year.

COUNTY ATTORNEY: And why was that? You didn't like her?

MRS. HALE: I liked her all well enough. Farmers' wives have their hands full, Mr. Henderson. And then—

COUNTY ATTORNEY: Yes—?

MRS. HALE: [*Looking about.*] It never seemed a very cheerful place.

COUNTY ATTORNEY: No—it's not cheerful. I shouldn't say she had the home-making instinct.

MRS. HALE: Well, I don't know as Wright had, either.

COUNTY ATTORNEY: You mean that they didn't get on very well?

MRS. HALE: No, I don't mean anything. But I don't think a place'd be any cheerfuller for John Wright's being in it.

COUNTY ATTORNEY: I'd like to talk more of that a little later. I want to get the lay of things upstairs now.

[He goes to the left, where three steps lead to a stair door.]

SHERIFF: I suppose anything Mrs. Peters does'll be all right. She was to take in some clothes for her, you know, and a few little things. We left in such a hurry yesterday.

COUNTY ATTORNEY: Yes, but I would like to see what you take, Mrs. Peters, and keep an eye out for anything that might be of use to us.

MRS. PETERS: Yes, Mr. Henderson.

[The women listen to the men's steps on the stairs, then look about the kitchen.]

MRS. HALE: I'd hate to have men coming into my kitchen, snooping around and criticizing.

[She arranges the pans under sink which the County Attorney had shoved out of place.]

MRS. PETERS: Of course it's no more than their duty.

MRS. HALE: Duty's all right, but I guess that deputy sheriff that came out to make the fire might have got a little of this on. [*Gives the roller towel a pull.*] Wish I'd thought of that sooner. Seems mean to talk about her for not having things slicked up when she had to come away in such a hurry.

MRS. PETERS: [*Who has gone to a small table in the left rear corner of the room, and lifted one end of a towel that covers a pan.*] She had bread set.

[Stands still.]

MRS. HALE: [*Eyes fixed on a loaf of bread beside the breadbox, which is on a low shelf at the other side of the room. Moves slowly toward it.*] She was going to put this in there. [*Picks up loaf, then abruptly drops it. In a manner of returning to familiar things.*] It's a shame about her fruit. I wonder if it's all gone. [*Gets up on the chair and looks.*] I think there's some here that's all right, Mrs. Peters. Yes—here; [*Holding it toward the window*] this is cherries, too. [*Looking again.*] I declare I believe that's the only one. [*Gets down, bottle in her hand. Goes to the sink and wipes it off on the outside.*] She'll feel awful bad after all her hard work in the hot weather. I remember the afternoon I put up my cherries last summer.

[She puts the bottle on the big kitchen table, center of the room. With a sigh, is about to sit down in the rocking chair. Before she is seated realizes what chair it is; with a slow look at it, steps back. The chair which she has touched rocks back and forth.]

MRS. PETERS: Well, I must get those things from the front room closet. [*She goes to the door at the right, but after looking into the other room, steps back.*] You coming with me, Mrs. Hale? You could help me carry them.

[They go in the other room; reappear, Mrs. Peters carrying a dress and skirt, Mrs. Hale following with a pair of shoes.]

MRS. PETERS: My, it's cold in there.

[She puts the clothes on the big table, and hurries to the stove.]

MRS. HALE: [*Examining her skirt.*] Wright was close. I think maybe that's why she kept so much to herself. She didn't even belong to the Ladies Aid. I suppose she felt she couldn't do her part, and then you don't enjoy things when you feel shabby. She used to wear pretty clothes and be lively, when she was Minnie Foster, one of the town girls singing in the choir. But that—oh, that was thirty years ago. This all you was to take in?

MRS. PETERS: She said she wanted an apron. Funny thing to want, for there isn't much to get you dirty in jail, goodness knows. But I suppose just to make her feel more natural. She said they was in the top drawer in this cupboard. Yes, here. And then her little shawl that always hung behind the door. [*Opens stair door and looks.*] Yes, here it is.

[*Quickly shuts door leading upstairs.*]

MRS. HALE: [*Abruptly moving toward her.*] Mrs. Peters?

MRS. PETERS: Yes, Mrs. Hale?

MRS. HALE: Do you think she did it?

MRS. PETERS: [*In a frightened voice.*] Oh, I don't know.

MRS. HALE: Well, I don't think she did. Asking for an apron and her little shawl. Worrying about her fruit.

MRS. PETERS: [*Starts to speak, glances up, where footsteps are heard in the room above. In a low voice.*] Mr. Peters says it looks bad for her. Mr. Henderson is awful sarcastic in a speech and he'll make fun of her sayin' she didn't wake up.

MRS. HALE: Well, I guess John Wright didn't wake when they was slipping that rope under his neck.

MRS. PETERS: No, it's strange. It must have been done awful crafty and still. They say it was such a—funny way to kill a man, rigging it all up like that.

MRS. HALE: That's just what Mr. Hale said. There was a gun in the house. He says that's what he can't understand.

MRS. PETERS: Mr. Henderson said coming out that what was needed for the case was a motive; something to show anger, or—sudden feeling.

MRS. HALE: [*Who is standing by the table.*] Well, I don't see any signs of anger around here. [*She puts her hand on the dish towel which lies on the table, stands looking down at table, one half of which is clean, the other half messy.*] It's wiped to here. [*Makes a move as if to finish work, then turns and looks at loaf of bread outside the breadbox. Drops towel. In that voice of coming back to familiar things.*] Wonder how they are finding things upstairs. I hope she had it a little more red-up[1] up there. You know, it seems kind of *sneaking*. Locking her up in town and then coming out here and trying to get her own house to turn against her!

MRS. PETERS: But Mrs. Hale, the law is the law.

MRS. HALE: I s'pose 'tis. [*Unbuttoning her coat.*] Better loosen up your things, Mrs. Peters. You won't feel them when you go out.

[*Mrs. Peters takes off her fur tippet, goes to hang it on hook at back of room, stands looking at the under part of the small corner table.*]

MRS. PETERS: She was piecing a quilt.

---

[1]*Red-up*: (slang) readied up, ready to be seen.

[She brings the large sewing basket and they look at the bright pieces.]

MRS. HALE: It's a log cabin pattern. Pretty, isn't it? I wonder if she was goin' to quilt it or just knot it?

[Footsteps have been heard coming down the stairs. The Sheriff enters followed by Hale and the County Attorney.]

SHERIFF: They wonder if she was going to quilt it or just knot it!

[The men laugh; the women look abashed.]

COUNTY ATTORNEY: [*Rubbing his hands over the stove.*] Frank's fire didn't do much up there, did it? Well, let's go out to the barn and get that cleared up.

[The men go outside.]

MRS. HALE: [*Resentfully.*] I don't know as there's anything so strange, our takin' up our time with little things while we're waiting for them to get the evidence. [*She sits down at the big table smoothing out a block with decision.*] I don't see as it's anything to laugh about.

MRS. PETERS: [*Apologetically.*] Of course they've got awful important things on their minds.

[Pulls up a chair and joins Mrs. Hale at the table.]

MRS. HALE: [*Examining another block.*] Mrs. Peters, look at this one. Here, this is the one she was working on, and look at the sewing! All the rest of it has been so nice and even. And look at this! It's all over the place! Why, it looks as if she didn't know what she was about!

[After she has said this they look at each, then start to glance back at the door. After an instant Mrs. Hale has pulled at a knot and ripped the sewing.]

MRS. PETERS: Oh, what are you doing, Mrs. Hale?

MRS. HALE: [*Mildly.*] Just pulling out a stitch or two that's not sewed very good. [*Threading a needle.*] Bad sewing always made me fidgety.

MRS. PETERS: [*Nervously.*] I don't think we ought to touch things.

MRS. HALE: I'll just finish up this end. [*Suddenly stopping and leaning forward.*] Mrs. Peters?

MRS. PETERS: Yes, Mrs. Hale?

MRS. HALE: What do you suppose she was so nervous about?

MRS. PETERS: Oh—I don't know. I don't know as she was nervous. I sometimes sew awful queer when I'm just tired. [*Mrs. Hale starts to say something, looks at Mrs. Peters, then goes on sewing.*] Well, I must get these things wrapped up. They may be through sooner than we think. [*Putting apron and other things together.*] I wonder where I can find a piece of paper, and string.

MRS. HALE: In that cupboard, maybe.

MRS. PETERS: [*Looking in cupboard.*] Why, here's a birdcage. [*Holds it up.*]
Did she have a bird, Mrs. Hale?

MRS. HALE: Why, I don't know whether she did or not—I've not been here
for so long. There was a man around last year selling canaries cheap,
but I don't know as she took one; maybe she did. She used to sing
real pretty herself.

MRS. PETERS: [*Glancing around.*] Seems funny to think of a bird here. But
she must have had one, or why would she have a cage? I wonder what
happened to it.

MRS. HALE: I s'pose maybe the cat got it.

MRS. PETERS: No, she didn't have a cat. She's got that feeling some people have about cats—being afraid of them. My cat got in her room
and she was real upset and asked me to take it out.

MRS. HALE: My sister Bessie was like that. Queer, ain't it?

MRS. PETERS: [*Examining the cage.*] Why, look at this door. It's broke. One
hinge is pulled apart.

MRS. HALE: [*Looking too.*] Looks as if someone must have been rough with
it.

MRS. PETERS: Why, yes.

[She brings the cage forward and puts it on the table.]

MRS. HALE: I wish if they're going to find any evidence they'd be about
it. I don't like this place.

MRS. PETERS: But I'm awful glad you came with me, Mrs. Hale. It would
be lonesome for me sitting here alone.

MRS. HALE: It would, wouldn't it? [*Dropping her sewing.*] But I tell you what
I do wish, Mrs. Peters. I wish I had come over sometimes when *she*
was here. I—[*Looking around the room.*]—wish I had.

MRS. PETERS: But of course you were awful busy, Mrs. Hale—your house
and your children.

MRS. HALE: I could've come. I stayed away because it weren't cheerful—
and that's why I ought to have come. I—I've never liked this place.
Maybe because it's down in a hollow and you don't see the road. I
dunno what it is but it's a lonesome place and always was. I wish I
had come over to see Minnie Foster sometimes. I can see now—

[Shakes her head.]

MRS. PETERS: Well, you mustn't reproach yourself, Mrs. Hale. Somehow
we just don't see how it is with other folks until—something comes
up.

MRS. HALE: Not having children makes less work—but it makes a quiet
house, and Wright out to work all day, and no company when he did
come in. Did you know John Wright, Mrs. Peters?

MRS. PETERS: Not to know him; I've seen him in town. They say he was
a good man.

MRS. HALE: Yes—good; he didn't drink, and kept his word as well as most, I guess, and paid his debts. But he was a hard man, Mrs. Peters. Just to pass the time of day with him—[*Shivers.*] Like a raw wind that gets to the bone. [*Pauses, her eye falling on the cage.*] I should think she would'a wanted a bird. But what do you suppose went with it?

MRS. PETERS: I don't know, unless it got sick and died.

[*She reaches over and swings the broken door, swings it again. Both women watch it.*]

MRS. HALE: You weren't raised round here, were you? [*Mrs. Peters shakes her head.*] You didn't know—her?

MRS. PETERS: Not till they brought her yesterday.

MRS. HALE: She—come to think of it, she was kind of like a bird herself—real sweet and pretty, but kind of timid and—fluttery. How—she—did—change. [*Silence; then as if struck by a happy thought and relieved to get back to everyday things.*] Tell you what, Mrs. Peters, why don't you take the quilt in with you? It might take up her mind.

MRS. PETERS: Why, I think that's a real nice idea, Mrs. Hale. There couldn't possibly be any objection to it, could there? Now, just what would I take? I wonder if her patches are in here—and her things.

[*They look in the sewing basket.*]

MRS. HALE: Here's some red. I expect this has got sewing things in it. [*Brings out a fancy box.*] What a pretty box. Looks like something somebody would give you. Maybe her scissors are in here. [*Opens box. Suddenly puts her hand to her nose.*] Why—[*Mrs. Peters bends nearer, then turns her face away.*] There's something wrapped up in this piece of silk.

MRS. PETERS: Why, this isn't her scissors.

MRS. HALE: [*Lifting the silk.*] Oh, Mrs. Peters—it's—

[*Mrs. Peters bends closer.*]

MRS. PETERS: It's the bird.

MRS. HALE: [*Jumping up.*] But, Mrs. Peters—look at it! Its neck! Look at its neck! It's all—other side *too*.

MRS. PETERS: Somebody—wrung—its—neck.

[*Their eyes meet. A look of growing comprehension, of horror. Steps are heard outside. Mrs. Hale slips box under quilt pieces, and sinks into her chair. Enter Sheriff and County Attorney. Mrs. Peters rises.*]

COUNTY ATTORNEY: [*As one turning from serious things to little pleasantries.*] Well, ladies, have you decided whether she was going to quilt it or knot it?

MRS. PETERS: We think she was going to—knot it.

COUNTY ATTORNEY: Well, that's interesting, I'm sure. [*Seeing the birdcage.*] Has the bird flown?

MRS. HALE: [*Putting more quilt pieces over the box.*] We think the—cat got it.

COUNTY ATTORNEY: [*Preoccupied.*] Is there a cat?

[*Mrs. Hale glances in a quick covert way at Mrs. Peters.*]

MRS. PETERS: Well, not *now*. They're superstitious, you know. They leave.

COUNTY ATTORNEY: [*To Sheriff Peters, continuing an interrupted conversation.*] No sign at all of anyone having come from the outside. Their own rope. Now let's go up again and go over it piece by piece. [*They start upstairs.*] It would have to have been someone who knew just the—

[*Mrs. Peters sits down. The two women sit there not looking at one another, but as if peering into something and at the same time holding back. When they talk now it is in the manner of feeling their way over strange ground, as if afraid of what they are saying, but as if they cannot help saying it.*]

MRS. HALE: She liked the bird. She was going to bury it in that pretty box.

MRS. PETERS: [*In a whisper.*] When I was a girl—my kitten—there was a boy took a hatchet, and before my eyes—and before I could get there— [*Covers her face an instant.*] If they hadn't held me back I would have— [*Catches herself, looks upstairs where steps are heard, falters weakly*]—hurt him.

MRS. HALE: [*With a slow look around her.*] I wonder how it would seem never to have had any children around. [*Pause.*] No, Wright wouldn't like the bird—a thing that sang. She used to sing. He killed that, too.

MRS. PETERS: [*Moving uneasily.*] We don't know who killed the bird.

MRS. HALE: I knew John Wright.

MRS. PETERS: It was an awful thing was done in this house that night, Mrs. Hale. Killing a man while he slept, slipping a rope around his neck that choked the life out of him.

MRS. HALE: His neck. Choked the life out of him.

[*Her hand goes out and rests on the birdcage.*]

MRS. PETERS: [*With rising voice.*] We don't know who killed him. We don't *know*.

MRS. HALE: [*Her own feeling not interrupted.*] If there'd been years and years of nothing, then a bird to sing to you, it would be awful—still, after the bird was still.

MRS. PETERS: [*Something within her speaking.*] I know what stillness is. When we homesteaded in Dakota, and my first baby died—after he was two years old, and me with no other then—

MRS. HALE: [*Moving.*] How soon do you suppose they'll be through looking for the evidence?

MRS. PETERS: I know what stillness is. [*Pulling herself back.*] The law has got to punish crime, Mrs. Hale.

MRS. HALE: [*Not as if answering that.*] I wish you'd seen Minnie Foster when she wore a white dress with blue ribbons and stood up there in the choir and sang. [*A look around the room.*] Oh, I *wish* I'd come over here once in a while! That was a crime! That was a crime! Who's going to punish that?

MRS. PETERS: [*Looking upstairs.*] We mustn't—take on.

MRS. HALE: I might have known she needed help! I know how things can be—for women. I tell you, it's queer, Mrs. Peters. We live close together and we live far apart. We all go through the same things—it's all just a different kind of the same thing. [*Brushes her eyes; noticing the bottle of fruit, reaches out for it.*] If I was you I wouldn't tell her her fruit was gone. Tell her it *ain't.* Tell her it's all right. Take this in to prove it to her. She—she may never know whether it was broke or not.

MRS. PETERS: [*Takes the bottle, looks about for something to wrap it in; takes petticoat from the clothes brought from the other room, very nervously begins winding this around the bottle. In a false voice.*] My, it's a good thing the men couldn't hear us. Wouldn't they just laugh! Getting all stirred up over a little thing like a—dead canary. As if that could have anything to do with—with—wouldn't they *laugh!*

[*The men are heard coming down stairs.*]

MRS. HALE: [*Under her breath.*] Maybe they would—maybe they wouldn't.

COUNTY ATTORNEY: No, Peters, it's all perfectly clear except a reason for doing it. But you know juries when it comes to women. If there was some definite thing. Something to show—something to make a story about—a thing that would connect up with this strange way of doing it—

[*The women's eyes meet for an instant. Enter Hale from outer door.*]

HALE: Well, I've got the team around. Pretty cold out there.

COUNTY ATTORNEY: I'm going to stay here a while by myself. [*To the Sheriff.*] You can send Frank out for me, can't you? I want to go over everything. I'm not satisfied that we can't do better.

SHERIFF: Do you want to see what Mrs. Peters is going to take in?

[*The County Attorney goes to the table, picks up the apron, laughs.*]

COUNTY ATTORNEY: Oh, I guess they're not very dangerous things the ladies have picked out. [*Moves a few things about, disturbing the quilt pieces which cover the box. Steps back.*] No, Mrs. Peters doesn't need supervising. For that matter, a sheriff's wife is married to the law. Ever think of it that way, Mrs. Peters?

MRS. PETERS: Not—just that way.

SHERIFF: [*Chuckling.*] Married to the law. [*Moves toward the other room.*] I just want you to come in here a minute, George. We ought to take a look at these windows.

COUNTY ATTORNEY: [*Scoffingly.*] Oh, windows!

SHERIFF: We'll be right out, Mr. Hale.

> [*Hale goes outside. The Sheriff follows the County Attorney into the other room. Then Mrs. Hale rises, hands tight together, looking intensely at Mrs. Peters, whose eyes make a slow turn, finally meeting Mrs. Hale's. A moment Mrs. Hale holds her, then her own eyes point the way to where the box is concealed. Suddenly Mrs. Peters throws back quilt pieces and tries to put the box in the bag she is wearing. It is too big. She opens box, starts to take bird out, cannot touch it, goes to pieces, stands there helpless. Sound of a knob turning in the other room. Mrs. Hale snatches the box and puts it in the pocket of her big coat. Enter County Attorney and Sheriff.]*

COUNTY ATTORNEY: [*Facetiously.*] Well, Henry, at least we found out that she was not going to quilt it. She was going to—what is it you call it, ladies?

MRS. HALE: [*Her hand against her pocket.*] We call it—knot it, Mr. Henderson.

CURTAIN

1916

David Ives (B. 1950)

Time Flies

Characters

HORACE
MAY
DAVID ATTENBOROUGH
A FROG

> [*Evening. A pond. The chirr of treetoads, and the buzz of a huge swarm of insects. Upstage, a thicket of tall cattails. Downstage, a deep green loveseat. Overhead, an enormous full moon.]*
>
> [*A cloud cuckoo sounds, like the mechanical "cuckoo" of a clock.]*
>
> *Lights come up on two mayflies: Horace and May, buzzing as they "fly" in. They are dressed like singles on an evening out, he in a jacket and tie, she in a party dress—but they have insect-like antennae; long tube-like tails; and on their backs, translucent wings. Outsized hornrim glasses give the impression of very large eyes. May has distinctly hairy legs.*

HORACE & MAY: Bzzzzzzzzzzzzzzzzzz . . .

[Their wings stop fluttering, as they "settle."]

MAY: Well here we are. This is my place.
HORACE: Already? That was fast.
MAY: Swell party, huh.
HORACE: Yeah. Quite a swarm.
MAY: Thank you for flying me home.
HORACE: No. Sure. I'm happy to. Absolutely. My pleasure. I mean—
you're very, very, very welcome.

[Their eyes lock and they near each other as if for a kiss, their wings fluttering a little.]

HORACE: *[Cont'd.]* Bzzzzzzzz . . .
MAY: Bzzzzzzzz . . .

[Before their jaws can meet: "cuckoo!"—and Horace breaks away.]

HORACE: It's that late, is it. Anyway, it was very nice meeting you—I'm
sorry, is it April?
MAY: May.
HORACE: May. Yes. Later than I thought, huh.

[They laugh politely.]

MAY: That's very funny, Vergil.
HORACE: It's Horace, actually.
MAY: I'm sorry. The buzz at that party was so loud.
HORACE: So you're "May the mayfly."
MAY: Yeah. Guess my parents didn't have much imagination. May, mayfly.
HORACE: You don't, ah, live with your parents, do you, May?
MAY: No, my parents died around dawn this morning.
HORACE: Isn't that funny. Mine died around dawn too.
MAY: Maybe it's fate.
HORACE: Is that what it izzzzzzzz . . . ?
MAY: Bzzzzzzzz . . .
HORACE: Bzzzzzzzzzzzzzz . . . *[They near for a kiss, but Horace breaks away.]*
    Well I'd better be going now. Good night.
MAY: Do you want a drink?
HORACE: I'd love a drink, actually . . .
MAY: Let me just turn on a couple of fireflies.

*[May tickles the underside of a couple of two foot-long fireflies hang-
ing like a chandelier, and the fireflies light up.]*

HORACE: Wow. Great pond! *[Indicating the loveseat:]* I love the lilypad.
MAY: That was here. It kinda grew on me. *[Polite laugh.]* Care to take the
    load off your wings?

HORACE: That's all right. I'll just—you know—hover. But will you look at that . . . !

[Turning, Horace bats may with his wings.]

MAY: Oof!
HORACE: I'm sorry. Did we collide?
MAY: No. No. It's fine.
HORACE: I've only had my wings about six hours.
MAY: Really! So have I . . . ! Wasn't molting disgusting?
HORACE: Eugh. I'm glad that's over.
MAY: Care for some music? I've got The Beatles, The Byrds, The Crickets . . .
HORACE: I love The Crickets.
MAY: Well so do I . . .

[She kicks a large, insect-shaped coffee table, and we bear the buzz of crickets.]

HORACE: [*As they boogie to that:*] So are you going out with any—I mean, are there any other mayflies in the neighborhood?
MAY: No, it's mostly wasps.
HORACE: So, you live here by your, um, all by yourself? Alone?
MAY: All by my lonesome.
HORACE: And will you look at that moon.
MAY: You know that's the first moon I've ever seen?
HORACE: That's the first moon I've ever seen . . . !
MAY: Isn't that funny.
HORACE: When were you born?
MAY: About 7:30 this morning.
HORACE: So was I! Seven thirty-three!
MAY: Isn't that funny.
HORACE: Or maybe it's fate. [*They near each other again, as if for a kiss:*] Bzzzzzzz . . .
MAY: Bzzzzzzzzz . . . I think that moon is having a very emotional effect on me.
HORACE: Me too.
MAY: It must be nature.
HORACE: Me too.
MAY: Or maybe it's fate.
HORACE: Me too . . .
MAY: Bzzzzzzzzzz . . .
HORACE: Bzzzzzzzzzzzzzz . . .

[They draw their tails very close. Suddenly:]

A FROG: [*Amplified, over loudspeaker.*] Ribbit, ribbit!
HORACE: A frog!
MAY: A frog!

HORACE & MAY: The frogs are coming, the frogs are coming! [*They "fly" around the stage in a panic. Ad lib:*] A frog, a frog! The frogs are coming, the frogs are coming!

[*They finally stop, breathless.*]

MAY: It's okay. It's okay.
HORACE: Oh my goodness.
MAY: I think he's gone now.
HORACE: Oh my goodness, that scared me.
MAY: That is the only drawback to living here. The frogs.
HORACE: You know I like frog films and frog literature. I just don't like frogs.
MAY: And they're so rude if you're not a frog yourself.
HORACE: Look at me. I'm shaking.
MAY: Why don't I fix you something. Would you like a grasshopper? Or a stinger?
HORACE: Just some stagnant water would be fine.
MAY: A little duckweed in that? Some algae?
HORACE: Straight up is fine.
MAY: [*As she pours his drink:*] Sure I couldn't tempt you to try the lily pad?
HORACE: Well, maybe for just a second.

[*Horace flutters down onto the love seat:*]

Zzzzzzz . . .
MAY: [*Handing him a glass:*] Here you go. Cheers, Horace.
HORACE: Long life, May.

[*They clink glasses.*]

MAY: Do you want to watch some tube?
HORACE: Sure. What's on?
MAY: Let's see. [*She checks a GREEN TV GUIDE.*] There is . . . "The Love Bug," "M. Butterfly," "The Spider's Stratagem," "Travels with My Ant," "Angels and Insects," "The Fly" . . .
HORACE: The original, or Jeff Goldblum?
MAY: Jeff Goldblum.
HORACE: Euch. Too gruesome.
MAY: "Born Yesterday" and "Life on Earth."
HORACE: What's on that?
MAY: "Swamp Life," with Sir David Attenborough.
HORACE: That sounds good.
MAY: Shall we try it?
HORACE: Carpe diem.
MAY: Carpe diem? What's that?
HORACE: I don't know. It's Latin.
MAY: What's Latin?
HORACE: I don't know. I'm just a mayfly.

["Cuckoo!"]

And we're right on time for it.

[May presses a remote control and David Attenborough appears, wearing a safari jacket.]

DAVID ATTENBOROUGH: Hello, I'm David Attenborough. Welcome to "Swamp Life."

MAY: Isn't this comfy.

HORACE: Is my wing in your way?

MAY: No. It's fine.

DAVID ATTENBOROUGH: You may not believe it, but within this seemingly lifeless puddle, there thrives a teeming world of vibrant life.

HORACE: May, look—isn't that your pond?

MAY: I think that is my pond!

HORACE: He said "puddle."

DAVID ATTENBOROUGH: This puddle is only several inches across, but its stagnant water plays host to over 14 gazillion different species.

MAY: It is my pond!

DAVID ATTENBOROUGH: Every species here is engaged in a constant, desperate battle for survival. Feeding—meeting—mating—breeding—dying. And mating. And meeting. And mating. And feeding. And dying. Mating. Mating. Meeting. Breeding. Brooding. Braiding—those that can braid. Feeding. Mating.

MAY: All right, Sir Dave!

DAVID ATTENBOROUGH: Mating, mating, mating, and mating.

HORACE: Only one thing on his mind.

MAY: The filth on television these days.

DAVID ATTENBOROUGH: Tonight we start off with one of the saddest creatures of this environment.

HORACE: The dung beetle.

MAY: The toad.

DAVID ATTENBOROUGH: The lowly mayfly.

HORACE: Did he say "the mayfly?"

MAY: I think he said the lowly mayfly.

DAVID ATTENBOROUGH: Yes. The lowly mayfly. Like these two mayflies, for instance.

HORACE: May—I think that's us!

MAY: Oh my God . . .

HORACE & MAY: *[Together:]* We're on television!

HORACE: I don't believe it!

MAY: I wish my mother was here to see this!

HORACE: This is amazing!

MAY: Oh God, I look terrible!

HORACE: You look very good.

MAY: I can't look at this.

DAVID ATTENBOROUGH: As you can see, the lowly mayfly is not one of nature's most attractive creatures.

MAY: At least we don't wear safari jackets.

HORACE: I wish he'd stop saying "lowly mayfly."

DAVID ATTENBOROUGH: The lowly mayfly has a very distinctive khkhkhkhkhkhkhkhkhkkh . . . —[*the sound of TV static.*]

MAY: I think there's something wrong with my antenna . . . [*She adjusts the antenna on her head.*]

HORACE: You don't have cable?

MAY: Not on this pond.

DAVID ATTENBOROUGH: [*Stops the static sound.*] . . . and sixty tons of droppings.

HORACE: That fixed it.

MAY: Can I offer you some food? I've got some plankton in the pond. And some very nice gnat.

HORACE: I do love good gnat.

MAY: I'll set it out, you can pick.

[*She rises and gets some food, as:*]

DAVID ATTENBOROUGH: The lowly mayfly first appeared some 350 million years ago . . .

MAY: That's impressive.

DAVID ATTENBOROUGH: . . . and is of the order Ephemeroptera, meaning, "living for a single day."

MAY: I did not know that!

HORACE: "Living for a single day." Huh . . .

MAY: [*Setting out a tray on the coffee table.*] There you go.

HORACE: Gosh, May. That's beautiful.

MAY: There's curried gnat, salted gnat, Scottish smoked gnat . . .

HORACE: I love that.

MAY: . . . gnat with pesto, gnat au naturelle, and Gnat King Cole.

HORACE: I don't think I could finish a whole one.

MAY: "Gnat" to worry. [*They laugh politely.*] That's larva dip there in the center. Just dig in.

DAVID ATTENBOROUGH: As for the life of the common mayfly . . .

HORACE: Oh. We're "common" now.

DAVID ATTENBOROUGH: . . . it is a simple round of meeting, mating, meeting, mating—

MAY: Here we go again.

DAVID ATTENBOROUGH: —breeding, feeding, feeding . . .

HORACE: This dip is fabulous.

DAVID ATTENBOROUGH: . . . and dying.

MAY: Leaf?

HORACE: Thank you.

[*May breaks a leaf off a plant and hands it to Horace.*]

DAVID ATTENBOROUGH: Mayflies are a major food source for trout and salmon.

MAY: Will you look at that savagery?

HORACE: That poor, poor mayfly.

DAVID ATTENBOROUGH: Fishermen like to bait hooks with mayfly looka-likes.

MAY: Bastards!—Excuse me.

DAVID ATTENBOROUGH: And then there is the giant bullfrog.

FROG: [*Amplified, over loudspeaker*] Ribbit, ribbit!

HORACE & MAY: The frogs are coming, the frogs are coming!

> [*They "fly" around the stage in a panic—and end up "flying" right into each other's arms.*]

HORACE: Well there.

MAY: Hello.

DAVID ATTENBOROUGH: Welcome to "Swamp Life."

> [*David Attenborough exits.*]

MAY: [*Hypnotized by Horace.*] Funny how we flew right into each other's wings.

HORACE: It is funny.

MAY: Or fate.

HORACE: Do you think he's gone?

MAY: David Attenborough?

HORACE: The frog.

MAY: What frog? Bzzzz . . .

HORACE: Bzzzzz . . .

DAVID ATTENBOROUGH'S VOICE: As you see, mayflies can be quite affectionate . . .

HORACE & MAY: Bzzzzzzzzzzzz . . .

DAVID ATTENBOROUGH'S VOICE: . . . mutually palpating their proboscises.

HORACE: You know I've been wanting to palpate your proboscis all evening?

MAY: I think it was larva at first sight.

HORACE & MAY: [*Rubbing proboscises together.*]
Zzzzzzzzzzzzzzzzzzzzzzzzzzz . . .

MAY: [*very British, "Brief Encounter."*] Oh darling, darling.

HORACE: Oh do darling do let's always be good to each other, shall we?

MAY: Let's do do that, darling, always, always.

HORACE: Always?

MAY: Always.

HORACE & MAY: Zzzzzzzzzzzzzzzzzzzzzzzzzzzzzzzzzzz!

MAY: Rub my antennae. Rub my antennae.

> [*Horace rubs May's antennae with his hands.*]

DAVID ATTENBOROUGH'S VOICE: Sometimes mayflies rub antennae together.

MAY: Oh yes. Yes. Just like that. Yes. Keep going. Harder. Rub harder.

HORACE: Rub mine now. Rub my antennae. Oh yes. Yes. Yes. Yes. There's the rub. There's the rub. Go. Go. Go!

DAVID ATTENBOROUGH'S VOICE: Isn't that a picture. Now get a load of mating.

> *[Horace gets into mounting position, behind May. He rubs her antennae while she wolfs down the gnat-food in front of her.]*

HORACE & MAY: Bzzzzzzzzzzzzzzzzzzzzzzzzzzzzzzzzzzzzzzzzzzzzz!

DAVID ATTENBOROUGH'S VOICE: Unfortunately for this insect, the mayfly has a lifespan of only one day.

> *[Horace and May stop buzzing, abruptly.]*

HORACE: What was that . . . ?

DAVID ATTENBOROUGH'S VOICE: The mayfly has a lifespan of only one day—living just long enough to meet, mate, have offspring, and die.

MAY: Did he say "meet, mate, have offspring, and DIE"—?

DAVID ATTENBOROUGH'S VOICE: I did. In fact, mayflies born at 7:30 in the morning will die by the next dawn.

HORACE: [*Whimpers softly at the thought.*]

DAVID ATTENBOROUGH'S VOICE: But so much for the lowly mayfly. Let's move on to the newt.

> *["Cuckoo!"]*

HORACE & MAY: We're going to die . . . We're going to die! Mayday, mayday! We're going to die, we're going to die! [*Weeping and wailing, they kneel, beat their breasts, cross themselves, daven, and tear their hair.*]

> *["Cuckoo!"]*

HORACE: What time is it? What time is it?

MAY: I don't wear a watch. I'm a lowly mayfly!

HORACE: [*Weeping.*] Wah-ha-ha-ha!

MAY: [*Suddenly sober.*] Well isn't this beautiful.

HORACE: [*Gasping for breath.*] Oh my goodness. I think I'm having an asthma attack. Can mayflies have asthma?

MAY: I don't know. Ask Mr. Safari Jacket.

HORACE: Maybe if I put a paper bag over my head . . .

MAY: So this is my sex life?

HORACE: Do you have a paper bag?

MAY: One bang, a bambino, and boom—that's it?

HORACE: Do you have a paper bag?

MAY: For the common mayfly, foreplay segues right into funeral.

HORACE: Do you have a paper bag?

MAY: I don't have time to look for a paper bag, I'm going to be dead very shortly, all right?

> *["Cuckoo!"]*

HORACE: Oh come on! That wasn't a whole hour!

["Cuckoo!"]

Time is moving so fast now.

["Cuckoo!"]

HORACE & MAY: Shut up!

["Cuckoo!"]

HORACE: [*Suddenly sober.*] This explains everything. We were born this morning, we hit puberty in mid-afternoon, our biological clocks went BONG, and here we are. Hot to copulate.

MAY: For the one brief miserable time we get to do it.

HORACE: Yeah.

MAY: Talk about a quickie.

HORACE: Wait a minute, wait a minute.

MAY: Talk fast.

HORACE: What makes you think it would be so brief?

MAY: Oh, I'm sorry. Did I insult your vast sexual experience?

HORACE: Are you more experienced than I am, Dr. Ruth? Luring me here to your pad?

MAY: I see. I see. Blame me!

HORACE: Can I remind you we only get one shot at this?

MAY: So I can rule out multiple orgasms, is that it?

HORACE: I'm just saying there's not a lot of time to hone one's erotic technique, okay?

MAY: Hmp!

HORACE: And I'm trying to sort out some very big entomontological questions here rather quickly, do you mind?

MAY: And I'm just the babe here, is that it? I'm just a piece of tail.

HORACE: I'm not the one who suggested TV.

MAY: I'm not the one who wanted to watch "Life on Earth." "Oh—Swamp Life. That sounds interesting."

FROG: Ribbit, ribbit.

HORACE: [*Calmly.*] There's a frog up there.

MAY: Oh, I'm really scared. I'm terrified.

FROG: Ribbit, ribbit!

HORACE: [*Calling to the frog.*] We're right down here! Come and get us!

MAY: Breeding. Dying. Breeding. Dying. So this is the whole purpose of mayflies? To make more mayflies?

HORACE: Does the world need more mayflies?

MAY: We're a major food source for trout and salmon.

HORACE: How nice for the salmon.

MAY: Do you want more food?

HORACE: I've lost a bit of my appetite, all right?

MAY: Oh. Excuse me.

HORACE: I'm sorry. Really, May.

MAY: [*Starts to cry.*] Males!

HORACE: Leaf? [*He plucks another leaf and hands it to her.*]

MAY: Thank you.

HORACE: Really. I didn't mean to snap at you.

MAY: Oh, you've been very nice.

[*"Cuckoo!" They jump.*]

Under the circumstances.

HORACE: I'm sorry.

MAY: No, I'm sorry.

HORACE: No, I'm sorry.

MAY: No, I'm sorry.

HORACE: No, I'm sorry.

MAY: We'd better stop apologizing, we're going to be dead soon.

HORACE: I'm sorry.

MAY: Oh Horace, I had such plans. I had such wonderful plans. I wanted to see Paris.

HORACE: What's Paris?

MAY: I have no fucking idea.

HORACE: Maybe we'll come back as caviar and find out. [*They laugh a little at that.*] I was just hoping to live till Tuesday.

MAY: [*Making a small joke*] What's a Tuesday? [*They laugh a little more at that.*] The sun's going to be up soon. I'm scared, Horace. I'm so scared.

HORACE: You know, May, we don't have much time, and really, we hardly know each other—but I'm going to say it. I think you're swell. I think you're divine. From your buggy eyes to the thick raspy hair on your legs to the intoxicating scent of your secretions.

MAY: Eeeuw.

HORACE: Eeeuw? No. I say woof. And I say who cares if life is a swamp and we're just a couple of small bugs in a very small pond. I say live, May! I say . . . darn it . . . live!

MAY: But how?

HORACE: Well I don't honestly know that . . .

[*Attenborough appears.*]

DAVID ATTENBOROUGH: You could fly to Paris.

MAY: We could fly to Paris!

HORACE: Do we have time to fly to Paris?

MAY: Carpe diem!

HORACE: What is carpe diem?

DAVID ATTENBOROUGH: It means "bon voyage."

HORACE & MAY: And we're outta here!

[*They fly off to Paris as . . .]*
[*Blackout.*]

THE END

1997

David J. LeMaster (B. 1966)

The Assassination and Persecution of Abraham Lincoln

Characters

ABRAHAM LINCOLN
JOHN WILKES BOOTH
EDWIN BOOTH, AKA ELVIS PRESLEY
UNION SOLDIER

Scene

Curtain up on a cheap room at the Motel 6. Abraham Lincoln bursts in, slams and bolts the door, then peers through the curtains to make sure he hasn't been followed. He is covered in blood. Lincoln pulls a suitcase out from under a double bed and rummages through its contents. Then he grabs the push-button phone and punches in a number.

LINCOLN: Mary? It's me. Did we pull it off? Good. Now listen, Booth is on his way, so skip town fast. No, go to Singapore first. You don't want the media following you. Right. I'll meet you in the Bahamas on the 20th. That's right. We don't have to worry about this Civil War thing anymore. From now on it's gonna be margaritas and sunshine.

(We hear three sharp knocks on the door. Lincoln hangs up, pulls an Uzi from his suitcase, and leaps over the bed to the door. He makes three sharp knocks in reply.)

BOOTH: (*outside*) Sockdolagizing all over the place!
LINCOLN: Sic semper tyranus!

(Enter John Wilkes Booth, a black man wearing a cheap polyester suit. Booth glances out the window as he shuts and bolts the door.)

LINCOLN: Anybody outside, Booth?
BOOTH: We're cool.
LINCOLN: Help me get this off.

(They peel away the bloodstained clothing to reveal a special effects jacket. Lincoln wears a Hard Rock Cafe T-shirt.)

BOOTH: (*pointing to Uzi*) What's that?
LINCOLN: Protection.
BOOTH: Protection? Come on, Abe. You don't know how to use this thing.

LINCOLN: I know good enough.

BOOTH: Put it down, you're gonna hurt someone.

LINCOLN: You telling me I don't know how to use a gun?

BOOTH: Just be careful, dude, that's all.

LINCOLN: Mind your own business, actor boy. Now how do we get out'a here?

BOOTH: Will you calm down? I'm the man with the plan.

LINCOLN: Well the man with the plan better start planning me onto the five o'clock to the Bahamas.

BOOTH: You got the money?

LINCOLN: I got the money.

BOOTH: In small, unmarked bills?

LINCOLN: In Susan B. Anthony dollars. What do you think, you muddle-headed dolt?

BOOTH: Relax. Soon as my brother Edwin gets here, we'll get this show on the road.

LINCOLN: Eddie? You said nobody else knew.

BOOTH: Chill, daddy-oh. We got it all worked straight.

LINCOLN: Chill? What kind of rhetoric is that? (*Mumbles.*) Actors. Look, you got any quarters? I want a Dr. Pepper.

BOOTH: You can't get a Dr. Pepper, you idiot! You're supposed to be dead. Now sit your ass down and relax. Here. How about some music?

(Booth turns on a radio.)

ANNOUNCER'S VOICE: Flash! The President of the United States has been shot! President Abraham Lincoln was announced dead at 9:00 this morning after receiving a mortal wound to the head during a performance at Ford's Theater in Washington. Vice President Johnson has assumed the Presidency and promises the American people he will stand tall in Lincoln's place.

JOHNSON'S VOICE: (*Southern drawl*) Ladybird and I will do our best to serve this nation's darkest hour . . .

(Lincoln shoots the radio with his Uzi.)

LINCOLN: I always hated that son of a bitch!

BOOTH: Chill, man! You're gonna get the cops up here! You want the pigs blowing your cover and carting you to the pen?

LINCOLN: I haven't the slightest idea what you just said.

BOOTH: Look, why don't you lie down with Mr. Valium and take some Z's, comprende?

LINCOLN: I beg your pardon?

BOOTH: Sit your butt down, lanky boy, and shut the hell up! (*Lincoln sits.*) Now. We've got some planning to do. You sure Mrs. Lincoln knows where to go?

LINCOLN: She's going to Singapore first.

BOOTH: Good, we don't want nobody following her.

LINCOLN: Booth?

BOOTH: What?

LINCOLN: Do you really think we pulled it off?

BOOTH: What are you worried about? You heard it yourself on the radio.

LINCOLN: But the acting. Was I good?

BOOTH: You were alright.

LINCOLN: Alright?

BOOTH: Yeah. Alright. (*quickly*) Now look, the Union pigs are gonna be outside the hotel room waiting for me, but I'm gonna double cross them.
I'm sending my brother Edwin. And they'll never suspect, because—

LINCOLN: What do you mean "alright"?

BOOTH: Huh?

LINCOLN: Are you patronizing me?

BOOTH: What are you talking about?

LINCOLN: You said my acting was alright.

BOOTH: Yeah. It was alright.

LINCOLN: That's all?

BOOTH: What do you expect me to say?

LINCOLN: I don't care—anything but alright.

BOOTH: It was fine.

LINCOLN: Fine?

BOOTH: What?

LINCOLN: I'm fine?

BOOTH: You were alright. You were fine. You were extraordinary. YOU'RE
GONNA WIN THE FREAKIN' ACADEMY AWARD! WHAT THE
HELL DO YOU WANT ME TO SAY?

LINCOLN: (*pause*) Tell me I was good.

BOOTH: (*pause*) You were good.

LINCOLN: (*pause*) You're just saying that.

BOOTH: No, really. You were fine. Er . . . good.

LINCOLN: Will you give me some criticism?

BOOTH: What?

LINCOLN: I need some—

BOOTH: Look, we gotta finish these plans.

LINCOLN: I want to know what to work on for next time.

BOOTH: Next time?

LINCOLN: If there's a Civil War in the Bahamas.

BOOTH: There ain't gonna be no Civil War—

LINCOLN: But if there is. Tell me what to work on.

BOOTH: Well. (*pause*) You don't die very well.

LINCOLN: What do you mean?

BOOTH: Forget it.

LINCOLN: No. Tell me!

BOOTH: It's just that you didn't die real well, that's all.

LINCOLN: That's all? But that's the only thing I did!

BOOTH: Can we do the plans now?

LINCOLN: What was wrong with it?

BOOTH: Nothing. I—look Abe, it's just that your leap from the balcony was too much, okay?

LINCOLN: Too much? But I was dying.

BOOTH: Whatever. People don't die that way.

LINCOLN: What do they do?

BOOTH: I don't know—they just die, that's all. They don't jump off the balcony. And they don't give soliloquies.

LINCOLN: They do in Shakespeare.

BOOTH: This ain't freakin' Shakespeare! And for God's sake, it didn't have to go fifteen minutes. Five minutes would've been plenty.

LINCOLN: Rubbish. Damned Method Actor.

(There's a knock on the door. Lincoln grabs the Uzi and leaps across the bed.)

BOOTH: *(wrestling with him)* Put that thing down! What's the matter with you? Did you shoot up before we left the theater?

LINCOLN: They're not taking me back alive!

BOOTH: No one's taking you back! It ain't the Union troops—it's my brother.

(He opens the door and in walks Edwin Booth, aka Elvis Presley. He wears a red, white, and blue tuxedo.)

ED: Thank you very much.

BOOTH: Mr. President, this is my brother, Ed.

LINCOLN: Say, you look familiar. Don't I know you?

ED: Well, I—

(Lincoln accidentally fires the Uzi. Edwin drops dead.)

LINCOLN: Oops.

BOOTH: You just shot my brother!

LINCOLN: You were right.

BOOTH: Right?

LINCOLN: People don't deliver soliloquies when they die. They just drop dead.

BOOTH: You dirty rat! You done killed my brother! What are we gonna do now?

LINCOLN: Why are you asking me? I thought you were the man with the plan.

BOOTH: Plan? I'll tell you one thing, I didn't plan on you putting the hit on my number one man.

LINCOLN: Sorry. Guess I got carried away.

BOOTH: *(looks out window)* Damn! It's the Union pigs!

LINCOLN: They're not taking me alive!

BOOTH: *(frantic)* Chill, man! We can detour to Mexico and meet Whitman . . .

LINCOLN: Who's Whitman?

BOOTH: Dealer friend. Writes poetry about grass.

LINCOLN: Forget it. I'm not trusting you and your hippie friends any-more.

BOOTH: Then you're on your own. I'm out'a here!

LINCOLN: Where are you going?

BOOTH: I ain't going to jail for you! I'm turning myself in.

LINCOLN: Like hell you are.

(Lincoln shoots Booth. Pause. Now there are two dead bodies.)

LINCOLN: *(pause)* Damn.

VOICE OUTSIDE: Booth! We know you're in there! Come out with your hands up!

LINCOLN: *(panicking)* Give me two minutes.

VOICE: You got about sixty seconds and we're coming in to get you!

(Lincoln looks around room, then sees Elvis. He puts on the tux and tries imitating Elvis's walk in front of the mirror. Enter a Union soldier in a Civil War uniform.)

SOLDIER: Alright, John Wilkes Booth, we got you surrounded and I—Oh! It's you! Edwin Booth.

LINCOLN: *(as Elvis)* Hi. How you doing.

SOLDIER: Oh! I'm your biggest fan!

LINCOLN: Thank you very much.

SOLDIER: *(sees bodies)* Why look at this! You've killed your own brother!

LINCOLN: Had to. He killed the President of the United States.

SOLDIER: Oh, Mr. Booth. What a great man you are.

LINCOLN: Thank you very much.

SOLDIER: *(shouts out doorway)* Hey fellas! Edwin Booth shot his brother and some other guy cuz they killed Mr. Lincoln!

VOICES: Hooray!

SOLDIER: Mr. Booth. May I have your autograph? It's for my daughter—

LINCOLN: Sure. No problem.

(Lincoln puts his arm around the soldier and they exit. Lights down. We hear the radio announcer's voice.)

ANNOUNCER: And now, in his new "I Killed the Man Who Assassinated Abraham Lincoln" Tour, America's greatest heartthrob—Edwin Booth!

(Spotlight on Lincoln. He has completed the transformation into Elvis and sings "A Hunk, a Hunk of Burning Love." Lights fade with the song.)

(Blackout.)

CURTAIN

1996

Jacquelyn Reingold

Creative Development

Characters

DOUG BELLOWS, 65. The creative director for an important film company. Animated, intense, volatile.

DIANE/ISIS, 30. Posing as a playwright, really a goddess. Bright, sharp, strong.

TIME: *Now.*
PLACE: *Here.*
SETTING: *A nice office. Plastic palm tree. Doug Bellows sits at his desk. He picks up a piece of paper, looks at it for a second, puts it down. A woman enters. She wears a coat.*

DOUG: Hello, hello. Come in, come in.
DIANE: Hi.
DOUG: Have a seat. Nice to meet you.
DIANE: Thank you for calling.
DOUG: Always like to meet young writers. Take off your coat.
DIANE: That's ok.
DOUG: You cold? [*She nods.*] Damn, I'm sweating up a storm up here. Water? [*He opens a bottle of Evian, she pulls a glass out of her bag.*]
DIANE: Thank you.
DOUG: Well. Hmm. [*He pours some water into her glass. They drink.*] So uh uh [*He looks at his paper.*] Dierdre.
DIANE: Donna.
DOUG: Yes. I'm Doug.
DIANE: Right.
DOUG: Bellows.
DIANE: Yes.
DOUG: Let's be frank, Donna, your play is not a movie.
DIANE: Oh?
DOUG: No, your play, I'm afraid, is definitely a play. And a play is almost never going to be a movie.
DIANE: Well, I thought . . .
DOUG: Now I didn't actually see your play.
DIANE: Oh?
DOUG: Oh, I tried, but it was raining, dear.
DIANE: Uh huh.

DOUG: Do you know what it's like to get a cab in the rain? It's hell.

DIANE: Maybe you could come another night.

DOUG: I thought it was over. [*He looks at his paper.*]

DIANE: It's been extended.

DOUG: Oh, well. How did that happen?

DIANE: Word of mouth, people liking it, that sort of thing.

DOUG: I see. Well, I'm sure it'll close soon, don't you think?

DIANE: No, actually I'm hoping it'll run for a very long time.

DOUG: Ha ha ha, I doubt that.

DIANE: I'd be happy to get you tickets.

DOUG: It's my wife, she can't make it.

DIANE: Maybe you could come without her. [*She pulls a ticket out of her bag.*]

DOUG: Now, Donna, the point is, regardless, it's not a movie. I've read the coverage. [*He holds the paper over his head, he chuckles.*] And it's not a movie. I mean what does it have? Live people talking to each other? Ha. Now, is there anyone famous in it?

DIANE: No.

DOUG: I know this may be hard to hear, and you seem like a particularly lovely young person. See, I used to be in the theatre, I was an actor once, a very good one, very, you know, good, and well I gave it up and I'm much better off now. It's really a pleasure to meet you. Sure you won't take off that coat? [*She shakes her head no.*] Can I get you anything? Cappuccino?

DIANE: Thank you, I have my own. [*She pulls a cappuccino out of her bag.*]

DOUG: Hmm. So. Uh. [*He presses his buzzer.*] Cappuccino, one. Donna, now. Hmm, I'm sure your play was nice, very uh interesting, but I bet it didn't pay the rent, did it, and how many people actually saw it, right? I know you wouldn't be here if you weren't interested in writing movies. Everyone wants to go to the movies, and everyone wants to do movies. It's well, something magical.

> [*A hand appears in the doorway holding a cappuccino. He retrieves it. Diane offers him a shaker of cinnamon from her bag.*]

DOUG: Uh. Thanks.

DIANE: Mr. Bellows.

DOUG: Doug, please.

DIANE: Doug, you have some foam. On your mouth.

DOUG: Oh. Thank you. So you gotta understand the hell we're in here. The people I work for are big powerful people, and they want big powerful movies. High concept. Now your play, if we made it into a movie, which we never would, would be an art film, and no one wants an art film and if they say they do they're a big fat liar. Ha! Let me introduce you to someone. [*He presses a buzzer.*] Send in Stew. I'm gonna do you a big favor.

> [*A door opens. Stew's shadow is seen.*]

DOUG: Stew, this is a writer, a playwright. [*Stew leaves.*] Never turn down a meeting, that's how things happen. So, where was I?

DIANE: My play.

DOUG: Right. By the way, how did you get it produced?

DIANE: Excuse me?

DOUG: How did you get that theatre to do your play? What exactly did you have to do?

DIANE: I think they liked it.

DOUG: Really? Huh. See I used to be in the theatre, I was a director, did some very interesting, you know, unusual non literary, I mean non linear work, maybe you know of it. Anyway, now I'm lucky enough to be here and help out playwrights like yourself. 'Cause I can tell by the cut of your coat I make a pretty penny more than you, dear. Would you like to read some screenplays? We have quite a collection.

DIANE: Have you produced any of these?

DOUG: What?

DIANE: What movies have you actually produced here?

DOUG: Donna! Are you with me?

DIANE: Yes.

DOUG: I'm going to tell you something very important now. About how to sell a movie. Are you listening?

DIANE: I'm listening.

DOUG: [*Clearly.*] The only way to make a movie is to make one that's already been made. You got it?

DIANE: Maybe you could say it again. A little louder.

DOUG: The only way to make a movie is to make one that's already been made! Like like Gump. [*He jumps up.*] Gump. Do you have a *Gump*? I gotta get a Gump.

DIANE: Um.

DOUG: Gump. I need a Gump. Do you have a Gump Gump Gump.

DIANE: Are you all right?

DOUG: Yes Gump I'm all right Gump of course I'm all right why wouldn't I be all right?

DIANE: I'm going to go out on a limb here and tell you it's very important that you see my play.

DOUG: What? What are you talking about?

DIANE: We could go right now.

DOUG: What?

DIANE: I strongly suggest it.

DOUG: No.

DIANE: How about another play?

DOUG: Excuse me?

DIANE: Why not?

DOUG: Look, I think I've made my point here. Are you interested in pitching or what? Do you have any big ideas?

DIANE: My play.

DOUG: You're not getting the message. Why are you not getting the message?

DIANE: Come to my play.

DOUG: No way.

DIANE: I'm warning you.

DOUG: You're warning me—very funny—the nerve. This is my office.

DIANE: What are you afraid of, huh?

DOUG: Afraid? What do I have to be afraid of?

DIANE: Then why not?

DOUG: Because because I don't go to the theatre. All right? Why should I? No one goes. Who goes? Tourists? Other people in the theatre? It's pathetic, it's elitist, it's too expensive, you can't eat popcorn, you can't go to the bathroom until intermission and nowadays a play doesn't even have an intermission. Does yours?

DIANE: No.

DOUG: See? I have a very small bladder. [*She hands him a urinal from her bag. He grabs it and uses it for emphasis.*] Hell no I won't go. It's dying, it's dead. You know that. Everyone does. So give it up. Wake up. Donna!!! Wake up!! There is no theatre anymore, it's a dinosaur on its last fart. Who goes . . . no one! Stop with the plays, start with the block-busters. Gump Gump Gump! [*Very calm:*] So, I'm sure if you have something like like that movie I mentioned I'm sure we could work together, collaborate. Very nicely. Very successfully.

DIANE: Bellows.

DOUG: Yes?

DIANE: I'm not really a playwright.

DOUG: Thank God, I didn't think you were. You certainly don't act like one.

DIANE: My name isn't Donna.

DOUG: Oh?

DIANE: It's Diane.

[*Thunder and lightning as she pulls off her coat, revealing a mini toga. She is a powerful goddess.*]

DIANE: Diane Isis. You just failed the last test.

DOUG: Very funny ha ha.

DIANE: I'm not kidding, Doug.

DOUG: Who put you up to this, Stew? That guy. [*He presses a buzzer.*]

DIANE: There is no more Stew.

DOUG: Yeah, right, good one.

DIANE: Do you hear that? [*She opens her bag, we hear lovely singing.*] Those are the muses, all nine of them, they've been listening to your every word, and they can't believe what they've heard.

DOUG: Oh, I'm shaking. What did I do?

DIANE: Impersonated a creative director.

DOUG: I am a creative director.

DIANE: Ha!

DOUG: Is this some kind of a pitch? A feminist Spartacus remake? Well, it's not working.

DIANE: Bellows! Did you think you could get away with it? Did you think no one was watching? Calling in thousands of playwrights to humiliate them, to convince them to stop writing plays and start writing movies?

DOUG: Now look Dierdre Donna Diane I have another meeting in a minute so . . .

DIANE: You're telling writers what to do? Isn't that a little upside down, Doug? Shouldn't it really be the other way around, Doug?

[A ferocious wind blows. Doug holds onto his desk for dear life.]

DOUG: What the hell was that?

DIANE: That was Calliope exhaling.

DOUG: Ok ok, this meeting is over.

DIANE: This meeting has just begun!!!!

DOUG: What are you after? A deal? Well fine, let's hear it.

DIANE: Your deal days are done, Doug. You've turned the artistic world upside down and we're here to set it straight and the first casualty is you.

DOUG: Have we met before?

DIANE: You hear that? [*We hear hissing.*] Those are the sisters; they're morphing into something a little more s-s-sinister.

DOUG: Hey, I'm just doing my job.

DIANE: We know all about your job, what you really do here. The underground network, the antitheatre lobbying effort, the I Won't Go To The Theatre Newsletter. And we are not amused. We know you've converted millions, and raised money into the billions. We know who you contributed to in the last election. We know all about you.

DOUG: I got nothing to hide. Maybe that was me, but I'm not killing the theatre, I'm just helping it go easy. I'm protecting audiences all over the world from an intolerable night out. What are you gonna do? Fire me? Go ahead. There'll be someone else here tomorrow.

DIANE: Why'd you do it, Doug? Fear? Was that it? Afraid of seeing something that might make you uncomfortable? Well, you're about to learn the real meaning of the word. Sisters!

[From out of her bag emerge nine women of all shapes and sizes. They all wear mini togas with a large M on them, and have snakes in their hair.]

DOUG: Well, uh hello, uh, ladies.

DIANE: Prepare for your final treatment. We have come for our revenge.

MUSES & DIANE: [*They roar at him.*] Rah!

[The lights change.]

DOUG: Now hang on, let's be reasonable here.

[They surround him, and they tie him up.]

MUSES: [*They roar.*] Rah!

DOUG: Now now look what are you doing? I mean, I get it, ok? You made your point. Hey! Please. I'm just human, right? I mean do you know how hard it is to make a living in the theatre?

[They pull out their weapons. One has a giant paintbrush, one has a musical instrument, one has a big pair of toe shoes, another a chisel. Diane pulls out a mirror. They start to create something.]

DOUG: Ok, what do you want? I'll let you make an art film, ok? You can make that Dierdre's play into a very arty art film. We can work together, do things from the inside. I know where you're coming from. I used to be in the theatre. I was a producer. Not for profit!

[The Muses and Diane have created an instant stage for Doug.]

DIANE: Ok, Bellows. Create.

DOUG: What?

DIANE: You're in a theatre, you're on the stage.

DOUG: What?

DIANE: You've got an audience.

[House lights come up.]

DOUG: Oh my God, I do.

DIANE: It's live. Create. Write a poem, recite a play, do a dance. They're waiting.

DOUG: [*To audience.*] Uh. Hello. Uh. [*To Diane*] Ok, I'll call those playwrights. I'll call every playwright and apologize. Diane? Oh God, Diane? [*To audience*] Ha ha ha. Uh. Uh. [*To Diane*] I'll cancel the committee. I was wrong. I admit it. I was a jerk. Diane? [*To audience*] Uh uh. [*The Muses as audience start to cough, unwrap candy wrappers, shuffle, and answer their ringing cell phones.*] [*To Diane*] Think of my wife. My kids. I have daughters, one does modern dance, the other plays the piano, I swear. Uh . . . Uh . . . I can't. Please. I can't. I'm not creative. I'm not. I have no ideas. None. None.

DIANE: This is your life now, Doug. For eternity this is what you will be: an actor/director/producer on stage without a play. Forever.

DOUG: Oh God. Look, ok, this is very hard for me, but I'll go to the play. I will, I'll go to that Donna's play. Please! Forgive me. My life is hell. You have to understand. I'm the one who turned down Gump. [*He sobs.*] It's true. For ten years I said no to Gump. And look what happened.

DIANE: Doug, wasn't that some years ago?

DOUG: Yes, but but I haven't been able to get past it.

MUSE 1: [*A young muse speaks*] Wow.

MUSE 2: [*A large muse speaks*] Gump.

MUSE 3: [*An old muse*] That's bad.

MUSE 4: [*A dim muse*] Really bad.

MUSE 5: [*A loud muse*] Yeah.

MUSE 6: [*A silly muse*] I can't believe he did that.

MUSE 7: [*A fast muse*] Talk about stupid.

MUSE 8: [*A sloppy muse*] Dumb.

MUSE 9: [*A muse-like muse*] Pathetic.

ALL MUSES: [*All the muses*] Maybe he's suffered enough.

> *[They look to Diane, she thinks.]*

DOUG: I have. Really. I have. And look, uh ladies, I mean we've come a long way since you were last here. We've developed, creatively. Right? I mean, compassion and all that, forgiveness. [*They look at each other.*] I said I'd go to the play. I mean isn't that the point? I mean. I will go. Why we can all go. I mean, have you seen that play? [*The muses look away, embarrassed.*] We can go together: you, me; man, uh women; the past, the present. Group rate. How's that?

> *[The lights brighten. A reprieve.]*

DIANE: Hmm. Untie him.

> *[They start to slowly untie him. Diane puts on her coat.]*

DOUG: Oh thank you, thank you. You won't regret it. From now on I'll be different. I swear. Very different.

DIANE: Hmm, Doug.

DOUG: Yeah?

DIANE: One more thing.

DOUG: What is it, dear?

DIANE: I have this idea.

DOUG: Really?

DIANE: For a movie. Blockbuster. I thought I'd just try it out on you.

DOUG: Oh?

DIANE: It's about a guy who dresses as a woman. An unattractive woman.

DOUG: It's been done.

DIANE: Exactly. It takes place on a sinking boat.

DOUG: That's been done, sounds good.

DIANE: Special effects from a natural disaster.

DOUG: Yeah.

DIANE: A plot from Shakespeare.

DOUG: I'm listening.

DIANE: A fatal illness.

DOUG: Uh huh.

DIANE: And the thing is . . . the main character, the one dressed as the very unattractive woman, he's also dumb.

DOUG: Oh.

DIANE: Very dumb.

DOUG: Yeah?

DIANE: Stupid.

DOUG: Uh huh.
DIANE: Ugly.
DOUG: I see.
DIANE: And we can call it . . .
DOUG: What? What?
DIANE: We can call it. Frump.
DOUG: FRUMP! I love it! We'll make it.
DIANE: Tie him up! [*They roar.*] Rah!

[*Diane throws off her coat, weapons come out. Blackout.*]

THE END

1997

Milcha Sanchez-Scott (B. 1955)

The Cuban Swimmer

Characters

MARGARITA SUÁREZ	the swimmer
EDUARDO SUÁREZ	her father, the coach
SIMÓN SUÁREZ	her brother
AÍDA SUÁREZ	the mother
ABUELA	her grandmother
Voice of Mel Munson	
Voice of Mary Beth White	
Voice of Radio Operator	

Setting. The Pacific Ocean between San Pedro and Catalina Island.
Time. Summer.
Live conga drums can be used to punctuate the action of the play.

Scene I

Pacific Ocean. Midday. On the horizon, in perspective, a small boat enters upstage left, crosses to upstage right, and exits. Pause. Lower on the horizon, the same boat, in larger perspective, enters upstage right, crosses and exits upstage left. Blackout.

Scene II

Pacific Ocean. Midday. The swimmer, Margarita Suárez, is swimming. On the boat following behind her are her father, Eduardo Suárez, hold-

ing a megaphone, and Simón, her brother, sitting on top of the cabin with
his shirt off, punk sunglasses on, binoculars hanging on his chest.

EDUARDO:

> (*Leaning forward, shouting in time to Margarita's swimming.*) *Uno, dos,
> uno, dos. Y uno, dos*[1] . . . keep your shoulders parallel to the water.

SIMÓN: I'm gonna take these glasses off and look straight into the sun.

EDUARDO: (*Through megaphone.*) *Muy bien, muy bien*[2] . . . but punch
those arms in, baby.

SIMÓN: (*Looking directly at the sun through binoculars.*) Come on, come
on, zap me. Show me something. (*He looks behind at the shoreline and
ahead at the sea.*) Stop! Stop, Papi! Stop!

> (*Aída Suárez and Abuela, the swimmer's mother and grandmother,
> enter running from the back of the boat.*)

AÍDA AND ABUELA: *Qué? Qué es?*[3]

AÍDA: *Es un* shark?[4]

EDUARDO: Eh?

ABUELA: *Que es un* shark *dicen?*[5]

> (*Eduardo blows whistle. Margarita looks up at the boat.*)

SIMÓN: No, Papi, no shark, no shark. We've reached the halfway mark.

ABUELA: (*Looking into the water.*) *A dónde está?*[6]

AÍDA: It's not in the water.

ABUELA: Oh, no? Oh, no?

AÍDA: No! *A poco* do you think they're gonna have signs in the water to
say you are halfway to Santa Catalina? No. It's done very scientific. *A
ver, hijo,* explain it to your grandma.

SIMÓN: Well, you see, Abuela—(*He points behind.*) There's San Pedro. (*He
points ahead.*) And there's Santa Catalina. Looks halfway to me.

> (*Abuela shakes her head and is looking back and forth, trying to
> make the decision, when suddenly the sound of a helicopter is heard.*)

ABUELA: (*Looking up.*) *Virgencita de la Caridad del Cobre. Qué es eso?*[7]

> (*Sound of helicopter gets closer. Margarita looks up.*)

MARGARITA: *Papi, Papi!*

> (*A small commotion on the boat, with everybody pointing at the heli-
> copter above. Shadows of the helicopter fall on the boat. Simón looks
> up at it through binoculars.*)

> *Papi—qué es?* What is it?

---

[1] *Uno, dos, uno, dos. Y uno, dos:* One, two, one, two. And one, two.
[2] *Muy bien, muy bien:* Very good, very good.
[3] *Qué? Qué es?:* What? What is it?
[4] *Es un shark?:* Is it a shark?
[5] *Que es un shark dicen?:* Did they say a shark?
[6] *A dónde está?:* Where is it?
[7] *Virgencita de la Caridad del Cobre. Qué es eso?:* Virgin of Charity. What is that?

EDUARDO: (*Through megaphone.*) Uh . . . uh . . . uh, *un momentico . . . mi hija*[8] . . . Your papi's got everything under control understand? Uh . . . you just keep stroking. And stay . . . uh . . . close to the boat.

SIMÓN: *Wow, Papi!* We're on TV, man! Holy Christ, we're all over the fucking U.S.A.! It's Mel Munson and Mary Beth White!

AÍDA: *Por Dios!*[9] Simón, don't swear. And put on your shirt.

> (*Aída fluffs her hair, puts on her sunglasses and waves to the helicopter. Simón leans over the side of the boat and yells to Margarita.*)

SIMÓN: Yo, Margo! You're on TV, man.

EDUARDO: Leave your sister alone. Turn on the radio.

MARGARITA: *Papi! Qué está pasando?*[10]

ABUELA: *Que es la televisión dicen?* (*She shakes her head.*) *Porque como yo no puedo ver nada sin mis espejuelos.*[11]

> (*Abuela rummages through the boat, looking for her glasses. Voices of Mel Munson and Mary Beth White are heard over the boat's radio.*)

MEL'S VOICE: As we take a closer look at the gallant crew of *La Havana* . . . and there . . . yes, there she is . . . the little Cuban swimmer from Long Beach, California, nineteen-year-old Margarita Suárez. The unknown swimmer is our Cinderella entry . . . a bundle of tenacity, battling her way through the choppy, murky waters of the cold Pacific to reach the Island of Romance . . . Santa Catalina . . . where should she be the first to arrive, two thousand dollars and a gold cup will be waiting for her.

AÍDA: Doesn't even cover our expenses.

ABUELA: *Qué dice?*

EDUARDO: Shhhh!

MARY BETH'S VOICE: This is really a family effort, Mel, and—

MEL'S VOICE: Indeed it is. Her trainer, her coach, her mentor, is her father, Eduardo Suárez. Not a swimmer himself, it says here, Mr. Suárez is head usher of the Holy Name Society and the owner-operator of Suárez Treasures of the Sea and Salvage Yard. I guess it's one of those places—

MARY BETH'S VOICE: If I might interject a fact here, Mel, assisting in this swim is Mrs. Suárez, who is a former Miss Cuba.

MEL'S VOICE: And a beautiful woman in her own right. Let's try and get a closer look.

> (*Helicopter sound gets louder. Margarita, frightened, looks up again.*)

MARGARITA: Papi!

---

[8]*Un momentico . . . mi hija*: Just a second, my daughter.

[9]*Por Dios!*: For God's Sake!

[10]*Papi! Qué está pasando?*: Dad! What's happening?

[11]*Que es la televisión dicen? Porque como yo no puedo ver rada sin mis espejuelos*: Did they say television? Because I can't see without my glasses.

EDUARDO: (*Through megaphone.*) Mi hija, don't get nervous . . . it's the press. I'm handling it.

AÍDA: I see how you're handling it.

EDUARDO: (*Through megaphone.*) Do you hear? Everything is under control. Get back into your rhythm. Keep your elbows high and kick and kick and kick and kick . . .

ABUELA: (*Finds her glasses and puts them on.*) Ay sí, es la televisión . . . (*She points to helicopter.*) Qué lindo mira . . . (*She fluffs her hair, gives a big wave.*) Aló América! Viva mi Margarita, viva todo los Cubanos en los Estados Unidos![12]

AÍDA: *Ay por Dios*, Cecilia, the man didn't come all this way in his helicopter to look at you jumping up and down, making a fool of yourself.

ABUELA: I don't care. I'm proud.

AÍDA: He can't understand you anyway.

ABUELA: *Viva* . . . (*She stops.*) Simón, *cómo se dice viva?*[13]

SIMÓN: Hurray.

ABUELA: Hurray for *mi Margarita y* for all the Cubans living *en* the United States, *y un abrazo* . . . Simón, *abrazo* . . .

SIMÓN: A big hug.

ABUELA: *Sí*, a big hug to all my friends in Miami, Long Beach, Union City, except for my son Carlos, who lives in New York in sin! He lives . . . (*She crosses herself.*) in Brooklyn with a Puerto Rican woman in sin! *No decente* . . .

SIMÓN: Decent.

ABUELA: Carlos, no *decente*. This family, *decente*.

AÍDA: Cecilia, *por Dios*.

MEL'S VOICE: Look at that enthusiasm. The whole family has turned out to cheer little Margarita on to victory! I hope they won't be too disappointed.

MARY BETH'S VOICE: She seems to be making good time, Mel.

MEL'S VOICE: Yes, it takes all kinds to make a race. And it's a testimonial to the all-encompassing fairness . . . the greatness of this, the Wrigley Invitational Women's Swim to Catalina, where among all the professionals there is still room for the amateurs . . . like these, the simple people we see below us on the ragtag *La Havana*, taking their long-shot chance to victory. *Vaya con Dios!*[14]

(*Helicopter sound fading as family, including Margarita, watch silently. Static as Simón turns radio off. Eduardo walks to bow of boat, looks out on the horizon.*)

EDUARDO: (*To himself.*) Amateurs.

---

[12]*Aló América! Viva mi Margarita, viva todo los Cubanos en los Estados Unidos!* Hello America! Hurray for my Margarita, hurray for all the Cubans in the United States!

[13]*Cómo se dice viva?*: How do you say "viva" [in English]?

[14]*Vaya con Dios!*: Go with God. [God bless you.]

AÍDA: Eduardo, that person insulted us. Did you hear, Eduardo? That he called us a simple people in a ragtag boat? Did you hear . . . ?
ABUELA: (*Clenching her fist at departing helicopter.*) *Mal-Rayo los parta!*[15]
SIMÓN: (*Same gesture.*) Asshole!

> (*Aída follows Eduardo as he goes to side of boat and stares at Margarita.*)

AÍDA: This person comes in his helicopter to insult your wife, your family, your daughter . . .
MARGARITA: (*Pops her head out of the water.*) *Papi?*
AÍDA: Do you hear me, Eduardo? I am not simple.
ABUELA: *Sí.*
AÍDA: I am complicated.
ABUELA: *Sí, demasiada complicada.*
AÍDA: Me and my family are not so simple.
SIMÓN: Mom, the guy's an asshole.
ABUELA: (*Shaking her fist at helicopter.*) Asshole!
AÍDA: If my daughter was simple, she would not be in that water swimming.
MARGARITA:
> Simple? *Papi* . . . ?

AÍDA: *Ahora,* Eduardo, this is what I want you to do. When we get to Santa Catalina, I want you to call the TV station and demand an apology.
EDUARDO: *Cállete mujer! Aquí mando yo.*[16] I will decide what is to be done.
MARGARITA: *Papi,* tell me what's going on.
EDUARDO: Do you understand what I am saying to you, Aída?
SIMÓN: (*Leaning over side of boat, to Margarita.*) Yo Margo! You know that Mel Munson guy on TV? He called you a simple amateur and said you didn't have a chance.
ABUELA: (*Leaning directly behind Simón.*) *Mi hija, insultó a la familia. Desgraciado!*
AÍDA: (*Leaning in behind Abuela.*) He called us peasants! And your father is not doing anything about it. He just knows how to yell at me.
EDUARDO: (*Through megaphone.*) Shut up! All of you! Do you want to break her concentration? Is that what you are after? Eh?

> (*Abuela, Aída and Simón shrink back. Eduardo paces before them.*)

> Swimming is rhythm and concentration. You win a race *aquí.* (*Pointing to his head.*) Now . . . (*To Simón.*) you, take care of the boat, Aída *y Mama* . . . do something. Anything. Something practical.

> (*Abuela and Aída get on knees and pray in Spanish.*)

> *Hija,* give it everything, eh? . . . *por la familia. Uno . . . dos . . .* You must win.

> (*Simón goes into cabin. The prayers continue as lights change to indicate bright sunlight, later in the afternoon.*)

---

[15]*Mal-Rayo los parta!*: To hell with you!
[16]*Cállete mujer! Aquí mando yo*: Quiet! I'm in charge here.

Scene III

Tableau for a couple of beats. Eduardo on bow with timer in one hand as he counts strokes per minute. Simón is in the cabin steering, wearing his sunglasses, baseball cap on backward. Abuela and Aída are at the side of the boat, heads down, hands folded, still muttering prayers in Spanish.

AÍDA AND ABUELA:

> (*Crossing themselves.*) *En el nombre del Padre, del Hijo y del Espíritu Santo amén.*[17]

EDUARDO: (*Through megaphone.*) You're stroking seventy-two!

SIMÓN: (*Singing.*) Mama's stroking, Mama's stroking seventy-two . . .

EDUARDO: (*Through megaphone.*) You comfortable with it?

SIMÓN: (*Singing.*) Seventy-two, seventy-two, seventy-two for you.

AÍDA: (*Looking at the heavens.*) *Ay*, Eduardo, *ven acá*,[18] we should be grateful that *Nuestro Señor*[19] gave us such a beautiful day.

ABUELA: (*Crosses herself.*) *Sí, gracias a Dios.*[20]

EDUARDO: She's stroking seventy-two, with no problem (*He throws a kiss to the sky.*) It's a beautiful day to win.

AÍDA: *Qué hermoso!*[21] So clear and bright. Not a cloud in the sky. *Mira! Mira!*[22] Even rainbows on the water . . . a sign from God.

SIMÓN: (*Singing.*) Rainbows on the water . . . you in my arms . . .

ABUELA AND EDUARDO: (*Looking the wrong way.*) Dónde?

AÍDA: (*Pointing toward Margarita.*) There, dancing in front of Margarita, leading her on . . .

EDUARDO: Rainbows on . . . *Ay coño!* It's an oil slick! You . . . you . . . (*To Simón.*) Stop the boat. (*Runs to bow, yelling.*) Margarita! Margarita!

(On the next stroke, Margarita comes up all covered in black oil.)

MARGARITA: *Papi! Papi* . . . !

(Everybody goes to the side and stares at Margarita, who stares back. Eduardo freezes.)

AÍDA: *Apúrate*, Eduardo, move . . . what's wrong with you . . . *no me oíste*,[23] get my daughter out of the water.

EDUARDO: (*Softly.*) We can't touch her. If we touch her, she's disqualified.

AÍDA: But I'm her mother.

EDUARDO: Not even by her own mother. Especially by her own mother . . . You always want the rules to be different for you, you always want to be the exception. (*To Simón.*) And you . . . you didn't see it, eh? You were playing again?

---

[17]*En el nombre del Padre, del Hijo y del Espíritu Sanco amén*: In the name of the Father, the Son, and the Holy Ghost, Amen.

[18]*Ven acá*: Look here.

[19]*Nuestro Señor*: Our father [God].

[20]*Sí, gracias a Dias.* Yes, thanks be to God.

[21]*Qué hermoso!*: How beautiful!

[22]*Mira!*: Look.

[23]*Apúrate . . . no me oíste*: Finish this! . . . didn't you hear me?

SIMÓN: *Papi,* I was watching . . .

AÍDA: (*Interrupting.*) *Pues,* do something Eduardo. You are the big coach, the monitor.

SIMÓN: Mentor! Mentor!

EDUARDO: How can a person think around you? (*He walks off to bow, puts head in hands.*)

ABUELA: (*Looking over side.*) *Mira como todos los* little birds are dead. (*She crosses herself.*)

AÍDA: Their little wings are glued to their sides.

SIMÓN: Christ, this is like the La Brea tar pits.

AÍDA: They can't move their little wings.

ABUELA: *Esa niña tiene que moverse.*[24]

SIMÓN: Yeah, Margo, you gotta move, man.

> (*Abuela and Simón gesture for Margarita to move. Aída gestures for her to swim.*)

ABUELA: *Anda niña, muévete.*[25]

AÍDA: Swim, *hija,* swim or the *aceite*[26] will stick to your wings.

MARGARITA: Papi?

ABUELA: (*Taking megaphone.*) Your *papi* say "move it!"

> (*Margarita with difficulty starts moving.*)

ABUELA, AÍDA AND SIMÓN: (*Laboriously counting.*) *Uno, dos* . . . *uno, dos* . . . *anda* . . . *uno, dos.*

EDUARDO: (*Running to take megaphone from Abuela.*) *Uno, dos* . . .

> (*Simón races into cabin and starts the engine. Abuela, Aída and Eduardo count together.*)

SIMÓN: (*Looking ahead.*) *Papi,* it's over there!

EDUARDO: Eh?

SIMÓN: (*Pointing ahead and to the right.*) It's getting clearer over there.

EDUARDO: (*Through megaphone.*) Now pay attention to me. Go to the right.

> (*Simón, Abuela, Aída and Eduardo all lean over side. They point ahead and to the right, except Abuela, who points to the left.*)

FAMILY: (*Shouting together.*) *Para yá!*[27] *Para yá!*

> (*Lights go down on boat. A special light on Margarita, swimming through the oil, and on Abuela, watching her.*)

ABUELA: *Sangre de mi sangre,*[28] you will be another to save us. En Bolon-dron, where your great-grandmother Luz Suárez was born, they say one

---

[24]*Esa niña uene que moverse:* That girl has to move.

[25]*Anda niña, muévete:* Come on girl, move!

[26]*Aceite:* oil.

[27]*Para yá:* Over there.

[28]*Sangre de mi sangre:* blood of my blood.

day it rained blood. All the people, they run into their houses. They cry, they pray, *pero* your great-grandmother Luz she had *cojones* like a man. She run outside. She look straight at the sky. She shake her fist. And she say to the evil one, "*Mira . . . (Beating her chest.) coño, Diablo, aquí estoy si me quieres.*"[29] And she open her mouth, and she drunk the blood.
BLACKOUT

Scene IV

Lights up on boat. Aída and Eduardo are on deck watching Margarita swim. We hear the gentle, rhythmic lap, lap, lap of the water, then the sound of inhaling and exhaling as Margarita's breathing becomes louder. Then Margarita's heartbeat is heard, with the lapping of the water and the breathing under it. These sounds continue beneath the dialogue to the end of the scene.

AÍDA: *Dios mío.* Look how she moves through the water . . .

EDUARDO: You see, it's very simple. It is a matter of concentration.

AÍDA: The first time I put her in water she came to life, she grew before my eyes. She moved, she smiled, she loved it more than me. She didn't want my breast any longer. She wanted the water.

EDUARDO: And of course, the rhythm. The rhythm takes away the pain and helps the concentration.

(Pause. Aída and Eduardo watch Margarita.)

AÍDA: Is that my child or a seal . . .

EDUARDO: Ah, a seal, the reason for that is that she's keeping her arms very close to her body. She cups her hands, and then she reaches and digs, reaches and digs.

AÍDA: To think that a daughter of mine . . .

EDUARDO: It's the training, the hours in the water. I used to tie weights around her little wrists and ankles.

AÍDA: A spirit, an ocean spirit, must have entered my body when I was carrying her.

EDUARDO: *(To Margarita.)* Your stroke is slowing down.

(Pause. We hear Margarita's heartbeat with the breathing under, faster now.)

AÍDA: Eduardo, that night, the night on the boat . . .

EDUARDO: Ah, the night on the boat again . . . the moon was . . .

AÍDA: The moon was full. We were coming to America . . . *Qué romantico.*

(Heartbeat and breathing continue.)

EDUARDO: We were cold, afraid, with no money, and on top of everything, you were hysterical, yelling at me, tearing at me with your nails. *(Opens*

---

[29]*Mira . . . coño, Diablo, aquí estoy si me quieres:* Look . . . damn it, Devil, here I am if you want me.

his shirt, points to the base of his neck.) Look, I still bear the scars . . . telling me that I didn't know what I was doing . . . saying that we were going to die . . .

AÍDA: You took me, you stole me from my home . . . you didn't give me a chance to prepare. You just said we have to go now, now! Now, you said. You didn't let me take anything. I left everything behind . . . I left everything behind.

EDUARDO: Saying that I wasn't good enough, that your father didn't raise you so that I could drown you in the sea.

AÍDA: You didn't let me say even a good-bye. You took me, you stole me, you tore me from my home.

EDUARDO: I took you so we could be married.

AÍDA: That was in Miami. But that night on the boat, Eduardo . . . We were not married, that night on the boat.

EDUARDO: *No pasó nada!*[30] Once and for all get it out of your head, it was cold, you hated me, and we were afraid . . .

AÍDA: *Mentiroso!*[31]

EDUARDO: A man can't do it when he is afraid.

AÍDA: Liar! You did it very well.

EDUARDO: I did!

AÍDA: *Sí.* Gentle. You were so gentle and then strong . . . my passion for you so deep. Standing next to you . . . I would ache . . . looking at your hands I would forget to breathe, you were irresistible.

EDUARDO: I was?

AÍDA: You took me into your arms, you touched my face with your fingertips . . . you kissed my eyes . . . *la esquina de la boca y* . . .

EDUARDO: *Sí, Sí,* and then . . .

AÍDA: I look at your face on top of mine, and I see the lights of Havana in your eyes. That's when you seduced me.

EDUARDO: Shhh, they're gonna hear you.

(Lights go down. Special on Aída.)

AÍDA: That was the night. A woman doesn't forget those things . . . and later that night was the dream . . . the dream of a big country with fields of fertile land and big, giant things growing. And there by a green, slimy pond I found a giant pea pod and when I opened it, it was full of little, tiny baby frogs.

(Aída crosses herself as she watches Margarita. We hear louder breathing and heartbeat.)

MARGARITA: Santa Teresa. Little Flower of God, pray for me. San Martín de Porres, pray for me. Santa Rosa de Lima, *Virgencita de la Caridad del Cobre*, pray for me . . . Mother pray for me.

---

[30]*No pasó nada!:* Nothing happened.
[31]*Mentiroso!:* Liar!

Scene V

Loud howling of wind is heard, as lights change to indicate unstable weather, fog and mist. Family on deck, braced and huddled against the wind. Simón is at the helm.

AÍDA: *Ay Dios mío, qué viento.*[32]

EDUARDO: (*Through megaphone.*) Don't drift out . . . that wind is pushing you out. (*To Simón.*) You! Slow down. Can't you see your sister is drifting out?

SIMÓN: It's the wind, *Papi.*

AÍDA: Baby, don't go so far . . .

ABUELA: (*To heaven.*) *Ay Gran Poder de Dios, quita este maldito viento.*[33]

SIMÓN: Margo! Margo! Stay close to the boat.

EDUARDO: Dig in. Dig in hard . . . Reach down from your guts and dig in.

ABUELA: (*To heaven.*) *Ay Virgen de la Caridad del Cobre, por lo más tú quieres a pararia.*

AÍDA: (*Putting her hand out, reaching for Margarita.*) Baby, don't go far.

(*Abuela crosses herself. Action freezes. Lights get dimmer, special on Margarita. She keeps swimming, stops, starts again, stops, then, finally exhausted, stops altogether. The boat stops moving.*)

EDUARDO: What's going on here? Why are we stopping?

SIMÓN: *Papi,* she's not moving! Yo Margo!

(*The family all run to the side.*)

EDUARDO: *Hija!* . . . *Hijita!* You're tired, eh?

AÍDA: *Por supuesto* she's tired. I like to see you get in the water, waving your arms and legs from San Pedro to Santa Catalina. A person isn't a machine, a person has to rest.

SIMÓN: Yo, Mama! Cool out, it ain't fucking brain surgery.

EDUARDO: (*To Simón.*) Shut up, you. (*Louder to Margarita.*) I guess your mother's right for once, huh? . . . I guess you had to stop, eh? . . . Give your brother, the idiot . . . a chance to catch up with you.

SIMÓN: (*Clowning like Mortimer Snerd.*) Dum dee dum dee dum ooops, ah shucks . . .

EDUARDO: I don't think he's Cuban.

SIMÓN: (*Like Ricky Ricardo.*) *Oye,* Lucy! I'm home! Ba ba lu!

EDUARDO: (*Joins in clowning, grabbing Simón in a headlock.*) What am I gonna do with this idiot, eh? I don't understand this idiot. He's not like us, Margarita. (*Laughing.*) You think if we put him into your bathing suit with a cap on his head . . . (*He laughs hysterically.*) You think anyone would know . . . huh? Do you think anyone would know? (*Laughs.*)

---

[32]*Ay Dios mío, qué viento:* Oh my God, what wind.

[33]*Ay Gran Poder de Dios, quita este maldito viento:* By the great power of God, keep the cursed winds away.

SIMÓN: (*Vamping.*) *Ay, mi amor.* Anybody looking for tits would know.

(*Eduardo slaps Simón across the face, knocking him down. Aída runs to Simón's aid. Abuela holds Eduardo back.*)

MARGARITA: *Mía culpa!*[34] *Mía culpa!*

ABUELA: *Qué dices hija?*

MARGARITA: *Papi*, it's my fault, it's all my fault . . . I'm so cold, I can't move . . . I put my face in the water . . . and I hear them whispering . . . laughing at me . . .

AÍDA: Who is laughing at you?

MARGARITA: The fish are all biting me . . . they hate me . . . they whisper about me. She can't swim, they say. She can't glide. She has no grace . . . Yellow-tails, bonita, tuna, man-o-war, snub-nose sharks, *los baracudas* . . . they all hate me . . . only the dolphins care . . . and sometimes I hear the whales crying . . . she is lost, she is dead. I'm so numb, I can't feel. *Papi! Papi!* Am I dead?

EDUARDO: *Vamos*, baby, punch those arms in. Come on . . . do you hear me?

MARGARITA: *Papi* . . . *Papi!* . . . forgive me . . .

(*All is silent on the boat. Eduardo drops his megaphone, his head bent down in dejection. Abuela, Aída, Simón, all leaning over the side of the boat. Simón slowly walks away.*)

AÍDA: *Mi hija, qué tienes?*

SIMÓN: Oh, Christ, don't make her say it. Please don't make her say it.

ABUELA: Say what? *Qué cosa?*

SIMÓN: She wants to quit, can't you see she's had enough?

ABUELA: *Mira, para eso. Esta niña* is turning blue.

AÍDA: *Oyeme, mi hija.* Do you want to come out of the water?

MARGARITA: *Papi?*

SIMÓN: (*To Eduardo.*) She won't come out until *you* tell her.

AÍDA: Eduardo . . . answer your daughter.

EDUARDO: *Le dije* to concentrate . . . concentrate on your rhythm. Then the rhythm would carry her . . . ay, it's a beautiful thing, Aída. It's like yoga, like meditation, the mind over matter . . . the mind controlling the body . . . that's how the great things in the world have been done. I wish you . . . I wish my wife could understand.

MARGARITA: *Papi?*

SIMÓN: (*To Margarita.*) Forget him.

AÍDA: (*Imploring.*) Eduardo, *por favor.*

EDUARDO: (*Walking in circles.*) Why didn't you let her concentrate? Don't you understand, the concentration, the rhythm is everything. But no, you wouldn't listen. (*Screaming to the ocean.*) Goddamn Cubans, why, God, why do you make us go everywhere with our families? (*He goes to back of boat.*)

---

[34]*Mia Culpa!:* It's my fault.

AÍDA: (*Opening her arms.*) *Mi hija, ven,* come to *Mami.* (*Rocking.*) Your *mami* knows.

> (*Abuela has taken the training bottle, puts it in a net. She and Simón lower it to Margarita.*)

SIMÓN: Take this. Drink it. (*As Margarita drinks, Abuela crosses herself.*)
ABUELA: *Sangre de mi sangre.*

> (*Music comes up softly. Margarita drinks, gives the bottle back, stretches out her arms, as if on a cross. Floats on her back. She begins a graceful backstroke. Lights fade on boat as special lights come up on Margarita. She stops. Slowly turns over and starts to swim, gradually picking up speed. Suddenly as if in pain she stops, tries again, then stops in pain again. She becomes disoriented and falls to the bottom of the sea. Special on Margarita at the bottom of the sea.*)

MARGARITA: *Ya no puedo* . . . I can't . . . A person isn't a machine . . . *es mi culpa* . . . Father forgive me . . . *Papi! Papi!* One, two. *Uno, dos.* (*Pause.*) *Papi! A dónde estás* (*Pause.*) One, two, one, two. *Papi! Ay, Papi!* Where are you . . . ? Don't leave me . . . Why don't you answer me? (*Pause. She starts to swim, slowly.*) *Uno, dos, uno, dos.* Dig in, dig in. (*Stops swimming.*) *Por favor, Papi!* (*Starts to swim again.*) One, two, one, two. Kick from your hip, kick from your hip. (*Stops swimming. Starts to cry.*) Oh God, please . . . (*Pause.*) Hail Mary, full of grace . . . dig in, dig in . . . the Lord is with thee . . . (*She swims to the rhythm of her Hail Mary.*) Hail Mary, full of grace . . . dig in, dig in . . . the Lord is with thee . . . dig in, dig in . . . Blessed art thou among women . . . *Mami,* it hurts. You let go of my hand. I'm lost . . . And blessed is the fruit of thy womb, now and at the hour of our death. Amen. I don't want to die, I don't want to die.

> (*Margarita is still swimming. Blackout. She is gone.*)

Scene VI

Lights up on boat, we hear radio static. There is a heavy mist. On deck we see only black outline of Abuela with shawl over her head. We hear the voices of Eduardo, Aída, and Radio Operator.
EDUARDO'S VOICE: *La Havana!* Coming from San Pedro. Over.
RADIO OPERATOR'S VOICE: Right, DT6-6, you say you've lost a swimmer.
AÍDA'S VOICE: Our child, our only daughter . . . listen to me. Her name is Margarita Inez Suárez, she is wearing a black one-piece bathing suit cut high in the legs with a white racing stripe down the sides, a white bathing cap with goggles and her whole body covered with a . . . with a . . .
EDUARDO'S VOICE: With lanolin and paraffin.
AÍDA'S VOICE: *Sí* . . . *con lanolin and paraffin.*

> (*More radio static. Special on Simón, on the edge of the boat.*)

SIMÓN: Margo! Yo Margo! (*Pause.*) Man don't do this. (*Pause.*) Come on . . . Come on . . . (*Pause.*) God, why does everything have to be so hard? (*Pause.*) Stupid. You know you're not supposed to die for this. Stupid. It's his dream and he can't even swim. (*Pause.*) Punch those arms in. Come home. Come home. I'm your little brother. Don't forget what Mama said. You're not supposed to leave me behind. *Vamos*, Margarita, take your little brother, hold his hand tight when you cross the street. He's so little. (*Pause.*) Oh Christ, give us a sign . . . I know! I know! Margo, I'll send you a message . . . like mental telepathy. I'll hold my breath, close my eyes, and I'll bring you home. (*He takes a deep breath; a few beats.*) This time I'll beep . . . I'll send out sonar signals like a dolphin. (*He imitates dolphin sounds.*)

> (*The sound of real dolphins takes over from Simón, then fades into sound of Abuela saying the Hail Mary in Spanish, as full lights come up slowly.*)

Scene VII

Eduardo coming out of cabin, sobbing, Aída holding him. Simón anxiously scanning the horizon. Abuela looking calmly ahead.

EDUARDO: *Es mi culpa, sí, es mi culpa.*[35] (*He hits his chest.*)

AÍDA: *Ya, ya viejo.*[36] . . . it was my sin . . . I left my home.

EDUARDO: Forgive me, forgive me. I've lost our daughter, our sister, our granddaughter, *mi carne, mi sangre, mis ilusiones.*[37] (*To heaven.*) *Dios mío*, take me . . . take me, I say . . . Goddammit, take me!

SIMÓN: I'm going in.

AÍDA AND EDUARDO: No!

EDUARDO: (*Grabbing and holding Simón, speaking to heaven.*) God, take me, not my children. They are my dreams, my illusions . . . and not this one, this one is my mystery . . . he has my secret dreams. In him are the parts of me I cannot see.

> (*Eduardo embraces Simón. Radio static becomes louder.*)

AÍDA: I . . . I think I see her.

SIMÓN: No, it's just a seal.

ABUELA: (*Looking out with binoculars.*) *Mi nietacita, dónde estás?* (*She feels her heart.*) I don't feel the knife in my heart . . . my little fish is not lost.

> (*Radio crackles with static. As lights dim on boat, voices of Mel and Mary Beth are heard over the radio.*)

MEL'S VOICE: Tragedy has marred the face of the Wrigley Invitational Women's Race to Catalina. The Cuban swimmer, little Margarita

---

[35] *Es mi culpa, sí, es mi culpa:* It's my fault, yes, it's my fault.

[36] *Ya, ya viejo:* Yes, yes, old man.

[37] *Mi carne, mi sangre, mis ilusiones:* My flesh, my blood, my dreams.

Suárez, has reportedly been lost at sea. Coast Guard and divers are looking for her as we speak. Yet in spite of this tragedy the race must go on because . . .

MARY BETH'S VOICE: (*Interrupting loudly.*) Mel!

MEL'S VOICE: (*Startled.*) What!

MARY BETH'S VOICE: Ah . . . excuse me, Mel . . . we have a winner. We've just received word from Catalina that one of the swimmers is just fifty yards from the breakers . . . it's, oh, it's . . . Margarita Suárez!

(Special on family in cabin listening to radio.)

MEL'S VOICE: What? I thought she died!

(Special on Margarita, taking off bathing cap, trophy in hand, walking on the water.)

MARY BETH'S VOICE: Ahh . . . unless . . . unless this is a tragic . . . No . . . there she is, Mel. Margarita Suárez! The only one in the race wearing a black bathing suit cut high in the legs with a racing stripe down the side.

(Family cheering, embracing.)

SIMÓN: (*Screaming.*) Way to go, Margo!

MEL'S VOICE: This is indeed a miracle! It's a resurrection! Margarita Suárez, with a flotilla of boats to meet her, is now walking on the waters, through the breakers . . . onto the beach, with crowds of people cheering her on. What a jubilation! This is a miracle!

(Sound of crowds cheering. Lights and cheering sounds fade.)

BLACKOUT

1984

Writers on the Art

Sherman Alexie and Diane Thiel
(B. 1966 and B. 1967)

A Conversation with
Sherman Alexie

DIANE THIEL: Can you say a bit about working in different genres in your writing, and often crossing genres in a single book? A signature element in your books seems to be a fusion of forms. One wonders while reading: "Is this a poem or short story?" What distinctions do you see between genres? Do you think some distinctions are rather artificial? Has your relationship with the different forms changed at all in the evolution of your work?

SHERMAN ALEXIE: I suppose, as an Indian living in the United States, I'm used to crossing real and imaginary boundaries, and have, in fact, enjoyed a richer and crazier and more magical life precisely because I have fearlessly and fearfully crossed all sorts of those barriers. I guess I approach my poetry the same way I have approached every other thing in my life. I just don't like being told what to do. I write whatever feels and sounds right to me. At the beginning of my career, I wrote free verse with some formal influences, but I have lately been writing more formal verse with free verse influences. I don't feel the need to spend all my time living on either the free verse or the formal reservation. I want it all; hunger is my crime.

DT: And what about the fusion of poetry and story in your work, in *The Business of Fancydancing: Stories and Poems*, and in *One Stick Song* in particular. Could you tell me a bit more about crossing those barriers? Not many writers defy the genres, and I'm curious about your decision to collect the stories and poems together as you have. And also about your path towards the novels and screenplays. Did you feel you needed a larger or different kind of canvas to tell certain stories?

SA: The original decision to include poems and stories in the first collection, *The Business of Fancydancing*, was made by the Hanging Loose Press editors. I was only twenty-three years old when that book was accepted for publication, and didn't really know how to put a book together (I still don't know how!), so it was really an editorial decision. I guess those Hanging Loose guys understood my work was a blend of poetry and fiction, and since I was such a baby writer then,

I think that fusion is just natural, maybe even reflexive. I have to work hard now to make a poem completely identifiable as a poem, and not as a hybrid. Of course, I still love hybrids. I'm a hybrid. So I think it was the Hanging Loose editors who helped me define myself as a poet. They're still my poetry publishers, and I'm very curious what they'll do with my next book, which will be mostly formal poems. I think my path toward novels and screenplays was, number one, the simple effort to make more money so I could be a full-time writer. But heck, I haven't published a novel in seven years, so I'm not sure I can be described as a novelist. I think I'm a poet with short story inclinations. And since screenplays and movies are poetic in structure and intent, I find that I'm much more comfortable writing screenplays than I am writing novels. I am currently working on my first nonfiction, a big book about four generations of Indian men in my family, and our relationship with war, and I've broken it down into fiction, nonfiction project, and poetry, so I'm really looking for a hybrid work here. In some sense, I feel this new book is a summation of all my themes until now. After this book, I think I'll be looking in some radical new directions.

DT: Could you speak a bit about converting literature for the screen? What are the different demands of the work in print and the work on the screen? What is your process? What useful advice have you received along the way? Was there any "advice" that you instinctively did not agree with?

SA: Although I have written two produced movies, and worked on screenplays for a half-dozen unproduced flicks, I still haven't figured out what works or what doesn't. I don't think the audiences for movies are nearly as forgiving or ambitious as the audiences for poetry or fiction. Ninety-nine percent of all movies ever made, from the most independent to the most capitalistic, from the crappy ones to the classics, are identical in structure. If poets worked like film-makers, we'd all be writing sonnets, only sonnets, and nothing else! Just try to make a movie out of "The Wasteland" or *Portrait of the Artist as a Young Man*. I want to make movies that are much more like poems, so I'll be making them myself for extremely low budgets. The best advice I've ever received: "Sherman, quit wasting your time in Hollywood!" Of course, I have completely ignored that advice.

DT: In *First Indian on the Moon*, the poem "The Alcoholic Love Poems" ends with the lines "All I said was 'When I used to drink, you're exactly the kind of Indian I loved to get drunk with.' Oh all my life in the past tense." How does the recognition of "past tense" in this poem affect your writing? Do you often feel as if you are writing about past selves, past injuries? Can you discuss how past meets present in your work?

SA: In my dictionary, "Indian" and "nostalgic" are synonyms. As colonized people, I think we're always looking to the past for some real and imaginary sense of purity and authenticity. But I hate my nostalgia. I think I'm pop-culture obsessed because I hope it's an antidote for the disease of nostalgia. So I think the past and present are always duking it out in my work. The Lone Ranger and Tonto will always be fistfighting.

DT: The title poem of your first book, *The Business of Fancydancing*, is a sestina, and I notice that an interest in using the various forms of poetry has persisted in your body of work. Who were your early influences of "formal" poetry? Why did you feel drawn to it? What do you think are some of the possibilities using form provides?

SA: Although I would certainly be defined as a free verse poet, I have always worked in traditional and invented forms. Though I've never recognized it before, the fact that the title poem of my first book is a sestina says a lot about my varied ambitions. My earliest interest in formalism came from individual poems, rather than certain poets. Marvell's "To His Coy Mistress," Roethke's "My Papa's Waltz," Gwendolyn Brooks's "We Real Cool," and Langston Hughes's "A Dream Deferred" are poems that come to mind as early formal poems I admired. Speaking both seriously and facetiously, I think I've spent my whole career rewriting "My Papa's Waltz" with an Indian twist. Lately, as I've been writing much more formally, with end rhyme, a tenuous dance with meter, and explicit form, I've discovered that in writing toward that end rhyme, that accented or unaccented syllable, or that stanza break, I am constantly surprising myself with new ideas, new vocabulary, and new ways of looking at the world. The conscious use of forms seems to have freed my subconscious.

DT: That's exactly how I feel about using form—that it has the power to free the subconscious. I've actually thought about Roethke's poem when reading your work. For me, too, it was one of the poems that startled me into poetry early on. It's an interesting poem to teach because of the range of reaction to it. Some—those who focus on the waltz and the horseplay—feel the tone to be much lighter. Others—those who concentrate more on the whisky on his breath, the way the child "hung on like death," and the ear scraping a buckle—feel that it's much darker. I think that the tug of the two different tones creates the true charge in the poem.

SA: I think the poem is incredibly sad and violent, and its sadness and violence is underscored by its gentle rhymes and rhythms. It's Mother Goose on acid maybe. I think that gentle music is a form of denial about the terror contained in the poem, or maybe it's the way kids think, huh? My dad wasn't violent, but he would leave us to go drinking, and would sometimes be gone for a few weeks. He was completely undependable and unpredictable. My wife's father was a scary and unpredictable alcoholic, charming and funny one moment, violent and caustic the next. So Roethke's poem, I think, is all about the unpredictability of the alcoholic father.

DT: I find the way the personal fuses with the political a very evocative element in your work. The love poem, for instance, is often simultaneously a political poem. Sometimes this is suggestive, but other times it is quite direct, even in the very title—as in "Seven Love Songs Which Include the Collected History of the United States of America." Could you discuss this fusion and how it evolved in your work?

SA: I've stated in other places that Indians are politicized from birth. I was five or six years old, standing in line to get free government food on the reservation, when I had my first political thought: "Hey, I'm in this line because I'm an Indian!" Of course, I was having a great time in that line with my very funny and highly verbose siblings and parents. I would guess my family, pound for pound, is one of the funniest in the world! So I was taught to fuse the political and the artistic, the poem and the punchline. It seems to me it is just as much nature as nurture. In terms of love, I was involved in a long-term love affair with a white woman, and our races and our political positions were always a subject of discussion and dissent. I am never, not even in my most intimate moments, completely free of my tribe.

DT: The poet Michael S. Harper (with whom I studied years ago) has a book entitled *History Is Your Own Heartbeat*. I've always been particularly interested in exploring history in a poem, but doing so via a very personal current. Was it a conscious choice for you—to take on all that history in your work, or did it just slowly become your subject matter? What writers influenced you, in the way the personal and the historical mesh?

SA: Generally speaking, I think Indians have a much longer memory than white Americans. Or perhaps we Indians hold more passionate grudges! But I think my work has been more autobiographical than historical. So maybe I've been a personal historian. A poet-memoirist. In the link between personal and world history, I think other Native American poets have influenced me most—Simon Ortiz, Adrian C. Louis, Joy Harjo, Leslie Silko, just to name a few, who are constantly aware of history. In Ortiz's book-length poem *From Sand Creek*, he weaves his personal history with the history of genocide in the United States, and creates a stunning brand of confessional poetry. Simon seems to be confessing in a royal voice, with a tribal "we" and not a narcissistic "I." I hope that's what I'm doing with my poems.

DT: I've been thinking as we talk that perhaps the reason you're drawn to form in poetry might have something to do with your attraction to repetition and refrains. Many of your poems employ a kind of elliptical repetition—in your chapbook *Water Flowing Home*, for instance, the poem "This Woman Speaks" has this kind of elliptical nature:

> This woman speaks, this
> woman, who loves me, speaks
> to another woman, her
> mother, this daughter
> speaks to her mother

Could you comment on your use of repetition and the cultural aspects of this?

SA: In my tribe, and in the Native American world, in general, repetition is sacred. All of our songs go on for hours: "This Indian will be coming around the mountain when he comes, when he comes, when he comes . . . " So I think repetition appeals to me on that tribal level, and it also appeals to me on a simple musical level. I want my poems to sound like tribal songs, and with repetition, I can sometimes make English sound like Salish. I also think that in terms of spirituality and prayer, repetition can sound a note of desperation. Think of Hopkins, "Pitched past pain." God can feel so far away. So we sinful slobs have to keep screaming until God pays attention.

DT: When I heard you read in New Mexico, I was struck by the performative aspect. I know you've been involved in a number of poetry slams and have held the title of Heavyweight Poetry Champion (or something like that). Do you think of a poem as something meant to be performed, and what are the different ways you've developed to make a poem come alive in the air?

SA: Story-tellers were telling stories long before they had the means to record them or write them down, so I think performance is primal. I know it feels primal to me. When I'm really doing well onstage, I feel almost as crazy and wonderful as I do when I'm writing the stuff. As a story-teller, I also feel a responsibility to my audience. I want them to feel as strongly about the work as I do. I want them to know how much I both love and hate it. If a poem is funny, I want to hear the laughter. If it's sad, I want to hear the tears.

DT: How did your "stand-up" readings develop? Was it something you always did, or did it develop as a kind of backlash to the often dry, humorless readings that can be a part of the literary world? Would you consider yourself an extrovert? Or do you just don that persona when you are performing?

SA: Most of the readings I've been to are so damn boring! We've got a lot of competition out there in the world. I have to be at least as good as Eminem or I'm dead! In my personal life, I'm an introvert. I spend most of my time alone, with my thoughts for company, and much prefer a book and a bathtub to any gathering of messy human beings. As a public performer, I "act." It's a strange thing. I become a slightly larger and more exaggerated version of myself.

DT: I hear a great deal of humor in your fiction and drama (and in your performances), but it's often more subtle in your poetry. How do you feel about humor in poetry, in general?

SA: I think my poems are very funny, but readers are not trained to laugh at poems. And I think funny poems are seriously devalued in the poetry world. I'd love to edit an anthology of humorous poems that are serious and great by any standard. I'd call it "Funny Poems." I think Auden is hilarious. I think Lucille Clifton is very funny. And Frost is to my mind an incredibly bitter Bob Newhart.

DT: There are many references to the dream world in your work, even when it's not explicitly a dream being explored. "Dead Letter Office," for instance, begins with a very believable occurrence—receiving a letter written in your native tongue that needs translating—but as the poem goes on, the experience feels increasingly surreal, and you traipse after the translator, "Big Mom," for years, "holding some brief letter from the past." I chose that poem as an example because it's not directly about a dream, and yet it feels decidedly like one.

SA: I was hydrocephalic at birth, had serious brain surgery at six months of age, and had epileptic seizures and was on serious sedatives until age seven, so I certainly have a more scarred and ragged brain than most. I don't know how to speak of it medically, but I'm sure my brain damage gives me all sorts of visions! I've always been nightmare-prone and insomniac, so sleep and the lack of sleep, and dreams and nightmares have always been my primary obsession. I was taking phenobarbital before I went to Kindergarten, so I was probably destined to be a poet, enit?

2004

Rhina P. Espaillat (B. 1932)

Bilingual/Bilingüe

Recent interest in the phenomenon known as "Spanglish" has led me to reexamine my own experience as a writer who works chiefly in her second language, and especially to recall my father's inflexible rule against the mixing of languages. In fact, no English was allowed in that midtown Manhattan apartment that became home after my arrival in New York in 1939. My father read the daily paper in English, taught himself to follow disturbing events in Europe through the medium of English-language radio, and even taught me to read the daily comic strips, in an effort to speed my learning of the language he knew I would need. But that necessary language was banished from family conversation: it was the medium of the outer world, beyond the door; inside, among ourselves, only Spanish was permitted, and it had to be pure, grammatical, unadulterated Spanish.

At the age of seven, however, nothing seems more important than communicating with classmates and neighborhood children. For my mother, too, the new language was a way out of isolation, a means to deal with the larger world and with those American women for whom she sewed. But my father, a political exile waiting for changes in our native country, had different priorities: he lived in the hope of return, and believed that the new home, the new speech, were temporary. His theory was simple: if it could be said at all, it could be said best in the language of those authors whose words were the core of his education. But his insistence on pure Spanish made it difficult, sometimes impossible, to bring home and share the jokes of friends, puns, pop lyrics, and other staples of seven-year-old conversation. Table talk sometimes ended with tears or sullen silence.

And yet, despite the friction it caused from time to time, my native language was also a source of comfort—the reading that I loved, intimacy within the family, and a peculiar auditory delight best described as echoes in the mind. I learned early to relish words as counters in a game that could turn suddenly serious without losing the quality of play, and to value their sound as a meaning behind their meaning.

Nostalgia, a confusion of identity, the fear that if the native language is lost the self will somehow be altered forever: all are part of the subtle flavor of immigrant life, as well as the awareness that one owes gratitude to strangers for acts of communication that used to be simple and once imposed no such debt.

Memory, folklore, and food all become part of the receding landscape that language sets out to preserve. Guilt, too, adds to the mix, the suspicion that to love the second language too much is to betray those ancestors who spoke the first and could not communicate with us in the vocabulary of our education, our new thoughts. And finally, a sense of grievance and loss may spur hostility toward the new language and those who speak it, as if the common speech of the perceived majority could weld together a disparate population into a huge, monolithic, and threatening Other. That Other is then assigned traits and habits that preclude sympathy and mold "Us" into a unity whose cohesiveness gives comfort.

Luckily, there is another side to bilingualism: curiosity about the Other may be as natural and pervasive as group loyalty. If it weren't, travel, foreign residence, and intermarriage would be less common than they are. For some bilingual writers, the Other—and the language he speaks—are appealing. Some acknowledge and celebrate the tendency of languages to borrow from each other and produce something different in the process. That is, in part, the tendency that has given rise to "Spanglish."

It's dangerous, however, to accept the inevitable melding of languages over time as a justification for speaking, in the short run, a mix that impoverishes both languages by allowing words in one to drive out perfectly good equivalent words in the other. The habitual speaker of such a mix ends by speaking not two, or even one complete language, but fragments of two that are no longer capable of standing alone or serving the speaker well with any larger audience. As a literary device with limited appeal and durability, "Spanglish," like other such blends, is expressive and fresh. But as a substitute for genuine bilinguality—the cultivation and preservation of two languages—I suspect it represents a danger to the advancement of foreign speakers, and a loss to both cultures. My father sensed as much in 1939, and stubbornly preserved my native language for me, through his insistence that I be truly bilingual rather than a traveler across boundaries that "Spanglish" has made all too permeable.

My father, who never learned to think in English, was persuaded that the words of his own language were the "true" names for things in the world. But for me that link between fact and word was broken, as it is for many who grow up bilingual. Having been taught to love words and take them seriously as reflections of reality, I felt it a loss to learn that, in fact, words are arbitrary, man-made, no more permanent than clothing: somewhere under all of them reality is naked.

Disconcerting as it is, however, to lose the security of words that are perceived as single keys to what they unlock, it is also exhilarating to see oneself as the maker of those words, even if they are now impermanent, provisional artifacts that have value for us only because they're ours. Anybody who has ever gone hunting for that one right and elusive word knows what bilingualism feels like, even if he's never left his native country or learned a word in any language but his own. There is a sense in which every poet is bilingual, and those of us who are more overtly so are only living metaphors for the condition that applies to us all. We use a language that seems deceptively like the language of the people around us, but isn't quite. The words are the same, but the weight we give them, the connections we find among them, the criteria we use to choose this one rather than that one, are our own.

At a recent poetry reading I closed with a poem in Spanish, and a member of the English-speaking audience approached me afterward to remark how moved she had been by that poem, and how she wished I had read others.

"Where did you learn Spanish?" I asked.

"I don't speak any Spanish," she replied. "What I understood was the music of what you read."

It occurred to me, during our subsequent conversation, that poetry may be precisely what is almost lost, not in translation, but in the wording, the transit from experience to paper. If we succeed in salvaging anything, maybe it is most often in the music, the formal elements of poetry that do travel from language to language, as the formal music of classic Spanish poetry my father loved followed me into English and draws me, to this day, to poems that are patterned and rich and playful.

It's occurred to me since that conversation that a poem in Spanish may have more in common with a poem in English—or any other language—than with a grocery list, say, or a piece of technical writing that happens to use Spanish words. There is something in poetry that transcends specific language, that makes it possible for transplanted people like me to recognize the songs of the Other as his own even before he understands them fully. Poetry may be used to draw very small circles around itself, identifying its speaker as a member of a narrowly delineated group and looking at "outsiders" with eyes that discern less and less detail as distance increases. But it may also be used to draw very large circles, circles that will draw in rather than exclude, as in Edwin Markham's apt four-line metaphor titled "Outwitted":

> He drew a circle that shut me out—
> Heretic, rebel, a thing to flout.
> But Love and I had the wit to win:
> We drew a circle that shut him in.

1998

Robert Frost (1874–1963)

Poetic Metaphor (from "Education by Poetry")

I do not think anybody ever knows the discreet use of metaphors, his own and other people's, the discreet handling of metaphor, unless he has been properly educated in poetry.

Poetry begins in trivial metaphors, pretty metaphors, "grace" metaphors, and goes on to the profoundest thinking that we have. Poetry provides the one permissible way of saying one thing and meaning another. People say, "why don't you say what you mean?" We never do that, do we, being all of us too much poets. We like to talk in parables and in hints and in indirections—whether from diffidence or some other instinct.

I have wanted in late years to go further and further in making metaphor the whole of thinking. I find someone now and then to agree with me that all thinking, except mathematical thinking, is metaphorical, or all thinking except scientific thinking. The mathematical might be difficult for me to bring in, but the scientific is easy enough.

What I am pointing out is that unless you are at home in the metaphor, unless you have had your proper poetical education in the metaphor, you are not safe anywhere. Because you are not at ease with figurative values: you don't know the metaphor in its strength and its weakness. You don't know how far you may expect to ride it and when it may break down with you. You are not safe in science; you are not safe in history.

1930

Charlotte Perkins Gilman (1860–1935)

Why I Wrote "The Yellow Wallpaper"

Many and many a reader has asked that. When the story first came out, in the *New England Magazine* about 1891, a Boston physician made protest in *The Transcript*. Such a story ought not to be written, he said; it was enough to drive anyone mad to read it.

Another physician, in Kansas I think, wrote to say that it was the best description of incipient insanity he had ever seen, and—begging my pardon—had I been there?

Now the story of the story is this: For many years I suffered from a severe and continuous nervous breakdown tending to melancholia—and beyond. During about the third year of this trouble I went, in devout faith and some faint stir of hope, to a noted specialist in nervous diseases, the best known in the country. This wise man put me to bed and applied the rest cure, to which a still-good physique responded so promptly that he concluded there was nothing much the matter with me, and sent me home with solemn advice to "live as domestic a life as far as possible," to "have but two hours' intellectual life a day," and "never to touch pen, brush, or pencil again" as long as I lived. This was in 1887.

I went home and obeyed those directions for some three months, and came so near the borderline of utter mental ruin that I could see over.

Then, using the remnants of intelligence that remained, and helped by a wise friend, I cast the noted specialist's advice to the winds and went to work again—work, the normal life of every human being; work, in which is joy and growth and service, without which one is a pauper and a parasite—ultimately recovering some measure of power.

Being naturally moved to rejoicing by this narrow escape, I wrote "The Yellow Wallpaper," with its embellishments and additions, to carry out the ideal (I never had hallucinations or objections to my mural decorations) and sent a copy to the physician who so nearly drove me mad. He never acknowledged it.

The little book is valued by alienists and as a good specimen of one kind of literature. It has, to my knowledge, saved one woman from a similar fate—so terrifying her family that they let her out into normal activity and she recovered.

But the best result is this. Many years later I was told that the great specialist had admitted to friends of his that he had altered his treatment of neurasthenia since reading "The Yellow Wallpaper."

It was not intended to drive people crazy, but to save people from being driven crazy, and it worked.

The Forerunner, October 1913

Susan Glaspell (1882–1948)

Creating Trifles

We went to the theater, and for the most part we came away wishing we had gone somewhere else. Those were the days when Broadway flourished almost unchallenged. Plays, like magazine stories, were patterned. They might be pretty good within themselves, seldom did they open out to— where it surprised or thrilled your spirit to follow. They didn't ask much of *you*, those plays. Having paid for your seat, the thing was all done for you, and your mind came out where it went in, only tireder. An audience, Jig[1]

---

[1]*Jig:* the nickname of George Cram Cook (1873–1924), Glaspell's husband, who was the central founder and director of the Provincetown Players, perhaps the most influential theater company in the history of American drama.

said, had imagination. What was this "Broadway," which could make a thing as interesting as life into a thing as dull as a Broadway play?

There was a meeting at the Liberal Club—Eddie Goodman, Phil Moeller, Ida Rauh, the Boni brothers, exciting talk about starting a theater. . . .

He [Jig] wrote a letter to the people who had seen the plays, asking if they cared to become associate members of the Provincetown Players. The purpose was to give American playwrights of sincere purpose a chance to work out their ideas in freedom, to give all who worked with the plays their opportunity as artists. Were they interested in this? One dollar for the three remaining bills.

The response paid for seats and stage, and for sets. A production need not cost a lot of money, Jig would say. The most expensive set at the Wharf Theater[2] cost thirteen dollars. There were sets at the Provincetown Playhouse which cost little more. . . .

"Now, Susan," he [Jig] said to me, briskly, "I have announced a play of yours for the next bill."

"But I have no play!"

"Then you will have to sit down tomorrow and begin one."

I protested. I did not know how to write a play. I had never "studied it."

"Nonsense," said Jig. "You've got a stage, haven't you?"

So I went out on the wharf, sat alone on one of our wooden benches without a back, and looked a long time at that bare little stage. After a time the stage became a kitchen—a kitchen there all by itself. I saw just where the stove was, the table, and the steps going upstairs. Then the door at the back opened, and people all bundled up came in—two or three men, I wasn't sure which, but sure enough about the two women, who hung back, reluctant to enter that kitchen. When I was a newspaper reporter out in Iowa, I was sent down-state to do a murder trial, and I never forgot going into the kitchen of a woman locked up in town. I had meant to do it as a short story, but the stage took it for its own, so I hurried in from the wharf to write down what I had seen. Whenever I got stuck, I would run across the street to the old wharf, sit in that leaning little theater under which the sea sounded, until the play was ready to continue. Sometimes things written in my room would not form on the stage, and I must go home and cross them out. "What playwrights need is a stage," said Jig, "their own stage."

Ten days after the director said he had announced my play, there was a reading at Mary Heaton Vorse's. I was late to the meeting, home revising the play. But when I got there the crowd liked "Trifles," and voted to put it in rehearsal next day.

THE ROAD TO THE TEMPLE

1927

---

[2] *Wharf Theater:* the makeshift theater that Cook created from an old fish-house at the end of a Provincetown wharf.

Credits

Ackerman, Diane. "The Truth about Truffles," from *A Natural History of The Senses*. Copyright © 1990 by Diane Ackerman. Used by permission of Random House, Inc.

Alexie, Sherman. "Indian Education," from *Old Shirts and New Skins*, American Indian Studies, UCLA, The Regents of the University of California. Copyright © 1993 by Sherman Alexie. Reprinted by permission of Sherman Alexie. *Smoke Signals* (excerpt) Copyright © 1998 by Sherman Alexie. Reprinted by permission of Hyperion and the author.

Alexie, Sherman and Diane Thiel. "A Conversation with Sherman Alexie." First appeared in *Crossroads: Journal of the Poetry Society of America*. Copyright © 2004 by Diane Thiel.

Auden, W. H. "Musée des Beaux Arts," from *Collected Poems By W. H. Auden*. Copyright © 1940 and renewed Copyright © 1968 by W. H. Auden. Used by permission of Random House, Inc. and Faber & Faber.

Bishop, Elizabeth. "One Art," from *The Complete Poems, 1927–1979*. Copyright © 1979, 1983 by Alice Helen Methfessel. Reprinted by permission of Farrar, Straus and Giroux, LLC.

Bishop, Elizabeth. First draft of Elizabeth Bishop's "One Art." Special Collections, Vassar College Libraries. All rights reserved.

Chatwin, Bruce. From *In Patagonia*. Reprinted with permission of Simon & Schuster Adult Publishing Group. Copyright © 1977 by Bruce Chatwin.

Connell, Evan S. From *Mrs. Bridge*. Copyright © 1959 by Evan S. Connell. Reprinted by permission of Don Congdon Associates, Inc.

Cope, Wendy. "Lonely Hearts," from *Making Cocoa for Kingsley Amis*. Copyright © 1986. Reprinted by permission of Faber & Faber.

D'Aguiar, Fred. "A Son in Shadow." First appeared in *Harper's* magazine Vol. 298, No. 1786, March 1999. Copyright © 1999 by Fred D'Aguiar. Reprinted by permission of the author.

Espaillat, Rhina P. "Bilingual/Bilingüe," (poem and essay) from *Where Horizons Go*. Poem first published in *Northeast*; copyright © 1998 by Rhina P. Espaillat. Essay first published in *Where Horizons Go*. Reprinted by permission of the poet.

Finch, Annie. "Sapphics for Patience," from *Eve*, Story Line Press, 1997. Copyright © 1997 by Annie Finch. Reprinted by permission of the poet.

Frost, Robert. "The Mending Wall," "Out, Out—," "The Road Not Taken," from *The Poetry of Robert Frost*, edited by Edward Connery Lathem. Copyright © 1916, 1930, 1939, Copyright © 1969 by Henry Holt and Company, LLC.

Gioia, Dana. "My Confessional Sestina," from *The Gods Of Winter*. Copyright © 1991 by Dana Gioia. Reprinted with the permission of Graywolf Press, St. Paul, Minnesota.

Gwynn, R. S. "Shakespearean Sonnet." Copyright © 2001 by R.S. Gwynn. Reprinted by permission of the poet.

Harjo, Joy. "She Had Some Horses," from *She Had Some Horses*. Copyright © 1983, 1997 Thunder's Mouth Press. Appears by permission of the publisher, Thunder's Mouth Press, a division of Avalon Publishing Group.

Ives, David. "Time Flies," from *All in the Timing*.

Kennedy, X. J. "John While Swimming in the Ocean," from *Brats*, Margaret K. McElderry Books. Copyright © 1986 by X.J. Kennedy. Reprinted by permission of the poet.

Kincaid, Jamaica. "Girl," from *At the Bottom of the River*. Copyright © 1983 by Jamaica Kincaid. Reprinted by permission of Farrar, Straus & Giroux, LLC.

LeGuin, Ursula K. "The Wife's Story." Copyright © 1982 by Ursula K. Le Guin; first appeared in *Compass Rose*. Reprinted by permission of the author and the author's agents, the Virginia Kidd Agency, Inc.

LeMaster, David. "The Assassination and Persecution of Abraham Lincoln," Copyright © 1996 by David LeMaster. Reprinted by permission of the author and Brooklyn Publishers (www.brookpub.com).

Lessing, Doris. "A Woman on a Roof," from *Stories*. Copyright © 1963 Doris Lessing. Reprinted by kind permission of Jonathan Clowes Ltd., London, on behalf of Doris Lessing.

Lim, Shirley Geok-lin. "Pantoum for Chinese Women," from *Monsoon History*, 1994. Copyright © 1994 by Shirley Geok-lin Lim. Reprinted by permission of the poet.

Lindner, April. "Spice," from *Skin*, Texas Tech University Press. Copyright © 2002. Reprinted by permission of the poet.

Mason, David. "Acrostic from Aegina," from *Arrivals*, Story Line Press, www.storylinepress.com. Copyright © 2004. Reprinted by permission of the poet.

Index of Authors, Titles, and First Lines of Poems